Contents at a Glance

Part V: SAP Careers

Table of Contents

About the Authors

Dr. Michael Missbach, Manager of the Cisco SAP Competence Center, focuses on best practices for SAP HANA and other mission-critical applications in public and private cloud scenarios. Earlier, he worked as IT Superintendent for ALCOA. He has also written books on SAP hardware, SAP system operation, adaptive SAP infrastructures, SAP on Windows, and SAP on the cloud.

Dr. George Anderson, senior architect and program manager for Microsoft Services, specializes in designing and deploying mission-critical SAP and Microsoft Dynamics solutions. A certified SAP technical consultant, PMI PMP, and Six Sigma black belt, he has also written books on SAP implementation, performance testing, and project management.

Acknowledgments

This book is the product of voluntary work completed over many nights, weekends, and airplane flights. We wish to extend a special thank you to all of our customers and colleagues who selflessly provided so much help in the form of insight, tips, contributions, reviews, and constructive criticism. Without their support, we would not have been able to write this book.

In particular, we would like to call out the following people: Sean Donaldson and Len Landale from secure-24 and Steffi Dünnebier from Grand-consult for their contributions to the topic of systems management; Gerhard Lausser for his insights on Nagios; Antonie Katschinsky from Cap Gemini for much of the introduction on simplified finance; Cameron Gardiner from Microsoft for his deep expertise around SAP and the cloud; and Andreas Jenzer, Jeff Davis, Sebastian Lenz, and Stefan Schiele for their proofreading and SAP application and technical insight. The practical experience of all of our advisors added much of the enduring value of this book, and their support was a great source of encouragement.

We Want to Hear from You!

As the reader of this book, you are our most important critic and commentator. We value your opinion and want to know what we're doing right, what we could do better, what areas you'd like to see us publish in, and any other words of wisdom you're willing to pass our way.

We welcome your comments. You can email or write to let us know what you did or didn't like about this book—as well as what we can do to make our books better.

Please note that we cannot help you with technical problems related to the topic of this book.

When you write, please be sure to include this book's title and author as well as your name and email address. We will carefully review your comments and share them with the author and editors who worked on the book.

Email: consumer@samspublishing.com

Mail: Sams Publishing
         ATTN: Reader Feedback
         800 East 96th Street
         Indianapolis, IN 46240 USA

Reader Services

Visit our website and register this book at informit.com/register for convenient access to any updates, downloads, or errata that might be available for this book.

Introduction

Now that we've covered the basics of SAP and what it means "The world of SAP and our world in general have gone through major upheavals in the last few years, and I was excited to share with SAPlings and veterans alike just how much had changed." This is how George Anderson started the introduction of the 4th edition of this book in 2011. And it reflects exactly how I felt when he and Sams asked me to take over as the primary author for this newest edition: thrilled! And honored as well. Seriously! Actually, George and I shared the work to rewrite and edit this 5th edition. We introduced many more screen shots and other graphics, and revised the format while preserving the most teachable aspects of earlier editions.

In addition, we added a tremendous amount of new material. From the introduction of new technologies such as in-memory HANA databases and hosting platforms to SAP's new user interfaces, newly acquired cloud-based Software as a Service solutions, new reporting applications, and more, we've essentially rewritten many of the hours from the ground up.

Because the IT world in general has changed so dramatically, we found it useful to provide a broader foundation than ever before. We've incorporated new topics such as the Internet of Things, new mobile device technologies, and how social media and big data are changing the IT playing field. And we've briefly covered data security threats and other developments alongside plausible or possible future trends. Our goal in doing so was to help you think more deeply about where SAP fits in, where the gaps are, and therefore where some of the biggest future challenges might be found.

So thank you for picking up the latest and yes, best ever, edition of *Sams Teach Yourself SAP in 24 Hours*. We are confident you'll find it worth your time.

The hours are organized into five easy-to-consume sections. Part I naturally starts with an introduction to all the basics. Part II covers SAP's new and older business applications and components. In this way, the stage is set for us to explore SAP from a business user perspective (Part III) and then from an IT professional's perspective (Part IV). Part V concludes with three hours devoted to helping you start or grow a career in SAP.

Along the way, we have covered what we think matters most to SAP newcomers. For our business user readers, we've put together several hours that walk through actual business transactions. We explore what it means to create sales orders, check on customer records, update employee personnel records, and more. We provide lists of business transaction codes used in SAP's Business Suite to execute common business transactions. And we explore reporting and query processes executed not only from SAP ERP itself but also from SAP's Business Objects and other applications. In this way, prospective SAP business users will get a better feel for what a day-in-the-life looks like for many SAP end users.

For our technical readers, we've returned to providing deeper content, and we've done something we hope is especially helpful. Feedback from readers let us know that it has become quite difficult and confusing to navigate the SAP Service Marketplace, Developer Network, Help Portal, and various blogs to find the basic installation guides, essential technical information, and so on. So we've added detailed step-by-step "how to locate" material alongside the technical details.

We also quickly walk through the installation of the trial version of SAP, covering both on-premise and in-the-cloud installations. With a "real" SAP system on hand, you'll be able to better apply in real-time what we explore together across these 24 hours. We also explore the world of the SAP developer, look at what it means to prepare for technical upgrades, and explore steps necessary for managing an SAP implementation project. By covering SAP technology from several different perspectives, including cutting-edge insight related to SAP and cloud computing, even our more experienced technical readers will be better positioned to make a difference at work.

Armed with new insight and awareness, we suspect our readers will be more effective than ever. You'll be that rare person who is broad enough to understand the big picture and smart enough to realize you still have a long journey ahead of you. But with this knowledge alone, you'll be well on your way to transforming yourself, your career, and your future.

What's Covered

This book covers what you need to know to understand SAP's core products and components, which are often collectively referred to simply (and vaguely!) as "SAP." Though this is a beginner's book, it provides a well-rounded and current outlook on SAP today. As career SAP professionals, your authors, contributors, and technical editors have made sure that this book reflects the real world.

This latest edition continues to target the two largest audiences of those interested in learning about SAP: business users and IT professionals. Readers will appreciate how the book is arranged around these two very different types of skill sets and interests. And by providing an overview to each area coupled with actionable steps or guidance, we believe you will find this to yet again be the most useful and teachable *Teach Yourself SAP in 24 Hours* to date.

The book begins with the basics, introducing terminology regarding SAP and its business applications, technology underpinnings, and project implementation considerations. From there begins the process of carefully building on your newfound knowledge to piece together the complex world of SAP's applications and components. The pace of the book is designed to provide a solid foundation up front so you can grasp the more advanced topics covered in later hours. In this way, even a novice should quickly understand what it means to plan for, deploy, and use SAP. With this understanding, you'll also begin to appreciate the roles that so many people play in SAP projects and ongoing maintenance—how executive leadership, project management, business applications, technical deployment, and the application's business users all come together to create, use, and manage SAP over its lifecycle.

The first several chapters establish a deeper foundation than past editions, bringing readers up to speed before breaking matters down into areas targeted at business users or IT professionals. The book's hours are also organized more clearly, making it even easier for readers interested in a particular subject area to quickly locate the material that's most interesting to them. And as in the previous edition, each chapter concludes with a real-world case study that enables readers to put their new-found knowledge to the test.

What's Really New

Beyond important structural changes and a clear focus on business users and IT professionals, this latest edition of *Teach Yourself SAP in 24 Hours* includes new content reflecting

- ► SAP's newest cloud-based and other products and acquisitions, including Ariba, Concur, Fieldglass, hybris, and SuccessFactors

- ► The strategy behind HANA, along with business cases explaining when and how to benefit from it

- ► Where SAP Simple Finance fits into SAP's application portfolio

- ► Much deeper and broader technology platform details

- ► Reporting applications beyond SAP ERP's legacy reporting capabilities, including Business Objects Explorer, Crystal Reports, Xcelcius, Web Intelligence, and more

- ► Improved real-world SAP project implementation, migration, and upgrade guidance

- ► Use of SAP Solution Manager to address systems management and monitoring well beyond traditional CCMS

- ► New ideas and next steps related to career development

To give you a sense of how SAP businesses work with SAP at their desks every day, the book also includes real-world transactions used to run common SAP business scenarios. Several of these scenarios are detailed, whereas others simply reflect the kind of work that users might regularly perform in SAP CRM, ERP, PLM, SCM, and SRM systems.

Who Should Read This Book

This book is for people new to SAP, as well as for experienced people interested in filling in some of their own SAP knowledge gaps. Because the past five years have seen tremendous changes in the SAP application landscape, even the most seasoned SAP professionals will still benefit from Hours 3, 5, 6, 8, 13, 14, 18, 19, 20, and 21 (as well as significant portions of Hours 4, 7, 10, and 16).

From all of us at Sams, we hope you enjoy this read. More importantly, we hope this material helps give you the jump-start you need to make a difference in the world around you. Thank you again for adding our latest book to your personal library.

Conventions Used in This Book

Each hour starts with "What You'll Learn in This Hour," a brief list of bulleted points highlighting the hour's contents. Each hour also includes a summary highlighting key takeaways. Finally, each hour concludes with a case study with questions and answers relevant to the material in that hour.

PART I

Introduction to SAP

HOUR 1
SAP Explained

What You'll Learn in This Hour:

▶ History of the software company SAP SE

▶ SAP's business applications and industry solutions

▶ Components, modules, and transactions

▶ SAP client concept

▶ What it means to run SAP

This hour sets the stage by introducing the software company SAP and providing its brief history. Then, we explore SAP's application legacy and unique collection of acronyms so we will be able to speak the same language. A synopsis of SAP's current technologies and applications wraps up Hour 1.

Overview of SAP: The Company

A beginner's guide to SAP would be incomplete without a review of how the company evolved to its dominant leadership position. Headquartered in Walldorf, Germany, SAP SE is the largest enterprise applications provider and one of the world's largest software companies. Although SAP and its enterprise competitors are all distinctly different from one another, they are markedly similar. Most provide enterprise-class business software, business analytics and data warehousing solutions, solutions for small and large businesses, platforms for web and application development, integration software to tie systems together, and so on.

Each competitor helps sustain SAP; SAP counts Oracle as its largest database vendor, for example, and Microsoft provides SAP's most popular operating systems in both the datacenter and the office. IBM is SAP's largest consulting partner, and both Microsoft and IBM provide business intelligence solutions used by SAP's applications.

SAP was founded nearly 40 years ago in Mannheim, Germany, by a group of former IBM engineers with a singular vision: to develop a software package that married a company's diverse business functions together. The idea was to help companies replace 10 or 15 different business applications—such as financial systems (running accounts payables and receivables), warehousing applications, production planning solutions, plant-maintenance systems, and so on—with a single integrated system. Even better, these former IBMers wanted to create a system that embodied all the best practices that various types of businesses and industries had to offer. In the process, it was envisioned that this new software package would minimize a great deal of complexity and provide businesses with more real-time computing capabilities. This vision became real when Systems, Applications, and Products in Data Processing (SAP, or in German: *Systemanalyse und Programmentwicklung*) opened its doors in 1972. Those of us working in the SAP ecosystem have long referred to the company and its products interchangeably using a single word best spelled out as S-A-P (pronounced "ess aye pea," not "sap").

SAP's goal from day one was to change the world, and the company continues to deliver on that goal. Beyond its initial vision, the company's leaders created a multilingual and multinational platform capable of easily changing to accommodate new business process standards and techniques. Today, SAP is used by more than a million business users working for nearly 150,000 customers across 120 countries. Its 50,000 employees and 2,000 SAP implementation and support partners are busy building and implementing software in 40 different languages and 50 currencies. All these SAP business solutions are running on a growing number of computing platforms, thanks to advances in cloud computing.

To this last point, SAP has helped revolutionize the technology foundation for enterprise applications. Although it wasn't the first to support cloud computing, it purposefully broke away from the monolithic mainframe-based technology models prevalent in business applications in the 1960s and 1970s in the name of "choice." Since day one, SAP has architected its software solutions to run on a variety of different hardware platforms, operating systems, and database releases. Through this flexibility and openness, SAP in turn gave its customers flexibility and choice. Such a revolutionary departure from the norm created a tipping point in enterprise business software development and delivery that helped propel SAP to the forefront of IT and business circles by the early 1990s.

New entrants to the enterprise software field also grew popular during the 1990s, including Baan, Oracle Corporation, PeopleSoft, and JD Edwards. Soon afterward, smaller players began gaining ground, including Great Plains and Navision. Although still widespread, mainframe applications had simply grown too burdensome and expensive for many firms, and the enterprise software industry jumped at the chance to replace those aging legacy systems. IT organizations in companies around the world were just as anxious, finding it easier and cheaper to support a growing number of standardized hardware platforms.

In the same way that new enterprise software companies were gaining traction, new databases from vendors such as Oracle, Sybase, and Informix offered attractive alternatives to the old mainframe IMS and DB2 offerings. And new operating systems helped create low-cost mission-critical computing platforms for these new databases and applications. By the mid-1990s, when

SAP began supporting the Microsoft Windows operating system and SQL Server databases, followed soon afterward by the Linux operating system, SAP's place in the enterprise software market was firmly planted: The company's founders had completely delivered on their vision of a multinational, multilingual business solution capable of running on diverse platforms operated and maintained by equally diverse IT organizations. SAP had not only grown into a multibillion-dollar company by that time, but it had succeeded in changing the world of user productivity and organizational efficiency.

SAP Business Applications

From a business applications software perspective, SAP is nearly all things to nearly all businesses. SAP's application software foundation is built on the concepts of specialization and integration. Each software component or application within the SAP family of products and services meets a particular need, facilitating day-to-day financial and resource management (SAP Enterprise Resource Planning [ERP]), addressing product lifecycle planning requirements (SAP Product Lifecycle Management [PLM]), supporting internal company procurement (SAP Supplier Relationship Management [SRM]), interconnecting different systems to ease integration headaches (SAP NetWeaver Process Integration [SAP NetWeaver PI]), enabling customer relationship management (SAP Customer Relationship Management [CRM]), and so on. Divided by SAP into the SAP Business Suite (comprising all the business applications) and SAP NetWeaver (components of which essentially enable the SAP Business Suite, like a portal product, development tools, and business intelligence tools), all of these products and more are explained in future lessons; suffice it to say here that many SAP applications or components, many products, and therefore many potential SAP solutions can be assembled and customized for almost any business.

Components, Modules, and Transactions

It's important to understand the differences between SAP components, modules, and transactions. SAP uses the term *components* interchangeably with the term *business application*, and most of the time, this latter term is shortened to *application*. On the other hand, SAP modules provide specific functionality within a component. The Finance module, Production Planning module, and the Materials Management module are good self-explanatory examples. These individual SAP modules combine to create the SAP ERP component. It is within a particular module that a company's business processes are configured and put together.

Business processes are also called business scenarios. A good example is order-to-cash. It comprises many different transactions, from writing up sales orders in the system to managing purchase requisitions and purchase orders, "picking" inventory to be sold, creating a delivery, and invoicing the customer for the order. Each transaction is like a step in a process (step one, step two, and so on). When all these transactions are executed in the right order, a business process like order-to-cash is completed. Many times, these transactions are all part of the same module. In other cases, a business process might require transactions to be run in several different modules, maybe even from several different components (see Figure 1.1).

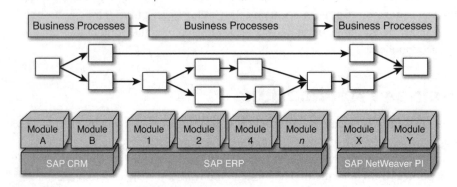

FIGURE 1.1
SAP components are made up of modules, which in turn comprise transactions used to execute high-level business processes and even higher-level mega processes.

Cross-Application Business Processes

The fact that SAP's transactions can be combined helps create broad and capable platforms for conducting business. In this way, SAP allows companies to obtain greater visibility into their sales, supply chain, and manufacturing trends or to allow new methods of entering or tracking such trends (to maximize revenue and profit) by extending business processes in several different directions. A good example again is order-to-cash, which is essentially a "back office" accounting process. By combining multiple SAP applications, a company can create a more capable extended version of this business process, something called a cross-application process, mega process, or extended business process.

Our simple order-to-cash process can become much more powerful in this way. For example, we might initiate our process through SAP's Enterprise Portal, which allows a broad base of a company's users or even its partners and suppliers to access the company's SAP system using a simple browser. Once in the system, the user might "punch through" to SAP ERP to actually place an order. Through the business logic enabled at the business process level, control might be passed to the SAP CRM application to determine a particular customer's buying preferences or history. CRM's business logic might then direct or influence the business process in a particular way, perhaps to help the salesperson increase the customer's order size or affect the order's gross margin. Next, SAP's Supply Chain Management (SCM) system might be accessed to revise a supply chain planning process for a set of potential orders, looking to optimize profitability as the system seeks to balance the needs of many different customers with the organization's access to materials, people, and other resources. SAP NetWeaver Business Warehouse might next be queried to pull historical data related to the customer's credit-worthiness in light of specific economic conditions or to assess sales patterns within a particular geography or during a particular season. After these details are analyzed, the extended business process might turn control over to SAP's Crystal Solutions to create company-internal reports. Simultaneously, SAP ERP or SAP NetWeaver Portal might be used to drive and track the pick-list process, order fulfillment and shipping process, and finally the accounts receivables processes to conclude the overall business process.

SAP Industry Solutions

Beyond enabling broad-based business processes, SAP is also well known for reflecting industry best practices in its software. By adopting SAP best practices rather than inventing their own, companies can more efficiently and effectively serve their customers, constituents, and other stakeholders. This is a big reason why SAP has been so successful: SAP stays abreast of many different industries, making it easy for companies in those industries to adopt not only SAP's software but that industry's best practices as well.

SAP's industry solutions were historically (and today are still loosely) divided into three areas: Manufacturing, Service Industries, and Financial/Public Services. There are actually 25 different groups of industries, such as Aerospace & Defense, Automotive, Banking, Chemicals, Consumer Products, Healthcare, Higher Education & Research, High Tech, Insurance, Media, Mill Products, Mining, Public Sector, Retail, Telecommunications, Utilities, and more. For the complete list, point your browser to http://go.sap.com/solution.html or just search for "SAP industry solutions" using your favorite search engine.

One of the nice things about these industry solutions is that they are simply "installed" atop SAP's other products. The Oil & Gas industry solution, for example, is installed on top of SAP ERP, and it allows ERP to be quickly configured for O&G business transactions that aren't standard in the out-of-the-box SAP ERP solution. If we didn't have the O&G industry solution, each O&G customer would have to pay someone to create, configure, test, and deploy that specific functionality. Such customizations, as we will learn, are expensive to develop and often more expensive to maintain over time. And when it comes time to upgrade SAP ERP one day, such customizations not only complicate matters but often benefit from being re-developed from scratch in the upgraded system.

Connecting the Dots

As touched on earlier, applications such as SAP ERP can be broken down into many different modules. A module's discrete functionality addresses a specific business function (which again is composed of many specific business transactions). Individually, each module is used to manage a business area or functional area for which a particular department may be responsible. Prior to extending a line of credit, for instance, a company's Accounts Receivables group may run a business transaction using the Finance module of SAP ERP to check a customer's credit and on-time payment history. Likewise, the Shipping department will regularly run a business transaction in the Materials Management module to check inventories at a particular warehouse. Other departments may be responsible for managing payables, real estate, sales estimates, budgeting, and so on. Together, all the various departments in the company work together to do the business of the company, using SAP across the board. In this way, the company benefits from a great amount of consistency between departments while giving the company's management the high-level visibility it needs to make all the strategic decisions necessary to keep the business in good shape.

Do you see a common thread? SAP's products satisfy the needs of enterprises, big and small, enabling them to tend to the business of running the business. SAP's software products are all about the "big picture"—about conducting business by connecting people, resources, and processes around the globe. SAP and its enterprise application competitors—Oracle, Microsoft, Sage Group, NetSuite, IBM, Epicor, Infor Global Solutions, Workday, salesforce.com, and many others—enable this capability at scale, integrating many otherwise discrete functions under a single umbrella. Note that SAP, Oracle, and Microsoft own the bulk of market share and mind share in much of the enterprise applications software space, followed closely by Sage Group, Epicor, Infor, and NetSuite.

The SAP Client Concept

We need to look at one more concept before we think about what it means to actually run SAP. In the world of SAP, the term *client* has special meaning. Clients are essentially self-contained business entities or units within each SAP system; using a common web browser or one of SAP's special user interfaces called the SAPGUI (pronounced "sap goo ee"), you log in to a client or legal entity configured within SAP, and it is this client that you actually use to run business transactions and so on. Each system—SAP ERP, CRM, SCM, and so on—has a unique system-specific client you log in to. Contemporary organizations thus have multiple production clients (one production client per SAP component), and each component contains several nonproduction clients. These are used for demonstration purposes and to develop and test the business functionality that will one day be put into the production client and handed over to the company's end users.

A client has its own separate master records and own set of "tables" (covered in Hour 3, "SAP Technology Basics"). The best way to grasp this might be to think about a really large company, such as ExxonMobil, General Motors, or Honeywell. Within each of these large multinational organizations, for example, you might have three, four, or even ten or more other companies or business units. Each SAP client might be tied to a different business unit; really big companies might have two or three production clients for a single SAP component, like ERP. For example, the company might structure its clients around discrete business groups (Chevrolet, Cadillac, and

GMC) or by geography (South America, Africa, Australia, and Europe). In this way, a Chevrolet business user might log in to the Chevy client to do her work, whereas business users over at Cadillac might instead log in to the Caddy client on the same SAP system to do their work.

In the end, having multiple clients can be a really good thing. For example, the Chevy client might be specifically configured for business processes and languages and currencies that only the Chevy business unit uses. And when those processes need to be changed, there's no need to coordinate with other business units, which saves time and provides the Chevy business unit with an extra bit of agility. The financials and other aspects of each business represented by the different clients can be easily rolled up, too, so that the multinational organization as a whole can easily report on its cross-company financial status, inventory levels, and so on.

Having multiple clients can represent a whole lot of extra work or duplicated work, too. Hosting different business processes and ways of working means there's less standardization across a multinational organization that has chosen to operate as different legal or business entities. Training systems need to be deployed for each unique client. End users can't seamlessly transfer between business units without requiring time to ramp up on how business is conducted in their new job. Data details will vary over time, too, creating scenarios where the same part of a vehicle might have several different part numbers and descriptions, depending on the client being used.

These trade-offs are all manageable and all part of developing the right business solution for a particular organization at a particular point in time. Regardless of the number of clients, the good news is that SAP makes it easy to keep clients separate and to remember which ones to access. When you need to log in to SAP, you choose the specific client you wish to log in to. Each client is assigned a unique three-digit number, which you may be required to know and type in at login time. This makes it easy to distinguish between clients you use for different lines of business, different geographies, or various testing purposes. Note that SAP security will prevent you from accidentally logging in to unauthorized clients; to access a particular client, you need to have a user ID and the appropriate permissions and authorizations setup.

A programmer developing new features in the SAP system might log in to client 100 to do some programming, log in to client 200 in another system to review and test new business logic, and log in to client 500 in yet another system to check out the new training system where his code is being used to teach others how to use SAP. In the same way, an end user might log in to client 300 in the production system to do his day-to-day work and occasionally log in to client 200 in a test system to check on the status of new functionality he requested be developed for production.

Remember this: In the broader world, the term *client* can mean several things, including an individual PC or workstation. For our purposes, however, we use *client* in the manner used by SAP: to describe a logically discrete legal entity or separate business entity within an SAP system—and try to avoid using this term to describe PCs and workstations.

Summary

This hour introduced you to the world of SAP. You gained an understanding of SAP's history and some of the specific business application and technology terms used in the world of SAP. When all is said and done, remember that the real work done by SAP is done by its components or applications; this has little to do with technology but rather involves business processes that have been specifically configured for a company. Business processes are often industry-unique. Fortunately, SAP's large number of industry solutions helps companies implement industry best practices. Also keep in mind that business processes are basically individual SAP business trans-actions strung together to do the actual work of running a business. Transactions are associated with specific modules, but business processes may consist of transactions from different modules. Cross-application or mega business processes consist of transactions spanning multiple modules and even multiple SAP components. We are now ready to turn our attention in Hour 2, "SAP Business Basics," to the core business fundamentals behind SAP. First, though, let's take a look at a case study.

Case Study: Hour 1

This case study winds its way through each hour and is designed to help you review and synthe-size what you have learned and to help you to think ahead as you seek to put your knowledge into practice. You can find answers to the questions related to this case study in Appendix A, "Case Study Answers."

Situation

MNC Inc., or simply MNC, is a large multinational mining, milling, and manufacturing com-pany with operations in 20 countries. Its customers are located around the world. Although MNC is a fictional amalgamation of many real-world companies that use SAP, the challenges it faces are relevant to those faced by contemporary organizations today. Ongoing financial transparency issues, lack of supply chain visibility, and recent concerns with falling worldwide sales and lost market opportunities have re-emphasized to the MNC executive board its need to replace its collection of more than 30 legacy business applications with a single well-integrated business application. The board is particularly concerned with business-unit agility as well as the organization's requirement to support several different languages and currencies. The board has also heard horror stories about expensive customization and is curious about whether SAP might have a relevant industry solution to build upon. Finally, with 100,000 Windows-based end users spread out across 500 different offices and 20 countries, the board is also concerned with how it can possibly get all of its people using a single application. The board members need to understand more clearly SAP's client concept as well. By walking the board through the follow-ing questions, your task is to help the MNC leadership team understand SAP's ability to address this first set of questions and priorities.

Questions

1. Outside of SAP, which other enterprise software companies might MNC also be investigating?

2. Which SAP applications or components might the board be most interested in first learning about?

3. Which SAP industry solutions might prove especially useful to MNC?

4. Given the large number of people (future SAP end users) that MNC employs, what might be the challenges faced, and how could SAP software be helpful?

5. Given the board's interest in business-unit agility, how might SAP's client concept be beneficially employed?

6. Will language and currency support issues be a problem for SAP?

SAP Business Basics

What You'll Learn in This Hour:

▸ SAP business roadmap

▸ Business architecture and blueprinting

▸ Mapping business needs to SAP applications

▸ Four perspectives to addressing business needs

▸ How SAP technologies support business needs

▸ How SAP enables a sampling of business scenarios

Though SAP provides a number of applications and underlying technologies to meet a company's business needs, those needs or business requirements must first be understood and then mapped to and delivered by software applications. Discovering, defining, and mapping needs back to a company's business vision and forward to an application strategy is the subject of business analysis, or "business architecture." A roadmap can be created to help an organization navigate this process. In this hour, we explore the basics of business architecture and developing a business roadmap. You'll see firsthand how business requirements connect an organization's vision and its people to the SAP and other business applications they ultimately use to run the business.

The SAP Business Roadmap

Before we can talk about SAP's applications and technologies, we need to understand the purpose and role of business architecture in general and the business roadmap in particular. Business architecture represents the highest level of abstraction, where the company's business vision is deconstructed into required business functions. When these business requirements are understood, they can be translated into a set of fundamental business processes (or workstreams), which in turn are married to more specific business functionality (like creating purchase orders or managing the new-hire process) that SAP and other applications provide.

Business Architecture

Sometimes business architecture is described as addressing the high-level *who, what, where,* and *when* questions. The business roadmap, on the other hand, is the tool used to bring all this together into a logical process. It maps the people who will eventually use SAP itself or SAP's data and reports to the business applications that provide the data and reports. During a new implementation, the business roadmap helps an organization stay on course. Later, after SAP has been installed and is being used, tools and processes similar to the business roadmap help the organization navigate necessary changes to how they conduct business.

As with building a house without plans, a company will never achieve its long-term vision or effectively take care of its day-to-day business needs without a good business roadmap. The business roadmap takes the outputs of strategic vision and business architecture to describe the company's business requirements, business functions, and applications that provide that functionality. Another way to look at this is that the roadmap shows how specific business functionality is ultimately delivered to meet a company's business requirements and fulfill its vision (see Figure 2.1). In doing so, the business roadmap takes the first steps in making technology relevant to business operations; it synthesizes business matters into what eventually becomes an SAP-derived technology-enabled business solution. In this way, SAP's applications and underlying technologies simply represent the tools used by the business to arrive at the roadmap's destination.

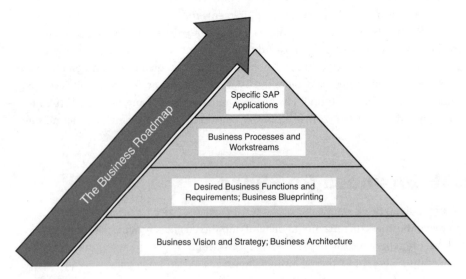

FIGURE 2.1
The business roadmap connects vision and strategy with the SAP applications used to run the business.

Traditional Business Concerns

Businesses provide goods or services. Many of these businesses exist to create value on behalf of the company and its owners in the form of profit, stockholder value, and the like. Other types of firms like nonprofits and charitable organizations are in business to serve a socially desirable purpose such as feeding hungry children or taking care of the needy. Regardless of its purpose, however, if a business cannot recoup its costs, it fails.

At the core of business architecture, and indeed business, is what the business does (what it sells or provides). Auto companies sell cars, oil companies sell oil, and charitable organizations provide goods and services to those who want them. How well a company performs its service is another matter entirely, though. Many different dimensions come into play, from financial aspects to matters of sales, marketing, supply chain/logistics, product lifecycle management, payroll, and so on. All these dimensions boil down to two simple tenets: maximizing revenue (or sales) and minimizing expenses (or costs), as explored next.

SAP's Purpose: To Run the Business

At the end of the day, SAP applications are used to run the business. But a closer look reveals how SAP also affects financial fundamentals; a well-implemented SAP business solution helps organizations increase their top-line revenue and shave their bottom-line expenses. For example, from a revenue perspective, SAP helps to

- ▶ Identify and manage new markets (via SAP Customer Relationship Management [CRM], Business Warehouse, and Business Intelligence)

- ▶ Innovate in terms of products and services to address new markets (via SAP Composite Applications, Product Lifecycle Management, and CRM)

- ▶ Improve a company's relationship with its existing customers to sell more goods per customer, establish a deeper sales relationship, or gain a "greater share of wallet" (via SAP CRM, Business Intelligence, and Enterprise Resource Planning [ERP])

In the same way, SAP enables cost reductions as it helps to

- ▶ Increase business operations efficiency by streamlining business processes, maximizing asset productivity, minimizing unproductive time, and so on (via SAP ERP)

- ▶ Reduce a company's cost of raw materials through vertical consolidation (via SAP Supply Chain Management)

- ▶ Reduce a company's cost of goods, materials, labor, and more through increased visibility and business process transparency (via SAP Supply Chain Management and ERP)

- ▶ Reduce costs of internal operations (via SAP Supplier Relationship Management)

- ▶ Maximize inventory and supplier discounts (via SAP ERP)

- ▶ Reengineer a company's service delivery processes (via SAP ERP)

- ▶ Reduce the company's "cost of change" by more quickly identifying opportunities to improve its cost model and optimize inefficient processes (via SAP Business Warehouse and Business Intelligence)

- ▶ Enhance how the company manages, delivers, optimizes, tracks, and improves on its products and services—or the processes used to drive its products and services (via SAP ERP)

Companies that increase sales while reducing costs realize greater business success than their industry counterparts, but companies that can better manage the risks of change have an even better shot at beating the competition.

Managing Business Risk

With every change introduced into a business comes the opportunity to make minor missteps and major blunders. To counter the negative impact inherent in such errors (in judgment, leadership, product marketing, sales strategies, partnerships, alliances, and more), a smart organization proactively identifies, manages, and mitigates risks. This applies to efforts aimed at increasing revenue or decreasing costs.

Contingency plans are especially important. An SAP implementation is far-reaching and complex, explaining in part why SAP projects may fail to be completed on time and on budget or may fail to initially deliver on promised value. Such complex endeavors require organizations to create Plan B, Plan C, and so on. Knowing and preparing for changes to Plan A makes the difference between a successful business solution and a business solution that simply cannot deliver the transformation promised by SAP in the first place. Successfully developing and executing against this kind of deployment mindset brings up another dimension of business architecture and the SAP business roadmap in particular: business agility (covered next).

Business Agility: Keeping the Future in Mind

Business agility speaks to a firm's ability to transform its products, services, supply chain, sales strategy, technical enablers, and so on in such a way as to more nimbly meet customer demand. Agility isn't so much about the present as it is about the unknown future; an agile organization beats its less agile competition because it can more quickly close the gap between present-day capabilities and needs and desired capabilities and needs. A good business roadmap, therefore, must reflect matters of business agility that enable an organization to work more efficiently, more quickly, more nimbly, and more effectively. These in turn need to be mapped to enabling SAP applications and technologies.

Increasing business agility is easier said than done. To change means to fight the inertia behind "the way things have always been done." Fighting inertia means changing how people and organizations work and how business processes are handled; the status quo might be markedly affected. As too many firms find out the hard way, maintaining the status quo is no way to run a business. Indeed, implementing SAP is often seen as a way of disrupting the status quo and reinventing how the work of running the business is optimized, divided, and addressed. Optimization is probably the key because in the end decision making is streamlined, resulting in

- Better and faster CRM

- More effective and less expensive supply chain management

- Increased transparency and compliance with regulations

- Improved cost versus risk metrics and outcomes

- Measurable business-enabling return on investment (ROI)

Only a well-developed business-enabling roadmap has a chance of transforming the business through increased revenue or decreased costs. But it's the next step that's most crucial. If business architecture and strategy is our house's foundation, the actual SAP business process development process, described by SAP as "business blueprinting," is our house's framing.

Business Blueprinting

Business blueprinting entails defining a firm's to-be business processes, identifying gaps between the current state and the to-be state, determining how well SAP's templates can be applied, identifying and prioritizing the need for customizations to these templates, and then locking down the scope of work necessary to make all this happen. Organizational matters come into play, as do the organization's original goals (and making revisions to those goals, as business realities dictate). In short, business blueprinting serves as the culmination of the initial roadmap development work.

SAP calls out this process of blueprinting in its Accelerated SAP (ASAP) project implementation methodology. Blueprinting follows a number of tasks related to project preparation. When blueprinting is completed, each SAP application is specifically configured to turn the envisioned business processes into real-life usable workstreams made up of strings of customized customer-unique business transactions. This phase of ASAP, called realization, consumes most of the project's time and budget. (Several iterations of functional, integration, and other types of testing consume a whole lot of time, people, and other resources.) Once realization is completed, final preparation, go-live support, and running SAP post go-live round out the ASAP project lifecycle methodology. The SAP project lifecycle, ASAP, and other matters of project management methodology are covered in more detail in Hour 4, "SAP Project Basics," and Hour 15, "An SAP Project Manager's Perspective."

The Business Perspective

As already noted, developing a sound business perspective is a critical first step in solving a business problem or tending to a business need. The business perspective articulates why a particular problem needs to be solved or an opportunity needs to be explored. Developing a firm's unique business perspective means working through the following:

▶ The identification of business-relevant stakeholders

▶ Long-term strategy enablement

▶ Short-term business objectives

▶ Core competencies

▶ Competencies other than the core competencies (and thus opportunities for partnering, developing alliances, or contracting out specific services)

▶ Procurement and other sourcing strategies (and how those strategies and relationships might change over time)

▶ SAP globalization and localization realities (where the emphasis tends to shift back and forth between enabling global consistency and roll-up financial reporting, for example, along with addressing the currency and language requirements for local user communities)

The most relevant stakeholders at this level are those involved in strategically aligning and executing the actual business processes or workstreams necessary for survival. Therefore, business executives and other officers of the board, along with functional managers and team leads, business analysts, and any other line-of-business leaders must be included in developing and communicating the business view.

How SAP Technologies Support Business Needs

With the business perspective behind us, the next several tasks of business blueprinting can be addressed. Matters such as developing the underlying architecture and designing the IT platform need to be considered and completed. In this way, the business roadmap will actually align to business goals predicated on responding in an agile manner to changing markets, new business needs, increased governance, and so on—all of which requires an agile technology platform. Technology basics are detailed in Hour 3, "SAP Technology Basics," which in turn sets the stage for developing the technology roadmap detailed in Hour 16, "A Technology Professional's Perspective on SAP."

Working with Stakeholders

Building a business roadmap is impossible without understanding the various stakeholders and their particular perspectives. Therefore, a quick look at stakeholders is warranted. In general, stakeholders are those who are most affected by the problems or concerns of an organization and therefore have significant interest in some aspects of a proposed solution. They can represent the entire company (such as the board of directors) or a just a few people within a particular team or specific function (such as IT, the finance group, or the sales and marketing team).

By directly engaging stakeholders and extracting their priorities and concerns initially as well as over the course of an implementation, the SAP project sponsor along with the SAP project manager may together effectively plan and execute a successful project. When the right people are involved from the onset and given a "voice" throughout, the project will more likely solve the problems outlined in the first place.

There is no one best way to engage stakeholders. Common methods include kick-off and regularly scheduled follow-up meetings, function-specific workshops, and executive milestone or status meetings. Regular email updates reflecting changes in the project plan, scope, resources, and so on might be appropriate, as well. Frequency of communication tends to be more important than the actual length of time spent providing updates.

It's also important to give stakeholders access at some level to the repositories of data used to track and maintain all the business, functional, project management, and technical decisions made, problems resolved, contact information, and similar such details. By being completely transparent and ensuring that stakeholders feel recognized and "in the know," a project team has a much better chance of building and maintaining the critical buy-in necessary to successfully pursue and complete a complex implementation such as SAP.

As we conclude our discussion about business blueprinting, you've no doubt noticed how business blueprinting views SAP strictly from a business perspective. This is only one of four dimensions of an SAP implementation, however. The three remaining dimensions are functional, technical, and project implementation. Each of these perspectives is detailed in the next few pages.

Other Perspectives: Mapping Business Needs to SAP Applications

Because of the variety of stakeholders involved in implementing, using, and supporting SAP, a single perspective can never resonate completely with everyone. Few people have the breadth of experience necessary to grasp all the complexities of implementing SAP or other complex business solutions. Therefore, other views into how these business solutions are developed, managed, and enhanced over time can prove helpful. Functional, technical, and project implementation perspectives are all effective views in this regard. For IT stakeholders, a perspective into a business solution's business dimensions, functional requirements, and project perspectives will help fill in their knowledge gaps. In the same way, a functional perspective followed by a more technical view, both of which are supported by an end-to-end project implementation perspective, allows nearly any stakeholder to envision a business solution in its entirety, as discussed next.

The Functional Perspective

The functional perspective is the easiest to grasp for individuals familiar with how to run a business. It is the most difficult to grasp for nonfunctional experts, however. This perspective addresses the *what* surrounding a solution—not *how*, or *when*, or *with what*, but simply *what*. It answers the question "What will a particular business process do?" In this way, the functional perspective or view addresses the following:

▶ It describes or communicates the flow of work (business process workflows or workstreams) in a stepwise fashion. The functional perspective asks what steps are necessary to execute a business process and thereby achieve a particular end state.

▶ It describes the properties or qualities to be exhibited by the business process. Thus, the functional perspective seeks to identify the characteristics and properties that each business process must reflect and to what degree these are reflected.

▶ It addresses these matters of workflows and characteristics from technology-independent and SAP-independent perspectives; a good functional perspective doesn't even mention SAP because it's simply not dependent on a particular application vendor's solutions.

As you can imagine, the key stakeholders for such a view are the end users who will ultimately execute the business process as part of their daily work. Business process designers, line-of-business leaders, and others involved with the functionality to be embodied by the solution are important stakeholders, too.

The Technical Perspective

The technical perspective or view addresses the "how" part of the solution equation. It gives legs to the functional view in that the technical perspective describes how the business solution will be enabled through technology. Important considerations include the following:

▶ Focusing on the key dimensions of the system; identifying and then establishing how the system will deliver the performance, availability, scalability, security, agility, systems manageability, and so on required by the business.

▶ Describing the solution's overall components in terms of business applications and other SAP components, data and relevant dependencies, interface requirements, underlying technical infrastructure, and all the underlying relationships and integration points necessary to enable the functional perspective described earlier.

▶ Providing to the extent possible a technology-independent perspective as to how technology helps enable the functional perspective.

Primary technical perspective stakeholders include enterprise and technical architects, solution developers and programmers, infrastructure and other technology specialists, and other technology-focused suppliers, vendors, and partners. Business architects also typically find this view useful.

The Project Implementation Perspective

The project implementation perspective is simple to comprehend. It answers questions related to what solution will be built, over what time period, and leveraging what resources. This implementation-specific view accomplishes the following:

▶ Describes and details the deployment plan, which in turn encompasses organizational and third-party resources, timelines, constraints (business, functional, technical, and other), and so on.

▶ Describes the SAP products and components to be used to fulfill the company's strategic vision and tactical functional needs, including to the extent to which these needs are fully developed and delivered.

Common implementation view stakeholders are project managers and coordinators, technical specialists, developers/programmers, testers, business process owners, executives, business leaders, power users, and more.

There's often a strong temptation to align specific views with certain disciplines or areas of expertise. Perhaps most obviously, the business and functional views might be lumped into business concerns, whereas the technical view might be seen as an "IT" thing and the implementation view as a "project management" thing. Avoid creating these silos and instead remember that a successful SAP implementation depends on the company and its partners working well together. Break down the walls, build teams that cross boundaries, and be sure each team has a voice in the overall implementation.

Combining the Four Perspectives

The four perspectives described this hour work to marry together a business solution's purpose (*why*) with its functions (*what*), technical underpinnings (*how*), and implementation details (*with what*). Breaking down a solution into these perspectives allows a firm to communicate across business and technology boundaries.

You probably noticed, however, that references to specific SAP products and components were lacking in this hour. There's good reason for this: A solid business roadmap should be developed well before a specific ERP solution is decided on. Like putting the cart before the horse, planning a roadmap based on the business solutions offered by a particular software vendor (SAP included) makes no sense at all. Figure out what the business needs to accomplish first and then determine how SAP and other vendors in the application solution space might best address those needs. In the succeeding hours, we cover the SAP-specific details necessary to move from conceptual roadmaps to firm implementation plans, technology platforms, and functional business solutions.

A Sampling of SAP Business Processes

To give you a sense of why a company spends so much time and money and invests in so many people to introduce SAP, this section covers several common business processes. In each scenario, you'll see how a company's end users use an SAP application in the course of their day-to-day job running the company's business. For even greater detail, see Hour 11, "Using SAP ERP to Do Your Job."

Performing Employee Self-Service Functions

One of the most common business scenarios involves employees viewing and changing their own personnel records. SAP NetWeaver Portal provides special views called iViews that enable employees to easily create, display, and change their own personnel records (assuming that they've been given these privileges). An employee might change her home address or telephone number, for instance, or update her contact information after a relocation. In other cases, she might be curious about when her paycheck will be deposited or might want to view the company's updated organization chart in the wake of a management shake-up. These kinds of self-service business transactions used to be completed by dedicated human resource representatives; to reduce costs and empower users, these functions are part of SAP's Employee Self-Service (ESS) functionality today. A sample ESS process might include the following:

1. Log in to SAP NetWeaver Portal's Welcome page.

2. Choose the Working Time option and then select Record Working Time.

3. Choose Leave Request.

4. Examine the Leave Request's overview.

5. Choose the Personal Information option and select Personal Data.

6. View the home address on record.

7. Choose the Bank Information option.

8. Choose Benefits and Payment and then select Paycheck Inquiry.

9. Log out of the portal.

These kinds of transactions are so typical that they're also used by the SAP EP-ESS Benchmark.

Balancing the Books

SAP ERP was born out of the need to marry core manufacturing, distribution, and warehousing functions with a single overarching financial system. Accounts and other financial analysts employed by the company use this functionality to pay the company's bills, balance the books, and so on. One of the most long-lived and useful SAP business scenarios within the finance and accounting function involves displaying, posting, and eventually balancing financial documents. The SAP Financial Accounting Benchmark illustrates this process well:

1. Use the SAPGUI to log in to SAP ERP's main screen.

2. Call Post Document.

3. Create a customer item.

4. Create a general ledger (GL) account item.

5. Choose the Post option.

6. Call Display Document.

7. Enter the previously posted document's number.

8. Double-click the first line of the document.

9. Call Customer Line Item Display.

Enter relevant data, choose Execute, and then:

1. Select the first line.

2. Call Post Incoming Payments.

3. Enter header data.

4. Choose Process Open Items.

5. Select an item in the resulting list.

6. Scroll to the end.

7. Select the last item.

8. Deactivate all selected items.

9. Choose Post.

After the documents have been posted, an accountant or a financial analyst might execute a similar process for a different general ledger or in support of another of the company's business units. Given SAP's long history and understanding of finance and accounting, new SAP finance users are often quite fond of the new-found power and capabilities they have with SAP ERP.

Selling from Stock

Like the other two business scenarios outlined this hour, the sell-from-stock business process is also common. Incidentally, it is the business scenario modeled by the most popular SAP benchmark, the SAP SD Benchmark. This scenario is typically executed by a company's sales team member, such as an inside sales representative. The rep uses SAP ERP either directly via the traditional SAPGUI fat client or by way of a web browser using the SAP NetWeaver Portal or perhaps a Microsoft SharePoint site. The basic sell-from-stock process consists of six transactions:

1. Run VA01 to create an order with five line items.

2. Run VL01N to create a delivery for the previously created order.

3. Use VA03 to display the order.

4. Change the delivery and then "post goods issue" using VL02N.

5. Use VA05 to list the last 40 orders created for one sold-to party.

6. Create the invoice for the order using VF01.

For other examples of how SAP is used in the course of a normal day at work, see Hour 11 and Hour 12, "Using Other SAP Business Suite Applications." In the meantime, by walking through the sample business scenarios above, we've wrapped some much-needed context around what we have studied so far.

Summary

The concepts outlined in this hour have prepared you to develop a high-level business roadmap. When you better understand SAP's applications and technologies, you'll be positioned to actually marry a company's business vision and needs with SAP's applications and thus create the underpinnings of an SAP-derived business solution. Before such a marriage is possible, however, the business's strategic and more-immediate business needs must be identified, prioritized, and communicated. This includes goals and requirements related to increasing revenue, decreasing costs, and managing the risk of change. We also discussed the importance of facilitating business agility, the company's ability to nimbly transform itself in response to changing business drivers and operational realities. Finally, we investigated the four high-level perspectives or dimensions by which a business problem may be viewed: business, functional, technical, and project implementation.

Case Study: Hour 2

Consider the following case study and questions related to developing a business roadmap for SAP. You can find answers to the questions related to this case study in Appendix A, "Case Study Answers."

Situation

In a benchmark of its competitors, MNC has found that it seriously lags behind in several areas. MNC's customer base does less repeat buying, tends to exhibit less product loyalty, and costs more to service than similar customer-competitor relationships. Furthermore, the business landscape is clearly evolving to one favoring a more direct sales model for MNC's commodity goods. Opportunities for growth capable of outpacing the competition seem reasonable, so MNC's board of directors is encouraged more than ever to pursue its tentative ERP implementation plans. To that end, you have been selected to join a task force to identify important startup concerns. Using the knowledge you gained this hour, answer the following questions.

Questions

1. Given the early and tentative nature of this ERP project, is it safe to assume that SAP will be selected?

2. To help the team align, you have suggested reviewing MNC's partially completed business roadmap. What four high-level areas do you expect to find called out in this roadmap?

3. Which primary tenet of business aligns best with MNC's problem of a lack of repeat buyers?

4. What four perspectives or views should the task force explore?

5. Which perspective addresses the "what" surrounding a business solution?

6. What does the technical perspective specifically address?

HOUR 3
SAP Technology Basics

What You'll Learn in This Hour:

▶ Hardware platforms for SAP systems

▶ Technology performance and maturity

▶ What you need to know about servers and storage

▶ Essential operating system considerations

▶ Database basics

▶ Traditional and contemporary infrastructure providers

Now that we've covered the basics of SAP and what it means to run a business using SAP, we need to spend some time discussing the basic mechanics "under the hood." This hour investigates several commonly used infrastructure-related technical terms and takes an introductory look at the three core technologies necessary to support any SAP application: hardware, operating systems, and databases. We conclude the hour with an outlook on the new "simplified" concept introduced by SAP. Even if you have a strong technology background, this hour is probably worth your time.

SAP Technology

Hour 2, "SAP Business Basics," covered the concept of business architecture. Now let's turn our attention to technology architecture. Whereas business architecture covers logical business processes and workstreams, technology architecture is about the technologies under the covers used to support business processes. It describes in a vendor-independent way the technologies that need to come together to do something useful. In our case, hardware, operating systems, databases, and application-specific technologies come together to create a foundation for a business application. When the application atop this foundation is SAP, we call this layered combination of technologies *SAP Basis*.

More generically, we often refer to this "stack" of technologies as the *SAP computing platform*, *solution stack*, or *technology stack*. These interchangeable terms speak to the layers of technology that combine to create the *basis* of an SAP system. The technology underneath SAP is like the foundation of a house. An improperly built foundation weakens the ability of your SAP system to weather storms, survive changing business needs, and meet the expectations of its occupants (the SAP end-user community).

We can extend the concept of technology architecture to include more than just SAP's foundation. Client devices like laptops, tablets, smartphones, and traditional PCs and printers play a key role in technology architecture. So does all the network infrastructure tying everything together—the wireless hot spots and routers and even old-school modems used to connect all our "front-end" client devices with the "back-end" SAP application. These front-end technology specifics are covered in later hours. For now, let's focus on the core foundation underneath SAP, starting with server and disk hardware.

Hardware Basics

In spite of the promises of cloud computing and virtualization, business processes need something to be executed. This is why hardware is still the most basic component of an SAP system. Hardware comprises the servers (industry-grade computers), storage systems (ranging from internal disk arrays to cloud-based virtualized storage space), and network gear (such as fabric interconnects, switches, and routers). All this hardware must work together to create an effective infrastructure for SAP. Improperly addressing technology architecture or skimping on a piece of hardware might create a weak link or potential point of failure, which in turn might cause problems down the road. For this reason, proper hardware architecture and design (what SAP terms *sizing*) is absolutely critical.

All the major hardware vendors sell systems that fit all types of SAP application needs, big and small. Choosing a hardware partner simply based on name recognition is a good place to start. Cisco, HP, IBM, and to a lesser extent Dell and Oracle are well-known providers of physical hardware you can unbox, rack, and set up yourself in your datacenter. However, things are changing, and the way you procure a hardware platform today can be very different from how it was only a few years ago. For example, converged infrastructures like Flexpod,[1] vBlock,[1] or VersaStack[1] are delivered "ready to run," and providers such as Amazon, Microsoft, Virtustream, T-Systems, Freudenberg-IT, and even SAP itself offer Infrastructure as a Service (IaaS) for SAP applications. Many other IaaS cloud providers are jumping on this bandwagon[2] as well, adding to an already complicated ecosystem of technology architecture methods and practices.

---

[1] Integrated platforms using Cisco servers and network together with NetApp, EMC, or IBM storage.

[2] See http://global.sap.com/community/ebook/2012_Partner_Guide/partner-list.html#.

We cover IaaS and other cloud delivery methods in Hour 19, "SAP and the Cloud." For now, keep in mind that any proposed hardware solutions, regardless of source, need to be vetted against one another, against an SAP shop's risk profile, and ultimately against the kinds of workloads reflected by SAP. After all, not all clouds are mature enough or even capable of supporting mission-critical SAP workloads, and not all SAP workloads are actually critical to business operations.

Servers

Thanks to the massive improvements in CPU power, the share of the server hardware in the total cost of ownership (TCO) of a single SAP system has significantly shrunken. However, due to the ever-growing number of SAP solutions deployed by companies and the introduction of in-memory appliances by SAP, the number of servers in a complete SAP landscape has risen as the price per server has been reduced.

Depending on size and configuration, investment in servers certified for SAP[3] for a complete system landscape could range from a few thousand dollars to several million (not including follow-on annual maintenance, which also adds up). The same server computing power hosted in the cloud, on the other hand, can range from the legendary 99 cents per hour for a single VM with ephemeral storage to several hundred dollars an hour for a dedicated instance with persistent storage and backup necessary for a productive SAP HANA instance. Actually, the costs become a pay-as-you-go proposition, changing one-time capital expenditures (CAPEX) into recurring operational expenditures (OPEX). This can be an attractive change to the bean counters, even if the "total cost of operation" would be higher than the traditional TCO. However, although cloud looks cheap, depending on workload size and duration (days, months, years), traditional hosting may give a better business case than cloud.

Server and other SAP infrastructure costs can vary significantly, but companies have at their disposal various financial methods to calculate which approach is best for them. But how can you determine the necessary size and compare the offerings of the various hardware vendors and cloud providers, each claiming to have "the best server for SAP"? To answer this question, we must first clarify the meanings of *performance* and *maturity* of SAP systems.

SAP System Performance

From a business point of view, SAP performance is essentially determined by the response time of the system because during this period, the user cannot proceed with the actual business process. Therefore, short response times are the ultimate objective of every SAP system. Average response

---

[3] See http://www.saponwin.com/pub/hardware.asp?l=vendor&sl=41&i=41&la=en for Windows and http://scn.sap.com/docs/DOC-8760 and http://scn.sap.com/docs/DOC-55015 for Linux.

times below one second are generally perceived as good, whereas anything longer is generally regarded as disruptive for the workflow.

From the user's point of view, the response time is the period during which the user must wait after having pressed the Enter key until a system response is displayed on screen. From a data-center or cloud provider viewpoint, response time is the average time from the arrival of the processing request at the application server until the moment when the response from the application server is transferred to the network. Therefore, Internet round trip time and the processing on the end device must be considered.[4]

Every transaction has a minimum response time. This value can be achieved only after the system has "warmed up"—that is, when the buffers are filled. So don't expect top performance from an SAP system after a reboot.

From a technical point of view, SAP performance depends on the ratio of the available resources to the current transaction load. Even with a relatively low average system load, the randomly distributed user activities now and then temporarily cause a CPU usage of 100% and thus lead to wait times. These wait times are so short, however, that the user will hardly notice them.

Figure 3.1 shows an example of the measured CPU load at certain points in time on a system with an average CPU load of only 50%.

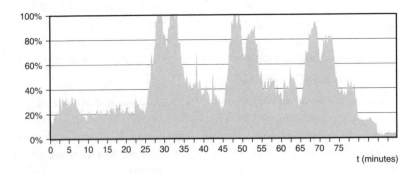

FIGURE 3.1
Example of CPU load distribution at 50% average utilization.

The greater the number of users, the greater the likelihood that the Enter key is pressed at the same time. Figure 3.2 shows the situation with an average CPU load of approximately 70%.

---

[4] CCMS transaction DINOGUI displays the execution time of the dialog step on the servers. DIALOG also includes the runtimes on the network up to the SAPGUI.

Here, the 100% peaks are actually small plateaus, and the result is that some users must sometimes wait a little longer for the SAP system to respond.

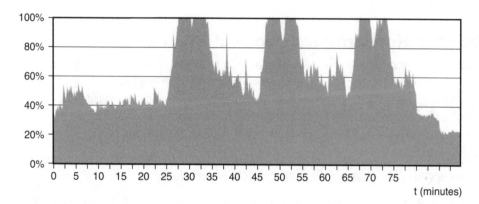

FIGURE 3.2
CPU load distribution with an average of approximately 70% utilization.

In Figure 3.3, despite an average CPU load of only 80%, the 100% plateaus have become so wide that long periods of unsatisfactory response times—and dissatisfied users—can hardly be avoided.

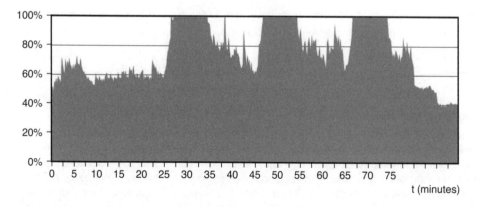

FIGURE 3.3
CPU load distribution with an average of approximately 80% utilization.

But how can the measured or projected transaction load be transformed into an actual tool for modeling server load and performance? The most common method or process is called "sizing."

For decades, the SAP Quicksizer[5] has been a proven tool for ensuring that load peaks do not turn into prolonged 100% plateaus. To avoid hardware vendor lock-in, the Quicksizer transforms the transaction load into units of measure that are independent of CPU type, computer technology, and manufacturer.

SAPS: The Horsepower of an SAP System

Although the size of main memory and disk space can be specified in terabytes (TB), SAP had to develop its own unit of measure for system throughput: the SAP Application Performance Standard (SAPS). Similar to the more generic tpmC performance ratings provided by the Transaction Processing Council (TPC), the SAPS unit of measurement is based on the Sales & Distribution (SD) module of SAP ERP and is the most popular SAP benchmark.

One hundred SAPS corresponds to the processing of 2,000 order items per hour, which requires 6,000 user interaction steps (screen changes) or 2,400 SD transactions.

SAPS can be regarded as the horsepower of an SAP system. Having said that, SAPS has as much in common with the practical usage of the SAP SD module as horsepower does with the strength of an actual horse.

One benefit of the definition of SAPS is that it is release independent; 100 SAPS is always equal to 2,000 order items per hour, regardless of the release of the application. This results in a paradox situation: Despite extended functionality provided with every new release, the "consumed" number of SAPS of a 1,000-user system does not change from R/3 3.1 to ERP 6.6 as long there are no additional changes in customization, usage of functions, and so forth.

However, the hardware that was able to support these 1,000 users with release 3.1 might support fewer than 100 users with release ERP 6.6 because elaborated features consume significantly more CPU power.

NOTE
_____

The Donkey and the Bag

The situation just described can be compared with a situation in which a farmer's donkey had to carry a 50-gallon bag. As long as the farmer filled the bag with hay, the donkey ran fast. After a while, however, the farmer made a "release change" to denser grain. The bag still had the same 50-gallon capacity, but it was much heavier, and it slowed down the donkey significantly. After the farmer found gold and other minerals on his property and changed the content of the bag to ore, the poor old donkey could only creep along. The takeaway here for IT departments, however, is that thanks to advanced technology, today's "server donkeys" are stronger than elephants compared to their ancestors.

_____

[5] See service.sap.com/quicksizing; note that SAP S-user credentials are necessary to access the tool.

Customers who use the opportunity of an SAP release change to move their SAP system from a legacy platform to a private or public cloud just have to tell the cloud provider the number of SAPS they required on the old platform. This will enable the savvy cloud vendor to properly size and select the right cloud infrastructure.

It is wise to stencil the SAPS rating of a server on its enclosure or have the SAPS numbers at least on file. Unfortunately, this good practice has often been forgotten after the dust of the RFP battle has settled. In such a case, you have to derive them from the benchmark numbers measured by the hardware vendors and published by SAP[6] (keeping in mind that application customizations and other changes naturally affect the SAPS a particular solution actually requires).

Be aware that benchmark numbers are derived from configurations highly tuned over weeks or even months by experienced benchmark specialists. And realize that no hardware vendor has the time, budget, and other resources needed to run benchmarks for a complete server portfolio running with every supported database.

However, the database accounts for less than 10% of the server load in the SD benchmark, whereas the CPU load caused by the SAP application instances is over 90%. So even if a specific database might provide 10% more ERP performance, this will result in only a 1% better overall SAPS number in a two-tier benchmark. So all database solutions—if tuned well enough—will deliver almost identical benchmark results for SAP ERP solutions.

No rule is without exception. For HANA, SAP's in-memory database, SAPS numbers are meaningless because the server hardware is determined by the memory footprint, which determines the number of CPUs needed. SAP only certifies servers with a fixed ratio of CPUs to memory; at this writing, for actual Intel "Haswell" CPUs, a server with four CPUs can support 1.5TB for analytical applications but 3TB for transactional applications.

For HANA as an appliance, SAP supports only certain enterprise-class Intel E7 CPUs; cheaper Intel E5 CPUs are supported under the "tailored datacenter integration." Restricted to servers with two CPUs and without performance guaranty, E5-based HANA systems are a "good enough" choice for development systems.

What Is the Best Platform for SAP?

Since SAP was founded, there has been a battle about which platforms and architectures represent the best technology for SAP's applications. Forty years ago, the mainframe was the only platform for SAP R/2; 10 years later, UNIX enabled the development of R/3. Since then, Windows and Linux have also proven themselves to be capable SAP platforms. If we define *maturity* as the

---

[6] See sap.com/solutions/benchmark/sd2tier.epx.

sum of scalability, stability, availability, and other architecture attributes, every platform essentially follows a similar maturity path (see Figure 3.4).

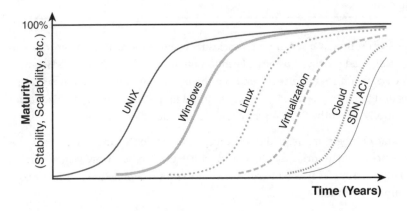

FIGURE 3.4
Maturity of platforms for SAP applications over time.

Together with the operating systems, the CPU technologies have evolved. Within the Itanium initiative, the reliability features of UNIX CPUs went into Intel E7 x86 CPU design. Today the majority of all SAP installations worldwide run on x86 architectures, mostly from Intel— approximately 55% on Windows and 15% on Linux at this writing. Also, SAP code in general is developed only on x86.

Practical experience has demonstrated that x86 servers are "good enough" for even the largest and most mission-critical SAP systems, making proprietary CPU architecture and operating systems obsolete despite all their undisputed benefits.

One essential aspect should not be forgotten when discussing the merits of the server vendors: the experienced experts of their SAP competence centers providing advice and consulting and most essential root cause analysis if the system runs into trouble. Such expertise, however, doesn't come cheaply.

Two-Tier Versus Three-Tier

Broadly speaking, two options for implementing an SAP server infrastructure are possible:

▶ **Two-tier:** SAP application and database tier sharing the same server and operation system and a presentation tier on a PC, laptop, or mobile device

▶ **Three-tier:** SAP application and database tier on separate servers within the same datacenter network and a presentation tier on a client or mobile device

Which of the two options is the most cost-effective architecture? Obviously, having fewer servers and OS instances requires lower costs to acquire, administer, and maintain. In the past, however, there was not much choice because a single server couldn't provide sufficient resources. For larger systems, the resources necessarily had to be distributed over a database server and several application servers.

Thanks to tremendous performance improvements, this issue has become largely irrelevant. Today, a single blade server can easily provide enough power to run the application and database layers simultaneously for more than 20,000 SAP users as a "central system." Consultants who still claim that dedicated database servers are mandatory are only demonstrating that they are not quite up-to-date.

However, there is still one reason for a dedicated database server, but it is financial in nature more than technical. In cases where the database licenses are acquired from the database vendor, the number of CPU sockets or cores of the server determines the database license fees. Most database vendors do not distinguish between CPU cores utilized for the database and those for SAP business processes in a central system. Consequently, vendors will charge not only for the 20% to 40% cores used for the database in a two-tier setup but also for the cores used for the SAP application layer. In this case, it makes sense to run the SAP database on a dedicated server so that only the cores on this server are counted toward database licenses. It makes even more sense to consolidate multiple databases on the same server to benefit from leveraging effects.

If the database licenses are acquired as part of the SAP license, the number of cores the system utilizes does not affect the fee. SAP licenses are mostly bound to user numbers and sometimes to memory but rarely to CPUs. So a central system will not influence the license fees but has the technical advantage that the system automatically balances the CPU resources between database and application. Also, the exchange of data between database and SAP application is interprocess communication rather than crossing the network.

"Big Iron" Versus Blades

In general, the tremendous improvements in SAP performance are mostly related to increased CPU clock frequency. However, improvements in compiler and I/O architecture can compensate for higher clock speeds. Current mass-market x86 CPUs can provide the same or better SAPS per thread as highly clocked proprietary RISC CPUs. Because SAP processes are mostly single threaded, this has a direct effect on the end-user experience.

As Figure 3.5 shows, the SAPS ratings of today's commodity two- and four-socket blades exceed the performance numbers of much larger servers released just a few years ago. Therefore, the technical need for "big iron" has simply become obsolete for most SAP implementations.

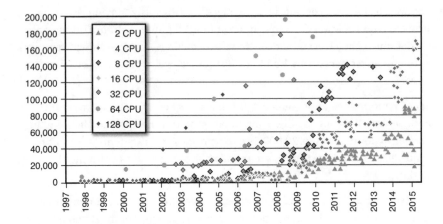

FIGURE 3.5
Note how the SAPS benchmark numbers per server have increased over the years.

Memory: Fast but Volatile

As the old IT saying goes, you can never have too much memory. This adage culminates with HANA in-memory databases demanding easily several terabytes of main memory. With HANA, the memory becomes the new frontier for server architecture, and this is true for both memory size and memory speed.

Unfortunately, main memory is volatile by nature and loses all its content immediately in the event of an electrical power outage. To avoid this effect, all databases certified for SAP write log files to nonvolatile storage such as SSD, flash drives, or disk drives.

SAP HANA also writes all changed memory pages by default every five minutes to nonvolatile storage. To avoid the sand glass displayed during such a savepoint, SAP specifies throughputs of up to 100,000 I/Os per second as KPI for a HANA validation. To reach this extraordinarily high throughput, SSD or flash devices can be used. Because they are still expensive, most vendors optimize their disk-based storage arrays as a cost-effective alternative for the persistency layer.

Storage: Hard Disks and Other Disks

In the past, one of the biggest cost drivers for datacenter infrastructure was the amount of disk space demanded by the SAP system. Due to the relatively small capacity of the individual disks, plenty of "spindles" were necessary to fulfill the demand of disk space even for moderate-sized SAP systems. However, all the spindles working in parallel also granted the necessary throughput.

Like SAPS numbers, disk capacity has developed almost in parallel with Moore's Law for CPUs. Unfortunately, there has been no commensurate improvement in disk throughput for random I/O because the physical I/O of a disk is restricted by mechanical parameters (rotation speed and positioning time of the write/read arm).

Ironically, the development of advanced compression technologies has allowed databases to shrink dramatically, but the I/O demand hasn't shrunk at the same rate. This results in an unfortunate paradox: Today, a disk subsystem needs many more disk drives to grant the necessary throughput than it would need for the necessary capacity.

Solid-state drives (SSD) using nonvolatile flash memory have significant advantages compared to electromechanical, hard-disk drive (HDD). While the mechanical nature of hard disks introduces seek time delays, for SSD the physical location of data is irrelevant. Most importantly, SSD technology offers significantly higher I/O performance:

- **HDD:** Small reads, 180 IOPS; small writes, 280 IOPS

- **Flash SSD:** Small reads, 1,075 IOPS; small writes, 2,100 IOPS

- **DRAM SSD:** Small reads, 4,091 IOPS; small writes, 4,184 IOPS

Even with all the benefits of SSD, there is also a drawback: price. At the time of writing, a HANA system with SSDs is 70% more expensive than the same configuration using traditional hard drives for the persistency layer. Due to patents on key manufacturing processes, the further decline in cost will be modest.

Storage Networks

Using the internal disks of a server to store mission-critical data has a drawback: You miss out on the flexibility and leveraging of virtualization and high-availability features of centralized storage arrays.

Storage area networks (SANs) are still the most robust and well-performing connections between servers and storage subsystems. Network-attached storage (NAS) systems have also proven their merits for SAP.

From the point of view of resource pooling typical for private and public clouds, both solutions have the drawback that additional interface cards have to be installed in the database server. SANs use HBAs, and NAS might need additional NICs to avoid SAP slowdown.

Technologies like Cisco's Unified Computing System (UCS) merge the SAN and LAN infrastructures using converged network adapters (CNA). A CNA acts simultaneously as both Fibre Channel HBA and Ethernet NIC, matching to unified switches. In this manner, any server can be deployed as a database with an FC storage server at any time. A straightforward benefit of UCS is the reduction in cabling and network components by at least half. Instead of redundant pairs of NICs and FC HBAs, only a single pair of CNAs is necessary. A less obvious benefit is that fewer components generate less heat. Also, eliminating any component helps reduce device failure and management overhead.

Cloud Storage

The most contemporary method of providing storage to SAP is via cloud-based disk space. Providers such as Amazon, Microsoft, and Rackspace all sell virtualized storage at pennies per gigabyte. Although cheap by any standard, the biggest challenge with cloud storage is the relatively low bandwidth and high latency of Internet connections (to access that storage!) compared to the internal network of the provider's datacenter. If you decide on a "cloud first" strategy, it is wise to procure both server and storage resources from the same cloud provider.

SAP System Landscapes

An *SAP system* refers to a collection of instances identified by a single system identifier (SID). For example, an SAP Enterprise Resource Planning (ERP) production system named PRD consists of one database, one set of central services, and anywhere from 1 to perhaps 100 application server instances (with 2 to 10 being most common, depending on the workload that needs to be supported and each physical server's capabilities). Similarly, you might configure another set of SAP instances and a database instance to create a single SAP CRM production system.

NOTE

Instances and Processes

In an SAP context, an instance is a self-contained unit, which comprises its own processes and memory, profiles, and executables. Instances write their own trace files and can be started and stopped autonomously. A single SAP system with multiple instances can run distributed over several computers. However, you can also easily install and execute several instances of one or more SAP systems on a single server.

For obvious reasons, the focus of SAP system architectures and operation is on the productive systems that provide business users with the necessary functionality to do their jobs. However, SAP recommends the deployment of additional, nonproductive systems to ensure the stable operation of each mission-critical business solution. This includes:

- A development (DEV) system for customizing, parameterizing, and implementing customer-specific developments

- A quality assurance (QA) system for validating customer development, SAP updates, database, and operating system patches before they are implemented in the production system

Thus, only tested versions of operating system, databases, and application code are executed on the production system to ensure a stable, reliable, and optimal performing operation. Each of these systems has its own set of database and application instances; they are therefore entirely independent systems coupled via the SAP Transport Management System (TMS).

Larger enterprises deploy additional installations for training, integration, staging, pre-production purposes, or so-called sandbox systems for testing new processes.

Most of these systems are relatively small because the number of users and transactions is usually very limited. The QA system, however, should be the same size as the production system to enable meaningful stress tests.[7]

With the stateless computing architecture and service profiles described later, the same resources can also easily be used as a technical sandbox and serve the purpose of fail-over infrastructure for production, if required.

Training and sandbox systems do not store sensitive data; therefore, they can be easily deployed in public clouds even if QA and production systems will be hosted in a private cloud. A special configuration is necessary when development systems are deployed in a public cloud to connect the SAP transport management system over wide area network (WAN) connections.[8]

UNIX and Linux OSs store their SAP binaries, log files, profiles, and libraries in a directory named /usr/sap. Windows stores its SAP files in x:\usr\sap. In UNIX and Linux systems, /sapmnt is mounted as an NFS (network file system) mount, and the /usr/sap/<SID> is a local file system. In Windows, the x:\usr\sap directory is shared as SAPMNT and is accessible as \\servername\ sapmnt. For Windows servers hosting multiple instances of SAP on a single OS installation, all SAP instances must be installed to the same SAPMNT directory; there can be only one SAPMNT share.

An optional but highly recommended service called SAPOSCOL runs the OS collector and allows SAP to gather OS-related performance and other statistics, such as CPU utilization, memory utilization, disk I/O activity, and more. Another Windows service called SAPService<SID> (where <SID> is the system identifier of the SAP instance) exists for each instance of SAP on the OS. This service is started with the sapstartsrv.exe executable. It calls the SAP start profile, which tells the system how to start SAP. Only after SAP is fully up and running can end users connect to it and do their work.

---

[7] See *mySAP Toolbag* by George Anderson.
[8] See page 21 of the *SAP on AWE Operations Guide* v1.5 (aws.amazon.com/sap).

SAP Work Processes

SAP uses the OS to run eight different kinds of work processes, as detailed in Table 3.1. You will sometimes see them collectively referred to as DVEBMSG. The D equates to dialog work processes, V is for update work processes (differentiated by V1 and V2 priority types, designating version), E is for enqueue, B is for background/batch jobs, M is the message service, S is used for print spooling, and G represents the SAP gateway. The instance profile for each SAP instance describes how many of each type of process will start at system startup time. (The instance profile is a simple text file sitting atop the OS and is discussed in the section "SAP OS-Level Profiles.") You can see which work processes your OS is running by executing a special OS-specific utility or by using SAP's own transactions SM50 and SM66. Although we are getting ahead of ourselves, this ability to see the status of SAP work processes is important: Beyond providing a view into the system's workload, it also reveals in real time the status of the instance and the overall system in terms of what each work process is doing. SM50 shows you only the work processes of a single application server, whereas SM66 is a global window into what is happening with every active work process running across an entire SAP system.

TABLE 3.1   SAP Work Processes

Work Process Type	Description
Dialog	D: Processes real-time information in the foreground
Background	B: Background processing for long-running processes, reports, and batch jobs
Synchronous update	V1: Processes immediate updates to the database
Asynchronous update	V2: Processes updates to the database on a lower priority than V1 (that is, when time permits)
Enqueue	E: Manages database locks
Message	M: Manages communication between application servers
Spool	S: Manages print jobs (the print spool)
Gateway	G: Communicates with other SAP and non-SAP systems

SAP OS-Level Profiles

Each SAP instance has three profiles: the default profile, start profile, and instance profile. Profiles are text files that are imported into and maintained by the SAP database and used to start and run the instance. The default profile contains information common to all SAP instances of a particular SAP system. For example, the production system might include a database, a central instance, and six application servers; all of these instances use the same default profile. The start profile calls the executables to start SAP, and this would be pretty similar for each instance.

Finally, the instance profile contains detailed instance-specific information. In the instance profiles of two of your application servers, you might define a bunch of batch work processes (for example, to create batch servers). Other instance-specific detailed information might include specific memory configuration parameters, buffer settings, and more. Use SAP transaction RZ10 to change and maintain all these profiles and to access a handy list of all available profile parameters.

Database Basics for SAP

With hardware and operating system details behind us, it is now time to turn our attention to the role of the database underneath an SAP business application. The same care that goes into choosing a hardware platform and OS should be used when choosing a database. Depending on your platform and SAP version, you might be restricted to only one or a few database choices (which underscores the importance of viewing your SAP infrastructure as a holistic computing platform). SAP supports most mainstream databases, including Microsoft SQL Server (and ultimately its cloud counterpart, SQL Azure), IBM DB2, Oracle (including real application clusters [RAC]). Since the acquisition of Sybase, SAP offers also ASE and IQ together with HANA. Many customers say it's a pity that SAP announced the end of the further development of MaxDB (formerly SAPDB), which was known for low license fees and even lower required administration effort.

Microsoft SQL Server runs only on Windows-based operating systems. Oracle, ASE, and IQ are supported on Windows, Linux, and all the major UNIX operating systems. DB2 is supported on all these platforms as well as IBM's legacy mainframe systems.

Most IT departments prefer SAP database platforms that they currently support and with which they already have familiarity and experience. Sticking with only those platforms can be an expensive mistake because much of the traditional work performed by a database administrator (DBA) is just not necessary in the world of SAP. That is, SAP "abstracts" a lot of the complexity out of managing and maintaining the underlying database.

A Quick Database Primer

Whichever database you choose, enterprise applications such as SAP are essentially made up of programs and data that are both used by and created by those programs. The data is organized in a meaningful way within a database, making it easy for the programs to access and find the data necessary to do something useful, such as run a financial report or create a sales order. In the case of most SAP components, such as ERP, the programs and data reside together in the same database.

Each component generally requires its own database (although exceptions exist). For example, a "production environment" consisting of SAP ERP, SAP NetWeaver Enterprise Portal (EP), and SAP hybris consists of three different production databases.

The database plays a key role in each SAP system because it houses all the data used by that particular SAP component or application. In the simplest form, a database is composed of tables, columns (called *fields*), and rows (called *records* or *data*). The basic structure of a database is quite similar to the structure of spreadsheets like Microsoft Excel, where columns (fields) store row after row of records (data). The biggest difference between a database and a spreadsheet is just that databases can contain multiple (and extremely large) tables that are connected to one another through relationships. Therefore, a database can be thought of as a much more complex, and ultimately much more useful, spreadsheet.

Tables, Indexes, and Structure

An SAP database contains literally thousands of tables that store information. Some products, such as ERP, contain more than 40,000 tables, whereas less complex offerings such as SAP NetWeaver Process Integration (PI) might have fewer than 10,000. Note that in most SAP systems, 10% of the tables house 90% of the data, so some tables can grow quite large and are subject to constant change, whereas others tend to remain small and relatively static. All these tables are tied to each other through established relationships. It is precisely this series of connected multiple tables that creates what is known as a *relational database management system* (RDBMS).

Beyond housing raw data, databases house indexes, which are used to speed up the retrieval of data. An index might best be described as a table of contents or viewed as a copy of a database table reduced to only the key fields. The data in this reduced copy is sorted according to some predefined criteria that consequently enables rapid access to the data. Not all fields from the copied table exist in the index, and the index contains a pointer to the associated record of the actual table. You might be surprised to know that indexes can make up to 50% of the overall size of an SAP database!

SAP uses another concept called *transparent tables*, which are SAP database tables that contain data only at runtime. A transparent table is automatically created in a database when a table is activated in the ABAP/4 Data Dictionary. This transparent table contains the same name as your database table in the ABAP/4 Data Dictionary. Each of its fields also contains the same names as its database counterpart, although the sequence of the fields might change. The varying field sequence makes it possible to insert new fields into the table without having to convert it, all of which allows for more rapid access to data during runtime.

Finally, it's important to know a bit about *database structures*. Just remember that database structures are groups of internal fields that logically belong together. Structures are activated and defined in the SAP ABAP/4 Data Dictionary, and they contain data only temporarily (during the execution of a program). Structures are differentiated from database tables based on the following three criteria:

▶ A structure does not contain or reflect an associated ABAP/4 Data Dictionary table.

▶ A structure does not contain a primary key.

▶ A structure does not have any technical properties such as class, size, category, or buffering specifications.

Migration Without Risk

SAP systems can be moved easily from one vendor server platform to another, as long as the operating system and database didn't change. SAP stores all its own executables and configuration files together with the business data in the same database. So all you need to do for what SAP calls a homogenous migration is to dismount the volumes from the old server, mount on the new system, and boot. Even a mishmash of different operating systems can be used, although some need a more elaborate system setup.

Changing the operating system or database, however, requires more effort. The good news, however, is that such a heterogeneous migration will not change your business processes because they are coded in ABAP or Java, and both are platform independent. The only platform-dependent part of the classical SAP solutions is the so-called "kernel" or "Basis," a runtime to execute ABAP and Java. So changing the operating system of the SAP application servers just requires you to download and install the correct SAP kernel.

Changing the database, however, is a different story. Because the code and the way the data is structured is platform dependent, you have to do a complete export of the source database to flat file and import to the target platform when changing the OS or the DB or both.

In the past, such migration was a major project because of the extended downtime and some risk incurred with lack of experience. With today's powerful servers and storage arrays, the downtime for the export and import of several terabytes is a matter of hours rather than days. Today a migration project for a single productive instance is two weeks in most cases, and even system landscapes with hundreds of SAP systems have been migrated within a total project runtime of a few months, thanks to experienced consultants being able to perform RISC migration without risk

Future Developments

For more than 30 years, the traditional database concepts of Oracle, SQL, and DB2 have evolved to cope with the demand of SAP systems for performance, scalability, and stability. Summarizing several innovative architectural concepts described in the next hour, SAP HANA fundamentally changed the rules of the game. For example, column orientation made indexes mostly obsolete with HANA, shrinking the database footprint by 30% to 40%. HANA also features advanced compression technologies. For example, SAP's own productive ERP system shrunk from 7.1TB on DB2 down to 1.8TB when migrated to HANA.

To understand the next step, you must know that most of the 40,000 tables (mentioned earlier) in an ERP database are so-called aggregates, used to store precalculated sums and averages to accelerate system performance for repetitive calculations. Utilizing HANA's capability to calculate such sums and averages on-the-fly, aggregates become obsolete if the code of the SAP solution is adapted accordingly. Removing aggregates will not only further shrink the database but also simplify the data structure significantly.

The first available simplified SAP business process is "smart financials," already used in SAP's own sERP implementation, which reduce the database footprint further, from 1.8TB to only 0.5TB, by making obsolete all aggregates and indices.

The simplified database structure is expected to enable the data of all simplified SAP business solutions to be stored in a single HANA database, making the whole system landscape real time again and the need for data replication between such SAP applications obsolete.

However, it will take SAP quite a while to rewrite the code of all its applications to simplify them. It is good that SAP has announced support for all "classical" SAP solutions (and databases) until 2025.

Summary

This hour covered the key components of SAP infrastructure: hardware, operating systems, and databases. Beyond traditional methods of building the Basis layer or computing platform for SAP, we also looked at newer methods of providing this IaaS. And we looked at what it means to choose and partner with vendors that must work together to create a well-performing computing platform for SAP.

Case Study: Hour 3

Using your newly acquired hardware, operating system, and database knowledge, read through this hour's case study and address the questions that follow. You can find answers to the questions related to this case study in Appendix A, "Case Study Answers."

Situation

Your employer, MNC, runs the latest releases of SAP's applications on Microsoft Windows and SQL Server. MNC recently acquired Archaic Manufacturing Incorporated (AMI), a large competitor that also runs the latest releases of SAP's applications on a combination of UNIX and mainframe platforms, atop a mix of Oracle and DB2 databases, respectively. AMI's databases are huge by any standard. MNC wants to consolidate like-for-like systems between the two companies, in alignment with its own IT cost-reduction strategies. It is also looking for much faster business analytics and is asking about HANA. Finally, MNC also needs to understand how HANA might provide other advantages.

As one of the technology architects on the team, you have identified four options. The first is to do nothing and continue to have each IT team support its own systems. Second, the team could consolidate all its hardware and other gear as is into a single common datacenter. Third, the team could standardize computing platforms. Finally, the team could pursue some kind of strategy with the cloud. Assume that you have the necessary means, resources, and time to pursue any of these choices and answer the following questions.

Questions

1. Identify the primary advantage to the team's first choice, to doing nothing.

2. List several disadvantages or challenges related to doing nothing.

3. How might the second option, to consolidate existing assets into a single common datacenter, prove beneficial?

4. List some of the advantages of standardizing computing platforms.

5. If AMI's production landscape consists of SAP ERP, CRM, and PLM, and each of those consists of four instances, how many production systems does AMI currently support?

6. How might the team consider using HANA to MNC's advantage, and what would probably be HANA's chief disadvantage?

SAP Project Basics

What You'll Learn in This Hour:

▶ SAP project implementation basics

▶ Preplanning first steps prior to implementation

▶ Key project tasks and roles

▶ SAP realization resources and timelines

▶ The SAP project lifecycle

Even if you now understand the business and technology basics behind SAP, if you are new to the SAP world, you might still be unclear about what it means to plan for, install, and run SAP. This hour completes our "basics" discussions, as it describes an SAP project and much of what it entails.

Running an SAP Project: The Basics

If someone tells you a company is busy implementing SAP, be sure to ask what that really means. What exactly is the company deploying? SAP Enterprise Resource Planning (ERP), SAP Supply Chain Management (SCM), or SAP Customer Relationship Management (CRM)? Another SAP BusinessSuite or NetWeaver application? As you might remember from Hour 1, "SAP Explained," many companies around the world have already implemented SAP ERP but continue to add new SAP applications and features. Perhaps the company is deploying Business Objects, SuccessFactors, Ariba, Fieldglass, or SAP HANA. Meanwhile, other companies are extending SAP to include third-party applications (such as Microsoft Dynamics CRM and AX, the latter of which is another ERP package better suited to certain industries, geographies, or business environments).

Even if you don't specifically know which SAP product is being deployed, if you understand the business functionality being implemented, you can probably guess the application. Once you understand the functionality and its scope, you might turn your thoughts to how the project will be managed. How will business requirements be identified, and how will gaps in SAP's out-of-the-box solution be addressed? How long will the project take, and who will be involved? Although SAP's various software products and their purposes differ, an SAP implementation project requires a tremendous amount of preparation and project management to bring everything together.

To set the stage for success, the most important and immediate matter is getting all of an SAP project's stakeholders and necessary subject matter experts (SMEs) thinking and moving in the same direction. Company executives, business unit leaders, functional and technical specialists, end users involved in the project, the organization's IT department and project management office, a host of external consulting and integration partners, and many others all need to be mobilized to help organize and move an SAP project forward. Without good alignment between all these stakeholders and SMEs (see Figure 4.1), the project will never get off the ground, much less successfully reach the point where SAP is turned over to its end users to be used—a special day known as "go-live."

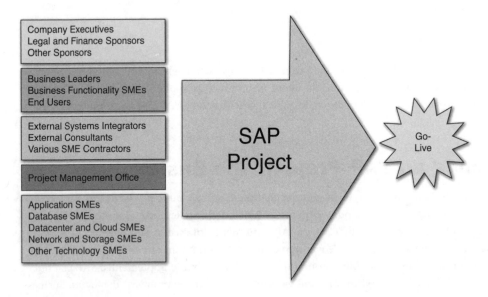

FIGURE 4.1
A variety of absolutely critical team, roles, and subject matter experts must come together to achieve go-live.

First Steps in Pursuing an SAP Project

Before an SAP project ever begins, an enormous amount of work goes into understanding whether the company (or organization) even needs such a thing. After all, SAP and its enterprise software counterparts are expensive and risky. And SAP projects consume huge quantities of time, people, and other resources that might be better invested elsewhere.

Most of the early work is best described as due diligence, validation, and preplanning. The specific first steps toward pursuing an SAP project often include the following:

- ▶ Identify the organization's pain points, including current business problems and lost business opportunities that might be solved by making some kind of change.

- ▶ Document the organization's business processes and issues with those processes that are at the root of the organization's pain points.

- ▶ Determine whether the issues with those processes (and the organization's pain) would be best remedied by a software system implementation.

- ▶ Create a "business case" (benefits, drawbacks, rough order of costs, timelines, risks, and so on) for implementing a new software system.

- ▶ Consider the organization's ability to adapt to a new software system (that is, a new way of working).

- ▶ Consider various software vendors by evaluating your organization's pain points against the software vendor's specific applications and solutions.

- ▶ Develop a fit/gap analysis for each software vendor that describes how well its solution out-of-the-box fits your company and addresses your pain points (fitness) and to what extent the solution would need to be customized (gaps).

- ▶ Select the software vendor (let's assume SAP was the best choice) based on out-of-the-box fitness, fewest number of gaps that would need to be developed or customized for your organization, SAP SE's ability to help your organization navigate the change necessary to adopt its software system, SAP's references in your specific industry or geography, overall estimated project costs (initial acquisition costs, implementation costs, and ongoing software maintenance costs), potential risks and their ability to be mitigated or managed, and more.

- ▶ Plan for the implementation in terms of business functionality, technical underpinnings, interfaces needed to communicate with other systems used by the business, training, and change management.

As you've surely realized by now, all of these preplanning and validation tasks take months to complete. Such an exercise represents a project in its own right, and indeed the preplanning steps really need to be managed like a project in order to yield the best choice. Once a decision is made to implement SAP, you're ready to begin working through the SAP project implementation lifecycle, discussed next.

The SAP Project Lifecycle

A lifecycle approach to implementing SAP helps illuminate the broad-brush phases or tasks associated with Accelerated SAP (ASAP)'s blueprinting phase (briefly introduced in Hour 2, "SAP Business Basics," and detailed later in Hour 15, "An SAP Project Manager's Perspective"). An SAP project lifecycle may be divided into seven phases or steps, each of which involves various roles and tasks:

1. Project initiation

2. Matching and prototyping

3. Design and construction

4. System integration testing

5. Business acceptance testing

6. Cut-over preparation

7. Stabilization

In terms of overall effort, understanding steps 2 through 5 is most useful. It's in these steps that most of a project's time and budget is spent. Deliverables or outputs associated with each step act as inputs into the subsequent step. Each step is also associated with particular objectives and goals. A sample timeline illustrating the SAP project lifecycle is shown in Figure 4.2.

Step 1: Project Initiation

Project initiation commences the SAP project lifecycle in terms of driving the planning and overall strategy of the project—how it will be staffed, executed, managed, and evaluated. This involves several tasks similar to ASAP's phase 1:

▶ Establishing objectives and scope

▶ Designing and staffing the implementation team

▶ Training the team

▶ Establishing controls and other project management processes

▶ Conducting the project's formal kickoff

Outputs include publishing a defined scope of work (project scope), filling out the team's roster of resources, aligning business units and their respective power users, establishing measurable success criteria, and creating the initial business templates to be used for prototyping.

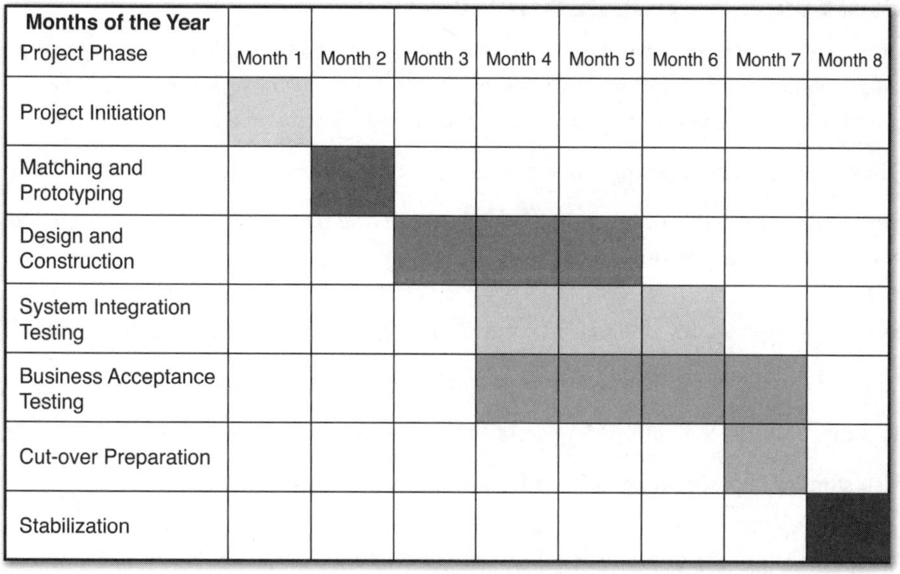

Months of the Year Project Phase	Month 1	Month 2	Month 3	Month 4	Month 5	Month 6	Month 7	Month 8
Project Initiation	▓							
Matching and Prototyping		▓						
Design and Construction			▓	▓	▓			
System Integration Testing				▓	▓	▓		
Business Acceptance Testing				▓	▓	▓	▓	
Cut-over Preparation							▓	
Stabilization								▓

FIGURE 4.2
The SAP project lifecycle provides a simple seven-step view into a project over time.

Step 2: Matching and Prototyping

In prototyping, functional experts and other row leaders work with power users and SAP component specialists to review SAP's solutions. Through this exercise, each functional team works to prototype a workable, albeit limited, business-specific SAP solution. Tasks associated with prototyping include the following:

▶ Developing and sharing a complete set of business scenarios

▶ Mapping the firm's unique business processes and workflows to the SAP solution being adopted

▶ Identifying gaps between SAP's capabilities and the organization's business requirements (performing a fit/gap analysis)

▶ Conducting initial integration testing (also called shakedown testing)

Outputs from these prototyping activities include a complete list of agreed-upon in-scope business scenarios, a document mapping work processes to SAP functionality and solution sets, a list of gaps in required and desired business functionality, and a set of integration test results showing whether the proposed solution is on track.

Step 3: Design and Construction

In step 3 of the SAP project lifecycle, the new functionality required by SAP's systems to meet a firm's business requirements is outlined from both technical and business perspectives. From a technical point of view, the teams responsible for design and construction do the following:

▶ Conduct reviews focused on the scope and design of all development items

▶ Document and complete all functional configuration and programming work required to meet a firm's business requirements

From a business perspective, the design and construction teams perform many tasks:

▶ Align new or updated business processes with row leader expectations

▶ Train power users in the various SAP workflows and business processes

▶ Publish standard operating procedures for workflows and business processes

Step 3 outputs consist mainly of published documents reflecting technical solution scope and design, standard operating procedures, and the entire process surrounding how to train power users and later the business end-user community in general.

Step 4: System Integration Testing

System integration testing (SIT) demonstrates that a system is capable of supporting the business's requirements. This massive undertaking requires a detailed schedule. Unit and functional testing are followed by testing with all necessary master and reference data (and mocked-up transactional data, as necessary).

Once individual functionality is proven, entire business processes are woven together and tested, culminating in a system integration test. Final outputs include the deployment of a "rollout system" capable of supporting the new SAP-derived business processes.

Step 5: Business Acceptance Testing

Business acceptance testing demonstrates that a newly configured SAP system is capable of supporting the company's business requirements. An extension of both SIT and user acceptance testing, business acceptance testing involves the following:

▶ User acceptance signoff

▶ End-user training signoff

▶ Standard operating procedures signoff

There are many different types of business acceptance testing, depending on the scope of a project. However, four types are prevalent throughout most SAP projects:

▶ **Unit/functional testing:** Validates each step of a business process or functional transaction to ensure that it operates as expected.

▶ **System integration testing (SIT):** Involves walking through all the steps in a business process to verify that the entire business process works as expected and then taking the tests up a notch to determine how well they work for a business group or an entire site. An example might include testing the sales-to-cash business process from ordering through procurement, shipping, delivery, and final billing.

▶ **User acceptance testing:** This type of testing is more detailed than system integration testing because it includes all real-world as well as what-if test cases. Instead of being performed by the business configurators (as is the case with SIT), row leaders and power users tend to drive the bulk of user-acceptance testing. Such testing might include ordering a mix of products from various sites and with various payment terms and shipping requirements to various distribution centers around the world—just as real users would presumably do one day.

▶ **Load, or stress, testing:** This type of testing (a form of which is also called volume testing) is required to ensure that business processes run well with other business processes—all under the load placed by hundreds or thousands (whatever is realistic) of SAP end users doing their work, just as they will one day do in production. This will validate whether the system scales when the system is under load or at what point the system no longer responds well (referred to as smoke testing). As you can imagine, load testing is especially useful to the technical and business teams tasked with ensuring that the SAP applications perform well.

Be careful to manage well the time spent prototyping; without a clear scope of work and meticulously managed marching orders, a team of expensive consultants and a slew of company-internal resources can be quickly consumed by prototyping that might never bear fruit. Carefully align this activity with the scope of work and manage it closely

Outputs from business acceptance testing include verification that all users are indeed trained and ready to work on the new system, that the new system and its business processes work as intended (that is, they work as described by the scope of work outlined initially, including the impact that subsequent change orders would have had on the system), and that all business test cases and other real-world scenarios are tested and signed off by the business.

Step 6: Preparation for Production Cut-Over

Production cut-over requires preparation like any other phase. Once all the preceding activities have been signed off on, a series of business-oriented and technology-oriented checks should be conducted. Only once all issues have been resolved or deemed noncritical can the system be cut over and go-live achieved. The following constitute several such checkpoints:

▶ Completed "transports" of all configuration and development changes, which are initiated in the development environment, tested in quality assurance (QA)/testing, and upon signoff transported from development directly into the production system

▶ Master data integrity check, to ensure that all master data is up to date, consistent, validated by the business, and present (Like configuration and development changes, master data is transported across the SAP system landscape, too.)

▶ Transaction data migration from legacy and other systems to the SAP system landscape, which gives SAP's end users the ability to look at recent albeit pre-SAP transactions (useful when accounts or shipping status needs to be validated shortly after go-live and the old systems have been retired)

▶ Stress/load testing, to ensure that the system scales well under the load of hundreds or thousands of users

▶ SAP Early Watch reporting, which entails SAP or a local SAP-approved partner connecting to the SAP system and running through a series of technical checks intended to validate stability, availability, and performance

The SAP support team also needs to develop and publish an SAP production support plan in preparation for production cut-over. This comprehensive plan provides a framework that defines how issues are captured, escalated, and managed; how performance is monitored; how business processes are monitored to ensure that their performance meets established service level agreements; and so on. The production support plan also includes a contingency plan—the firm's backup plans in case something goes horribly wrong and the system crashes or key functionality failure represents critical business disruption. Outputs are numerous and generally reflect the items listed earlier.

Just like the development and configuration aspects of developing a new system, transports will also consume a huge amount of time during an SAP implementation. Don't underestimate the human power required, not to mention the timing and coordination necessary between the functional consultants, row leaders, power users, and others. It's more work than you think. And it only gets worse after go-live.

Step 7: Operational Stabilization (Run)

Step 7 refers to work performed after the system goes "live" and is therefore the longest step or phase in terms of duration (lasting years, until the SAP system is finally retired and replaced). It maps well to ASAP's phase 6: Run (also called Run SAP). The team is busy on several fronts during this time. Simply initially supporting the end-user community and their respective business groups consumes many resources. Other team members are busy planning for the first several change waves (where new functionality that didn't make the cutoff in time for go-live will likely be introduced). Developers continue doing their work of developing, transporting, and testing changes and bug fixes alike, while the firm's project management office publishes its conclusions and lessons learned, measures and reports against the project's success criteria, obtains final signoffs for all outputs and other deliverables, and closes out the project. Still others focus on refining the tools used for monitoring and maintaining the system—from the lowest levels of the SAP technology stack to the applications, integration points, and bolt-on products necessary to run a business.

Operational stabilization outputs include finalizing and publishing all project documentation, publishing all end-user and technical team training materials, handing off operations support to the appropriate post-go-live teams, and finalizing all project actuals, resource status, and other communications mechanisms, including the project's lessons learned.

Organizing a Project by Tasks

Let's assume that your project planning tools and processes are in place and your business solution's blueprint has been established and agreed upon. The next step is to organize the teams responsible for doing the bulk of the project work, called *realization*. Although there are several ways to do this, it's important to first recognize the steps, tasks, and roles necessary to execute a large software project. To get and stay organized, SAP project teams might set up a Microsoft SharePoint team site or file server directory structure much like the following:

- ▶ **01 Pre-Sales:** Includes the initial request for proposal (RFP) published by the customer, various systems integrators (SIs) and others' responses to the RFP, contracts, expectations, initial plans that were discussed (what was sold), information related to solution demonstrations or proofs of concept (POCs), promises made, initial high-level schedule, initial gaps identified by the customer, and more.

- ▶ **02 Communications:** How communications and other materials will be shared between the stakeholders, contact lists, email distribution lists, web sites and other tools used for communication, schedules, initial success criteria communicated, expectations and norms around communications, and other such materials that explain how project communications will occur.

▶ **03 Project management:** Detailed project plans, resource plans, staffing models, task lists, typical PMO information, and also information on partners, ISVs, and others that are helping on the project.

▶ **04 Program management:** Includes strategic materials and decisions, how stakeholder management is to be performed, communications plans specific to executive leadership, steering committee meeting minutes, variations to plan, and weekly and monthly status reports.

▶ **05 Blueprints and analysis:** Include early decisions and supporting rationale for each of the SAP application's functional modules, along with changes determined along the way. (Detailed configuration and customization requirements are covered in their own respective areas.)

▶ **06 Configuration:** Includes standard configuration rules (not customizations but rather the out-of-the-box configuration performed on the system), fit/gap details, high-level solution design, detailed design, configuration standards, configuration workbook (reflecting meetings with BPAs, what was demonstrated, promised), final solution configuration (including trade-offs, add-ons/scope creep, and what was pushed out to a backlog of planned system updates post-go-live), necessary production system specs/how they might change, and technical details related to batch, reporting, and information/collateral related to the SAP industry solution (IS) that's being deployed.

▶ **07 Customizations:** Same as 06 Configuration but focused on the gaps (where gaps are akin to customization); includes customization standards, change management strategy and tools (how the development process will be managed), functional system documentation (organized by functional areas, such as FI, MM, PM, payroll, SCM), technical system documentation (again organized by functional areas but reflecting the technical details related to providing the software's functional needs), release notes, decisions, and trade-offs; the IS being deployed may also be tracked here if the IS represents customization more so than the core SAP solution.

▶ **08 Testing:** Akin to "quality," includes materials related to the overall project's test strategy, integration testing, QA testing, interface testing, performance testing, stress testing, and test matters related to training.

▶ **09 Defects:** Includes the strategy, tools, resolution processes, and escalation methods necessary to track the SAP system's defects found through testing. Thus this includes configuration, customization, data issues, and more, all combined into one bucket for easier tracking and status updates. Only the smallest of projects with very few customizations would attempt to track defects manually; the vast majority of SAP projects require a dedicated system for tracking and resolving such thing.

▶ **10 Technical Team:** Includes a diverse set of materials reflecting the entire SAP solution stack (from the SAP application itself down to the project's hosting or data center strategy). Server, operating system, and disk requirements, network details, SAP system landscape design, bolt-ons, cloud and on-premises decisions and resources, integration details, systems management strategy and details, and all of the traditional technical SAP application (formerly SAP Basis) details are included as well.

▶ **11 Data:** Includes the project's legacy data transformation and migration strategy, master and reference data strategy and processes, lists of legacy systems and their data sources and contacts/BPAs, transformation requirements and processes, templates for uploading data into the new system, tracking data issues and resolutions, how to prep for go-live (full data followed by incremental updates from the legacy systems), where automation is possible, cutover times/schedules, and so on.

▶ **12 Security:** Includes the project's security strategy; how users and roles will be managed; application, infrastructure, and physical security considerations; and decisions made.

▶ **13 Access Strategy:** Materials related to how the system(s) will be accessed and why certain decisions were made (fat, web, Citrix, using SharePoint, mobile apps, and so on).

▶ **14 Training:** Includes training plans, manuals, user guides, and other materials focused primarily on the end users who will be using the system.

▶ **15 Cutover and Go-Live:** Includes transition strategies and plans, details cutover checklists, includes go/no-go rules, and details on the specific success criteria and KPIs to be measured and monitored before and after go-live.

▶ **16 Post Go-Live:** Includes plans, checklists, and other materials used to achieve operational excellence once the system has been turned over to its end users.

Although this list doesn't attempt to be comprehensive, it should give you a good idea of the complexities and challenges inherent in an SAP project and its myriad tasks. Let's look at people next, based on the roles they hold in an SAP project.

Organizing a Project by Roles

A surprisingly diverse number of roles are typically necessary to develop, operate, and maintain an SAP environment. From a headcount perspective, the number of individuals could be considerably less than the number of roles (that is, a single person might fulfill multiple roles). SAP complexity and the size of the environment itself are key factors, as are the skills and experience levels of the individuals holding those roles. For instance, functional specialists might have knowledge of multiple functional modules, or technical specialists might have knowledge of multiple technical areas.

On the other hand, a single specialist may be unable to handle all the work associated with certain highly complex functional modules or work-intensive technical tasks. For example, operations teams often comprise four or more headcount, and development teams grow to handfuls of team members before settling down into maintenance activities post-go-live.

In an SAP environment, project roles are categorized into leadership roles, business or functional roles, technical roles, and general support roles, detailed next.

Leadership Roles

Quite a few leadership roles are important to an SAP project throughout its lifecycle, some of which include

▶ **Executive SAP business sponsor/leader:** Accountable to the business for the overall SAP solution from a business-enabling perspective; serves as the primary role accountable for overall system capabilities, performance, recoverability, and business operations; ultimately responsible for system-wide business and IT governance, including regulatory and audit compliance.

▶ **SAP program director:** Manages the project from a strategic or big-picture perspective, focusing on stakeholder management, communications, risk/issues management, executive relationships, contractual details, and the overall project's success in the context of the organization's business goals and environment.

▶ **SAP project manager:** Responsible for the project from a tactical perspective; manages time, schedules, scope, quality, risks, people, and other resources. See Hour 15 for details related to the SAP project manager's role, focus areas, and responsibilities.

▶ **SAP team manager:** Responsible for the SAP environment after go-live; coordinates analysis of new business requirements; coordinates collaboration between functional and technical roles; coordinates local and partner resources.

Business or Functional Roles

Functional roles are responsible for performing the business-enabling functional tasks associated with operating and maintaining the functionality of an SAP environment. These include the following roles and skills:

▶ **SAP functional architect or business analyst:** Responsible for the cross-module integrated solution of SAP in alignment with its respective functionality and business processes; verifies business needs and how those needs can be met; has excellent functional knowledge of specific SAP module(s), potentially including ISV and other partner modules/functionality;

specialized in a specific area/module/business process of SAP; responsible for depicting specific business processes as part of the SME's functional area expertise in SAP; works closely with the test manager and development lead to clarify questions about specific business processes.

▶ **SAP test manager:** Responsible for the testing processes, including coordinating test processes, consolidating test cases, and coordinating varying levels of integration testing and user acceptance testing (UAT); also analyzes test results and communicates outcomes and recommendations to the team.

▶ **SAP change management or "release" manager:** Coordinates application changes, verifies business needs and prioritization of new business demands for the system, and defines release cycles and each application's patch management strategy.

▶ **SAP functional support engineer:** Handles functional-related SAP support cases and support calls; triages and diagnoses problems, investigates resolutions, and resolves and communicates problem resolutions after go-live; and holds strong functional knowledge of specific SAP module(s) and related business processes.

Other functional roles exist and are detailed in subsequent chapters.

Technical Roles

A vast number of technical roles are responsible for performing the technical tasks associated with deploying, operating, and maintaining the technical platform and underpinnings of an SAP environment. Several key roles include the following:

▶ **SAP technical architect:** Prepares and conducts infrastructure analysis, sizing, and design; designs and executes technical deployment and management methodologies; designs and deploys integration components; and develops strategies for maintaining technology over its lifecycle.

▶ **SAP database administrator:** Performs database (Oracle, Microsoft SQL Server, SAP Sybase) administrative and maintenance tasks; and monitors database performance, sizing, and growth.

▶ **SAP development lead (one per functional area):** Responsible for the development strategy and ABAP and Java code quality; coordinates development work items; evaluates new hotfixes; develops work items, bug fixes, and regression fixes; and debugs application code.

▶ **SAP administrator:** Adds new users, deploys hotfixes, deploys SAP instances, and so on; conducts SAP-wide infrastructure monitoring administration; and monitors application availability, interfaces, performance, and error conditions.

▶ **SAP datacenter operator and systems management lead:** Owns the overall infrastructure and facilities environment from an ongoing operations perspective; executes backups and other routine computer operations and administration tasks; and monitors the hardware, OS, database computing environment, and interfaces to other systems underlying the SAP solution.

▶ **SAP technical support engineer:** Handles technical-related support calls, triages and diagnoses problems, and investigates resolutions after go-live; resolves and communicates problem resolutions; and possesses strong technical knowledge of the SAP solution stack.

Finally, many other roles are critical to deploying and managing SAP, several of which are discussed next.

General Support Roles

Beyond technical and functional roles, a number of additional supporting roles are necessary. These include the following:

▶ **SAP organizational change management lead:** Coordinates organizational change management communications; coordinates and communicates technical and functional changes; and helps measure and ensure the adoption of SAP, new business processes, and new ways of working by the end user community.

▶ **SAP security/audit lead:** Tests and monitors plans for implementing and maintaining SAP security and maintains and enforces security policies and procedures aligned with best and proven practices for assuring role-based segregation of duties; regularly audits roles for adherence to segregation of duties aligned with best and proven practices; serves as a security-specific liaison between the business and technical teams; manages role-based security by working with the business to understand needs; reviews security logs; serves in a compliance capacity, supporting both external and internal auditing, and provides a vehicle for exceptions through escalation to executive management.

▶ **SAP business continuity/disaster recovery (DR) lead:** Responsible for working with business areas and IT leads to create, test, and maintain the DR and business continuity plans; owns and is responsible for maintaining the SAP DR Crash Kit; manages risks and operational impact and establishes alternative plans to resume critical business operations; has expertise in application and IT infrastructure disaster planning; and is skilled in assessing complex ERP environments from a single-point-of-failure perspective to identify availability and recoverability gaps.

Surely, many other roles are necessary to plan for, deploy, and operate SAP. The previous lists of roles are intended only to provide a glimpse into the complexities and opportunities surrounding an SAP project.

Summary

In this hour, we walked through what it means to plan for and run an SAP project, including some of the basic project tasks, resources, and roles. And we walked through the SAP project life-cycle from a project and business user perspective. These fundamentals set the stage for many of the remaining hours in this book.

Case Study: Hour 4

Consider the following case study and questions. You can find answers to the questions related to this case study in Appendix A, "Case Study Answers."

Situation

With your experience implementing SAP at a competitor, your industry experience, and your MNC companywide contacts, it was no surprise you were appointed to the new ERP project direc-tor position at MNC. You are well aware that the executive management team has decided to implement SAP's ERP and supply chain applications, but these decisions haven't been commu-nicated broadly yet, and blueprinting just started. Your first day on the job finds you in a town hall meeting with many of your new team members and direct reports, several of whom asked the following questions.

Questions

1. What are we doing with SAP?

2. Once blueprinting is wrapped up, how will you structure the teams for the realization phase?

3. Several business unit VPs are curious about whether you're going to go with browser access or do some kind of thing with a fat client. What will you tell them?

4. Another person is asking about the SAP project lifecycle and wants to understand how it's structured. How would you most easily explain it?

5. One of your senior project managers is under the impression that the blueprinting phase will consume most of the project's time and budget. What is your response?

6. After the town hall meeting, an employee corners you in the elevator and asks whether his job in finance will be impacted.

PART II

SAP Applications and Components

Overview of SAP Applications and Components

What You'll Learn in This Hour:

▸ The past, present, and future of SAP solutions

▸ The core SAP Business Suite

▸ The role of SAP NetWeaver

▸ Solutions for small and midsize enterprises

▸ How to pick the right solution for your business

Predefined business processes are provided by the SAP Business Suite, NetWeaver, and a growing number of SAP cloud solutions for some of the largest and most well-known companies around the world. But SAP also boasts three different solutions for *small and medium enterprise* (SME) customers together with several appliances and database offerings. Even for experts, it is difficult to cope with the overwhelming number of components based on different technologies and ever-changing three- and four-letter acronyms. To best understand the future requires knowledge of the past; this hour starts with a brief overview into the SAP portfolio as well as a look at the SAP roadmap to achieve real real-time business solutions. The second half of this hour covers solutions for small and medium enterprises.

A Real-Time Vision

In 1972, when Hasso Plattner, Dietmar Hopp, Hans-Werner Hector, Klaus Tschira, and Claus Wellenreuther founded a company called Systems, Applications, Products in Data Processing (SAP), their vision was to develop standard software for business processes. The first versions materialized on thousands of punch cards, and the product eventually grew into an integrated business system called R/3.

Covering the basic business processes of a whole company in one monolithic application with a single database had the tremendous advantage that the result of any transaction became available for all users at literally the same moment. This real-time nature gave us the "R" in R/3. For example, every movement of capital and goods in and out of the company could be reflected in the company's bookkeeping in real-time, a feature largely unparalleled by previous business applications. And that was only the beginning.

Figure 5.1 illustrates how SAP complemented R/3 over time with solutions for data analysis (Business Warehouse [BW]), production planning (Advanced Planner and Optimizer [APO]), sales management (Sales Force Automation [SFA]), system administration (Computing Center Management System [CCMS]), and more. With the advent of the Internet, the Internet Transaction Server (ITS) and solutions for Internet-based sales (Online-Store) and purchasing (Business to Business [B2B]) were added to the SAP portfolio.

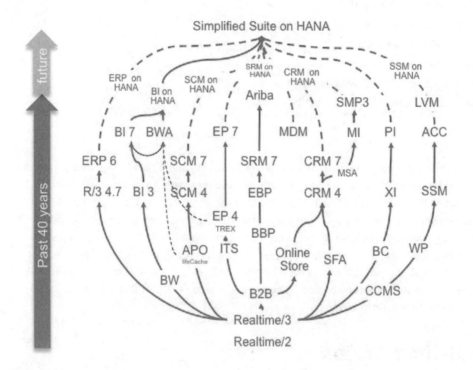

FIGURE 5.1
The evolution of SAP's application portfolio from legacy R/3 to contemporary in-memory solutions.

The purchasing solution was later enhanced as Business to Business Procurement (BBP) and Internet-based communication with third-party systems enabled by Business Connector (BC). SFA was developed into Customer Relationship Management (CRM), APO became Supply Chain Management (SCM), BBP evolved into Enterprise Buyer Professional (EBP) and later Supplier Relationship Management (SRM), BC into Exchange Infrastructure (XI) and then Process Integration (PI), and CCMS into SAP Solution Manager (SSM or SolMan).

SAP NetWeaver

With SAP NetWeaver, SAP extended its portfolio with the SAP Enterprise Portal (EP), Mobile Infrastructure (MI), Master Data Management (MDM), and NetWeaver Administrator (NWA). XI was renamed Process Integration (PI), and BW was renamed Business Intelligence (BI) and moved into the NetWeaver portfolio. Several other solutions were grouped into the SAP Business Suite. Finally, SAP's traditional ERP product R/3 Enterprise was renamed Enterprise Core Component (ECC).

To enable ad-hoc analysis, SAP combined the Live-Cache in-memory technology already developed for APO with its TREX indexing machine and called the solution BW Accelerator (BWA); it acted essentially as a high-performance "side car" to the BI solution.

A dedicated solution for data analysis became necessary because the performance of early platforms didn't allow running transactions and reports at the same time on the same system. While these solutions optimized for specific business processes became a great success, the concept of the integrated real-time system was broken since each of these solutions demands its own database instances to grant performance. Data generated in the different systems had to be replicated and consolidated. Because the extraction would have a negative effect on the response time of the transaction systems, the replication is usually done at night, with the effect that all reports reflect the "truth of yesterday" only.

Simplification: Real-Time Again

In the days of R/2 and R/3, SAP's goal was to create a real-time platform for business. In those early days, real time was pretty subjective, though, akin to processing that didn't require transactions to be "batched" and processed after hours when the user community was out of the office.

Eventually, real-time transactions became a commodity; all of the big software vendors could boast real-time business systems. But real-time didn't mean instantaneous, and more and more business scenarios demanded nearly instantaneous responses. Scientific studies at the Hasso Plattner Institute of the University of Potsdam resulted in the High-Performance Analytic Appliance (HANA), a hybrid in-memory database intended to replace the traditional databases used for SAP business applications.

During the announcement of HANA at Sapphire 2010, Hasso Plattner presented his vision of SAP HANA becoming a common database for SAP's entire enterprise software portfolio. Within this concept, the different software solutions would remain independent but share one single high-performance database (HDB).

Today, the unified database is still a vision due to the fact that the data table structures of the different solutions have become incompatible with each other over time. Therefore, any SAP solution still needs its own HANA instance (BW on HANA, ERP on HANA, CRM on HANA, and so on).

At the SAPPHIRE NOW conference in 2014, Hasso Plattner disclosed that SAP is on the way to simplifying the data structure of its solutions, radically replacing aggregates and indices with ad-hoc algorithms (stored procedures) running in HANA. Such "simplification" will not only reduce the number of tables in SAP solutions from several thousand to a few hundred but also enable SAP to make the data table structures of the different solutions compatible with each other again.

S/4HANA is the name chosen for the new Simple ERP. The S stands for *simple*, and 4 reflects the fourth generation. S/4HANA starts with Simple finance (as of this writing), and then comes Simple logistics (soon), and then the rest of ERP. SAP announced that S/4HANA will not make custom code using aggregates obsolete; rather, S/4HANA code will detect such access to tables not available anymore and redirect to the equivalent HANA view automatically.

As a welcome side effect, a unified data store for transactional and analytical data will make the current need for replication between the different database instances of the individual SAP applications obsolete and reduce the total physical storage footprint of a company significantly.

As more simplified SAP solutions based on the same reduced set of tables become available in the upcoming years, the vision of a single database to store all business process is in reach, enabling business process data available to all applications and users at the same moment again as they were more than 40 years ago.

Into the Cloud

With the acquisition of SuccessFactors for talent management, SAP added a first "cloud-only" solution. Later it added Ariba for business-to-business procurement, Fieldglass to manage the leased workforce and contingent workers, and then Concur for travel management. These Software as a Service (SaaS) solutions are "cloud only" by definition and utilize technologies that have nothing in common with classical SAP architecture. Nevertheless, they have to be connected and integrated with the "classical" SAP solutions implemented on premise or in public clouds. For this reason, we discuss these SAP cloud solutions together with the SAP business solutions that need to be integrated in Hour 8, "SAP on the Cloud and New SAP Solutions."

SAP Business Suite Components

Without a doubt, the SAP products sold as components of the SAP Business Suite are some of the company's most well known. Providing literally thousands of ready-to-run business processes for any department in an enterprise, the SAP Business Suite can be seen as an office package for enterprises. For years, large organizations have been deploying these solutions, which today are synonymous with SAP, including

- ▶ SAP Enterprise Resource Planning (ERP)

- ▶ SAP Customer Relationship Management (CRM)

- ▶ SAP Supply Chain Management (SCM)

- ▶ SAP Supplier Relationship Management (SRM)

Each of these is explored in the following sections. For more details, see Hour 7, "SAP ERP and Business Suite."

SAP Enterprise Resource Planning

Given its longevity, ERP is still the most deployed SAP solution. ERP deals with the fundamental business processes in every enterprise: financial accounting, production, and human resources. In other words, among other functions, SAP ERP ensures that orders can be accepted, fulfilled, tracked, and paid for.

SAP ERP is a bundle and consists of SAP ECC and SAP NetWeaver. Technically, ECC represents the newest incarnation of the famous SAP R/3. The business process logic is split into Enterprise Core and Enhancement Packages to make updates less intrusive.

Within the broad umbrella of SAP ERP solutions are basic business functions, including the following:

- ▶ **SAP ERP Financials:** Includes Financial Accounting, Treasury Accounting, Controlling, Treasury and Corporate Finance Management, Real Estate Management, and more. Built-in compliance for Sarbanes-Oxley and Basel II and Basel III enable companies to provide transparent financial reporting and corporate governance (necessary hassles, thanks to the Enron debacle and other such past events).

- ▶ **SAP ERP Operations:** Includes Procurement and Logistics Execution, Product Development and Manufacturing, and Sales and Service. These solutions take logistics to the next level, introducing sales, warehousing, procurement, transportation, and distribution into the realm of collaborative business solutions.

- ▶ **SAP ERP Human Capital Management (HCM):** Provides functions for payroll, time management, gratuities, incentives, statutory reporting, and cost planning. SAP HCM also provides solutions for e-recruitment, e-learning, and employee self-service.

- ▶ **SAP ERP Corporate Services:** Bundles many core company services into a neat package ranging from Project and Portfolio Management to Environment, Health, and Safety (EH&S) Management, Travel Management, Quality Management, and more.

- ▶ **SAP ERP Analytics:** A powerful business analytics function that marries financials, operations, and workforce-based analytics and reporting in one place.

As mentioned in Hour 4, "SAP Project Basics," SAP also offers a wide range of industry-specific solutions for more than 25 industries, from Aerospace & Defense to Wholesale Distribution. These industry solutions consist of modified and extended SAP ERP standard components.

SAP Customer Relationship Management

SAP CRM is also found in many customer installations. CRM provides processes for interactions with customers such as marketing, sales, service, and support transactions. With its focus on customers and improving top-line revenue, SAP CRM deployment has consistently grown in popularity and accounts for much of SAP's growth over the past few years.

Technically an offspring of R/3, SAP CRM implementations can become quite complex to fulfill today's sales, services, and marketing demands. For example the SAP Internet Sales scenario consists of the basic SAP CRM system, as well as SAP Internet Pricing and Configurator (IPC), SAP Biller Direct, a catalog system, SAP Knowledge Provider (KPro), and a permanent shopping basket. The acquisition of hybris[1] added multichannel e-commerce and product content management (PCM) software.

SAP Supply Chain Management

Most enterprises producing and distributing goods have implemented SAP SCM to streamline their supply chain. SCM enables companies to increase shareholder value by optimizing production schedules and minimizing the costs caused by inventory without the risk of jeopardizing customer satisfaction by running out of stock.

The core component of SCM is the SAP Advanced Planner and Optimizer (APO), which includes the following:

- ▶ Requirements forecasting on the basis of historical data by Demand Planning (DP)
- ▶ Cross-plant distribution of orders onto the available transport and production capacities by Supply Network Planning (SNP)
- ▶ Production Planning–Detailed Scheduling (PP-DS)
- ▶ Transportation Planning–Vehicle Scheduling (TP-VS)
- ▶ Vendor Managed Inventory (VMI)
- ▶ Availability-to-Promise (ATP), which provides multilevel availability checks that can be carried out against material stocks, production, warehouse and transport capacities and costs across plants, etc.

---

[1] See http://www.hybris.com/en/.

All these business processes demand complex optimization runs with a large number of characteristic combinations and demand extremely fast access to data, which is impossible to achieve with hard disks. For this purpose, SAP developed liveCache, one of the first in-memory databases, based on MaxDB (previously called SAPDB). In combination with special object-oriented technologies, the in-memory concept significantly accelerates the algorithmically highly complex, data-intensive, and runtime-intensive functions of APO.

Other components of SAP SCM include:

▶ SAP Event Management (EM), which provides functions for managing deviations between planning and reality

▶ SAP Inventory Collaboration Hub, which supports cross-enterprise integration for Supplier Managed Inventories (SMI) or Vendor Managed Inventories (VMI)

▶ The SAP Auto-ID Infrastructure (AII), which provides connectivity of RFID scanners to SAP SCM and can generate extremely high I/O loads

SAP Supplier Relationship Management

SAP SRM is SAP's venerable solution for managing the procurement and support of the goods and services a company needs to use internally to run day in and day out. Just as SAP CRM manages the relationship between a company and its customers, SAP SRM helps to optimize and manage the relationship between a company and its suppliers. As another one of SAP's more mature offerings, SRM integrates seamlessly with ERP and enables a high degree of collaboration between product buyers and parts suppliers. Bidding processes are streamlined, as well. SRM also ties into SAP SCM, extending and enabling tight integration with a company's supply chain.

With the acquisition of Ariba, SAP added a fully cloud-based SaaS solution for external order and payment processing as well as for sourcing and spend analysis. Many customers combine an on-premise SAP SRM system with Ariba in a hybrid model.

SAP NetWeaver Components

In some ways, SAP NetWeaver can be characterized as an operating system for enterprises. Like Microsoft Windows, it provides a user interface but also ways to store, search, and retrieve data; the components of SAP NetWeaver unify the user interface to the different core business systems and take care of communications between these systems.

Just as Windows provide the runtime for Outlook, Word, Excel and PowerPoint, NetWeaver provides the foundation for Business Suite. However, many specific products fall under the label of NetWeaver, too. The NetWeaver umbrella has become so crowded in the past few years that SAP has organized this collection of applications, utilities, and tools around six areas or themes:

▶ **Foundation Management:** Includes SAP NetWeaver Application Server (the platform for Business Suite), Identity Management (for user identity and system access), and SAP Solution Manager and SAP Landscape Virtualization Management (to manage SAP's implementation and operations throughout the system lifecycle).

▶ **Middleware:** Includes SAP NetWeaver Process Integration (used to integrate SAP and non-SAP applications and data sources together), partner adapters (to simplify complex system connections across business networks), and support of various industry-standard protocols (necessary to support business-to-business connections).

▶ **Information Management:** Includes SAP NetWeaver Master Data Management (for managing and synchronizing companywide data), SAP NetWeaver Business Warehouse and Warehouse Accelerator (SAP's long-time data warehouse and search solutions), and SAP Information Lifecycle Management (to efficiently manage legacy SAP systems in the name of legal compliance).

▶ **Team Productivity:** Includes user experience tools and applications like SAP NetWeaver Portal (which provides role-based web access to SAP's applications), SAP NetWeaver Mobile (access for mobile users), and SAP NetWeaver Enterprise Search (SAP's gateway to the enterprise's information).

▶ **Composition:** Includes tools to develop, monitor, and manage business processes using SAP NetWeaver Composition Environment, SAP NetWeaver Developer Studio (for more complex business applications), and SAP NetWeaver Visual Composer (for rapid model-based business application development, no coding required).

▶ **Business Process Management:** Comprises a subset of the SAP NetWeaver Composition Environment, including SAP NetWeaver Business Process Management (to specially model and run business processes) and SAP NetWeaver Business Rules Management (to create and manage the business rules that describe business processes).

Many of these NetWeaver components, tools, and utilities are discussed further in Hour 6, "SAP NetWeaver and HANA."

Small and Medium Enterprises

As you've seen this hour, SAP offers a wealth of big-business software solutions and a host of tools to extend, manage, and optimize these solutions. As we all know, however, there are dramatically more small and medium businesses than large ones. These smaller entities have different business requirements and smaller financial resources for the applications and tools they need to take care of business. With these differences in mind, SAP markets three different solutions for the SME market: SAP Business One, SAP Business ByDesign, and SAP Business

All-in-One (also called simply SAP All-in-One). Table 5.1 briefly compares these three different solutions.

TABLE 5.1   Comparing SAP's SME Solutions

SAP SME Solution	Business One	Business ByDesign	SAP All-in-One
Simple description	A single, integrated application to manage basic SME processes	SaaS-based integrated application to manage basic SME processes	A subset of the main SAP Business Suite solutions on a single system
Number of company employees/users	Up to 100	100–500	Up to 2,500
Country availability	40 countries	Limited to US, UK, Germany, France, India, and China	50 countries
Implementation type or method	On-premise	Hosted by SAP	On-premise or hosted
Implementation timeline	2–8 weeks	4–8 weeks	8–16 weeks
Transaction volume	Low	Moderate	High
Industry solutions	Several	Few	Many

While software giants like SAP, Oracle, and Microsoft dominate the ERP market, there are plenty of open source ERP options.[2] You can find an ERP system selection methodology available at Wikipedia.[3] However, according to Gartner, the open source ERP market share will likely hover around 5% through 2018 and beyond.[4]

For years, SAP has publicly stated that the SME market is where it expects to achieve much of the growth in its customer base. In 2007, SAP had a goal of achieving 100,000 customers by 2010, and the key to this was success in the SME space. By 2010, SAP had actually overachieved on this target, hitting 105,000 customers. As of this writing, SAP boasts nearly 150,000 customers. The SME market (and an aggressive acquisition strategy) played a big role in this success. Next, let's take a closer look at the three SME business solutions that helped make this milestone possible.

---

[2] See http://www.enterpriseappstoday.com/erp/10-open-source-erp-options.html.

[3] See http://en.wikipedia.org/wiki/ERP_system_selection_methodology.

[4] Gartner, "Predicts 2014: The Rise of the Postmodern ERP and Enterprise Applications World," December 5, 2013: https://www.gartner.com/doc/2633315.

SAP Business One

The idea behind Business One (B1) is to provide the basic financial, manufacturing, warehousing, and customer relations requirements of a small business in a single system. Typical B1 customers have fewer than 100 employees across five branches or locations and independent subsidiaries. SAP positions B1 also as a solution for multinational company *subsidiaries* because the solution is easily linked with SAP's Business Suite solution back at corporate headquarters; this strategy is often employed by multinational companies.

Business One is designed to be affordable. It is delivered to the customer via SAP's worldwide network of qualified business partners. A key selling point is the solution's relatively short implementation time. In fact, Business One implementations are typically measured in weeks. With such a small timeframe, it's easier to develop a quick estimate of the implementation cost, and the disruption and impact to the business are minimized.

B1 Implementation

Due to the relatively small numbers of users, Business One can be implemented together with the database on a single Windows server. Designed to be easily customized without the need for time-consuming technical training, it is assumed that there is no need for development or the quality assurance systems described in Hour 3, "SAP Technology Basics." System and functionality changes are implemented directly on the production system.

Leveraging either Microsoft SQL Server or IBM DB2 Universal Database Express edition, the database licensing costs are less than for SAP's enterprise-class offerings.

Several cloud providers are offering Business One for a monthly subscription fee.[5]

B1 Functionality and Features

Like its more capable big-business counterpart SAP ERP, B1 supports the key business processes necessary to run businesses of any size:

- Financial management
- Warehouse management
- Purchasing
- Inventory

- Manufacturing
- Banking
- Customer relations

---

[5] For example, SingTel is on their PowerOn cloud based on a VCE vBlock infrastructure.

Further, it allows for the implementation of a simple e-commerce solution, enabling an organization to market and sell goods and services online while providing integration with financials, inventory, and shipping information.

Where available, B1 provides country-specific localizations and a Drag & Relate feature for easy creation of reports. Integration with Microsoft Outlook supports management by exception alerting and business process workflow.

Because all data is stored in a single database, B1 provides almost instant access to all the business information—the kind of "real real-time" business SAP promised with HANA-based simplification.

As an already integrated system, there might be no need to integrate B1 with other solutions (although doing so is certainly possible). This all-encompassing nature results in savings in both integration costs and maintenance costs associated with maintaining multiple systems.

B1 Development

Acquired in 2002 from TopManage, Business One has no code or architecture common with the classical SAP applications. Therefore, development is different than in a traditional SAP ERP environment. Business One has its own *software development kit* (SDK). The SDK contains three *application programming interfaces* (APIs): the User Interface API, the Data Interface API, and the Java Connector. In addition, SAP partners have developed more than 430 industry-specific and other solutions that are handy in extending Business One's usefulness.

SAP Business ByDesign

SAP Business ByDesign (BBD) is SAP's SaaS-based integrated SME business management software. The code was written from the ground up, leveraging state-of-the-art concepts, and has nothing in common with other SAP solutions. BBD includes preconfigured best practices for managing financials, customer relationships, human resources, projects, procurement, and the supply chain.

BBD is hosted exclusively by SAP, so customers don't need to worry about maintaining hardware and software, running database backups, or implementing updates and fixes, but it becomes an issue when local laws demand to keep the data in the country.

BBD is designed for companies with 100 to 500 employees, supporting multiple locations and independent subsidiaries. At the time of writing, BBD customers pay $149 a month to SAP for each user (with a minimum of 25 users and lower pricing for self-service users). Like all other SaaS-based solutions, BBD's fee structure is based on a pay-as-you-go concept. You can easily add users as you grow.

SAP does not position ByDesign as a competitor to Business One or Business All-in-One. Rather, it is a solution intended for customers seeking to avoid investing in all the necessary infrastructure and support personnel associated with business software.

BBD Implementation and Adaptability

One of the primary targets of BBD was ease of configuration. Nontechnical users are expected to build business processes using visual modeling tools and web services. The underlying technology includes the NetWeaver Composition Environment (CE), Enterprise Services Repository, and Enterprise SOA—tools that make it possible for do-it-yourselfers to quickly model, test, and configure BBD. The concept was that a company deploying BBD does not necessarily require consultants for implementation. Instead, BBD's users can change their business processes themselves, using the provided tools.

BBD Functionality and Features

If there is one drawback to this do-it-yourself approach, it's the degree to which BBD can be customized. For example, even simple functionality like the capability to filter customers by country or zip code is not available.

The product supports moderately complex business processes. The functionality is most applicable to companies in the following industry sectors: automotive, consumer products, high tech, industrial machinery and components, manufacturing, mill products, professional services, and wholesale distribution. Service and support as well as business analytics are built in to BBD. Companies that need deep, industry-specific functionality in other industry verticals (or a highly customizable solution) should look elsewhere.

Advantages of BBD's SaaS Approach

Business ByDesign is exclusively hosted by SAP in its datacenter. In addition to providing the hardware and software, SAP also takes care of backups, infrastructure patching, health checks, and updates, so you don't need a technical staff to maintain BBD. However, you still need business process experts to implement the solution and adapt your company to the capabilities of the preconfigured business processes.

BBD Challenges

SAP invested a tremendous amount of time and money in making BBD a success. But although Business ByDesign has several good things going for it, a few obstacles have led to a relatively low adoption rate. First, some initial code stability issues allowed SAP's competitors the chance to attack its execution ability and ultimately its commitment to SaaS-based solutions. Second, BBD by its very nature does not enjoy the same specialized solution development opportunities SAP's partners provide for Business One or Business All-in-One. With little opportunity to bring in extra value, SAP partners have no incentive to sell Business ByDesign to SMEs. Also, experienced implementation consultants are rare.

Finally, BBD adopters are challenged by some missing "nifty detail" functionality. As an example, you can tag a contact at a customer as "left the company" or even "died." But this tagging has no effect for mailing lists. So you either have to delete such contacts completely (and accept that all the communication history will be lost) or accept that any marketing mail will be sent to contacts who are not available at your customer anymore.

SAP All-in-One

SAP All-in-One is essentially a lightweight subset of SAP ERP, BI, CRM, and SCM running in a single instance. It is designed to meet the needs of companies with 100 to 2,500 employees or subsidiaries of larger enterprises.

Built on the standard SAP NetWeaver platform, it is specifically designed to address the needs of midsize companies. This means that medium-size businesses receive the same benefits of SAP ERP as enterprise customers; however, the functionality is reduced to the core business processes of particular industries.

In conjunction with best practices, this approach allows for quicker, more predictable and therefore less costly implementations. Finally, All-in-One provides an intuitive user experience, based in large part on the use of the new SAP NetWeaver Business Client. Built on proven SAP technology, All-in-One can be virtualized and fits quite well with IaaS cloud services.

SAP All-in-One Functionality

If you turn back and review the goals of the SME solutions presented at the beginning of this hour, it should be obvious how well All-in-One meets the requirements of a small or medium business organization. The All-in-One solution includes core ERP processes such as analytics, planning, purchasing, inventory management, production, sales, financials and controlling, human resource management, and a host of industry-specific business processes.

In addition, All-in-One includes CRM functionality such as Account and Contact Management, Activity Management, Pipeline Performance Management, Campaign Management, and Segmentation. These solutions are enabled and delivered via preconfigured best practices from SAP. Further extensibility is made possible via partner solutions.

All-in-One provides enhanced business visibility and reporting, too. Boasting tight integration with Microsoft Excel, SAP makes it possible to access custom analytical reports in Excel—where users can manipulate, display, and analyze their data using Excel's familiar features and tools. This eliminates the need to pull reports from various systems or to integrate disparate systems in order to obtain a complete picture of the entire business. And with All-in-One's support for regulatory compliance (including documentation and reporting by country and industry for select regulations, including Sarbanes-Oxley in the United States), business transparency is easily achieved.

All-in-One Partners and Solution Centers

SAP All-in-One benefits from having an ecosystem of more than 1,000 qualified partners who have developed and delivered solutions designed to cover highly specific industry needs. Leveraging their industry specific skill, these partners have developed hundreds of "microvertical" solutions. This makes it apparent which solutions deliver the functions and processes appropriate to your industry. A sampling of All-in-One's solutions includes the following:

▶ **Automotive:** 72 qualified partner-developed solutions

▶ **Chemicals:** 58 qualified partner-developed solutions

▶ **Consumer products:** 83 qualified partner-developed solutions

▶ **Professional services:** 47 qualified partner-developed solutions

Again, partners play an important role in All-in-One. In addition to developing solutions, partners provide implementation and support, as well as customization expertise. The local SAP Solution Centers aids partners by providing deployment tools and methodologies; they also provide detailed documentation of business processes to help accelerate implementation.

All-in-One Features and Functionality

To compete in the SME market, SAP had to make All-in-One easier to use, configure, and administer compared to the SAP Business Suite. An important feature of Business All-in-One is its ability to provide a predictable cost of ownership, which starts with predictable implementation time and cost. This is realized by using SAP best practices during the implementation to simplify configuration of Business All-in-One, thereby making implementation time more predictable. The SAP best practices facilitate tested industry-specific business processes and operations; you're not building business processes from the ground up.

SAP provides a best practices library based on more than 35 years of customer implementations in more than 25 industries worldwide. You can take advantage of these lessons to implement documented, preconfigured business scenarios (in many cases specific to your industry). The documentation includes end-user training guides and configuration guides.

In addition, Business All-in-One is extensible via partner solutions, as you learned earlier this hour. Finally, remember that Business All-in-One is essentially SAP ERP and can be customized in the same manner to adapt to changing business needs in a rapid fashion—a key requirement for midsize businesses.

SAP Business All-in-One is built on the SAP NetWeaver platform, the same platform used by the SAP Business Suite. NetWeaver is based on industry-standard protocols that can be used to integrate Business All-in-One with third-party products. (It also provides the integration platform for SAP solutions.) In addition to supporting the development of enterprise *service-oriented architecture* (SOA)-based applications, NetWeaver provides a Java development environment and supports applications developed in the Microsoft .NET and IBM WebSphere development environments.

Companies that outgrow All-in-One can easily to migrate to the SAP Business Suite because it uses an identical technical platform. When moving from Business One or Business-by-Design, you have to start from scratch.

Selecting the "Best" SME Solution

The "best" solution depends on many factors, including cost, required functionality, features, preference for onsite versus hosted solutions, size, and complexity of the business processes to be configured. SAP provides a breadth of products, each targeted a bit differently at addressing these factors, as detailed next.

Cost

For obvious reasons, cost is probably the most important factor in the decision-making process, so it is crucial that the true cost be determined. Oftentimes, the initial cost for the acquisition of software licenses is a relatively small part of the total cost of ownership of any business software, due to the fact that discounts on list prices can be negotiated.

As for the "big" SAP Business Suite solutions, by far the biggest part of the initial costs of SAP's SME solutions relates to the consulting services for the implementation followed by proper user training. Even if you do not hire external expertise and follow a do-it-yourself approach, there are tasks that have to be done (and the time of internal resources is also not free). Such tasks include:

- ▶ Configuring the standard business processes delivered with the system to adopt to the demand of the company.

- ▶ Import of data from legacy systems. (Don't underestimate the effort for data cleansing!)

- ▶ Integration into the existing system landscape—from setup of printer queues to integration into the central SAP BW of the mother company.

▶ End-user training, which is often forgotten because organizations assume that the system is so intuitive that users do not need training. But even the most intuitive user interface demands that the user understand the business process. And due to the fact that SME solutions have reduced capabilities to adapt the solution to the existing business process, the users have to adapt to processes they are not used to. Practical experience demonstrates that productivity will drop significantly if users are confronted with new business processes without proper training.

As fewer business processes have to be adapted to special demands, data is cleaner to import, and systems require few interfaces, which in turn reduces implementation costs. Attempts to lower these costs by hiring cheaper consultants with less practical experience may result in additional consulting hours needed to train themselves on the job. Such is true independently if a solution is hosted on-premise or in the cloud.

Despite the initial outlay of cash, it's actually the ongoing costs that represent the greatest expense over a business solution's lifetime. The ongoing "operational" costs include:

▶ **Software maintenance fees:** The annual maintenance fee can be even higher than the cost of the initial licenses. In the case of SAP Business Suite and NetWeaver, for example, the 22% that customers pay for maintenance is based on list price and rarely if ever subject to discounts.

▶ **Administration and technical maintenance (patches and updates) of SAP software, databases, operating systems, virtualization software, hardware, etc.:** While solutions exist to manage and patch OS, virtualization software, and hardware for thousands of servers as if there were only one, the administration, patching, and updating of the SAP and DB must still be done for each SAP system individually.

Functionality

The solutions offered by SAP and its competitors may differ significantly in regard to functionality. The key here is to find a solution that meets the business's requirements. In most cases it is by far more expensive to write and maintain additional code to provide a missing business process than to acquire a "bigger" solution that provides this functionality out of the box.

Features

Many of features are meant to make an application easier to use. If two competing solutions provide approximately the same functionality, the solution that provides the feature set most applicable to your business is probably the best choice.

Hosted Versus On-Premise

A primary consideration is whether a business wants to house a solution on its premises or have it hosted by SAP or a partner. Business ByDesign is a hosted solution. For Business One and All-in-One, you can choose to run them on-premise or use the hosted solutions of providers that specialize in SMB solutions, like Singtel, Freudenberg-IT, and All-in-One, just to name a few.

Number of Employees

SAP has established guidelines concerning the size of a business appropriate for each of its solutions. Business One is generally targeted at companies with fewer than 100 employees. Part of this probably has to do with the underlying technology. Business One is designed to run on a single server and is therefore limited to some extent by the underlying computing platform. Business ByDesign is targeted at companies with between 100 and 500 employees; SAP requires that at least 25 users be licensed. At the high end, Business All-in-One is suitable for companies with between 100 and 2,500 employees.

Business Process Complexity

Business process complexity has to do with how customizable the software in question is. SAP Business All-in-One is very customizable. It is based on SAP ERP and runs on the NetWeaver platform. On the other hand, Business One is designed for companies with relatively straightforward business processes. It is important to keep in mind that SAP partners have built solutions for specific industries and verticals; therefore, a prepackaged solution might already exist for your specific industry or business.

Choosing SAP SME Offerings over Business Suite

Another way to describe SAP's SME offerings is to compare them to SAP's Business Suite. Small and medium enterprises choose *not* to implement the SAP Business Suite for multiple reasons, such as the following:

▶ The licensing costs associated with SAP Business Suite

▶ The complexity of SAP Business Suite, which directly drives the cost of consulting and other professional services necessary for implementation

▶ A lack of the IT professionals necessary to maintain and support the complexities of SAP Business Suite

▶ The long timeframes involved in implementing SAP Business Suite

▶ Risks associated with implementing the more costly, complex, and time-consuming SAP Business Suite

▶ Time and money required for training end users on how to use the more comprehensive and feature-rich SAP Business Suite solutions

Summary

In this hour, we reviewed the full gamut of SAP's big-company Business Suite and NetWeaver offerings. We concluded this hour by comparing and contrasting SAP's three small and medium business solutions with one another and with the SAP Business Suite.

Case Study: Hour 5

Consider this case study and the questions that follow. You can find answers to the questions related to this case study in Appendix A, "Case Study Answers."

Situation

MNC has a number of subsidiaries, many of which are classified as small and medium enterprises. All these subsidiaries roll up their financials to MNC corporate, and some have their own special business requirements. MNC has just acquired a new company that will operate as a subsidiary. This new subsidiary runs several business software packages that may or may not be particularly well suited for interfacing with MNC's corporate SAP ERP and other flagship Business Suite systems. Your job is to answer several questions from MNC corporate IT and select the most appropriate solution from SAP's broad lineup of business applications.

Questions

1. Which is the best solution from SAP if the subsidiary has fairly complex business processes and comprises more than 1,000 users?

2. What solution would be ideal if the subsidiary ran less-complex business processes and needed a fully deployed system in two to three weeks?

3. What is the best solution from SAP if the subsidiary consists of about 250 employees and seeks to deploy a system customizable by the subsidiary's own business users?

4. What is the best solution from SAP if the subsidiary has 2,500 employees and intends to double in size over the next year?

5. The CEO of the new subsidiary has expressed a reluctance to implement a business solution because the company really does not have the appropriate infrastructure or personnel to maintain it. What solution from SAP might you suggest?

SAP NetWeaver and HANA

What You'll Learn in This Hour:

▶ Overview of SAP NetWeaver

▶ Strategic benefits of SAP NetWeaver

▶ Designing a NetWeaver system using building blocks

▶ The speed of thought

▶ Why (and when) HANA is so fast

▶ Implementing HANA

This hour closely looks at both SAP's NetWeaver and HANA, including how they can be used individually and how they can be combined to create and support an SAP business application environment.

The Foundation for SAP

SAP NetWeaver provides the technology foundation for most of SAP's products and applications. Like the foundation of a building, these components supply the horizontal underpinnings on which SAP business solutions are built. In addition, SAP NetWeaver components and tools provide the vertical support necessary to tie applications together, extend SAP to mobile devices, and facilitate business analytics and reporting.

SAP HANA provides not only the technology for new business processes based on extremely fast ad-hoc analytics but also the foundation for the simplification and unification of all SAP solutions into a real real-time environment.

Prior to the introduction of SAP NetWeaver in 2004, a large part of the SAP technology stack was synonymous with the SAP computing platform. We often referred to this stack simply as the *SAP Basis layer*. And despite seeming complex at the time, the stack was indeed simple by today's standards. SAP was implemented as a client/server model, the code was written in SAP's proprietary Advanced Business Application Programming language (ABAP), and the systems could be extended by tax bolt-ons, faxing systems, and printing solutions.

Today, many still use the term *Basis*, but the relative simplicity of the client/server era that gave birth to SAP R/3 is long gone, and the complexities of the post-client/server era, in-memory databases, and the Intercloud are all around us. Basis has grown up and raised a family, but none of the offspring left for college or struck out on their own. And we're faced with managing and maintaining the whole lot.

The SAP NetWeaver Umbrella: Six Areas

SAP NetWeaver provides the foundation for Business Suite. But many specific products fall under the label of NetWeaver, too. The NetWeaver umbrella has become so crowded in the past few years that SAP finally organized this portfolio of applications, utilities, and tools around six areas (sometimes called domains or themes):

- ▶ Foundation management

- ▶ Middleware

- ▶ Team productivity

- ▶ Composition

- ▶ Business process management

- ▶ Information management

The first five areas are detailed next, while the topic information management will be covered later, in the discussion of HANA.

Foundation Management

The idea of *foundation management* speaks to both NetWeaver's unified platform atop which applications such as SAP CRM and ERP run and to two other products that are useful in ensuring a successful SAP implementation. These applications and tools include

- ▶ **SAP NetWeaver Web Application Server:** The base platform for the SAP Business Suite; an open, reliable, extensible, and scalable platform for business transformation.

- ▶ **SAP NetWeaver Identity Management:** Used to manage user identity and cross-system enterprise-wide access.

- ▶ **SAP Solution Manager (SolMan):** SAP's ubiquitous tool for managing SAP's implementations and operations. SolMan includes implementation and upgrade guidance, change control management and testing, root cause analysis, real-time solution monitoring, service level management, an avenue for centralized administration, and IT and application support.

Middleware

Middleware is traditionally about connecting different systems so that they can share data and support cross-application business processes. SAP's middleware software solution is called SAP NetWeaver Process Integration (PI) and was formerly called SAP Exchange Infrastructure. Although not the most capable or efficient middleware solution on the market, it nonetheless effectively integrates SAP's applications with one another.

Less effectively, SAP NetWeaver PI also ties non-SAP applications and data sources together with your SAP systems. Often this integration requires a third-party adapter. PI adapters are plentiful, though, and come in several flavors. Technology and protocol-specific adapters include the following and more:

- **IDOC:** Standard SAP interchange document format
- **RFC:** Standard SAP function calls
- **File/FTP:** Local and remote file systems, including FTP servers
- **HTTP(S):** Servers using the web protocol
- **SOAP:** Web services
- **JMS:** Messaging services
- **JDBC:** Relational databases
- **SMTP/POP3/IMAP:** Email servers
- **EDIFACT/ANSI X.12:** Electronic data interchange (EDI)
- **IBM 3270/5250:** Screen-based mainframe/midrange system access

Many application-specific adapters have been developed over the years for other enterprise resource planning, customer relationship management, business-to-business, supply chain management, and other systems. SAP's supported adapters include Ariba, Baan, BroadVision, IBM's venerable CICS, Clarify, i2, IBM IMS/TM, JD Edwards World and OneWorld, Lawson, Lotus Notes, Manugistics, Microsoft Dynamics CRM, PeopleSoft, Siebel, Vantive, and more.

In addition, SAP NetWeaver PI supports industry-specific *business-to-business* (B2B) adapters, such as the following:

- **HL7:** Healthcare data exchange standard
- **UCCnet and Transora:** Consumer products data exchange standard
- **SWIFT:** Financial transactions
- **CIDX:** Chemical process integration
- **RosettaNet:** High-tech process integration

Other EDI standards for the automotive, chemical, consumer products, paper, pharmaceutical, retail, and high-tech industries exist as well. Finally, SAP's middleware capabilities extend to technology standards. SAP NetWeaver supports several different technologies and standards, including:

- ▶ Java

- ▶ Microsoft .NET interoperability

- ▶ IBM WebSphere interoperability

- ▶ Web services

Given that middleware's purpose is to move and share data between source systems, let's take a closer look at how SAP turns data into information.

Information Management

Information management involves speeding up decision making by getting the right information to the right decision maker at the right time. SAP has three tools for accomplishing this:

- ▶ **SAP NetWeaver Master Data Management:** Supports customer data integration, enables global data synchronization and spend analysis, facilitates product content management, and helps companies sort out data needs of those in the midst of mergers and acquisitions.

- ▶ **SAP NetWeaver Business Warehouse (BW):** Provides a scalable enterprise data warehouse (and discussed in detail later in this hour).

- ▶ **SAP Information Lifecycle Management:** Enables companies to efficiently comply with legal and regulatory mandates related to managing their legacy SAP data's access, storage, and retention. (Yes, SAP has been around so long now that its own products often fall into the realm of legacy systems, too.)

With regard to efficiency, SAP NetWeaver also includes a domain or an area dedicated to team productivity, covered next.

Team Productivity

SAP's concept of team productivity includes *user experience* (UX) tools and applications intended to help individuals work more smartly and teams collaborate more efficiently:

- ▶ **SAP NetWeaver Portal:** With its intuitive web interface and role-based views into an organization's enterprise, NetWeaver Portal enables collaboration and knowledge sharing. Although not the most feature-rich portal, many companies today use SAP's portal nearly exclusively, to provide users personalized access to multiple SAP solutions with single sign-on (SSO).

▶ **SAP NetWeaver Enterprise Search (ES):** NetWeaver ES utilizes the Text Retrieval and Information Extraction (TREX) engine to search documents, from simple text files to Microsoft Word or PowerPoint, and index files that are stored in Lotus Notes, Microsoft Exchange, or Documentum. Besides searching such unstructured data, TREX can also index and aggregate structured business data, which made it a key component of HANA.

All these SAP NetWeaver applications and products can be extended and made more powerful through SAP's composition tools, as discussed next.

Composition

SAP NetWeaver Composition involves tools used to develop, monitor, and manage business processes that span multiple applications and technologies. We've covered several quasi-development tools already that SAP has aligned with other areas. With regard to the composition area, SAP outlines three toolsets used to "compose" (in this case, connect) applications that in turn support various business scenarios:

▶ **SAP NetWeaver Composition Environment (CE):** A Java development environment intended to build and run composite applications rapidly and efficiently. To cover SAP NetWeaver CE would require its own book. Suffice it to say that CE is powerful, necessarily complex, and quite useful when it comes to designing, implementing, and running composite applications.

▶ **SAP NetWeaver Developer Studio:** An open source Eclipse-based tool used to develop Java 2 Enterprise Edition (J2EE)-based, multi-tiered business applications. Whereas SAP NetWeaver CE is generally used to connect systems, Developer Studio is used to create full-featured systems based on Java and web services.

▶ **SAP NetWeaver Visual Composer:** Used to create ad-hoc "freestyle" user interfaces based on drag-and-drop technology. Therefore, there's no coding to do; rather, Visual Composer is model driven. Its ease of use makes this tool a favorite of business owners who seek to quickly create effective (if limited) user interfaces. A favorite development pattern is to create special iViews for SAP NetWeaver Enterprise Portal. Such an iView might bring together a bunch of data on a "page" that can be updated in any direction and used as a dashboard to reflect the status of a particular business process, for example.

A special kind of development pattern involves creating and managing business processes. SAP defines this as the sixth and final SAP NetWeaver area, described next.

Business Process Management

SAP NetWeaver Business Process Management (BPM) can be looked at as a subset of the SAP NetWeaver Composition Environment. BPM lets you model, execute, and monitor an organization's business processes based on a common process model. After composing and defining process steps, you set up business rules and exceptions. Then you model process flows, using industry-standard business process modeling notation, test and execute your process models, and set up user interfaces or interactive forms as desired. BPM also enables you to monitor these process flows over time to improve their speed and efficiency. All this functionality is made possible through three components:

▶ **Process composer:** Used by architects and developers to create and test business process models. Like a project plan or flowchart, each business process model walks through a specific set of steps where rules are defined and exceptions are noted.

▶ **Process server:** Executes the process models. This easy-to-use tool is tied into SAP NetWeaver Composition Environment.

▶ **Process desk:** Accessed by process users to perform their specific BP steps.

SAP System Landscape Management

SAP provides its own tools to manage SAP system landscape. The SAP Solution Manager (SSM) is the central system management system of SAP. It provides deeply detailed statistics collected from the individual SAP software instances within a landscape. In addition, some rudimentary statistics regarding the server platform are collected by the so-called SAPOSCOL agent that customers are asked to install on every server. SSM is also instrumental in generating the installation keys necessary to install an SAP instance. The System Landscape Directory (SLD), SAP Central User Administration (CUA), and the SAP NetWeaver Landscape Virtualization Management (LVM) complement the SSM.

LVM enables drag and drop of SAP systems onto available hardware resources. This feature is enabled by mounting the LUN on an external storage device where all the data, code, and configuration files of an SAP system are stored to a server. LVM can also deploy virtual machines and support the relocation of SAP instances between physical and virtual machines.

Non-productive systems can be "sent to sleep" simply by shutting them down and waking them up on demand to save energy, and additional application server instances can be started unattended if workload exceeds predefined limits. The SAP system and its database still have to be installed the "traditional way" for obvious reasons, however. As with the SSM, the basic functionality of LVM is free of license fees.

LVM can also automatically generate SAP test, training, and QA instances, utilizing the various cloning features available from enterprise storage vendors. This feature includes the necessary pre- and post-processing steps and involves an additional license fee.

Like its predecessor Adaptive Computing Controller (ACC), LVM depends on agents running on the OS to collect status and performance of a machine, and it interfaces to virtualization managers and storage arrays to perform its tasks. SAP Host Agent can be downloaded from the SAP service marketplace; the agents for the storage have to be provided by the storage vendors.

Bringing It All Together

So now that we have covered the history and components of SAP NetWeaver, let's work through some actual SAP implementations. As companies seek to address new business challenges through SAP NetWeaver technologies, they must gather requirements to determine the type of solution needed. SAP provides the SAP NetWeaver Master Guide for system administrators and technology consultants to assist with the implementation of their SAP NetWeaver systems. This guide is available at the SAP service market place at https://websmp106.sap-ag.de/ (see Figure 6.1) or, after you have logged in, via https://websmp105.sap-ag.de/~sapidb/01100035870000089 6802012E.pdf. Note that these documents are available only to those with valid SAP user IDs.

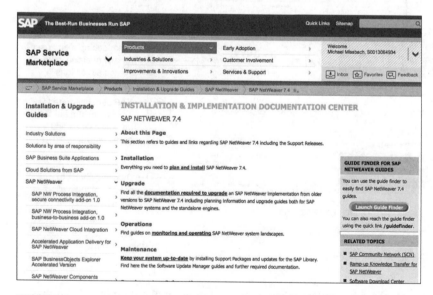

FIGURE 6.1
SAP NetWeaver 7.4 Master Guide, available online to SAP Service Marketplace users with valid user IDs.

The Master Guide provides a common reference for the entire SAP NetWeaver implementation cycle and is a valuable resource for those new to NetWeaver.

From SAPGUI and WebGUI to Fiori and Lumira

In addition to the classical user interface SAPGUI, which has to be installed at the end user's workstation, and the browser-based WebGUI, SAP has introduced a new proprietary user interface toolkit called UI5.

Based on this toolkit, SAP Fiori adds a collection of mini applications to access frequently used SAP software functions (see Figure 6.2). In essence, it's a universal replacement for SAPGUI, Business Explorer, BusinessObjects, and other interfaces. Like SAPGUI, Fiori is included in the license for the SAP application. Download an overview of Fiori from http://scn.sap.com/docs/ DOC-55614.

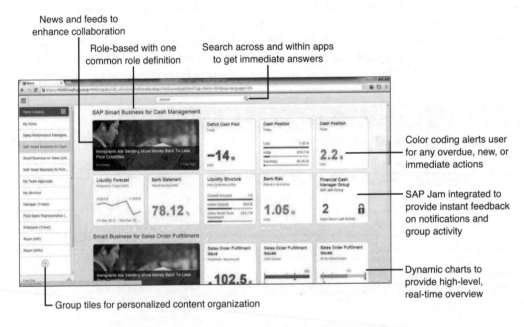

FIGURE 6.2
The SAP Fiori Launchpad (courtesy of SAP).

Lumira is a self-service tool for a broader audience than the traditional data miner. It features interactive charts and maps for analytics (see Figure 6.3). Not considered a traditional BI tool, Lumira falls under a new category, "information discovery," for users who don't know what they're looking for yet but want to be able to slice and dice bigger datasets. You can download a

30-day free trial of SAP Lumira Desktop Standard Edition; however, there is a specific licensing for data visualization.[1]

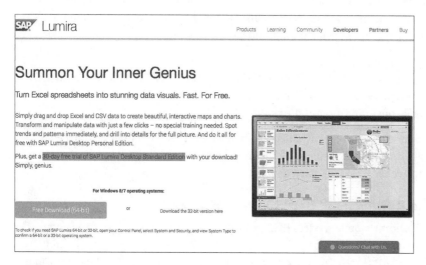

FIGURE 6.3
The Lumira download page (courtesy of SAP).

SAP Mobile Platform

SAP supports all its applications that run on the desktop (SAPGUI, WebBrowser, SAP Fiori, etc.) and SAP Mobile Documents also on all popular mobile platforms and form factors, including tablets, smartphones, and SMS-based apps. Prebuilt applications from SAP and partners are available in the SAP Store.[2] Some of these apps even compete with SAP's own solutions.

SAP's Mobile Portfolio

SAP has consolidated multiple mobile acquisitions to the SAP Mobile Platform 3.0 (SMP3)[3] as a mobile application development platform (MADP). This platform comprises Sybase Unwired Platform (SUP), Agentry (through the acquisition of SYCLO), and Mobiliser (through Sybase 365). SMP3 provides a Java gateway and a Java-based version of SAP Process Integration (PI) for data integration from various different systems.

---

[1] See http://saplumira.com/download/.

[2] See store.sap.com/mobile.

[3] See global.sap.com/campaigns/digitalhub-mobile-platform/index.html.

SMP3 provides authentication, connectivity, and administrative services. The enterprise mobility management (EMM) suite, called SAP Mobile Secure, includes mobile device management (MDM) by SAP Afaria, Mobile App Management by SAP Enterprise store and SAP Mobile App Protection by Mocana for app wrapping, SAP Mobile Documents for mobile content management, and telecom expense management built into SAP Afaria and offered by partners like Tangoe.

A machine-to-machine (M2M) platform handles the aggregation of M2M data, the analytics, and the solutions on top. SMP3 also offers mobile messaging (SMS, USSD, MMS), connected to more than 980 mobile operators around the world.

SMP3 is back-end agnostic, allowing customers to interface with SAP and non-SAP back-end databases and systems. SMP3 is optimized for SAP back-ends but has hundreds of deployments on IBM Maximo and other vendor systems as well.

Mobility on the HANA Cloud: SMP3 Versus HCPms

SAP HANA Cloud Platform mobile services (HCPms) will replace the SMP3 Enterprise Edition, Cloud Version (commonly referred to as SMP Cloud) as SAP's Platform as a Service offering. Running on top of the SAP HANA Cloud Platform as a real Mobile-as-a-Service (MaaS), customers don't have to worry about upgrades, backup, patching, scalability and so forth. SAP will take care of that.

Merging the two source-code baselines of SMP 3.0 and HCPms the bulk of the code is common between the two products and therefore exposes the same behavior. Therefore on-premises SMP 3.0 customers benefit from the features developed on HCPms with the next update. There are a few differences behind the scenes, but both applications are glued together by a single mobile SDK.

SAP NetWeaver BW

As the first sibling of SAP's classic R/3 solution, the SAP Business Information Warehouse (BW) is the most widely used SAP solution besides ERP. A dedicated data warehouse became necessary because the performance of early platforms made it cumbersome to run transactions and reports at the same time on the same server. (See Hour 13, "Using SAP for Reporting," for how SAP is used to support reporting).

In addition, the proliferation of SAP Business Suite solutions dedicated to the different departments in an enterprise made it mandatory to consolidate the transactional data of all these individual systems for reporting and analysis. However, splitting off BW from ERP generated the need to extract, transform, and load (ETL) data from the source system into the BW. This batch process puts such a high load on the source system that it usually runs at night to avoid negative effects on user response time during daytime operation. So any reports derived from BW are always based on the "truth of yesterday."

In contrast to an online transaction processing (OLTP) system, where all data records are stored in a normalized form for the sake of consistency, BW is an online analytical processing (OLAP) system, based on special data structures, known as multidimensional InfoCubes.

Roughly speaking, a dimension in an InfoCube corresponds to a classic report. In addition to the source data, it also provides key figures like sums and averages. These figures are calculated directly after the data is loaded and are therefore immediately available when a user makes a query. This way, a predefined BW report is displayed within seconds after a line-of-business manager calls it from the dashboard.

The Business Case for HANA

As described previously, an SAP BW system is fully capable of fulfilling the demands of enterprises for recurring daily, weekly, and monthly reports, as well as quarterly or annual closings. However, the design of multidimensional InfoCubes is a time-consuming task and requires specialized skills and experience. It can take weeks for a new type of report to become available to management, for example.

IT managers have nightmares about getting a call from a board member or senior director, asking for statistical data for an if-then analysis in the next 10 minutes. To solve this issue, SAP developed HANA, based on scientific research[4] at the Hasso Plattner Institute (HPI)[5]. SAP combined the technologies of TREX, MaxDB,[6] and P*TIME[7] to enable real-time business at the speed of thought. Some sources claim that the name HANA for the resulting hybrid database stands for "Hasso's New Architecture."[8]

The Speed of Thought

The average human reaction time to a simple stimulus has been measured at 220ms.[9] The average recognition reaction time is 384ms, however, because of the time necessary for understanding and comprehension. The recognition reaction time increases with the complexity of the context, up to a range of 550–750ms, which is assumed to be the speed of thought. With some exercising, the reaction time becomes shorter.

---

[4] *A Hybrid Row-Column OLTP Database Architecture for Operational Reporting* by Jan Schaffner, Anja Bog, Jens Krüger, and Alexander Zeier.

[5] Donated to the University of Potsdam by Hasso Plattner.

[6] Also known as ADABAS-D and SAPDB, acquired in 1997 from Software AG.

[7] See http://www.vldb.org/conf/2004/IND2P2.PDF.

[8] *Manager Magazine*, September 2012, and Vishal Sikka's blog: http://vishalsikka.blogspot.com/ October 2008.

[9] *Information Theory of Choice-Reaction Times* by D. R. Laming.

Any time longer than the speed of thought interval will be perceived as waiting time, causing the user's mind to unconsciously deviate to other topics. The further the mind is taken off the task at hand, the longer it takes to focus on the topic again after the waiting period. Such context switching between tasks is extremely exhausting for human brains. Response times in the range of the speed of thought allow the users to stay focused on one topic and be more productive and creative because tiresome context switches are avoided.

Most Relevant Versus Complete Answers

Part of the popularity of today's web search engines has to do with the fact that they magically deliver results at the speed of thought. Answers appear on the screen instantly, even before the user finishes entering a question. Why is such magic not available to enterprise business applications? The answer is the difference in the necessary completeness of the result between enterprise applications and surfing the web. The response of a web search displayed on the first page represents only the hits rated most relevant for the query.

A legal business report, on the other hand, must reflect all relevant data in its result. Whereas a web search just has to sift through an indexed dataset, a business application has to scan the complete dataset to guarantee completeness in addition to processing such complex aggregations.

Search engines like Google, Bing, or Baidu can be so astonishingly fast because the result of a search just has to be good enough for the common user. However, no tax authority will accept payment based on anything other than a complete scan through each and every accounting number. Therefore, some more advanced technologies than "just in-memory" are necessary to derive the complete answer for a business-grade system at the speed of thought.

In-Memory: A No-Brainer?

Given the fact that access to data in a computer's memory is orders of magnitude faster than to the data stored on disk, the concept of in-memory computing seems obvious. SAP followed this approach more than a decade ago, with the APO liveCache, a MaxDB running completely in main memory. Other SAP solutions using in-memory technology include Business Warehouse Accelerator (BWA), CRM Segmentation, and Enterprise Search.

Thanks to advances in microchip production technologies, large amounts of main memory are affordable today. Simply enlarging the main memory until it can keep a complete dataset of an application seems to be a straightforward strategy.

With the majority of databases used for SAP business applications being in the range of 1–3TB and considering the advanced compression features of state-of-the-art database systems, it should be easy to hold a complete dataset in the database memory buffer. Such an approach, however, will still not be sufficient to achieve the necessary performance for ad-hoc analysis. To enable business users to distill useful information from raw data in the blink of an eye, a deep understanding is necessary of how data is organized not only in main memory but in the CPU and intermediate caches.

Memory Is Slower Than CPU Cache

Even if main memory is several times faster than disk, it's still not as fast as the processor itself. At this writing, typical memory runs with clock speeds between 0.8 and 1.6GHz, and a typical x86 server CPU are rated for up to 4.0GHz (peak). Therefore, state-of-the-art CPU designs deploy different levels of caching to decrease the latency for repetitive access to the same piece of data.

To load a value from main memory, it has to be copied through intermediate caches until it reaches a register in the core. Accessing main memory can consume up to 80 times the number of CPU cycles of an access to the level 1 cache.

As the cache level lowers, the speed increases, but size decreases. Level 3 cache with a capacity of up to 45MB (Haswell generation Intel CPU) runs with a little more than half of the CPU clock speed. Level 2 and level 1 run at the same clock speed as the core itself, but level 2 can only store 256 and level 1 only 64KB of data.

In an ideal world, all data requested by the processor would be always available in the L1 cache. In the real world, however, "cache misses" happen, and the necessary data is not currently available in a certain cache level. Every cache miss slows down processes and wastes resources.

The worst case is a "full miss," when requested data has to be loaded from main memory. So even the fastest data transfer is futile if it delivers the wrong data. Therefore, data structures have to be optimized to maximize the likelihood that all the data necessary for the next computing step are in the same cache line.

Row Versus Column Orientation

To solve the issues described, the layout of the database tables have to be optimized to minimize the likelihood of cache misses. So what is the optimal layout of database tables? Whenever database structures are discussed, it is assumed that data is logically stored in two-dimensional tables, as in a spreadsheet.

In the physical world, however, all the bits and bytes representing data are stored and transmitted in one single string. Consequently, there are two ways to transform a table into a single string: You can either arrange one row of the table behind the other, or you can queue each column after the other. The first option is called row orientation, and the second is column orientation.

The Case for Row Orientation: OLTP

For good reasons, most databases used for business applications store data values in a row-oriented fashion. This way, much of the data belonging to the same business transaction (for example, order numbers, zip code of the customer who bought an item, part number of an item ordered, number of parts ordered, price per piece, total sum) are stored in adjacent memory blocks.

This row-oriented organization of data increases the likelihood that all data belonging to a single business transaction can be found in the same cache line, which reduces the number of cache misses. The fact that for decades row-oriented databases have enabled sub-second response times, even with disk-based storage, demonstrates that this concept fits well with OLTP systems.

The Case for Column Orientation: OLAP

Unfortunately, row-oriented storage is not well suited for reporting. Most reports do not need the complete dataset of any single business transaction; rather, only the part numbers, how many of them are bought on average, the total sum per order, and the zip code to calculate the revenue per sales area as an example.

In contrast to a typical business process, only a small number of attributes in a table are of interest for a particular query in a typical analysis. Loading every row into cache when only a fraction of data is really used is clearly not optimal for OLAP systems, even if they run completely in-memory.

Organizing a table such that columns are stored in adjacent memory blocks make it possible for only the required columns to be moved into cache, while the rest of the table can be ignored. This way, the cache has to keep only the data needed to process the request, significantly reducing the data traffic from main memory to CPUs, in between CPUs, and down through the whole cache hierarchy. Maximizing the likelihood that necessary data can be found in the level 1 cache will obviously speed up the processing and minimize the response time.

Analysis of database accesses in enterprise warehouse applications as well as practical experience show that column-oriented solutions like SAP IQ (former Sybase IQ) are an excellent choice for OLAP systems. The obvious disadvantage of these systems is that their performance with row-based transactions is poor. So what is good for business transactions is bad for reports and vice versa.

For many years, the only answer to this dilemma was to deploy two sets of applications with databases optimized either for OLTP or for OLAP. This not only doubles the amount of data to be stored and subsequently also the hardware and operation costs but also requires synchronization of data between the different systems.

The Secret Sauce: Two Engines Under One Hood

To combine the best of both worlds and support analytical as well as transactional workloads in one system, HANA combines the two different types of database architectures by means of two dedicated database engines:

▶ TREX for column-oriented, analytical operations

▶ P*TIME for row-oriented, transactional operations[10]

For each individual data table, the most suitable engine has to be selected at the time of creation. To grant optimal performance of a hybrid database, the access pattern has to be known in advance. Therefore, typical queries are analyzed with regard to their cache miss behavior. Together with the weight of the query, this is used to determine the optimal layout—either row or column. If necessary, the layout can be changed at a later time.

Both database engines can be accessed through SQL (JDBC/ODBC), MDX (ODBO), and BICS (SQL DBC) interfaces. HANA also provides a library of business functions and allows the execution of the application logic directly on the database, avoiding unnecessary moving of data to an external application server. A HANA-specific SQL script language can invoke such commands.

Compression

Advanced data compression technologies are implemented to reduce the demand for precious main memory and minimize the movement of data between memory and caches further. The compression factor depends mostly on the number of attributes in the source data. The higher the numbers of unambiguous attributes, the lower the compression factor, with almost no effect on already compressed data. The OS and the database itself also need some memory to run.[11]

A Sidecar for ERP

Obviously, the price of memory has come down considerably, but for huge amounts of memory, very large servers are necessary. According to SAP rules, a memory footprint of more than 3TB for scale-out HANA (SoH) exceeds the capabilities of commodity four-socket servers at this writing. Larger servers are available on the market, but their prices are significantly higher than for common two- and four-socket mass-market architectures. Also, cloud service providers rarely offer such "big iron."

For SoH systems, SAP offers a sidecar setup, where only the data necessary for fast ad-hoc reporting is stored in the HANA database, and all other data stays in a traditional OLTP database like SAP ASE (formerly Sybase ASE).

---

[10] Microsoft SQL Server 2014 for example solves this by adding a column store. An SAP IS-retail customer improved query performance by up to 5 times and reduced database size from 2.124TB to 0.892TB by using this feature.

[11] SAPnote 1872170 describes tools to extract the size from existing SAP installations, and SAPnote 1793345 describes a formula for "Greenfield installations": HANA memory = ((DB size / 2) * 1.2) + 50GB.

For analytical systems, new versions of HANA have the capability to keep "hot data" in HANA, "warm data" in SAP IQ (formerly Sybase IQ), and data rarely used in Hadoop. Both architectures keep the HANA footprint small, both in terms of physical size and total cost of ownership (TCO).

Truly Real-Time or the "Truth of Yesterday"?

As discussed earlier this hour, one of the obstacles for traditional data marts like SAP BW is that the extraction of data from the source system has to be done during the night shift to avoid negative impacts on the operation of the business systems during daytime. As a result, reports generated by such BWs reflect only the "truth of yesterday."

SAP HANA supports a replication method in which "triggers" on the source ERP system detect changes to the source database and replicate these changes to the HANA database in real time.

The ultimate vision, however, is to enable one single HANA database to become the single source of truth for all SAP applications of an enterprise. This way, the result of any transaction will be available for analysis in real time.

Volatile and Persistent Data Storage

Main memory is fast but volatile by nature and loses all its content immediately in case of an electrical power outage (as any book author knows when he has to reboot because his text processor hangs).

To avoid this effect, HANA has to make all data persistent on nonvolatile storage like SSD, flash, or disk drives. For this purpose, SAP implemented a MaxDB shadow server, which provides a persistence layer that is shared by both database engines.

Savepoints and Logs

The HANA main memory is divided into pages. Changed pages are asynchronously written by default every five minutes as a savepoint to nonvolatile storage. In addition, a database log synchronously captures all changes made by the transactions, ensuring that all committed transactions are permanent.

After a power failure or a maintenance shutdown, the database can be restarted like any other disk-based database. First, the database pages are restored from the last savepoint, and then the database logs are applied to restore the changes that have happened since this savepoint (rolled forward).

Persistency

To restore the database within a few minutes and to guarantee high performance during a savepoint, SAP specified an I/O throughput of 100,000 I/Os per second for scale-up appliances with internal storage and corresponding numbers for large scale-out HANA implementations with external storage.

To reach this extraordinarily high throughput, SSD or flash devices can be used; however, because they are still more expensive than traditional disks, most vendors offer disk-based storage arrays as a cost-effective alternative. Leveraging established disk array technologies also allows the utilization of proven data replication technologies for HA and DR scenarios.

HANA Studio

HANA Studio contains data-modeling and administration tools based on Eclipse and a set of libraries required for other applications to connect to the HANA database. Customers also use HANA Studio for maintenance and patching of the HANA database. The Software Update Manager (SUM) for HANA enables an automatic download and installation of software updates from the SAP service marketplace. Both HANA Studio and the client libraries are usually installed on a client PC or server.

HANA Delivery

As illustrated in Hour 3, "SAP Technology Basics" (refer to Figure 3.4), any new technology needs some time to stabilize and mature. Early adopters of HANA experienced a bumpy ride (much like the early days of Windows NT), with patches released sometimes twice a week to mitigate instabilities and even data losses. To keep support issues under control, SAP tried to minimize at least the trouble caused by the platform by restricting HANA to validated combinations of hardware and software delivered by certified SAP hardware partners, like Cisco, Dell, Fujitsu, Hitachi, HP, Huawei, Lenovo, NEC, SGI, and VCE—the name *High-Performance Analytic Appliance* indicates.

Hardware partners are responsible for the correct bill of material for hardware components, operating system, drivers, file system, etc., since they have to install and configure the HANA appliance prior to shipment. The term *appliance* usually implies that the customer does not have to take full responsibility for maintenance, patching, and updates of the HANA system after the handoff. However, in the case of HANA, the customer *must* take care of patching and updating themselves.

Tailored Datacenter Integration

Customers like the appliance model, assuming that the system, once delivered ready-to-run, does not need further patching and maintenance (or assuming simply that either SAP or the hardware vendor takes care for this). As soon as customers become aware that HANA has to be maintained by themselves like any other application, the fact that the appliance model prohibits the leveraging of existing datacenter infrastructure resources and standards becomes a major obstacle.

Responding to the demand of customers and cloud service providers to enable HANA to be integrated in their standard datacenter architectures, SAP offers Tailored Datacenter Integration (TDI) as an option to the appliance model.

The HANA TDI paradigm enables the operation of multiple HANA instances (multi-SID) for different clients (multi-tenant) on a shared infrastructure under the following conditions:

► Only HANA certified servers are supported.[12]

► Only HANA TDI certified storage is supported.[13]

► Only HANA certified installers can do the installation.

The only potential drawback of TDI is that SAP expects the customer to take responsibility for all the different components working together. However, vendors who grant the same level of support for TDI implementations following documented best practices and validated designs can mitigate this.

Utilization of existing enterprise storage, however, is challenging because of the extremely high I/O demand of HANA; just a few terabytes "left over" is not enough. Also, some storage arrays give priority to "read" over "write," which results in lower performance for HANA (which generates mostly writes) when mixed with other databases that are generating mostly reads.

On some storage arrays, this can be avoided by assigning dedicated engines and disks for HANA. Other arrays don't have this issue because they give writes priority over reads.

HANA Cloud Offerings

Several cloud options are available from SAP, as well as from a variety of cloud service providers:

► HANA Enterprise Cloud (HEC) is, despite its name, not a cloud service but a classical-hosting service for HANA. For certain solutions, SAP offers subscription pricing as an alternative to the perpetual license option that continues to be available.

► HANA Cloud Platform (HCP)[14] is aimed at development projects and provides HANA-based application services for a monthly subscription. The size ranges from 1GB up to about 1TB, orderable from the SAP Service Catalog Portal. Figure 6.4 shows the starter prices at this writing; for 1TB with HANA Platform Edition and app premium services, the monthly subscription fee is US$87,737.

► SAP HANA Infrastructure Services allows customers who have existing HANA licenses to utilize the HCP infrastructure. System sizes range from 64GB to 1TB of RAM.

► Partner Cloud, powered by HANA, allows you to run app servers and even non-SAP solutions on the same infrastructure. At this writing, SAP has certified 35 partners, including

---

[12] See http://scn.sap.com/docs/DOC-52522.

[13] See http://scn.sap.com/docs/DOC-48516.

[14] See http://hcp.sap.com/platform.html.

large service providers like Virtustream, T-Systems, Telstra, Suncore, Secure-24, NNIT, MKI, and Singapore Telecom; consulting companies like Accenture, Atos, CSC, Deloitte, and CapGemini; and specialized boutique providers like Freudenberg IT, Ciber, Finance-IT, OEDIV, Gisa, and Novis.

Technically, all HANA cloud offerings are based on the TDI model.

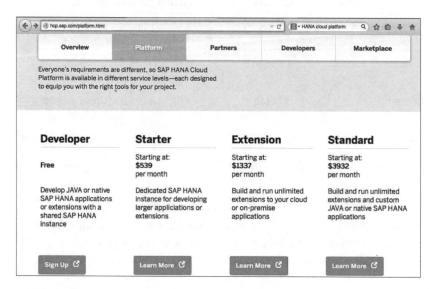

FIGURE 6.4
The HANA Cloud Platform subscription page (courtesy of SAP).

Business Cases for HANA

Though we've walked through many of the technical details of HANA, an important question still remains to be answered: What is the business case for HANA—that is, when and where does using HANA make sense? Without a doubt, the vision of a unified and simplified SAP landscape enabled by HANA is a convincing one for an IT department. However, the HANA licenses as well as the necessary technical infrastructure are still much more expensive than an SAP system running on a traditional database. Also without a doubt, business users around the world love faster reports and quicker access to insight. But would providing a report 100 times faster than usual help make a company 100 times more successful? If so, when is this true, and when is it probably a poor investment?

To answer this question, you need to apply some out-of-the-box thinking—especially out of the box of the IT department. One of the authors of this book supported a proof of concept

(PoC) exercise at a retailer selling pet nutrition. Table 6.1 shows the tremendous improvements achieved with HANA within this PoC.

TABLE 6.1 Typical Acceleration of BW Queries Achieved by HANA

Step	DB2	HANA	HANA Optimized Queries	Acceleration at Existing Queries	Acceleration at Optimized Queries
Front-end query call	4 minutes	2.8 minutes	20 seconds	Up to 1.5 times (+150%)	Up to 10 times (+900%)
Front-end navigation	6 minutes	30 sec	1 second	Up to 5 times (+500%)	Up to 20 times (+2,000%)
Back-end data update	9 hours		3 hours		Up to 3 times (+200%)
Back-end data activation	1.8 hours		10 minutes		Up to 10.8 times (+980%)

Line-of-business managers who went to the restroom, smoked a cigarette, and talked to colleagues while waiting on a report can now get this report in just a few seconds, thanks to HANA. However, what if the manager still spends time visiting the restroom, smoking a cigarette, and talking to colleagues, despite having reports in seconds, thanks to HANA? There would be no realized value in deploying HANA!

Actually, this company implemented HANA to solve one of the biggest pain points of any retail shop: a customer filling his shopping cart with all the cans of dog food available on the shelf, leaving behind a gap. Imagine the reaction of the next customer looking for the same brand of dog food. Thanks to HANA, out-of-stock situations at this retailer are now automatically detected down to the shelf by analysis of point-of-sales (POS) data in real time for each product and each shop.

Another example is analysis of the movements of people in an airport or a shopping mall. The airport or mall can combine HANA with Cisco location services utilizing existing Wi-Fi access points to triangulate the position of any customer carrying a smartphone to analyze such data in real time; such use can help detect congestion, enhance the shopping experience of the customers with information on special discounts offered by a nearby shop, and allow shops to enhance their revenue by analyze the traffic patterns. There are plenty of other examples, and an SAP design thinking workshop can help to discover good ones for your company.

Summary

From its inception, SAP NetWeaver was established to reduce the amount of time necessary to integrate disparate applications, reduce deployment and development time associated with new implementations, and minimize ongoing support and maintenance associated with in-place solutions. To enable real-time analytics, SAP has added HANA to this strategy to increase business agility across enterprises. Now that we have laid the groundwork with SAP NetWeaver, we're ready for Hour 7, "SAP ERP and Business Suite," and Hour 8, "SAP on the Cloud and New SAP Solutions."

Case Study: Hour 6

Consider this SAP case study and the questions that follow. You can find answers to the questions related to this case study in Appendix A, "Case Study Answers."

Situation

MNC has recently upgraded its SAP Business Warehouse system, and the company now wants to take advantage of some of BW's new features—and potentially use HANA as well. MNC has a number of financial and purchasing reports currently running in the enterprise that end users access via the BW Business Explorer (a BW add-on). MNC's purchasing department wants these reports to be available nearly instantaneously and also be available in traditional ways via email and using information broadcasting. MNC's end users have asked the company's SAP technical team to answer the following questions to assist with the design and implementation of the required new BW functionality. You are a member of the SAP technical team, tasked with satisfying the purchasing department's request. Based on the material in this hour, answer the following questions.

Questions

1. What are some of the strategic benefits that MNC may realize by implementing this new NetWeaver functionality, including HANA?

2. Of the six NetWeaver component areas or themes, which two focus on development?

3. What sources or guides can be used to assist with the planning and implementation of information broadcasting on the new SAP BW system?

4. Are BI scenarios different from BW scenarios?

5. Using SAP NetWeaver Process Integration, how might MNC connect SAP BW with its old legacy system that adhered to the chemical EDI standard?

SAP ERP and Business Suite

What You'll Learn in This Hour:

▶ The major components of SAP Business Suite

▶ A closer look at the four core SAP ERP scenarios

▶ What you should know about human capital management

▶ What CRM, SCM, SRM, and PLM are good for

▶ An introduction to SAP GRC and GTM

SAP ERP and the other components of SAP Business Suite provide essentially all of the business processes that company employees need day in and day out to do their jobs. SAP Enterprise Resource Planning (ERP) includes a number of modules or subcomponents that provide various kinds of critical business functionality, including finance-related tasks, logistics, human capital management, customer service, quality management tasks, and many others we look at this hour. As discussed in Hour 5, "Overview of SAP Applications and Components," SAP Business Suite's solutions are mostly offshoots of the classic R/3 system that provide prepackaged business processes specific to the principal line-of-business departments found in any enterprise. In principle, you can still run a company by deploying only ERP, but as soon as the sales department needs more than a basic sales and distribution solution, you will consider SAP CRM. A professionally managed buying department will soon ask for SAP SRM, and if your company produces more than a few very basic products and runs complex production processes, it will demand PLM and SCM. Finally, to ensure that the whole organization is in compliance with all the different rules and laws surrounding a global market, you'll need to add GRC as well. In this hour, we cover all these solutions and more.

NOTE

Online Transaction Processing

With the exception of SCM and PLM, SAP Business Suite solutions are online transaction processing (OLTP) systems. Their business processes are executed simultaneously by many online (real-time) users who use the system to run the business. An OLTP user might run business transactions to book an order, create a reservation, post a change to a material or warehouse requisition, delete an invalid accounting entry, or change an employee record to indicate that someone left the company. By their nature, these are small transactions. Combined across many users, though, Business Suite systems often represent some of the most heavily loaded and important business applications used in the course of running a business.

SAP ERP Business Scenarios

SAP ERP evolved from R/3 and comprises SAP ECC; the two are synonymous. ECC stands for ERP Central Component, although you will probably see the terms ERP Core Component and Enterprise Core Component incorrectly used across different websites, blogs, whitepapers, and other literature. Based on SAP NetWeaver, discussed in Hour 6, "SAP NetWeaver and HANA," SAP ERP supports open Internet, alongside Microsoft .NET and J2EE interoperability. By embracing a service-oriented architecture and leveraging a web-based computing platform, SAP ERP lends itself to enabling greater business agility than its predecessor.

As Figure 7.1 illustrates, the well-known R/3 modules providing basic ERP business processes have been grouped into four principal business scenarios within SAP ERP:

- SAP ERP Financials
- SAP ERP Operations
- SAP ERP Human Capital Management
- SAP ERP Corporate Services

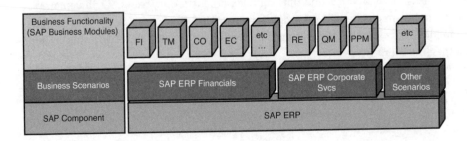

FIGURE 7.1
The SAP ERP component can be used to create several different business scenarios, each comprising SAP business modules.

Note that the core modules among R/3 and ECC are essentially the same; only the arrangement and specific configuration of each module helps differentiate R/3's somewhat vertically oriented deployment methodology over SAP ERP's more horizontally oriented and much-extended approach. Point your browser to http://www.sap.com/pc/bp/erp.html for additional information.

In principle, the deployment of the different modules is optional. For example, if a company is bringing in SAP to take care of financial accounting, controlling, and perhaps treasury cash management, they may use existing solutions for logistics offering, human capital management capabilities, and so forth. In this case you have to establish an integration project to connect SAP with these preexisting systems, using technologies and tools outlined in Hour 6.

Because SAP ERP is so tightly integrated, however, it's nearly impossible to maintain focus on a single SAP ERP module. Why? Because business processes still need occasional access to a certain amount of business rules, master data, and perhaps customer data outside a single module, and companies might find it easier and less expensive to include that basic information within SAP ERP instead of building and forever maintaining yet another interface to another system.

SAP ERP Financials

Without a doubt, Financials is the core of ERP, addressing core financial matters such as

- Financial and managerial accounting

- Enterprise controlling

- Treasury management

- Financial supply chain management

There is a module for each of these functions, and they are discussed in more detail next.

Financial and Managerial Accounting

The Financial and Managerial Accounting module enables companies of any size to centrally manage financial accounting data within an international framework of multiple companies, languages, currencies, and charts of accounts. SAP ERP complies with international accounting standards, such as Generally Accepted Accounting Principles (GAAP) and International Accounting Standards (IAS), and it fulfills the local legal requirements of many countries, reflecting fully the legal and accounting changes resulting from Sarbanes-Oxley legislation, European market and currency unification, and more. The Financial and Managerial Accounting module contains the following components:

- **General ledger accounting:** Ensures that the accounting data being processed fulfills all legal requirements in the countries where an enterprise is doing business.

- **Accounts payable:** Records and administers vendor accounting data.

▶ **Accounts receivable:** Ensures that the goods and services sold are paid by managing customer accounting data through a number of tools specializing in managing open items.

▶ **Asset accounting:** Supervises fixed assets and serves as a subsidiary ledger to the general ledger by providing detailed information on transactions specifically involving fixed assets.

▶ **Funds management:** Replicates a company's budget structure for the purpose of planning, monitoring, and managing company funds. Tasks include revenues and expenditures budgeting, funds movement monitoring, and insight into potential budget overruns.

▶ **Special purpose ledger:** Provides summary information from multiple applications at a level of detail specified according to business needs. This function enables companies to collect, combine, summarize, modify, and allocate actual and planned data originating from SAP or other systems.

Accounts payable and accounts receivable sub-ledgers are integrated both with the general ledger and with different components in the Sales and Distribution module. Accounts payable and accounts receivable transactions are performed automatically when related processes are performed in other modules.

Controlling

The Controlling module provides functions necessary for

▶ **Overhead cost controlling:** Focuses on the monitoring and allocation of your company's overhead costs and provides all the functions your company requires for planning and allocation. The functionality contained within the Controlling module supports multiple cost-controlling methods, giving you the freedom to decide which functions and methods are best applied to your individual areas.

▶ **Activity-based costing:** Enables you to charge organizational overhead to products, customers, sales channels, and other segments and permits a more realistic profitability analysis of different products and customers because you are able to factor in the resources of overhead.

▶ **Product cost controlling:** Determines the costs arising from manufacturing a product or providing a service by evoking real-time cost-control mechanisms (capable of managing product, object, and actual costing schemes).

▶ **Profitability analysis:** Analyzes the profitability of a particular organization or market segment (which may be organized by products, customers, orders, or a combination thereof).

Enterprise Controlling

Despite what its name implies, SAP's Enterprise Controlling module is not a kind of different controlling for large enterprises, but an extension of the cost accounting. The module is divided into the following components:

- **Business planning and budgeting:** Comprises high-level enterprise plans that allow for the adaptable representation of customer-specific plans and their interrelationships. This also takes into consideration the connections between profit and loss statements, balance sheet, and cash flow strategies.

- **Consolidation:** Enables a company to enter reported financial data online using data-entry formats and to create consolidated reports that meet company legal and management reporting mandates.

- **Profit center accounting:** Analyzes the profitability of internal responsibility or profit centers (where a profit center is a management-oriented organizational unit used for internal controlling purposes).

Treasury Management

The Treasury Management module provides functionality needed to control liquidity management, risk management and assessment, and position management. It includes the following components:

- **Treasury management:** Supports a company's financial transaction management and positions through back-office processing to the Financial Accounting module. It also provides a versatile reporting platform that your company can use to examine its financial positions and transactions.

- **Cash management:** Identifies the optimum liquidity needed to satisfy payments as they come due and to supervise cash inflows and outflows.

- **Market risk management:** Quantifies the impact of potential financial market fluctuations against a firm's financial assets. The Cash Management package, in combination with the Treasury Management package, helps a firm control for market risks, account for interest and currency exposure, conduct portfolio simulations, and perform market-to-market valuations.

- **Funds management:** Helps create different budget versions, making it possible to work with rolling budget planning. It's tightly integrated with the Employee Self-Services online travel booking function to track estimated and real costs.

Financial Supply Chain Management

With all the attention today on driving inefficiencies out of an organization's supply chain, it's little wonder that SAP continues to optimize functionality geared toward financially streamlining supply chains. The Financial Supply Chain Management (FSCM) module facilitates

▶ Credit limit management and control

▶ Credit rules automation and credit decision support

▶ Collections, cash, and dispute management

▶ Electronic bill presentment and payment

▶ Treasury and risk management

As you've probably noticed by now, there is quite a bit of overlap between particular solutions and modules. Although it can be confusing, this flexibility is one of SAP's greatest strengths: The ability to customize a business solution in this way makes it possible to create innovative business processes capable of meeting the needs of most any organization's finance and executive leadership teams. However, you should always keep in mind that customizing and adding homegrown code adds complexity that makes the system more difficult to maintain and ultimately more expensive to manage. If a line-of-business manager wants to implement a customized process, a smart business leader and development team will ask if the particular change will make the company more competitive. Perhaps it might be a smart change to make. Or perhaps a smarter approach would be to adopt the industry standard process delivered with the SAP solution by default.

SAP Manufacturing

SAP ERP provides several solutions that assist firms in achieving operational excellence through process efficiencies, business agility, and streamlined business operations. Essentially logistics, these solutions encompass all processes related to a firm's purchasing, plant maintenance, sales and distribution, manufacturing, materials management, warehousing, engineering, and construction. SAP Manufacturing and SAP ERP Operations (an aging but still useful term) include the following solutions:

▶ **Procurement and logistics execution:** Enables end users to manage their end-to-end procurement and logistics business processes as well as optimize the physical flow of materials.

▶ **Product development and manufacturing:** From production planning to manufacturing, shop floor integration, product development, and so on.

▶ **Sales and service:** Ranges from actual sales to managing the delivery of services and all the processes necessary to pay out commissions and other sales incentives.

SAP Manufacturing connects a firm's manufacturing processes with the rest of its business functions: logistics, financials, environmental health and safety (EHS) requirements, and more. It also allows a firm to manage its manufacturing operations with embedded Lean Sigma and Six Sigma, both of which help create and improve competitive advantage.

SAP manufacturing allows discrete and process manufacturing firms to better plan, schedule, re-sequence, and monitor manufacturing processes to achieve higher yields and greater profitability. This is accomplished through partner and supplier coordination, exception management, Six Sigma and Lean Six Sigma, compliance with EHS requirements, and so on—all facilitated by SAP Manufacturing. Through continuous improvement, SAP seeks to provide management and shop floor teams alike the ability to view and optimize real-time operations.

SAP ERP Operations

ERP Operations is still a mainstay. The bulk of the core functionality hails from the days of R/3 and include the following modules:

- ▶ **Sales and Distribution (SD):** Arms an enterprise with the necessary instruments to sell and deliver goods and services. An SD end user can access data on products, marketing strategies, sales calls, pricing, and sales leads at any time to facilitate sales and marketing activity.

- ▶ **Production Planning (PP):** Facilitates production planning, execution, and control from creating realistic and consistent planning figures to production order planning, repetitive manufacturing, or Kanban production control processing. Kanban is a procedure for controlling production and material flow based on a chain of operations in production and procurement.

- ▶ **Materials Management (MM):** Streamlines day-to-day management of the company's consumption of materials. It includes inventory management, warehouse management, purchasing, invoice verification, materials planning, and a purchasing information system.

- ▶ **Plant Maintenance (PM):** Manages preventive maintenance using different strategies, including risk-based maintenance and total productive maintenance as well as maintenance orders and equipment and technical objects.

SAP ERP Corporate Services

The final SAP ERP business solution, Corporate Services, assists companies with streamlining internal lifecycle processes. Modules of Corporate Services include the following:

▶ **Quality Management (QM):** Facilitates planning of inspections and quality control, as well as managing the necessary quality notifications, certificates, and test equipment to proactively manage the product lifecycle.

▶ **Project and Portfolio Management (formerly Project Management [PM]):** Focuses on managing the network of dependencies within a project and includes tracking and managing budget, scheduling, and other resource-based key performance indicators.

▶ **Real Estate Management:** Manages the real estate portfolio lifecycle, from property acquisition through building operations, reporting, maintenance, and disposal.

▶ **Enterprise Asset Management:** Addresses the design, build, operations, and disposal phases.

▶ **Travel Management:** Processes travel requests to manage planning, reservation changes, expense management, and specialized reporting/analytics.

SAP ERP Human Capital Management

SAP extended the R/3 Human Resources (HR) module into Human Capital Management (HCM) by adding a robust collection of integrated and self-described "talent management" capabilities. Several of these HCM services actually fall into two broad focus areas that SAP still tends to use as labels: Personnel Administration (PA) and Personnel Planning and Development (PD). Each addresses different aspects of a company's HR functions; the integration of the two creates a well-oiled HR machine that, when integrated with a firm's other business processes, creates a competitive advantage for the business.

The PA module of HCM manages functions such as payroll, employee benefits enrollment and administration, and compensation. Beyond personnel administration, SAP's Talent Management enables recruiters and managers to see into the various phases of employment, from employment advertising and recruitment through onboarding, employee development/training, and retention activities. It also provides a companywide profile of the firm's human capital (people), making it possible to seek out and manage the careers of people holding particular skills, jobs, or roles. Underlying solutions include

▶ **Enterprise compensation management:** Helps implement a company's pay, promotion, salary adjustments, and bonus plan policies. Functions managed by this solution include salary administration, job evaluations, salary reviews, salary survey results, compensation budget planning and administration, and compensation policy administration.

▶ **E-recruiting:** Helps companies manage their employee recruiting process. Recruitment initiates from the creation of a position vacancy through the advertisement and applicant tracking of potentials, concluding with the notification of successful and unsuccessful applicants and the hiring of the best candidate.

- ▶ **Time management:** Provides a flexible way of recording and evaluating employee work time and absence management. Companies can represent their time structures to reflect changing conditions, using the calendar as a basis. Flextime, shift work, and normal work schedules can be used to plan work and break schedules and manage exceptions, absences, and holidays.

- ▶ **Payroll:** Efficiently and accurately calculates remuneration for work performed by your employees, regardless of their working schedule, working calendar, language, or currency. Payroll also handles fluctuating reporting needs and the regularly changing compliance requirements of federal, state, and local agencies.

In addition, SAP HCM also provides tools to better manage people and traditional HR functions, including organizational management and workforce planning. Some of these include the following:

- ▶ **Organizational Management:** Assists in the strategizing and planning of a comprehensive HR structure. Through the development of proposed scenarios using the flexible tools provided, you can manipulate your company's structure in the present, past, and future. Using the basic organization objects in SAP, units, jobs, positions, tasks, and work centers are all structured as the basic building blocks of your organization.

- ▶ **SAP Enterprise Learning:** Helps a company coordinate and administer companywide training and similar events and also contains functionality to plan for, execute, confirm, and manage cost allocations and billing for your company's events.

- ▶ **SAP Learning Solution:** Provides a learning portal encompassing specialized learning management software and also tools to author tests and manage content through a customizable taxonomy and collaborate across an enterprise.

One of the highlights of nearly all SAP solutions is that they reflect the languages, currencies, and regulatory requirements of many different countries. Workforce Process Management (WPM) bundles country-specific HR topics including time entry, payroll, employee benefits, legal reporting, and organizational reporting to meet local regulations or country codes.

NOTE

Legal Patches Free of Charge within SAP Maintenance

In principle, HCM can run as a module inside ERP; however, many customers deploy HCM on a dedicated system. The reason is that legal patches that are relevant only for HR can be implemented much more easily on a dedicated HR system without causing trouble on the larger ERP system. The fact that SAP delivers such legal patches within the standard maintenance contract is one of the biggest benefits and differentiators of SAP.

Just imagine the situation of companies that deploy financial or HR software from vendors that do not provide such legal patches: Whenever a government in one of the countries these companies does business with issues a new law or legal rule (related to company or employer tax, paid time off, and so on), each of these companies has to adapt the code and test the solution itself. In certain cases, the software package will not even be capable of coping with the new laws.

For example, a recent change in a German law in regard to the per diem calculation rules for travel cost reimbursement couldn't be implemented in the Oracle application used by a major U.S. company. After months of trying to adapt the code, the only workaround was for the German employees to use an Excel spreadsheet to calculate their per diem spend and then enter the results manually into the system for more than a year until the calculation rules were adapted to the new law.

SAP HCM also facilitates a shared services center augmented by reporting and analytics capabilities. Self-service functionality includes or supports a number of roles and company needs, including the following:

- **Employee Self-Service (ESS):** Enables employees to maintain personal data, book travel, apply for vacation time, and more.

- **Manager Self-Service (MSS):** Provides a cockpit used by leadership to manage budgets, compensation planning, and profit/loss statements; sort and conduct keyword searches of employees' records; conduct the annual employee review process; and address other administrative matters quickly and from a centralized location.

- **Workforce Deployment:** Is geared for project teams. Teams are created based on projects, and individual team member competencies and availabilities may then be tracked along with time, tasks, and so on.

SAP added a first "cloud-based" solution with the acquisition of SuccessFactors for talent management. Later it added Fieldglass for management of leased workforce and contingent workers and Concur for travel management. These cloud solutions and others are discussed in Hour 8, "SAP on the Cloud and New SAP Solutions."

SAP Customer Relationship Management

Technically an early offspring of R/3, Customer Relationship Management (CRM) supports customer-related processes end to end. SAP CRM also augments typical back-end functions such as order fulfillment, shipping, invoicing, and accounts receivable. And it folds in and enables enterprise-wide customer intelligence—business intelligence specific to a company's customers and their needs. This increased velocity improves profitability per customer while helping address the business's strategic priorities.

CRM processes are typically built around the needs of a particular business unit or organizational entity. Key business scenarios that augment CRM's new customer support capabilities include

- **Marketing support:** Includes marketing resource management, campaign management, trade promotion management, market segment management, lead/prospect management, and marketing analytics.

- **Sales support:** Provides territory, account, and contact management as well as lead and opportunity management. Sales planning and forecasting help to identify and manage prospects. By leveraging quotation and order management, product configuration, contract management, incentive and commission management, time and travel management, and sales analytics, the team has the information it needs to keep customers happy while hopefully increasing sales volume and margins and decreasing the costs of doing all this.

- **Service support:** Assists post-sales services, including field service, Internet-enabled service offerings, service marketing and sales, and service/contract management. Customers benefit from improved warranty and claims management and effective channel service and depot repair services. And the service team benefits from insight gleaned from service analytics, which enables the team to maximize profit per customer.

- **Web channel support:** Increases sales and reduces transaction costs by turning the Internet into a service channel (or sales and marketing channel) geared toward effectively connecting businesses and consumers.

- **Interaction Center (IC) management support:** Complements and arms a company's field salesforce. This functionality supports marketing, sales, and service activities such as telemarketing, telesales, customer service, e-service, and interaction center analytics.

- **Partner channel management:** Provides processes for partner recruitment, partner management, communications, channel marketing, channel forecasting, collaborative selling, partner order management, channel service, and analytics.

- **Business communications management:** Features contact management across multiple locations and different communications mediums (including voice, text messaging, email, and others).

- **Real-time offer management:** Helps manage the complexities of marketing offers in real time, using SAP's advanced analytical real-time decision engine. This functionality also optimizes the decision-making process across different customer interaction channels, enabling a company to quickly and intelligently enhance its customer relationships.

Several additional industry-specific features round out SAP CRM. For example:

- **Leasing entities:** Provides end-to-end lease management, from identifying financing opportunities for new loans to remarketing existing leases and terminating leases.

- **Consumer products industry:** Provides customer trade promotions including brand management, activity planning, demand planning, budgeting, program execution, and promotion evaluation.

- **Media industry vertical:** Manages intellectual property (IP) and any resulting royalties.

- **Public sector:** Provides constituent services and tax and revenue management and more.

- **Pharmaceutical industry:** Supports the stages of drug commercialization.

- **Manufacturing vertical:** Features lean batch-management capabilities.

SAP CRM can become complex. For example, the call center solution Customer Interaction Center (CIC) relies on a corresponding interface to the PBX. Low response times are critical for CIC implementations because long wait times easily drive customers away.

Even more complex are web shops. In addition to the basic SAP CRM system, the SAP Internet Sales scenario also consists of the SAP Internet Pricing and Configurator (IPC), SAP Biller Direct, a catalog system, SAP Knowledge Provider (KPro), a permanent shopping basket, and more.

Finally, the recent acquisition of hybris by SAP added a multichannel e-commerce and product content management (PCM) software solution to SAP's software portfolio.

SAP Product Lifecycle Management

SAP Product Lifecycle Management (PLM) facilitates rapid development and delivery of the products addressing a host of change management challenges (from design to engineering, production ramp-up, and so on), post-sales service, and post-sales maintenance needs.

PLM's primary focus is on product development, but the solution also covers plant maintenance, quality assurance, hazardous substance management, industrial hygiene and safety, and environmental protection.

Although SAP PLM is a standalone solution, it is not an SAP system of its own. Instead, it uses a combination of functions from SAP ERP, SAP CRM, SAP SCM, and other components. Therefore, rather than requiring its own infrastructure, PLM is usually simply installed as an add-on to SAP ECC. The SAP Knowledge Warehouse (KW) can be used to store and distribute large files like scans, CAD drawings, video files, and so on.

PLM also serves as the foundation for the New Product Development and Introduction (NPDI) collaboration tool. Using NPDI, companies tie together people and information, effectively connecting sales, planning, production, procurement, maintenance, internal service provider, and other organizations to one another. SAP PLM's business benefits are both numerous and diverse. For example, SAP PLM may be deployed to

- Optimize the product development process while ensuring compliance with internal quality metrics, industry standards, and regulatory requirements.

- Reduce total costs related to planning for and deploying a new product.

- Measure and evaluate the progress of discrete product-oriented projects across different product lines.

- Leverage PLM's modular approach to product development and ramp-up, so as to incrementally meet your product's needs as it evolves through the product lifecycle.

- Maximize team productivity through the use of simple and effective role-based enterprise portal access.

- Make better and faster business decisions, taking advantage of powerful analytics across the product lifecycle (portfolio management, quality, occupational health and safety, maintenance management, and others).

You can use PLM to enable collaborative product development, engineering, and associated project and quality management. You can plug in your partners as you all seek to meet environmental, health, and safety requirements. And you can gain visibility across your enterprise by extending PLM via the entire SAP Business Suite—from CRM and SCM to SAP ERP and more. SAP PLM makes it possible to push new products through their development and engineering phases into manufacturing and ultimately into the hands of your customers faster and more profitably—so that you reap better margins and faster turnarounds than would otherwise be possible.

SAP Supply Chain Management

Generally speaking, a supply chain comprises three areas: supply, manufacturing, and distribution. The supply portion of a supply chain focuses on the raw materials needed by manufacturing, which in turn converts raw materials into finished products. The distribution aspect of a supply chain focuses on moving the finished products through a network of distributors, warehouses, and outlets. Strategic analysis and supply chain collaboration allow businesses to monitor and optimize the extended supply chain, spanning multiple parties inside and outside the organization.

SAP Supply Chain Management (SCM) provides for a great number of business scenarios but includes only a few technical components. SAP Advanced Planner and Optimizer (APO) is the core component of SCM, and it consists of the following modules:

- **APO Demand Planning (DP):** Forecasts future requirements on the basis of historical data. Different models can be created to simulate the balance of supply and demand to affect profitability, minimize inventory turns, and so on.

► **Supply Network Planning (SNP):** Optimizes the cross-plant distribution of orders onto the available transport and production capacities. Complemented by Production Planning–Detailed Scheduling (PP-DS) and Vendor Managed Inventory (VMI).

► **Availability-to-Promise (ATP):** Provides a multilevel availability check that can be carried out against material stocks, production, warehouse and transport capacities, costs across plants, and more.

► **Production Planning (PP):** Creates a production schedule that balances and reflects a supply plan with its point-in-time manufacturing capacity.

► **Purchasing Planning:** Models and develops various plans for balancing raw materials and other resources against the demand for products and generates a well-thought-out supply plan.

► **Transportation Planning–Vehicle Scheduling (TP-VS):** Optimizes transportation and handling processes.

► **Supply Chain Cockpit (SCC):** Analyzes company-specific supply chain elements and displays the results on a map, in a list, or in a number of table-based or graphical formats.

NOTE

liveCache: SAP's First In-Memory Database

All the supply chain processes described above demand complex optimization runs with a large number of characteristic combinations, which in turn demands extremely fast access to data that's impossible to achieve with traditional hard disks. Therefore, SAP developed liveCache, one of the first in-memory databases. In combination with special object-oriented technologies, the in-memory concept significantly accelerates the algorithmically, highly complex, data-intensive, and runtime-intensive functions of APO.

Beginning with SCM 7.12, the external liveCache can be migrated to an SAP HANA-integrated live-Cache, so the liveCache in this SCM system becomes part of the SAP HANA database.

Other components of SAP SCM include:

► **SAP Event Management (EM):** Provides functions for managing deviations between planning and reality.

► **SAP Inventory Collaboration Hub:** Supports cross-enterprise integration for Supplier-Managed Inventory (SMI) or Vendor-Managed Inventory (VMI).

► **SAP Auto-ID Infrastructure (AII):** Provides connectivity of RFID scanners to SAP SCM and can generate extremely high I/O loads.

▶ **SAP Object Event Repository (OER):** Implemented together with multiple local instances of SAP Auto-ID Infrastructure featuring Product Tracking & Authentication (PTA) to record uniquely identified objects like Electronic Product Codes (EPCs) for which information has been sent from AII. OER also has the capability of generating reports (business intelligence) for these data reads maintained in its repository.

SAP Supplier Relationship Management

Supplier Relationship Management (SRM) is the SAP component for purchasing and procurement departments, covering the complete process from placing an order to paying the invoice. Just as SAP CRM manages the relationship between a company and its customers, SAP SRM helps to optimize and manage the relationship between a company and its suppliers. Flexible approval procedures and tracking functions ensure that spending levels are monitored and controlled.

As another of SAP's more mature offerings, SRM integrates seamlessly with PLM, enabling a high degree of collaboration between product buyers and parts suppliers. Bidding processes are streamlined, as well. All this naturally impacts SAP ERP, too, because financial and logistics data are updated and shared between systems. SRM also ties into SAP SCM, extending and enabling tight integration with a company's supply chain.

The core component is SAP Enterprise Buyer Professional (EBP), which is enhanced by a catalog server. Optional components are SAP Content Integrator, SAP Bidding Engine for online auctions, SAP Supplier Self-Services (SUS), and SAP Live Auction Cockpit Web Presentation Server (LAC WPS) for online auctions.

SRM's business benefits revolve around sourcing, contract lifecycle management, and spend performance management:

▶ On-demand sourcing, which encourages or provides sustainable cost savings, 360-degree supplier insight, greater intercompany flexibility, and rapid time-to-value

▶ Compressed cycle times through faster request for payment (RFP)-to-receipt processes and online approvals

▶ Accelerated time-to-contract via automated contract creation and collaboration capabilities

▶ Consistent savings and revenue recognition enabled by contract visibility and awareness

▶ Reduced process costs, facilitated through simplification, process automation, and elimination of maverick buying

SAP SRM supports strategic purchasing and sourcing by

- ▶ Managing contracts relative to overall compliance with each contract's terms and conditions

- ▶ Creating and managing the internal procurement catalog

- ▶ Managing the supplier-selection process by analyzing each supplier's performance

- ▶ Providing electronic auction and bidding tools

- ▶ Aggregating the demand for particular materials and services across the enterprise

- ▶ Analyzing spending patterns through global spend visibility

With its tight integration with SAP PLM, SRM users benefit from the following:

- ▶ Streamlined access to engineering documentation and other materials that are useful in optimizing product quality, manufacturing processes, and more

- ▶ Better visibility into ERP back-end data, such as materials management processes, financial documents, and bills of materials (BOMs)

- ▶ PLM's tight integration with SRM's sourcing capabilities

Finally, SAP SRM streamlines procurement processes by improved collaboration with the following:

- ▶ **Product developers:** Allows data to be shared between trading partners and your own purchasing team to enable faster product development cycles.

- ▶ **Suppliers:** Gives suppliers access to your inventory and replenishment data so they can help you maintain your minimum required inventory levels.

By using SRM's breadth of capabilities, a firm can truly optimize, integrate, and automate procurement processes into its own day-to-day workflows. This helps the organization avoid missing out on supplies that are essential to conducting business.

Purchasing on the Cloud

With its acquisition of Ariba, SAP added a fully cloud-based SaaS solution for external order and payment processing, sourcing, and spend analysis. Ariba provides a supplier network with more than 1.5 million members; every two minutes, a new company adds itself to this network.

Even in the case that a product can't be found within the catalogs of the partners in the network, Ariba can be configured to search a site such as eBay, using criteria to consider only vendors where the product can be bought immediately and with a high customer feedback rating.

Many customers combine an on-premise SAP SRM system with Ariba in a hybrid model. In this case, Ariba needs to be integrated into the traditional SAP applications stack and the existing application workflow.

Other "goods" a company needs to procure are business travel and contingent workers Concur supports booking of business travel, and Fieldglass works with the management of leased workforce.

All purchase orders have to be processed in the bookkeeping and incoming goods department workflow, so all this SaaS have to be integrated into the SAP ERP bookkeeping system in order to be paid and accounted correctly. The effort to change the existing application logic to eliminate the old and replace it with a new cloud-based system should not be underestimated.

Governance, Risk, and Compliance

SAP Governance, Risk, and Compliance (GRC) enables enterprises to ensure that laws and rules like the Sarbanes-Oxley Act (SOX) are strictly followed throughout the organization in a way that can be audited by the relevant authorities. As part of GRC, Global Trade System (GTS) ensures that companies don't export something that is on a black list for certain countries. In addition, Environment, Health, and Safety (EH&S) manage the documents required for industrial hygiene and safety, and environmental protection, such as material safety data sheets and waste manifests. Access Control (formerly called Virsa Compliance Calibrator) supports the segregation of duties auditing.

With its integrated SAP ERP back end, SAP provides the visibility and transparency organizations demand in response to various regulatory body and internal control requirements. Because SAP GRC gives end users a tool to simply recognize critical risks and analyze risk–reward trade-offs, the time and expense required to implement this product is quickly recouped in cost savings. SAP GRC's business benefits include the following:

- **Well-balanced portfolios boasting well-vetted risk/reward analyses:** Through GRC's transparency, visibility, and companywide hooks, enables a firm's decision makers to make smart decisions—decisions based on risk and the probability of return.

- **Improved stakeholder value:** Yields preserved brand reputation, increased market value, reduced cost of capital, easier personnel recruiting, and higher employee retention.

- **Reduced cost of providing governance, risk, and compliance:** Provides enhanced business performance and financial predictability. SAP GRC gives executive leadership teams the confidence they need in their numbers and methods to quickly rectify issues.

- **Organizational sustainability:** Provides this despite the risks associated with poorly managed GRC, particularly legal and market ramifications.

All this amounts to increased business agility, competitive differentiation, and other brand-preserving and company-sustaining benefits.

Actually GRC should no longer be seen as an optional service but rather a mandatory part of doing business in a global world tainted by less-than-ethical businesses and business practices.

Global Trade Services

The component of SAP GRC known as SAP Global Trade Services (GTS) is also an SAP ERP Financials solution that further qualifies as an SAP Corporate Services solution and global supply chain enabler. GTS makes it possible for international companies to connect and communicate with various government systems, using a companywide trade process. In this way, SAP GRC GTS lets a business do the following:

- ▶ Meet international regulatory requirements

- ▶ Manage global trade by integrating companywide trade compliance across financial, supply chain, and human capital management business processes

- ▶ Facilitate and expedite the import/export process for goods traveling through different countries' customs organizations

- ▶ Facilitate increased supply chain transparency by sharing cross-border trade-related information with partners (insurers, freight handlers, and so on)

SAP GRC GTS thus enables a firm to mitigate financial and other risks associated with doing business around the globe. By ensuring compliance with international trade agreements, SAP GRC GTS customers can optimize their supply chain, reduce production downtime, and eliminate errors that otherwise yield expensive penalties. In a nutshell, SAP GRC GTS makes it possible for firms to do business across country borders and to do so more consistently and profitably.

Summary

This hour provided background about SAP R/3 and how it evolved into what is known today as SAP ERP. SAP ERP consists of several high-level solution offerings, including Financials, Operations, Human Capital Management (HCM) and its various solutions, and Corporate Services. An introduction to these core solutions areas was further bolstered by discussions of specific functional solutions and modules underpinning each SAP ERP solution offering.

As you can imagine, the complexity of the SAP business solutions discussed in this hour are much greater than reflected here. Indeed, each SAP component within the broader SAP Business Suite umbrella constitutes a complex SAP implementation project in its own right. The skills and knowledge you have gained in this hour have equipped you with a wide-ranging understanding of how each solution provides business benefit.

Case Study: Hour 7

Consider this SAP ERP case study and the questions that follow. You can find answers to the questions related to this case study in Appendix A, "Case Study Answers."

Situation

MNC is implementing SAP HCM and several SAP ERP logistics solutions. As a member of the development team, you have been asked to answer a number of questions posed by several of MNC's business stakeholders.

Questions

1. What does the acronym SAP ERP HCM stand for, and why is HCM a compelling solution for organizations today?

2. What are the components of SAP ERP Plant Maintenance?

3. What kind of business solutions does SAP ERP Operations address?

4. Why is there so much overlap among SAP ERP's business solutions, modules, and business processes?

5. For the most robust yet targeted set of SAP ERP analytics, what should MNC consider implementing?

6. Which features in SAP CRM augment your capability to support new customers?

7. Can an organization purchase SAP Manufacturing in the same way it can purchase one of the five SAP Business Suite components (like SAP CRM or SRM)?

8. How does SAP SRM's tight integration with PLM benefit your SRM users?

9. Which of the Business Suite components or products is the most mature?

10. What are the three general components of a supply chain?

HOUR 8

SAP on the Cloud and New SAP Solutions

What You'll Learn in This Hour:

- ▶ The different flavors of cloud services for SAP
- ▶ SAP's road to the cloud
- ▶ Running classic SAP solutions on the cloud
- ▶ HEC versus HPC
- ▶ New SAP solutions: SuccessFactors, Ariba, Fieldglass, Concur, and hybris

Despite its great tradition of in-house developments from R/3 to HANA, SAP has never been shy about acquiring other companies to extend its application portfolio and gain access to new technologies. Examples from the past include Business Objects, Kiefer & Veittinger, and Sybase's database technologies.

At this writing, Wikipedia lists 59 SAP acquisitions, with Concur Technologies being the latest. Among these acquisitions are several cloud-based Software as a Service (SaaS) solutions that were already successful on the market. With HANA Enterprise Cloud (HEC) and HANA Cloud Platform (HCP), SAP also added Platform as a Service (PaaS) and hosting services to its portfolio. In this hour, we provide a general overview of these solutions, how they fit into the big picture, how they are used, and the value they provide.

To business readers, it makes no difference whether SAP runs on premise (in a company's in-house datacenter) or out on the cloud somewhere, so you may skip the first half of this hour and move directly to the section "Newly Acquired SAP Solutions," which describes SAP's new solutions.

What Kind of Cloud?

Discussions about the cloud tend to contain a confusing variety of acronyms. Obviously, every vendor defines its own cloud according to the product portfolio it has available.

The cloud definitions of the National Institute of Standards and Technology[1] are so general that they are not much help in understanding cloud options. To understand the options relevant for SAP, it is helpful to take a look how other services are offered in the market.

An example that can in help understanding cloud concepts involves the provisioning of pizza for a family dinner. As most of us realize, there are several options available for obtaining pizza, ranging from genuine homemade to dining out and several options in between, as shown in Figure 8.1.

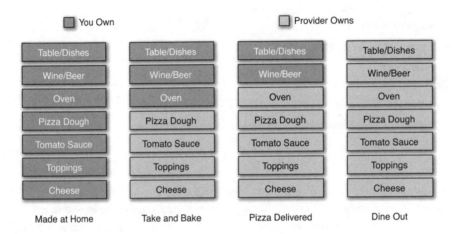

FIGURE 8.1
Different options for getting a pizza.

What distinguishes the different models (of cloud services as well as pizza) is the degree of the necessary infrastructure, supplies, and services you are able to control compared to the ones you have to "take-or-leave":

▶ In case of the traditional homemade pizza, you (or your grandma) can control the quality of all the ingredients, from flour to tomatoes, and you own all the kitchen equipment, down to the tableware.

▶ If you use frozen pizza, you outsource the hassle of preparing the dough, sauce, and toppings, but have to rely on the taste and quality of the ingredients used by your preferred brand. In addition, not all combinations of toppings and cheese are available, you can't choose the cheese from one vendor and the topping from another. The kitchen and dishes are still under your control (including the cleaning afterward).

---

[1] See http://csrc.nist.gov/publications/PubsSPs.html#800-145.

▶ If you choose pizza home delivery, you don't have to own an oven, but some of the other restrictions for frozen pizza apply: you can't choose the vendors for the ingredients. You depend on the capability of the service to deliver the pizza still hot, but you can still choose your preferred wine and tableware (and you still have to clean up afterward).

▶ If you decide to go with your family to a pizzeria, you take care of the reservation, the selection from the menu, and payment; you do not need to do any food preparation or cleanup. On the downside, you have to accept what's available on the menu and accept some longer waiting time until you get seated and served during prime time (which is called "oversubscription" in IT terms).

When it comes to SAP solutions and the IT services necessary to deliver them, it is important to distinguish between physical infrastructure (network, storage, or server) and software infrastructure (virtualization solutions, operating system, database, and application), where the actual ownership is represented by the license and maintenance contracts (see Figure 8.2).

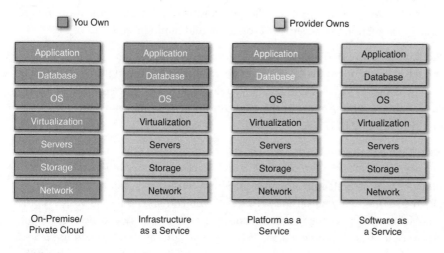

FIGURE 8.2
Different options for getting an SAP solution.

As with the pizza example, the different cloud offerings relevant to SAP can be classified by the ownership of the various layers necessary to deliver SAP as a service.

▶ In case of the traditional on-premise model, you own, manage, and maintain the complete infrastructure. Utilizing state-of-the-art private cloud virtualization and orchestration technologies provides the same flexibility as with the public counterparts. Being in a position to select from the portfolio of different hardware vendors competing against each other, you enjoy having access to the top expertise of their SAP competence centers for sizing and architecture optimization—worth hundreds of consulting hours free of charge—as a pre-sales service. Given the fact that a migration to another platform is not a big deal anymore, you can get prime attention if you run into trouble by claiming that you will move to another vendor and forcing the vendor to do the root cause analysis to prove that his part of the infrastructure is not causing the trouble. However, you also need the necessary skill in-house to operate and maintain the hardware and software you have acquired, and you have to pay license and maintenance fees for virtualization, the OS, the database, and the application.

▶ While in a classical hosting model you are still in a position to choose the hardware infrastructure, you don't have the hassle of dealing with the hardware vendors if you utilize an Infrastructure as a Service (IaaS) provider. The downside is that the hardware vendors are not available for root cause analysis when the system becomes unstable after an OS, database, or application patch if the service provider claims that the part he is responsible for runs stable. In regard to performance, you have to accept the level of resource over commitment you agreed to in the fine print. You pay only the hardware resources you consume but still have to "bring your own license" for the OS, database, and SAP solution, and you also have to bring the expertise to configure and maintain this part of the stack.

▶ Using a Platform as a Service (PaaS) is nearly the same as using an IaaS provider, but you don't have to worry about the operating system. And if you're using HANA Enterprise Cloud (HEC) or HANA Cloud Platform (HCP), you don't even need to be concerned about the database. You are still in control of the application licenses and can change the provider with little effort and little risk.

▶ If you decide to go with a genuine Software as a Service (SaaS) offering or transform the licenses of your classical SAP solutions into an SAP cloud license, you get rid of the responsibility for the complete infrastructure stack and can focus on utilizing the features provided by the solution for your business. However, you can order only the business processes available on the service menu; customization is restricted in most cases to adapting the user interface to your corporate design. In a way, you can say that you can use a SaaS solution without having IT skills. However, as with all the other cloud offerings, you still need in-house expertise or external consulting to integrate the different applications with each other and train your users in how to use the services provided.

With all the hype surrounding the cloud, it may be worth mentioning some of the most common challenges. Security is among the major concerns that come to mind. With the implications of the Patriot Act, many non-U.S. companies keep their sensitive data within the border of their country. However, nifty details like patch management can become a major headache, especially in hybrid scenarios where one vendor's patch cycles may not be coordinated with the customer, resulting in additional downtime. (For an in-depth discussion of security aspects, see our book *SAP on the Cloud*.[2])

SAP's Way to the Cloud

SAP customers don't like change—and for good reason. After all, mission-critical software is a conservative business, and SAP is the epitome of a conservative company. But even a company like SAP must eventually follow new trends like cloud computing to remain relevant and competitive.

In the past, SAP maintained a focus on developing solutions in-house complemented by solutions and technologies acquired externally. With a few exceptions, these solutions were tightly integrated in the portfolio and integrated with the standard technology. In any case, customers could choose to run these solutions on-premise or hosted by an SAP-certified provider.

It has been a long road from SAP's early efforts with service-oriented architecture (SOA) in 2004 (called Project Vienna). SAP's next cloud attempt was Business by Design, released in 2006. With the acquisition of SuccessFactors in 2011 and Ariba in 2012, SAP sent a signal to the market and its customers about its direction into on-demand software and cloud computing. Today, SAP follows a dual approach:

▶ Supporting the deployment of Business Suite and NetWeaver on IaaS and PaaS offerings from Amazon, Azure, and certified service providers with real experience in running mission-critical business applications, including their own HEC and HCP

▶ Acquiring established SaaS solutions to complement Business Suite, including Ariba, SuccessFactors, Fieldglass, and Concur

Given the current amount of change and transformation within SAP's cloud strategy, this section provides only a snapshot of the current initiatives on which SAP focuses.

Classic SAP Solutions on the Cloud

In principle, all the classic SAP Business Suite and NetWeaver solutions described in Hours 6, "SAP NetWeaver and HANA," and 7, "SAP ERP and Business Suite," can be implemented on IaaS and PaaS offerings.

At this writing, SAP has certified 220 partners for hosting, 105 for cloud, and 35 for HANA. Among them are large service providers like Virtustream, T-Systems, Telstra, Suncore, Secure-24, NNIT, MKI, and Singapore Telecom; consulting companies like Accenture, Atos, CSC,

---

[2] *SAP on the Cloud* by Missbach et al., Berlin: Springer, 2015.

CapGemini, Deloitte, and IBM; and specialized boutique providers like Freudenberg IT, Ciber, Finance-IT, OEDIV, Gisa, and Novis.[3]

SAP's own hosting organization was sold to T-Systems and Freudenberg IT in 2009. SAP does not own or operate Hana Enterprise Cloud itself, either, but acquires the services from Softlayer, an IBM company.

The most prominent cloud providers offering SAP solutions are Amazon and Azure, even though they can't offer anything other than IaaS. It has become a common practice in many enterprises to keep the mission-critical production systems on premise or at a classic full-service hosting provider, while utilizing cloud offerings for non-production systems that are needed only temporarily for development, testing, or training.

If you are a user, you will not see any difference in the way that the SAP Business Suite and NetWeaver solutions are operated; all the business processes should behave identically whether on premise or in the cloud, and the user interface should look exactly the same.

HEC Versus HCP

For the quite special demands of HANA, there are cloud options available from SAP (as well as from a variety of cloud service providers):

▶ **HANA Enterprise Cloud (HEC):** Despite its name, HEC is not a cloud service but a classical hosting service for HANA. SAP sells the service on its paper, but the infrastructure is actually hosted by Softlayer. For certain solutions, SAP offers a subscription pricing as an alternative to the perpetual license option that continues to be available.

▶ **HANA Cloud Platform (HCP)[4]:** HCP is a real subscription-based IaaS offering, aimed for development projects and providing HANA-based application services for a monthly subscription. Sizes ranging from 1 GB up to 1 TB can be ordered from the SAP Service Catalog Portal.

Both of these cloud offerings requires customers to buy their own HANA licenses. SAP recently announced that it would change the license model to a pay-as-you-go model, but the prices will rise from the "maintenance fee" of 22% to 50% of license list price per year.

Technically, all HANA cloud offerings are based on the so-called tailored datacenter integration (TDI) model that allows sharing server, storage, and networking resources.

---

[3] For a complete list of SAP Certified Outsourcing Operations Partners, see http://global.sap.com/community/ebook/2012_Partner_Guide/partner-list.html.

[4] See http://hcp.sap.com/platform.html.

Alternatively, SAP HANA App Services provides HANA instances with services for mobility, collaboration, security, systems management, and more—all orderable from the SAP Service Catalog Portal[5] (see Figure 8.3).

As discussed in Hour 6, "SAP NetWeaver and HANA," the HANA cloud offerings start at a very attractive price level for small development environments. With more features and options, the price rises significantly, as shown in Figure 8.3. Even with a monthly subscription fee, an annual contract is required. Note that system provisioning can take up to 48 hours.

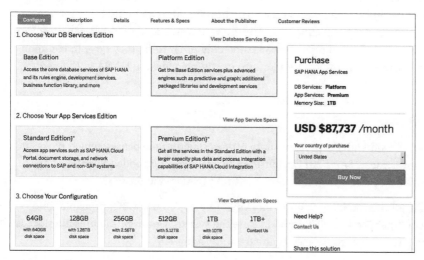

FIGURE 8.3
Subscription page for HANA App Services on the SAP Service Catalog Portal.[6]

NOTE

SAP on AWS and Azure

IT professionals will appreciate the extra level of deep technical and project management guidance provided in Hour 19, "SAP and the Cloud," with regard to how to run SAP on AWS and Azure. (We've also included an introduction to the SAP Cloud Appliance Library and Project Monsoon.) Enjoy.

---

[5] See http://marketplace.saphana.com/hcp.

[6] See http://marketplace.saphana.com/p/1808.

Newly Acquired SAP Solutions

Now that's we've discussed SAP's road to the cloud, we will introduce some of SAP SE's recent acquisitions, in the order in which they were acquired. With a few exceptions, these acquired companies provide SaaS solutions that are "cloud only."

The acquired companies discussed here all utilize technologies that have nothing in common with classic SAP architecture in regard to platforms, code, and user interfaces. This can be challenging for IT departments that must integrate these solutions into their existing software environment. It can also be challenging for end users, who have to adapt not only to a new look and feel but also to different naming conventions and business process concepts. Besides the fact that all of these solutions are owned and offered by SAP, the only other thing they have in common is HANA. They either already use the HANA platform or will be moved to HANA in the near future.

SuccessFactors

For most companies, the workforce represents up to 60% of operating expenses, which makes it their single largest investment. SAP's 2011 acquisition of SuccessFactors added talent management expertise and human resource management (HCM) to SAP's cloud assets.

SuccessFactors' HCM solutions are based on management by objectives (MBO) principles and promise that you don't need to know HR jargon to use the system. However, the user interface is quite different from SAP's standard UIs (see Figure 8.4 and Figure 8.5).

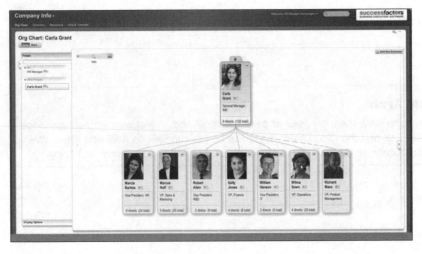

FIGURE 8.4
Example of the SuccessFactors Employee Central built-in organization chart (courtesy of SAP).

The SuccessFactors HCM Suite includes

- **Employee Central:** A self-service core HR and talent management solution

- **Recruiting:** Helps to attract, engage, and select candidates and measure the results

- **Onboarding:** Guides hiring managers and improves employees' job satisfaction, time to productivity, and first-year retention

- **Performance & Goals:** Communicates strategy and creates meaningful individual goals, streamlines the performance appraisal process, and enables meaningful feedback

- **Compensation:** Supports a company to pay people based on achievement and objective ratings

- **Succession & Development:** Enables planning for staffing changes

- **Learning:** A complete learning management solution (LMS) that enables instructor-led and formal and social online training; includes a Content-as-a-Service (CaaS) solution

- **Workforce Planning:** Provides workforce information and benchmarks to forecast the impact of business decisions.

- **Workforce Analytics & Reporting:** Delivers quantitative insights

- SAP added "Jam" (their private social network tool which combines collaboration and content creation) to the SuccessFactors portfolio.

In December 2013, SuccessFactors' Talent Management solution already had more than 4,000 customers with 25 million users, and the Learning Management System had more than 600 customers with 11.5 million users. Employee Central had 15 million users spanning 3,500 companies.

Integration with Payroll

Even if SuccessFactors' Compensation Management (see Figure 8.5) provided all the functionality needed to manage your employees' salaries, the actual payments would still need to be processed by SAP HCM's payroll (part of the core ERP system) or another third-party bookkeeping system.

Synchronizing the data between two systems has always been a complex activity. This should be considered when evaluating the compensation management of Successfactors compared to using the already built-in HCM integration of SAP ERP (more on this in Hour 19).

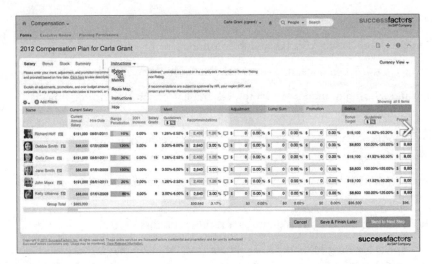

FIGURE 8.5
An example of SuccessFactors' compensation management (courtesy of SAP).

Ariba

From the first versions of R/3 and even R/2, the procurement process was an integral part of SAP's ERP solution, covering the complete process from placing an order to paying the invoice. To serve the specific demand of procurement departments, SAP soon split out a dedicated solution for enabling point-to-point purchasing connections between buyers and sellers.

See Hour 5, "Overview of SAP Applications and Components," especially Figure 5.1, to better understand how the name of the solution has changed over time from Business-to-Business procurement to SAP Enterprise Buyer Professional (EBP) and then Supplier Relationship Management (SRM)—enhanced by a catalog server, a bidding engine for online auctions, and more. However, the connection to each business partner had to be negotiated and set up separately.

In contrast to SAP's approach, focused on the demand of the buyer's departments for individual customers, Ariba succeeded in establishing a centralized trading platform for suppliers.

Founded in 1996 as one of the first startups utilizing the Internet for procurement processes, and acquired by SAP in 2012, Ariba provides a fully cloud-based SaaS solution for external order and payment processing as well as for sourcing and spend analysis. However, the biggest benefit that the more than 730,000 Ariba customers can capitalize on is a business network with more than 750,000 suppliers; Ariba claims that every two minutes, a company adds itself to this network.

And even in the event that a product can't be found within the catalogs of the partners in this huge network, Ariba can be configured to search other sites, such as eBay, using criteria to only consider vendors where the product can be bought immediately and with a high customer feed-back rating.

Ariba solutions are available by subscription and on-demand, so there's no software to install or maintain. All an end user needs is a web browser. Whether you want to buy (see Figure 8.6) or sell (see Figure 8.7), there is an easy step-by-step process available via Ariba Discovery.[7] Just click on Register Now to obtain an account and request a demo. It's free and takes only a few minutes.

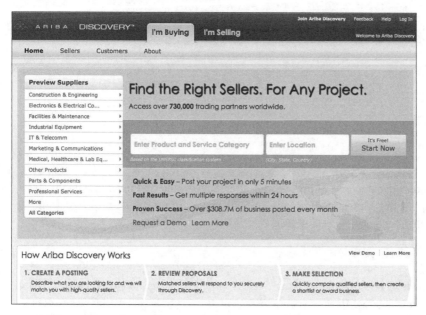

FIGURE 8.6
The Ariba Discovery portal for buyers (courtesy of Ariba).

For standard sellers, there is a fee to respond to postings based on the posting deal size: free up to US$1,000; $19 up to $50,000; $49 up to $100,000; $119 up to $1,000,000; and $149 over $1,000,000. Upgrading to the Advantage or Advantage Plus package brings free responses and other marketing opportunities.

---

[7] See https://service.ariba.com/Discovery.aw.

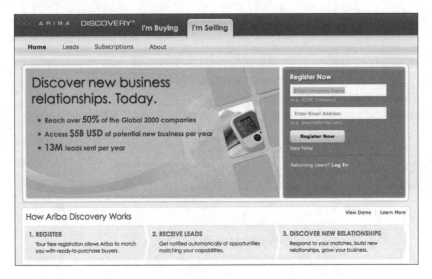

FIGURE 8.7
Ariba Discovery portal for vendors (courtesy of Ariba).

Because all purchase orders have to be processed in the bookkeeping and incoming goods department, Ariba has to be integrated into the SAP ERP system to make sure that everything procured is accounted correctly. (See Hour 19.)

Fieldglass

Another kind of goods or resources a company needs to procure is external staffing power; these resources range from individual freelancers or contingent workers to leased workforces capable of supporting a complete plant. The concept of engaging managed service providers (MSPs) to oversee the onsite contingent workforce emerged in the late 1980s and gained steam around the mid-1990s. During that same time, automated vendor management systems (VMS) propelled and enabled the MSP model.

Fieldglass, founded in 1999 and acquired by SAP in 2014, provides a cloud-based VMS used to manage a non-employee workforce of contingent workers (that is, independent contractors). The various business processes that such management comprises include procurement, creation of statements of work, project management, and payment management.

Figure 8.8 illustrates a variety of templates for job postings a project manager can use to select the proper skill set for a development task.

Figure 8.9 shows the Fieldglass management dashboard, where all activities from the hiring process to times sheets and budgetary reports down to employee reviews are available as structured workflows.

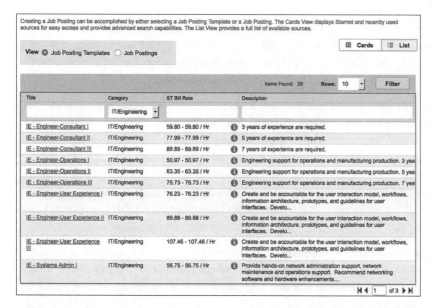

FIGURE 8.8
Fieldglass job posting template (courtesy of Cisco).

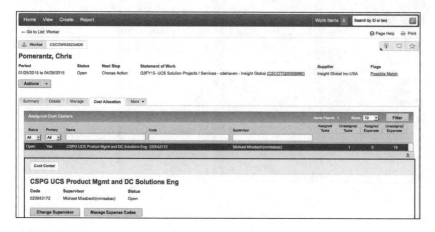

FIGURE 8.9
Fieldglass management dashboard (courtesy of Cisco).

As of early 2014, Fieldglass' client base included approximately 250 customers, many of them quite large or complex. SAP expects this business to grow as companies continue to shed traditional workforces and employ new staffing and resourcing models.

Concur

Travel and entertainment spend is the second-largest controllable cost for some companies—just behind payroll. Many highly paid experts have to spend a considerable amount of time organizing their travel and collecting all their travel receipts for reimbursement.

Concur's basic idea is to integrate corporate travel booking with expense tracking, so employees don't have to key in the same data multiple times in multiple systems. Electronic receipts from airlines, rental car companies, hotels, and restaurants are captured automatically and turned into expense line items, eliminating the hassle of filling out travel reports and improving accuracy significantly. If national tax laws permit, travelers just have to take photos of train tickets or taxi or restaurant bills with their smartphones and attach the images to expenses; in addition to the other benefits, this process saves greenhouse gases by preventing piles of paper from being processed abroad.

Figure 8.10 illustrates the Concur expense reporting process. The Travel & Expense app capture transactions directly from airlines, hotels, restaurants, and car companies and transforms them into expense line entries (left). Travelers can also add photos of receipts (middle) to the expense report. The last step is to forward the finished report to a manager for approval (right).

FIGURE 8.10
Generating a travel report with Concur Travel & Expense (courtesy of Concur).

Concur Travel & Expense supports multiple languages and currencies. Currency exchange rate and complex car-mileage allowances are automatically calculated, as are the tax rates of many countries. Interfaces for SAP business solution and other ERP systems are available.

Concur Travel & Expense is offered in multiple editions (Small Business, Standard, Concurforce, Professional, and Premium) and processes $50 billion in expense transactions per year.

In addition, Concur offers TripIt, a mobile travel organizer for individuals that is currently used by more than 5 million individuals (see Figure 8.11). Users simply forward all hotel, flight, car rental, and restaurant confirmation emails to plans@tripit.com, and TripIt transforms them into a detailed itinerary with dates, times, and confirmation numbers. In addition, directions, maps, weather, and other such information may be consolidated and centrally displayed for every trip.

FIGURE 8.11
TripIT's user interface (courtesy of Concur).

Like Ariba, Concur offers a test drive for 30 days free of charge[8] to help potential users become familiar with the look and feel of the solution.

SAP completed the acquisition of Concur in December 2014. While SAP will continue to fully support its customers currently using SAP Cloud for Travel and Expense through their current contract term, Concur's solution will be the offering of choice for customers moving forward.

hybris

In an interesting way, hybris represents an exception to the general trend of SAP acquiring established cloud solutions, because hybris is classic on-premise software that may be installed as an IaaS cloud offering. Founded in 1997 in Switzerland and acquired by SAP in 2014, hybris provides a suite of multichannel and product content management (PCM) software to complement SAP's classical CRM solutions.

Multichannel retailing considers the variety of channels consumers can choose today for shopping. Digitally savvy consumers are entering stores already well informed about a product's features and prices, and they expect store employees to know more than they do. Purchases may

---

8   See https://www.concur.com/en-us/free-trial?icid=en_us_trialtesttop.

be made in the store but are researched through other channels of communication, including online catalogs, television, mobile apps, and online stores like Amazon and eBay. To win connected consumers, all shopping channels from brick-and-mortar shops to telesales need to use the same information regarding products, prices, promotions, etc.

Many retailers also have to deal with multiple catalogs for different target audiences and languages. hybris supports multilevel hierarchies of catalogs, such that child catalogs can inherit a parent catalog's settings. On the other side, multichannel retailing solutions enable consumer-specific offerings, analyzing purchase patterns, social network affinities, website visits, loyalty programs, and so on—all of which increase the complexity of such solutions significantly.

The hybris Commerce Suite

The hybris Commerce Suite offers a single system for managing product content, commerce operations, and channels from mobile and online to in-store. Figure 8.12 gives you a glimpse of the catalog management capabilities of hybris.

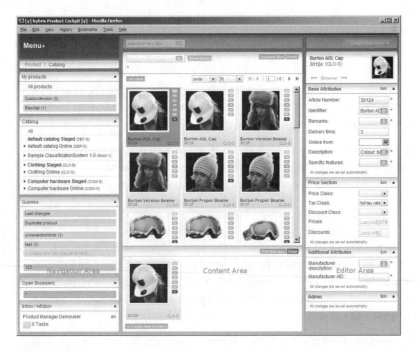

FIGURE 8.12
The hybris Product Cockpit manages product information and catalogs (courtesy of hybris).[9]

---

9   See http://www.lewiswire.com/de/lewiswire/Hybris/Hybris-Suite-40-Neue-Architektur-und-modernste-Technologie-legen-die-Messlatte-fr-E-Commerce-und-Master-Data-Management-Anwendungen-hher/n/5278.

hybris on the Cloud

Currently, hybris can use the cloud in a simple IaaS approach. According to a blog, SAP offers to run hybris on HANA for free, with the HANA Cloud Platform Developer Trial[10] at the time of writing. However, you should not expect good performance as the HANA cloud database is reachable via the relatively slow open-db-tunnel command, and the HANA instance is shared.

Summary

SAP has spent a significant amount of time and money over the past 15 years transforming itself from a purely on-premise software company to a company that offers a significant portion of its portfolio as software on demand.

In the first part of this hour, we discussed the different cloud flavors available for SAP and compared them with the classical on-premise and hosting models, using pizza as an example. We described SAP's road to the cloud and how classic SAP solutions look and feel for the user when running on the cloud, and we gave a short introduction to the HANA Enterprise Cloud and the HANA Cloud Platform.

In the second part of this hour, we described the purpose, focus, and functionality of new solutions acquired by SAP since the last edition of this book: SuccessFactors, Ariba, Fieldglass, Concur, and hybris. The majority of these are delivered exclusively from the cloud via the SaaS paradigm. Technical details of the integration of these new solutions into the classic SAP system landscape are provided in Hour 19.

Case Study: Hour 8

Consider this hour's case study regarding the new SAP applications and cloud solutions. Read through and respond to the questions that follow. You can find answers to the questions related to this case study in Appendix A, "Case Study Answers."

Situation

Like many other companies, MNC is considering the cloud as a sourcing and platforming option. You have been asked to study how to utilize the cloud in the most optimal way for MNC's SAP systems. You also need to evaluate questions regarding several of the newer SaaS and other solutions SAP has recently acquired.

---

[10] See http://scn.sap.com/community/developer-center/cloud-platform/blog/2013/12/14/run-Hybris-on-hana-cloud-database.

Questions

1. What type of cloud offerings can be considered for classic SAP solutions?

2. For what will MNC still be responsible when moving classic SAP solutions to the cloud?

3. Can MNC run only parts of their SAP systems on the cloud? If yes, which one should it start with?

4. Is the SAP HANA Enterprise Cloud (HEC) the only option for running HANA in the cloud?

5. What business processes does SuccessFactors offer?

6. How does Ariba complement SAP SRM?

7. What type of purchase is supported by Fieldglass?

8. How does Concur improve the accuracy of expense reports?

9. Which department would get the most benefit from hybris?

PART III

SAP for Business Users

A Business User's Perspective on Using SAP

What You'll Learn in This Hour:

▶ The SAP business user's role

▶ The special role of the SAP power user

▶ An overview of several SAP access methods

▶ What it means to use SAP's classic applications

▶ How to run several simple ERP transactions

SAP provides many of the most useful and popular business applications on the market today. Implementing these solutions requires a wealth of technical knowledge and project management know-how. But at the end of the day, the business experts using SAP to do their job really only care about how they will use SAP's applications to run their business. After addressing several business implementation basics this hour, we provide an overview of what it means to use some of SAP's most common user interfaces and applications. In subsequent hours, we go into more user interface–specific and SAP application–specific detail.

NOTE

SAP Applications Are Like Snowflakes

Part III, "SAP for Business Users," covers a lot of ground in a short amount of time. Unfortunately, much of what you'll read and see will not perfectly translate to your own SAP systems. Why? Because company-specific configuration and customization absolutely ensure that no two SAP applications are alike. In the same way that snowflakes differ, so too do all of the specific application implementations across the SAP ecosystem. For that reason, we've focused on some of the most generic business scenarios and mega business processes in the hopes that perhaps 80% of what you see will still be useful enough to get you through 100% of this journey.

Before SAP Is Deployed: The Business User's Role

Before a business expert or another SAP end user can ever access an SAP application to do some work, the application and its user interfaces need to be planned for, designed, implemented, tested, and deployed for use. Said another way, a company's business requirements need to be converted into business processes that can be executed using SAP's applications. The job of converting a firm's business requirements to functional specifications that may in turn be used to configure an SAP application and set of business processes is the responsibility of a special collection of business specialists. These business experts include row leaders, configuration specialists, power users, experience business users, and more. In the end, these people and their technical and project management counterparts together help make SAP's applications capable of running a company's business.

Many of these business experts are company-internal people with years of experience running the business using the legacy systems that SAP will eventually replace. Some of these internal experts will eventually step up to the role of "SAP power user," detailed later this hour. Other business experts come from outside the organization and are employed solely to help implement SAP. They're "hired guns" (consultants) with deep business domain experience. In the world of SAP consulting, they're also called functional business experts or business area leaders, business process analysts, or "row" leaders. Many of them have been SAP business application users in past lives, and they now use their hard-fought experience to help implement SAP solutions that keep their end-user colleagues' business needs in mind. Their role is outlined next.

Row Leaders: The Functional Business Experts

In SAP and other enterprise application implementations, the term *row* refers to a functional business domain. A typical SAP implementation involves 5 to as many as 20 rows—and therefore as many row leaders that together form the core functional team for the SAP implementation. Row leaders, the functional business experts who work with a company's power users to translate business requirements into functional specifications, are normally divided into two groups: functional row leaders and master row leaders.

A particular functional row leader might focus on SAP ERP's Materials Management module, for example. Another functional row leader might be put in charge of the finance and controlling functionality, and another the human capital management functionality. In every case, these row leaders are functional experts—the people others look to for guidance and expertise.

Master data row leaders, on the other hand, are primarily responsible for the data to be used in the SAP project implementation. Data includes things such as the firm's unique material or product numbers, stock numbers assigned to products, employee records, vendor records, names assigned to plants and storage locations, customer master data, and so on. Further differentiation between functional and master data row leaders includes the following:

▶ Functional row leaders are responsible for delivering overall solutions, consisting of work processes brought together to form systems for their rows. As they go about their work, functional row leaders help ensure that end-user site and user experience requirements are addressed. This might include verifying that desktop and laptop configurations meet the SAP user interface's minimum requirements, that other user experience or "usability" matters are addressed, and, most importantly, that the business functionality indeed delivers what's needed. The functional row leaders are also tasked with introducing and helping drive adoption and change management with the site's leadership; how well change is introduced into an organization is directly related to how well the organization will adopt those changes.

▶ Master data row leaders work with end users and leadership teams as well but from a different perspective. They are responsible for master data, including data cleanup and rationalization efforts. This means working through the data to remove old data that's no longer relevant to the business, to consolidate data (such that the same product code or identifying number is assigned to the same part or component regardless of site), and to develop a taxonomy that helps bring together all the data under a single unified umbrella. Master data row leaders also assist in work process development and deployment, helping functional teams understand how a business process changes based on the site, plant, or company code associated with the data being processed. (For instance, creating a sales order for a particular site might require special shipping and handling of master or reference data that is not needed for sales orders created for other sites.) The master data row leader also has a hand in end-user training and creating the documentation needed for both the business processes and the data.

Whereas the functional and master data row leaders get a lot of visibility, another team of specialists tends to do most of the work. These are the functional configuration specialists, many of whom work for the prime integrator and subsequently contract to the firm implementing SAP. Other specialists work for the firm itself, too, as discussed next.

Functional Configuration Specialists

Apart from the aforementioned, other key resources exist who are really customers to the project team but play a role within the project. They are the mirrors to the prime integrator's configuration specialists. These employees and other company-internal representatives help ensure that the prime integrator achieves what is described in the business blueprint. They are involved in helping define and validate the business blueprint, typically to the point of actually configuring functionality alongside their integration partner counterparts. They also play an important role in user acceptance testing, act as SAP application business liaisons, and provide other expertise from and to the business (primarily) and IT (occasionally).

The company-internal functional specialists are important, but it is rare for a single person to hold enough knowledge to single-handedly design and implement all the business processes germane to a particular functional area (such as finance, logistics, and human resource/ capital management). The company-internal functional specialists therefore lean heavily on one another, their external counterparts, and other key experts in their various roles (namely, power users).

The Role of the Power User

Within each functional business area or functional row are the business's power users. Power users are typically known as the company's internal business experts. Narumol in the Accounting Department might be "the queen of AP" when it comes to understanding how the company handles its accounts payables, for instance. If she's got the right attitude, sphere of influence, and network of company-internal business relationships, Narumol could make an ideal finance row power user.

In the context of an SAP implementation, the importance of power users can't be underestimated. As senior team members, power users are specialists in their respective business domains. They help define what an SAP system's business processes need to accomplish, what the SAP input and display screens should look like, and more:

- ▶ They participate with the technical team in defining and reviewing how the implementation's technical solutions will solve the firm's business problems.

- ▶ They help define and refine business processes alongside the functional specialists, leading business blueprinting, reviewing and approving identified solution gaps, and prioritizing potential changes.

- ▶ They are the experts on how the firm leverages and deploys global standards, where and how it maintains documentation, and so on.

- ▶ They serve as internal consultants to the consultants, coaching the implementation team in terms of how business is currently conducted.

- ▶ They provide ongoing support to the site's business group or department, often acting as a single point of contact relative to final questions or clarifications around their business areas.

As the experts in a site's or department's work habits and more formal business processes, power users are engaged in the implementation project throughout most if not all of the project lifecycle. They work with their respective teams to build buy-in for SAP, help in testing and validating the system from functional and performance perspectives, assist with training end users, and help ensure that documentation is accurate and complete. Power users need not only possess the required business knowledge and expertise to affect authentic change but also must be open-minded as new approaches to addressing the functional area's work are introduced, weighed, and potentially implemented. "Business as usual" has no place in a power user's attitude toward adopting SAP.

At the conclusion of a SAP implementation, you might think that the power users' importance would be diminished as they return to their regular jobs (now using the new system to get their work done). This is far from true. By the end of the implementation, power users have learned so much more about how their functional area fits and integrates into the firm's larger business scope that they're more valuable than ever. Power users become the experts in SAP functionality, as well; with their combination of business and SAP skills, power users are looked to as the experts long after go-live. Probably the greatest challenge organizations face after go-live is retaining their power users; many have been known to join the systems integrators and other consulting organizations with which they worked so closely over the previous months and years.

A Sampling of SAP Business Transactions

In Hour 2, "SAP Business Basics," we outlined three common SAP business processes—the kinds of business processes that end users might execute several times a day in the course of performing their jobs. The following pages include several individual transactions that make up one of those business processes as well as other business processes. We've also included screenshots to provide greater clarity as we further set the stage for what it means to use SAP as a business end user.

Logging On Using the SAP Logon Pad

To use the traditional SAP user interface (called the SAPGUI, covered in much more detail in Hour 10, "Using SAP's Traditional and New User Interfaces"), you need to log on. Most business users will access traditional SAP ERP and other SAP Business Suite applications by starting the SAP Logon Pad and then selecting the specific SAP application to connect to and use. In Figure 9.1, we've selected the CCC Production SAP instance; this is the system you might presumably log into everyday to do your work as a finance clerk, an inventory specialist, a warehouse worker, or a sales manager.

Keep in mind that while the SAPGUI has been around for years and is still arguably the king of SAP's user interfaces, a strong and growing number of access alternatives are available. Some of these alternatives simulate the look and feel of the SAPGUI in the form of a web interface, other alternatives provide even more powerful customization and simplification capabilities, and still others are optimized for mobile and other device types. See Hour 10 for more details.

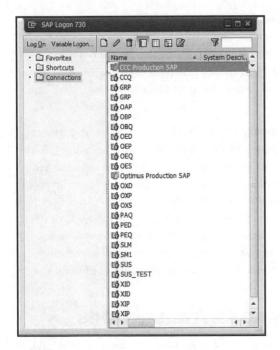

FIGURE 9.1
Use the SAP Logon Pad to select the appropriate SAP system to connect to and use.

Creating a New Sales Order

Let's say that you work in the sales department as an inside sales representative, and you need to create a sales order. Once you have logged into SAP ERP, you can run transaction /nVA01 (as you would have learned in your SAP role-based training) from the main SAP Easy Access home screen to create a sales order (see Figure 9.2).

Doing so takes you to the Create Sales Order screen (see Figure 9.3), where you now need to provide the initial order type and other data necessary to actually create a new sales order.

Next, you need to complete a much more detailed screen (see Figure 9.4). Note that the fields on this screen that appear in blue text are required fields, and the cursor has automatically been positioned to the first such field. In this case here, you need to enter a sold-to party and/or a ship-to party.

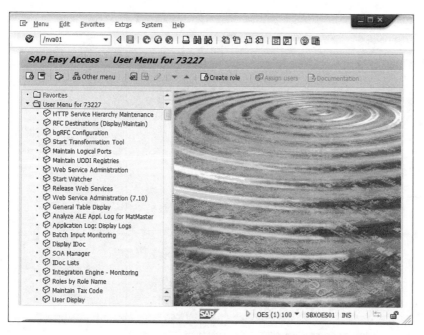

FIGURE 9.2
Run /nva01 from the Easy Access home screen.

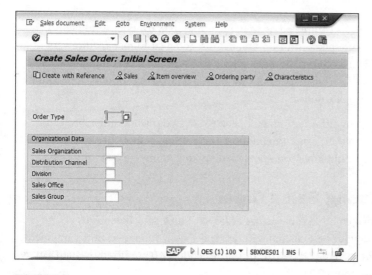

FIGURE 9.3
Enter the data necessary to complete this screen for a new sales order.

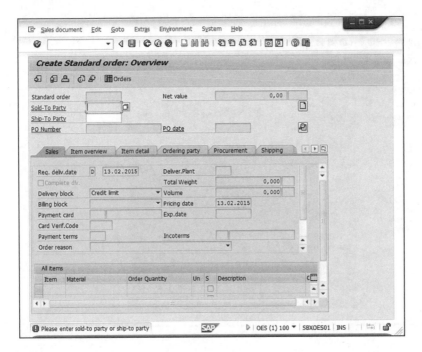

FIGURE 9.4
Enter additional data necessary to complete the sales order.

Many other items might need to be completed as well, including item overview and details, ordering party details, and procurement and shipping details. Some customers require very little detail to create a sales order, while other customers require much more; this varying level of detail reflects the customization and business rules that makes one SAP customer's application unique from other customers' applications.

After you provide all the necessary information, you need to save your work and submit the order by clicking the Save button, following a menu path, or pressing a shortcut key combination. Again, all these methods would have been passed along to you in your SAP training.

Displaying an Existing Sales Order

Let's say that you have finished creating a new sales order, and now your boss needs you to look up an existing order for one of your best customers. She's specifically interested in the payment terms. When you're logged into SAP ERP, you can run transaction VA03 to bring up the Display Sales Order: Initial Screen (see Figure 9.5).

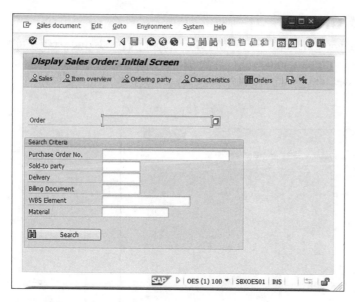

FIGURE 9.5
Run VA03 to display an existing sales order.

Once you enter a valid sales order number, you can display the details of that order. Halfway down the screen, for example, you can view the payment terms associated with this order (see Figure 9.6).

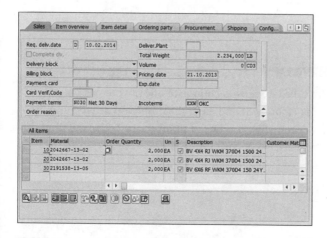

FIGURE 9.6
Note the payment terms and other details of this particular order.

Displaying a List of Orders

As an inside sales representative, you'll not only try to sell your company's goods and services to new customers but also be tasked with managing your existing customers. Run transaction VA05 to list any number of orders created for one of your customers (that is, one of your sold-to parties), as illustrated in Figure 9.7.

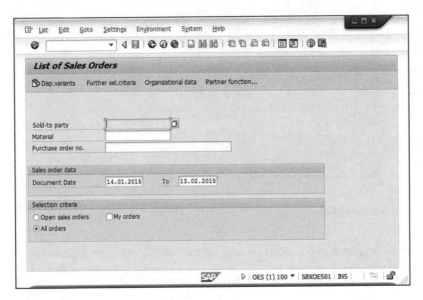

FIGURE 9.7
Run transaction VA05 to display a list of orders.

Changing Outbound Delivery

To wrap up this scenario, let's say you're asked to make a change to one of your customer's delivery dates. Run transaction VL02N (see Figure 9.8) and enter the outbound delivery number. If you don't know the specific number, you can enter a range of numbers, and SAP will display a list for your review (see Figure 9.9).

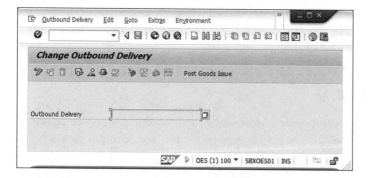

FIGURE 9.8
Run transaction VL02N to change outbound delivery details.

Delivery	Ship-to	Rou	Pick Date	TrpPlanDt	Loadg Da	GI Date	Deliv.Date	Load	Dl	No.Pk	O	W
50000191			01.01.2012	01.01.2012	01.01.2012	01.01.2012	01.01.2012			00000		
50000217			31.12.2012	31.12.2012	31.12.2012	31.12.2012	31.12.2012			00000		
50000275			18.04.2012	18.04.2012	18.04.2012	18.04.2012	18.04.2012			00000		
50000330			01.01.2012	01.01.2012	01.01.2012	01.01.2012	01.01.2012			00000		
50000397		CAM	16.04.2012	16.04.2012	16.04.2012	16.04.2012	16.04.2012			00000	C	C
50000600		CAM	07.05.2012	07.05.2012	07.05.2012	07.05.2012	07.05.2012			00000	A	
50000602		CAM	04.05.2012	04.05.2012	04.05.2012	04.05.2012	04.05.2012		Z1	00000		
50000756			14.05.2012	14.05.2012	14.05.2012	14.05.2012	14.05.2012			00000		
50000760		CAM	28.12.2012	28.12.2012	28.12.2012	28.12.2012	28.12.2012			00000		
50000792		CAM	23.04.2012	23.04.2012	23.04.2012	23.04.2012	23.04.2012			00000	A	
50000830			18.05.2012	18.05.2012	18.05.2012	18.05.2012	18.05.2012		Z1	00000	A	
50000972		CAM	01.06.2012	01.06.2012	01.06.2012	01.06.2012	01.06.2012			00000		
50000989		CAM	22.05.2012	22.05.2012	22.05.2012	22.05.2012	22.05.2012			00000	A	A
50001023			06.06.2012	06.06.2012	06.06.2012	06.06.2012	06.06.2012			00000		
50001048			01.12.2012	01.12.2012	01.12.2012	01.12.2012	01.12.2012			00000		
50001109			28.12.2012	28.12.2012	28.12.2012	28.12.2012	28.12.2012			00000		
50001110			13.06.2012	13.06.2012	13.06.2012	13.06.2012	13.06.2012			00000		
50001163		CAM	15.06.2012	15.06.2012	15.06.2012	15.06.2012	15.06.2012		Z1	00000	A	
50001199		CAM	29.05.2012	29.05.2012	29.05.2012	29.05.2012	29.05.2012			00000	A	A
50001202		CAM	19.06.2012	19.06.2012	19.06.2012	19.06.2012	19.06.2012		Z1	00000	A	
50001207			01.12.2012	01.12.2012	01.12.2012	01.12.2012	01.12.2012			00000		
50001311		CAM	20.06.2012	20.06.2012	20.06.2012	20.06.2012	20.06.2012			00000	A	A

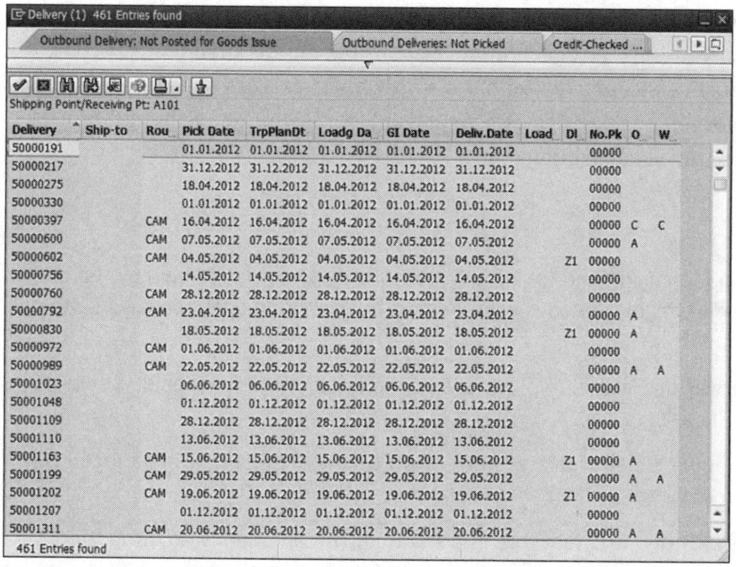

FIGURE 9.9
When you don't have a specific piece of data available, display a full list instead.

Summary

In this hour, we explored how a business user plans for, deploys, and uses SAP. We looked at the roles of various business users and others tasked with turning SAP's applications and components into a functional business solution—including row leaders and power users, specialists, and more. We also worked through several SAP ERP business transactions to further set the context around why SAP is implemented in the first place. In Hour 10, we will use what we've learned here to access SAP through a number of legacy and new user interfaces, to customize and even simplify the overall SAP user experience, and more.

Case Study: Hour 9

Review the following case study, which reflects a business user interested in not only using several different SAP applications but helping to implement one of these SAP solutions as well. You can find answers to the questions related to this case study in Appendix A, "Case Study Answers."

Situation

MNC needs to involve its most senior and experienced business users to help the firm understand its current business processes and actual business requirements. Someone should have been tagged for this long ago, but you have just been made responsible for identifying prospective power users across MNC's business teams, spread out over several sites. Each site represents a different MNC business group or function. You're also responsible for evaluating risks and providing an update to MNC's executive leadership team.

Questions

1. Given your late start in identifying and taking advantage of the knowledge held by the company's power users, what might be some risks related to the actual SAP business solutions currently being developed?

2. Explain how MNC's power users can help the SAP prime integrator's functional specialists get their jobs done.

3. With regard to the company's power users, what might be the biggest challenge faced by MNC's management team after go-live?

4. Although power users play an important role in an SAP implementation, who owns the job of converting a firm's business requirements to functional specifications that may in turn be used to configure SAP?

Using SAP's Traditional and New User Interfaces

What You'll Learn in This Hour:

▶ How to log on and off the traditional SAPGUI

▶ Session management and toolbars

▶ SAP screen elements and objects

▶ Tips for entering data in SAP screens

▶ SAP's new user interfaces: Fiori Launchpad, Screen Personas, and more

In this hour, we cover a number of user interfaces available to access your SAP applications. For starters, we look at the classic SAPzGUI, including how to log on to SAP's Business Suite applications and how to use screen elements and objects. We cover the fundamental elements of SAP screens and how to manage multiple user sessions, and then we discuss SAP's web-based user interfaces. We close with a review of SAP's newest user interfaces and other recent access tools and methods. At the end of this hour, you'll have a broad understanding of what it means to access an SAP application, when specific interfaces are required, and when certain tools or frameworks might be more advantageous than SAP's traditional access approaches.

The SAPGUI

SAP provides a number of tools and user interfaces for accessing its applications. The longstanding method for accessing SAP Business Suite components is through the SAPGUI, pronounced "sap goo ee." The SAPGUI must be installed on a laptop or desktop before it can be used to access SAP applications. The SAPGUI acts as the window into SAP's applications; it's the graphical user interface (GUI) to SAP. SAP calls this piece of software the *presentation layer* of an SAP solution.

The SAPGUI for Microsoft Windows is the most popular user interface available for SAP systems today. Also called the WinGUI, or the "fat client," this interface is the most capable but also eats up a chunky amount of disk space on your PC or laptop. It consumes a fair amount of memory to run well, too. Another SAP user interface, the Java GUI for SAP, is also a fat client. It provides non-Microsoft-based front-end clients, such as computers running Linux and UNIX, the ability to access SAP's Business Suite applications.

Once the SAPGUI is installed, there's still a fair amount of work to do to actually connect to and use an SAP application, as discussed next.

NOTE

SAPGUI: Behind the Scenes

The SAPGUI connects to the SAP central instance (where the SAP "executables" or "binaries" run) and then to an SAP application server (which hosts the application logic), which in turn talks to a back-end SAP database that holds all the programs, data, and so on. Regardless of your physical location, if you have authentic SAP credentials (a logon ID, a password, and a client to log in to) and a network connection to your SAP system, you can access SAP from pretty much anywhere around the world. The key is the ability to connect to the SAP central instance.

SAP User IDs and Sessions

Every SAP user is assigned a username or user ID (although you might see the occasional factory, warehouse, or distribution site where several workers share a single SAP user ID—but this is a poor practice from an auditing perspective). Your SAP security administrator sets your initial password when the ID is created, and the first time you sign in, you are forced to change it. In this way, your user ID is secure even from system administrators and others tasked with maintaining security.

Each time you connect to SAP via the SAPGUI or another user interface, you begin a user session. An SAP session simply means you have started the SAPGUI and established a connection with a particular SAP system—that is, you've successfully connected. You can have multiple sessions open with multiple SAP components (one for SAP ERP, another for CRM, and so on). You may also start multiple sessions within a single component. This can be useful if you're executing a long-running report, for example, and still want to process open orders in real time, read through a financial report, or simultaneously view the contents of your warehouse storage bins. Being able to be in multiple sessions enables you to multitask. By default, you can open up to six sessions at the same time, although the default can be increased by a knowledgeable SAP system administrator.

With your SAPGUI open and connected to SAP, you're ready to get to work. But let's step back a minute. SAP provides a tool that helps users connect to multiple systems—the SAP Logon Pad, covered next.

Using the SAP Logon Pad

End users who need to regularly access several different SAP components (such as SAP ERP alongside SAP CRM and perhaps occasional access to SAP PLM) should use the SAP Logon Pad. Through this simple utility (which needs to be installed on your desktop or laptop), you can quickly log on to different classic SAP systems.

Configure the SAP Logon Pad by manually keying in specific data needed for access (see Figure 10.1) or by asking your SAP system administrator to copy a preconfigured list of SAP servers (maintained in a saplogon.ini file) to your laptop, desktop, or other SAP-ready computer or device.

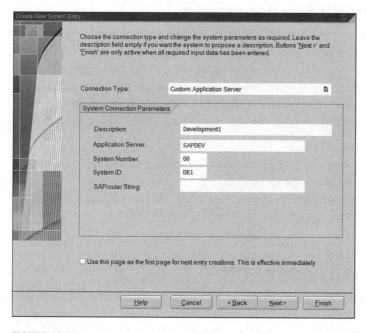

FIGURE 10.1
Configure the SAP Logon Pad for use by providing the information necessary to connect to an SAP Business Suite component.

To modify an entry that already exists in the SAP Logon Pad, right-click the SAP system's description and then select Properties. Update the SAP application server information needed to connect to the system. This information can also be obtained from your SAP administrator, and it includes the SAP application server computer's hostname or its TCP/IP address, its system ID (SID, a unique three-character identifier), and the two-digit system number. The SID and system number are assigned by the SAP administrator. Edit the description to reflect something meaningful (such as SAP ERP production system) and then click OK when you finish.

The next screen you see when first connecting to SAP is the SAP logon screen. Here, you need to provide the client number, your user ID, and the password initially assigned to you. Afterward, click the check mark in the upper-left corner or press the Enter key on your keyboard to continue.

Before you press Enter, you might need to provide a two-character logon language. Your system will likely be configured to default to a standard language for your organization (such as EN for English). If your organization requires multi-language support and the correct languages have indeed been installed or set up for your system, you can specify a different two-digit language code in the language box. Check with your administrator or business lead for the language-specific codes you might need in your case.

Understanding SAPGUI Session Basics

Remember that when you connect to SAP via the SAPGUI user interface, you have begun a user session. You can have multiple sessions, as discussed previously; the session number of the current session is displayed in the status bar on the bottom of the SAPGUI. Because each session uses system resources, your company will normally set limits on the number of sessions that you and your colleagues can create. Alternatively, your company might encourage the SAP user community to limit itself to only one or two sessions but not actually create a limit beyond the default of six.

You can create a session at any time and from nearly any screen in the system. You do not lose any data in the sessions that are already open when you create a new session, either. Create a new session by selecting System, Create Session. You will now have two sessions open on your computer. If you want to determine which session you are currently in, check the status bar at the lower right of your screen.

Ending a Session and Logging Off

When you finish using a session, it is a good idea to purposely end it. Each session uses system resources that can affect how fast the SAP system responds to your requests and those of your colleagues. Before you end a session, save any data or transactions you wish to keep. This is important because when you end a session, the system does not typically prompt you to save your data if you are in the middle of a transaction.

Ending a session is similar to creating a session. You select System, End Session (or enter /O as a shortcut). From the Overview of Sessions box, you can selectively close a session by selecting it and then clicking the End Session button. Give it a try.

If you've followed along and opened a number of SAPGUI sessions, select number 2 by single-clicking it and then click the End Session button. It might not initially appear that anything has happened, but the session does indeed close. To verify this, return to the Overview of Sessions box by entering the transaction code /O in the command field. Transactions 1 and 3 should still be listed, but number 2 should no longer be open. Follow the same steps to end session 3, leaving only session 1 open.

To terminate your SAP session or connection, you can select System, Logoff from the main menu. Alternatively, click the Windows X icon in the top-right corner of your SAPGUI window. You may also type in /NEX in the SAPGUI command field and press Enter. SAP prompts you with a window confirming shutdown of your SAP connection.

SAPGUI Elements and Other Basics

Despite its age, the SAPGUI for Windows remains the most common SAP user interface because it's functional. It's not always pretty, but it works. At the top of the SAGUI is the title bar, which displays the screen (or transaction) description for the window that is currently displayed.

Below the title bar, the drop-down menu bar contains all the menu options available. The menu bar changes from screen to screen to match the SAP transaction or function module that you are currently processing. The last two items on the menu bar, System and Help, remain constant on all SAP screens and contain the same submenu options.

Several useful buttons are available on what's called the standard toolbar. These buttons allow you to save your work, print, find text on the screen, create a new session, and more. All things considered, the SAPGUI is actually quite similar to any modern-day browser. Figure 10.2 shows the SAPGUI title bar, menu bar, and standard toolbar's buttons.

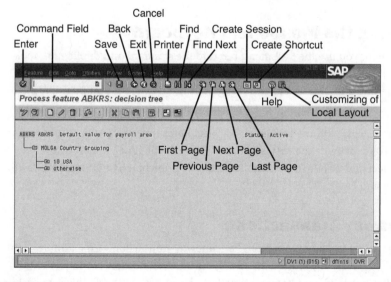

FIGURE 10.2
The standard elements of the SAPGUI title bar.

Another useful toolbar, the application toolbar, is located underneath the standard toolbar. This toolbar is screen specific; it changes depending on the screen you're displaying or the transaction you are currently processing. For example, if you are in the Finance module's Create Rental Agreement screen, the application toolbar contains buttons that enable you to copy or retrieve master data from SAP. If you are in the ABAP/4 Workbench Initial Editor screen, on the other hand, your application toolbar contains buttons for the Dictionary, Repository Browser, and Screen Painter.

SAPGUI Navigation Basics

To perform the tasks related to your job, you need to understand how to navigate the SAP system. For example, a salesperson needs to know how to enter a sales order and check on the status of an existing order. Menu paths and transaction codes are used to call transactions. You use the menu bar and toolbars, in conjunction with the mouse and keyboard, to complete a transaction and save the data.

Performing Tasks Using Menu Paths

When you first start using SAP, you are likely to use the SAP menus to navigate to the transactions required in your job or role. Your SAP user menu (or Easy Access menu) allows you to navigate through all the functions, areas, and tasks in SAP, down to the individual transactions. With menus, you can easily drill down into business-specific application transactions and other functions without having to memorize transaction codes.

Navigating Using the Mouse and Keyboard

After starting a transaction, you use the SAP menu bar and the standard and application toolbars to navigate through the screens required to complete the task. To select an entry from the SAP menu bar, click the menu to display the various options listed beneath that menu. A menu entry that contains an additional list of objects (submenus) includes an arrow.

You can also select menu items with the keyboard. To select items from the SAP menu bar using your keyboard, press F10 (to activate the menu bar) and then use the navigational arrow keys on your keyboard to select and display the menu. You choose a function by highlighting it with the arrow keys and pressing Enter.

Stopping Runaway Transactions

Occasionally, you might need to stop an "in flight" or runaway transaction—for example, right after you realize you just accidentally started the wrong business transaction or inadvertently kicked off a long-running batch job you have no time for. The easiest way to do this is to click the little icon in the upper-left corner of the SAPGUI, as shown in Figure 10.3, and select Stop Transaction.

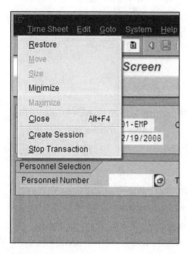

FIGURE 10.3
Click the upper-left icon to immediately stop an in-flight transaction.

Understanding and Using Fields

With your knowledge of what an SAP business transaction looks like, it's time to develop an understanding of how to interact with the SAP screens, to really use an SAP application. Let's start with the concept of an SAP screen itself. The screen is the visual contents you see within the SAPGUI after you have executed (or "called") a transaction. Most transactions require only a single screen to enter, display, or manipulate data. Complex transactions may require several screens.

As you enter data into the various data entry fields in an SAP screen and then save the data, you are essentially creating a record in the SAP database. For example, from within the SAP ERP 6.0 application, use the command field to navigate to transaction code /nFF7A. This transaction code takes you to the Cash Management and Forecast screen in the Financial Accounting module, where many data entry fields await completion by a finance clerk.

Most screens in the SAP system contain fields used to input data into the SAP system. These types of fields are often called *input fields*. Input fields vary in length (the number of keyboard characters you can type into them). The length of the rectangular box around an input field indicates the length of the longest valid data entry for that field. This simple limitation can be helpful to users unfamiliar with what might be expected in a particular input field.

When you place the cursor anywhere in an empty input field, the cursor appears at the beginning of the field. Because the cursor is located there, that particular field is said to be the active field. This is also helpful to the end user. Remember that the field can only hold data that fits into its rectangular box. After entry, the cursor remains in the input field until you press the Tab key to move the cursor to the next field, press the Enter key to check your entry, or click another input field.

Using Replace and Insert Modes

Your computer keyboard has a button called Insert in its top-right area, above the Delete button. This Insert key toggles between two writing modes. The Insert mode enables you to insert data into an existing field without typing over it. The Overwrite mode enables you to type over existing data in a field. The Overwrite mode is the SAP default.

You can tell which setting your SAP system is using by looking at the bottom-right area of your screen. In the box to the left of the system clock, you will see the abbreviation OVR for Overwrite mode or INS for Insert mode. This setting is based on an end user's preference. Keep in mind that with each new session you create, the default Overwrite mode setting is active unless you change it.

Displaying Possible Entries for an Input Field

Many fields are quite specific and only accept entries that have already been defined in the database (either by the system's developers or via another transaction) as valid entries for that field. If you are unsure of a valid entry (that is, the exact name of an entry that already exists in the table), you can click the Possible Entries button to select a valid entry from the list.

Any field containing a right arrow on the far-right side has a Possible Entry function. Give one a try. Use the transaction code /NFK10 to travel to the Vendor: Initial Screen Balances Display screen. This screen contains three input fields. Press Tab to navigate between them. You will see that as you travel from one field to another, the Possible Entries down arrow appears only when the field is active. You will also see that the Possible Entries down arrow is not present on the Fiscal Year field. Press Tab to return to the Company Code field. Use your mouse to select the Possible Entries arrow (keeping in mind that the Possible Entries Help button's down arrow disappears when the Possible Entries window opens). In this example, after selecting the Possible Entries down arrow for the Company Code field, you are presented with a list of possible entries that are acceptable and valid for that field. To select an item from a Possible Entries list, you can double-click it or use your mouse to highlight it once and then choose the green check mark icon. The list disappears, and the value selected is then present in your Company Code field.

See what happens when you enter a value that is not an item listed in the Possible Entries Help. Return your cursor to the Company Code field, type your initials, and press the Enter key.

A warning appears in the status bar area. This warning prevents you from progressing to additional screens until the issue is corrected.

Not all input fields have lists of possible entries. You cannot determine whether such a list is available for an input field until you place the cursor in the input field. Also, some fields that contain Possible Entries Help do not use a drop-down arrow even if the field is active. In these cases, press your keyboard's F4 key to retrieve the Possible Entries Help in any SAP field where it is available.

Sometimes the SAP system saves the last value entered in an input field into "memory." Even when you replace it with a new value, the old value is retained. To clear the SAP memory for an input box, press the exclamation point key (!) and press Enter; the input field is now clear.

Editing the Data in an Input Field

Now that you have an invalid entry in your Company Code field, you need to return to that field to correct the input. Place your cursor in the Company Code box and then select the Possible Entries Help down arrow for the Company Code field. Select any item from the list of possible entries and click the green check mark. Now your invalid entry is replaced by a valid one. Press Enter. SAP checks your entry to confirm that it is acceptable and removes the warning message from the status bar.

Understanding Required Input Fields

With certain SAP screens, some fields might require input data before you can proceed. These are called *required fields*, and in the early days of SAP, each required field contained a question mark (?). In later versions of SAP, these required fields instead contain a square with a check mark inside it.

Required fields are important to the logic of a business process. For example, it's impossible to edit an employee's address if the employee's name or number (for example) are not entered. Thus, name or number might be a required field. In the same way, a purchase order number or the date of an accepted delivery might be required fields.

Generally, if a screen does not contain a square with a check mark, you can navigate to the next screen without entering data in any fields. However, some screens that contain required fields are not marked in this way. For example, this situation can occur when you enter data in an optional field that has associated required fields.

No worries, though. If you have failed to enter all of the required fields on a screen and try to proceed to the next screen, the SAP system will display an error message in the status bar at the bottom of the SAPGUI screen. At the same time, you'll see the cursor jump to the first required field that needs the required data. Provide the data and then move on.

SAP provides field-level validation to ensure that your input data is "clean." After entering data into input fields on the screen, press the Enter key or click the green check mark on your SAP toolbar to check the validity of your entries. If your entries are valid, the system advances to the next screen in the task. If the system checks your entries and finds any errors—for example, entries in the wrong format—it displays a message in the status bar and positions the cursor in the field that you need to correct.

Once you've completed your work, you need to save it. The Save button appears on the standard toolbar at the top of the SAPGUI screen, and it looks like an open folder. When you are working through a business transaction that consists of several screens, the system temporarily stores the data you have already entered. After you complete all the necessary screens associated with your business transaction, save your data permanently by clicking the Save button. The Save button sends your data (or changes made to your data) to the SAP database, where it may then be processed.

Understanding SAPGUI Display Fields

Another type of SAP field is a display field. This type of field is not used to enter data but only to display it. Display fields are always shaded with a gray background to indicate that the field cannot be changed.

Display fields are typically used for values that were set according to some configuration in the system or by previous steps in business process. Fields are often assigned values based on configuration that occurs behind the scenes. For example, if you add a new employee to your Human Capital Management module, on the new-hire screen you will have a display field listing the employee's status as active. The system assigns and displays this value, and the user can't change it.

Some fields come preconfigured from SAP as display only, but you can also customize your system to change additional fields to display only. When you do so, users are unable to make changes to the data (either accidentally or intentionally).

In the same way, when system administrators run processes for maintaining the system, their screens often include date fields that store the current date. These are also display only. The system does not enable you to change the value in these fields because in most cases the values are used by the SAP system for accurate processing. Using the Human Capital Management example, if you hired a new employee and were able to change his hire date, the new employee's vacation time and other benefits would likely be incorrectly calculated.

SAPGUI Screen Objects

This section covers the different types of items you will see on SAP screens. Regardless of the SAP component's module you are processing in, the same types of screen objects generally appear on the different SAP screens.

SAP promotes itself being as logically designed and organized; a user can easily navigate through its system. The style of the SAP system is very different from the styles of many popular applications available on the market today, such as the Microsoft Office family of products. Often absent in SAP are the friendly pictures, detailed formatted text, and elaborate design. Most screens in SAP are designed in tabbed formats or tree structures, and the user navigates by "drilling down."

SAP Trees

You will soon become accustomed to using SAP trees to navigate through the SAP system. SAP menus are examples of SAP trees. SAP's logically devised environment centers on a basic tree structure. SAP trees appear similar to the structure you see in Windows Explorer. The tree structure is formulated so that you can drill down in the tree to reach deeper levels (branches) until you reach the endpoint (leaf). To use an SAP tree for navigation, you need to select the arrow to expand or compress the tree to view more or fewer selections, respectively. Older versions of SAP's applications used plus and minus signs, respectively, to expand and compress the tree.

Radio Buttons

When you are permitted only one option among several or many, you see a group of radio buttons provided rather than check boxes. A group of radio buttons accepts only one selection for the group. That is, you cannot mark more than one radio button in a group.

A mark placed in the circle indicates that the radio button is selected, and an empty circle indicates that the radio button is not selected. An example of a radio button is the designation of an employee in the Human Capital Management module as an employee or a contractor; you can select a person as one but not both.

Dialog Boxes

A dialog box is a window that pops up to provide information. Dialog boxes are also sometimes called information windows. Here are two situations in which a dialog box appears on your screen:

▶ The system needs more information from you before it can proceed.

▶ The system needs to give you feedback, such as messages or specific information about your current task.

For example, you might receive a dialog box on your screen when you are logging off SAP. If you select the SAP icon in the top-left corner of your screen and then click the Close button, you are prompted with a dialog box to confirm that you indeed want to log off the system.

Table Controls

A final object used in SAP screens is the table control. Table controls display data in a tabular format similar to a Microsoft Excel spreadsheet. Table controls are popular for displaying or entering single structured lines of data. Using them outside SAP can be tricky; several advanced concepts related to using the Clipboard to manipulate complex tables and screens are addressed in the next section.

Using the Windows Clipboard

You can transfer the contents of SAP fields (and, in some cases, the entire contents of an SAP screen) into your Windows Clipboard. Once it is in the Clipboard, data may be pasted into other SAP fields or into applications such as Microsoft Word and Excel.

To move data from a field, highlight the text and press Ctrl+X, move the cursor where you want the text, and then press Ctrl+V. The Cut (or Move) command is generally used on input fields. To copy data from a field, highlight the text and press Ctrl+C, move the cursor where you want the text, and then press Ctrl+V. The transferred data remains in the Clipboard until you use Cut or Copy again to move or copy new text onto the Clipboard.

But what if your data is "unselectable" and therefore unable to be easily copied and pasted into another application? You are not able to select certain data displayed on SAP screens using your mouse and the methods previously described. To see an example, return to your main SAP window and use the transaction code /nSE11 to travel to the SAP Data Dictionary initial screen. Place your cursor in the Object Name field and press the F1 key to launch the field-specific help. (If you do not have access to transaction code /nSE11, place your cursor in any SAP field and press the F1 key on your keyboard.) A window appears, giving detailed definitions and technical information for the field you selected.

Try to use the mouse to select the text displayed on this screen. You will see that you are unable to select the data. In cases like these, you need to add one more keyboard combination. Click once anywhere on the screen. Next press Ctrl+Y to change your mouse to a crosshair cursor. Use this cursor to select the desired text and follow the same steps as before: Ctrl+C to copy the text and Ctrl+V to paste the text.

Additional Legacy Interfaces

SAP has been Internet-enabled since 1996, so it's not surprising that a number of browser-based access methods are available. Compared to more contemporary access methods, though, these older methods are considered "legacy" access methods. Several of these include the WebGUI, JavaGUI, and NetWeaver Business Client, outlined next.

The WebGUI and JavaGUI

The SAPGUI is in reality a family of user interfaces. The default user interface is historically the SAPGUI for Windows. But's there's also the SAPGUI for HTML (also called the WebGUI), and there's another GUI written in Java called the JavaGUI.

Instead of using the fat SAPGUI client (called "fat" because it requires a hefty software installation on your desktop or laptop), access via a web browser has become much more popular in the past decade or so. Web browser access used to be meant for users running less-powerful desktops or laptops. Today, though, the idea of performing regular SAPGUI maintenance (including patches, upgrades, and all the other things that must be done to maintain any piece of software) isn't appealing, especially when thousands of individual desktops and laptops are involved. More importantly, web browsers are ubiquitous across PCs, smartphones, tablets, and more.

The SAPGUI for HTML runs on Windows, Linux, and Mac OS platforms; doesn't require a software installation per se (outside of the web browser itself); and works fine for most users. Truth be told, it doesn't perform as well as the SAPGUI for Windows; from a network bandwidth perspective; it's important to know that WebGUI is still not as efficient as its fat-client counterpart. But the ability to deploy-and-forget makes the SAPGUI for HTML a favorite of IT departments. It's easy to use and easy to maintain.

As of this writing, the most common web browser used by the WebGUI remains Microsoft's Internet Explorer (IE). For Windows-based client devices, IE works well. It's tested and used in the real world more than other browsers and therefore benefits from greater penetration and usability.

If your organization doesn't run Windows, or if you are not interested in running a web-based user interface such as the WebGUI, look to the SAPGUI for Java. Interestingly, the JavaGUI runs on Windows as well as Mac OS X, IBM AIX, and a number of Linux flavors (openSUSE, Fedora, Ubuntu, and more).

NOTE

A WebGUI Alternative for Mobile Devices

While the WebGUI can work on a number of platforms, including mobile devices, a software company called Synactive has also developed an SAP access utility called GuiXT for both Apple iOS and Android (along with a number of other handheld and RF mobile devices). GuiXT works with both Business Suite and NetWeaver components, and it gives developers the ability to quickly customize SAP transactions for small-screen footprints (which is excellent for environments where an SAP end user only needs to perform simple or repetitive tasks, for example).

The SAP NetWeaver Business Client

The SAP NetWeaver Business Client (NWBC) for the Windows platform was introduced several years ago. It is targeted at SAP's end users who need the power and familiarity of traditional SAPGUI-based transactions but also want to take advantage of new capabilities offered by a technology called Web Dynpro ABAP. NWBC affords a better user experience than its pure desktop (SAPGUI for Windows) and web (SAPGUI for HTML) counterparts. It does this by providing support for productivity-enabling user interface tools like worklists, side panels, and landing pages, along with the ability to be easily customized and personalized. And with its role-based access, low network bandwidth requirements, and support for single sign-on (SSO) across multiple SAP systems, the NWBC is a good choice for occasional users who have "power user" needs.

SAP's New User Interfaces and Tools

While the SAPGUI family is still the most popular of interfaces, SAP has been investing in and acquiring technologies to make using its applications easier. In the next few pages, we'll explore the SAP Fiori Launchpad, SAP Screen Personas, SAP Web IDE, SAP UI Theme Designer, and SAPUI5 and related frameworks.

SAP Fiori Launchpad

The SAP Fiori Launchpad was developed to help keep things simple for role-based users (users with specific needs defined by the role or job they occupy). It's fast, intuitive, and nearly ubiquitous. Built around HTML5, Fiori provides access to SAP's bread-and-butter applications ERP, HCM, and SCM, as well as many of SAP's new or acquired solutions, including Simple Finance, HANA, Ariba, SuccessFactors, Business Objects, and more. It works and looks the same on a PC, tablet, or smartphone, too. Such a consistent user experience helps SAP's end users remain in-the-know and productive as they move around from office to office, to their commute, to their home, and back again to the office.

SAP SE calls the SAP Fiori Launchpad an "aggregation" UI, where user tasks can be centralized, simplified, and personalized by individual end users to make their work lives easier. Each Fiori user organizes his or her individual launchpad into categories and further organizes those categories into folders, all of which remain consistent as the user experience moves between desktop, mobile, and other devices or platforms. Users can combine non-SAP content as well (which is important for business processes that span multiple applications—such as sales and procurement processes, supply chain processes, or human resource management processes that touch non-SAP as well as SAP applications). SAP Fiori is especially good at illustrating key performance indicators (KPIs) at a glance, as illustrated in Figure 10.4.

FIGURE 10.4
SAP Fiori allows users to quickly aggregate tasks and display key performance indicators.

SAP SE probably wants its user community to jump into Fiori even more than the users want to use it. Why? Because an intuitive user interface has escaped SAP for years, which means that companies using SAP have historically had to spend great amounts of time and money on user training, trying to convince their user communities to be happy about using SAP, and helping their organizations adopt SAP as their mission-critical software platform of choice.

Thus it's not surprising that SAP SE announced that Fiori will now be "included" with SAP—the company wants users to begin playing with and using it. Of course, "included" is not the same thing as "free." SAP Fiori Launchpad users still require an SAP user license. And because fewer than 30% of employees of a typical SAP customer have SAP user licenses, SAP SE is surely excited about driving additional license revenue.

Fiori is important for another reason, too: It's the hook for SAP to expand only user licensing and also to drive further HANA adoption. Rather than push HANA as the preferred database choice for SAP's applications, SAP SE can now use Fiori to help pull HANA into more of SAP SE's existing customer accounts.

Beyond the SAP Fiori Launchpad, SAP provides several other user interface tools (UI tools) that allow you to modify existing UIs and develop new ones. These include SAP Screen Personas, SAP Web IDE, SAP UI Theme Designer, and SAP's Floorplan Manager. SAP Screen Personas offers probably the most compelling set of capabilities and is explored in detail next, and the other UI tools are briefly outlined afterward.

SAP Screen Personas

Whereas SAP Fiori provides a consistent look and feel across mobile and traditional PC devices, SAP Screen Personas lets users and IT departments improve the usability and feel of the traditional SAPGUI. It's this create new-versus-modify existing UI perspective that is the primary difference between SAP Fiori and SAP Screen Personas.

SAP Screen Personas provides greater "productivity through personalization," as the company says. Easy to use, SAP Screen Personas employs drag-and-drop capabilities to personalize (and typically simplify) traditional SAPGUI screens.

End users can modify their own SAPGUI screens, removing the clutter they don't need to clean up and simplify how they work. They can combine content from multiple screens or tabs into a single screen. They can also convert items into simpler drop-down menus, automate repetitive keystroke combinations, and add external HTML-based content to the updated SAPGUI. Finally, customer IT organizations can easily apply thematic elements to the SAP user experience (background images, colors, logos, and so on) to create a more appealing UI. Figure 10.5 illustrates the powerful possibilities of SAP Screen Personas.

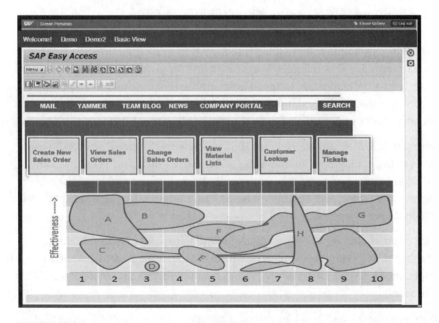

FIGURE 10.5
In this simple SAP Screen Personas customization, the user has included several key transactions, access to key resources, and an external HTML-based status graph—all in a single screen.

With SAP Screen Personas, SAP SE intends to decrease training time, make its user community happier, and help IT organizations spend less money on customizing the SAP experience, all with the goal of preserving its existing customer base and appealing to new customers. Like SAP Fiori, SAP Screen Personas is also included with each SAP user license.

SAP Web IDE

The SAP Web IDE (integrated development environment) is a web-based tool used by end users (rather than strictly development experts) to quickly prototype and create mobile, tablet, desktop, and browser-based user applications. Its modular architecture allows users and others to plug in their own SAPUI5 content (discussed later this hour)—for example, either on-premise or in the cloud. Development is handled in the cloud, too, so users don't have to load the SAP Web IDE locally or convince their IT department to provide infrastructure and management. You can purchase the SAP Web IDE through the SAP HANA marketplace or through the SAP HANA cloud platform.

SAP UI Theme Designer

The SAP UI Theme Designer lets you create common user experience (UX) themes across a diverse set of devices and technologies. For example, use the Theme Designer to create a consistent UX across Web Dynpro ABAP, SAP NetWeaver Business Client (NWBC), and other SAP user interfaces. To fast-track developing a theme, you can also choose to modify existing themes.

SAPUI5 and Other User Interface Frameworks

SAPUI5 is a UI framework that allows developers (not end users) to create new SAP user interfaces that can operate across mobile, tablet, and classic desktop environments. It is laser focused on helping developers create lightweight user interfaces for occasional SAP users rather than SAP's power users. UI frameworks are essentially development environments for creating new application user interfaces. SAP SE refers to the SAPUI5 UI framework as the "UI development toolkit for HTML5."

Other frameworks exist today, too, including the OpenUI5 and venerable Web Dynpro for ABAP. OpenUI5, the open source version of SAPUI5, is available at no cost (per the Apache 2.0 Open Source license) and thus appeals to open source development teams seeking to create modern application experiences. Web Dynpro for ABAP, on the other hand, has a decade-long history of helping organizations customize the classic SAPGUI. (a Web Dynpro for Java UI framework was actually available even earlier than the ABAP version but has since been discontinued in light of SAP's competition from newer frameworks with greater capabilities.)

Summary

In this hour, we explored what it means to log in and use an SAP application. We looked at the traditional SAPGUI in all its gory details, including SAP objects, controls, dialog boxes, radio buttons, and more. We then turned our attention to web-based and even newer access methods, such as the Fiori Launchpad, and concluded this hour with considerations related to SAP Screen Personas and other contemporary tools.

Case Study: Hour 10

Consider this case study regarding SAP's access methods and the questions that follow. You can find answers to the questions related to this case study in Appendix A, "Case Study Answers."

Situation

You have been asked to help familiarize a new SAP user with how to access MNC's core ERP and other applications, including trade-offs and advantages compared to several legacy and more contemporary methods.

Questions

1. What information will you need so that you can set up an entry for a new system in your SAP Logon Pad?

2. If you have never entered a sales order, what is the easiest way to find a sales order entry transaction?

3. Navigate the SAP menu to CCMS (by selecting Tools, CCMS). What type of screen object is the SAP menu structure?

4. Is the two-character language identifier necessary when logging on to SAP?

5. What is the primary difference between SAP Fiori Launchpad and SAP Screen Personas?

6. Name two modern UI frameworks that allow developers (rather than SAP's end users) to create new SAP user interfaces that operate across mobile, tablet, and classic desktop environments.

Using SAP ERP to Do Your Job

What You'll Learn in This Hour:

▶ Common SAP ERP Financials, Operations, Human Capital Management, and Corporate Services business transactions

▶ Modules and submodules typically used in the four business scenarios

▶ Additional important modules and submodules

▶ Other useful SAP ERP business transactions

This hour walks through the four core SAP ERP business scenarios and the modules and submodules that provide functionality for those scenarios. To provide context, we also include module-specific lists of common business transaction codes that end users in a particular scenario run on a regular basis in the course of working with the system. This hour gives a fairly realistic view of using SAP ERP to do your job.

The Four SAP Business Scenarios

As outlined in Hour 7, "SAP ERP and Business Suite," SAP ERP can be configured to support four common business scenarios that are relevant to nearly any business:

▶ SAP ERP Financials

▶ SAP ERP Operations

▶ SAP ERP Human Capital Management

▶ SAP ERP Corporate Services

Each scenario consists of a number of individual ERP modules that are used together to deliver the functionality associated with each business scenario. In turn, these business scenarios support typical line-of-business (LOB) processes such as asset management, corporate strategy and sustainability, customer sales and service, financial and managerial accounting, human resource management, information technology management, manufacturing, marketing, logistics, procurement, research and development, engineering, basic supply chain management, and much more.

To actually deliver these line-of-business processes, SAP consultants configure (and customize, if necessary) various SAP ERP modules, such as

- ▶ SAP CO (Controlling)

- ▶ SAP FI (Finance)

- ▶ SAP HCM (Human Capital Management, also known as human resources)

- ▶ SAP MM (Materials Management)

- ▶ SAP PM (Plant Maintenance)

- ▶ SAP PP (Production Planning)

- ▶ SAP PS (Project System)

- ▶ SAP QM (Quality Management)

- ▶ SAP SD (Sales and Distribution)

Although this list is not complete, it gives you an idea of the breadth of modules that can be configured and combined to create business processes, which in turn support SAP's four principal business scenarios. In the next few sections, we take a closer look at these four scenarios and their underlying modules, submodules, and business transactions.

SAP ERP Financials

Within SAP ERP Financials are four core areas: Financial and Managerial Accounting, Controlling, Treasury and Funds Management, and Financial Supply Chain Management. Several of these areas are explored next.

Financial and Managerial Accounting

Financial and Managerial Accounting involves general ledger, accounts payable, accounts receivable, asset accounting, and funds management processes that are delivered by configuring SAP ERP's FI and CO modules.

FI submodules include

- ▶ General Ledger

- ▶ Book Close

- ▶ Tax

- ▶ Accounts Receivable

- Accounts Payable
- Consolidation
- Special ledgers

CO submodules include

- Cost Elements
- Cost Centers
- Profit Centers
- Internal Orders
- Activity-Based Costing
- Product Costing

As you might expect, other modules or submodules can come into play here as well, but for simplicity this hour ignores them. Table 11.1 shows a sampling of common Financial and Management Accounting transaction codes (t-codes).

TABLE 11.1 Sample Financial and Management Accounting T-Codes

Functionality	T-Code	Description
Financials	XK01 and XK02	Create and change a vendor (centrally)
Financials	MK01 and MK02	Create and change a vendor (purchasing)
Financials	VD01 and VD02	Create and change a customer (sales)
Financials	FD32 and FD33	Change and display customer credit line
Financials	FCHU	Create reference for check
Financials	FB10	Invoice/credit fast entry
Financials	OBWW	Withholding tax
Financials	FD10	Customer account balance
Financials	FD11	Customer account analysis
Financials	FRCA	Settlement calendar
Financials	FV50	Park general ledger account items
Financials	F.07	General ledger: Balance carry forward
Financials	F.08	General ledger: Account balances

Functionality	T-Code	Description
Financials	F-04	Post with clearing
Financials	F-43	Enter vendor invoice
Financials	FBS1	Enter accrual/deferral documents
Controlling	KB11 and KB13	Enter and display reposting of primary costs
Controlling	KB21 and KB23	Enter and display activity allocations
Controlling	KB51 and KB53	Enter and display activity postings
Controlling	KB41 and KB43	Enter and display reposting of revenues
Controlling	KB66	Display indirect activity allocation reposting
Controlling	KB16NP	Display manual allocations
Controlling	KB17NP	Reverse manual allocations
Controlling	KB33	Display statistical key figures
Controlling	KO88	Actual settlement of a single order

While many more financial and controlling transactions are used to conduct day-to-day business, this table should give you an idea of the breadth of SAP's financial and management accounting function.

Treasury Management

The Treasury Management module can be further divided into the following submodules:

- ▶ Cash Management
- ▶ Cash Budget Management
- ▶ Market Risk Management
- ▶ Loans Management
- ▶ Funds Management
- ▶ Core Treasury Management

Table 11.2 shows a sampling of SAP's Treasury Management transaction codes.

TABLE 11.2 Sample Treasury Management T-Codes

Functionality	T-Code	Description
Treasury	FZ42	Customize customer application type
Treasury	FZ55	Customize insurance branch
Treasury	FZP2	Create legal person
Treasury	FZ56	Customize balance sheet indicator
Treasury	TBEX	Spreadsheet for market data
Treasury	FLQC1	Liquidity items
Treasury	FZB7	Statements
Cash Budget	OFO3	Transfer cash holdings
Cash Budget	OFGB	Funds management: Gradual FI data transfer
Cash Budget	FMR2	Actual/commitment per Company Code
Cash Budget	FMR3	Plan/actual commitment reports
Cash Budget	FMR5A	12 period forecast: Actual and plan
Cash Budget	OFG5	Funds management: Take over all documents

Financial Supply Chain Management

Financial Supply Chain Management (FSCM) is used to move cash between entities within an organization or between those entities and their external partners. It includes several important submodules:

- ▶ In-house Cash Management
- ▶ Credit Management
- ▶ Dispute Management
- ▶ Collections Management

Table 11.3 shows a sampling of SAP's FSCM transaction codes.

TABLE 11.3   Sample FSCM T-Codes

Functionality	T-Code	Description
FSCM In-House	IHC2 and IHC3	Change and display payment orders
FSCM In-House	IHC0	Payment order browser
FSCM In-House	IHC1IP	Create internal payment order
FSCM In-House	IHC1EP	Create external payment order
FSCM Collections	UDM_SUPERVISOR	Collections worklist for managers
FSCM Collections	UDM_SPECIALIST	Collections worklist for specialists
FSCM Collections	UDM_STRATEGY	Collection strategies
FSCM Collections	UDM_GENWL	Create worklist
FSCM Collections	UDM_PRDIST	Distribute worklist items
FSCM Collections	FDM_COLL01	Collections management
FSCM Collections	UDM_BP	Collections management business partner

SAP ERP Operations

The second principal SAP business scenario is SAP ERP Operations. This scenario is all about company operations such as logistics and ERP-specific supply chain matters, and it is built atop five popular SAP ERP modules: SD, PP, PM, MM, and QM (among others, such as warehouse management, product costing, global trade, transportation management, and more). Each of the five core modules is briefly explored next.

Sales and Distribution Module

The Sales and Distribution module is used to create and process sales orders; work through processes such as warehouse picking, packing, and shipping; perform pricing functions; bill customers; perform sales activities; and more. Key functional components include

- ▶ Sales
- ▶ Localization
- ▶ Foreign trade
- ▶ Billing
- ▶ Credit

▶ Electronic data interchange (EDI)

▶ Shipping

▶ Transportation

▶ Reporting

▶ Sales support

Table 11.4 shows a sampling of common SD transaction codes.

TABLE 11.4   Sample SD T-Codes

Functionality	T-Code	Description
SD Basics	V-41 and V-43	Create and change material price
SD Basics	V-44	Display material price
SD Basics	VOFO	Configure billing information
SD Basics	V-45	Create price list
SD Availability	CKAV	Check availability (Available to Promise)
SD Availability	CO06	Backorder processing
SD Credit	OVB5	Rqmts for creating a purchase requisition
SD Credit	OVB6	Rqmts for picking a delivery
SD Credit	OVB7	Rqmts for goods issue of a delivery
SD Billing	VF01 and VF02	Create and change a billing document
SD Billing	VF04	Maintain billing due list
SD Billing	VF21 and VF22	Create and change an invoice list
SD Billing	VF11	Cancel a billing document
Sales Activities	V+11	Create a direct mailing
Sales Activities	V+21	Create a sales prospect
Sales Activities	V+23	Create a business partner
SD Sales	VA01 and VA02	Create and change a sales order
SD Sales	VA21 and VA23	Create and display a sales quote
SD Sales	VA41 and VA42	Create and change a contract
SD Sales	VD53	Display customer material information

Functionality	T-Code	Description
SD Reporting	V.15	Display backorders
SD Reporting	VA35	List of scheduling agreements
SD Reporting	VA45	List of contracts
SD Reporting	VA05	List of sales orders

Production Planning and Control Module

The Production Planning and Control module (or simply Production Planning) enables a company to perform production capacity planning, address manufacturing shop floor functions, and develop the master scheduling and material requirements planning necessary to create a smooth-running production line. Key functional components include

▶ Material master

▶ Bills of material (BOMs)

▶ Routing recipes (how to plan to build something)

▶ Master recipes (how to build something)

▶ Master production planning and scheduling

▶ Material requirements planning (MRP)

▶ Production execution

▶ Demand management

▶ Forecasting

▶ Profitability analysis

Table 11.5 shows a sampling of common PP transactions. (Keep in mind that many other transactions spanning materials management, warehouse management, and other modules are also necessary to perform end-to-end production planning processes.)

TABLE 11.5 Sample PP T-Codes

Functionality	T-Code	Description
PP Master Data	MD01	MRP Run
PP Master Data	MD05	Individual display of MRP list
PP Scheduling	OPU3	Production order control parameters

Functionality	T-Code	Description
PP Scheduling	OPU4	Maintain capacity planning
PP Info System	MCPU	Production order analysis: Lead time
PP Info System	MCPS	Operations analysis: Lead time
PP Info System	MCPH	Work center analysis: Dates
PP Info System	MCPW	Material analysis: Lead time
PP Planning	PX03	Planning tool
PP Planning	PFSE	Call process flow scheduler
PP Demand Mgmt	MD70	Copy total forecast
PP Demand Mgmt	MDPH	Planning profile
PP Demand Mgmt	MD61	Create planned independent requirements
PP Demand Mgmt	MD83	Display customer independent requirements
PP MRP	MDL1 and MDL2	Create and change production lot
PP Recipes	CO53	Control recipe monitor
PP Recipes	CO53XT	Monitor control instructions/recipes
PP Process Orders	COR1 and COR2	Create and change process orders
PP Prod Orders	CO01 and CO02	Create and change production orders
PP Prod Orders	CO22	Orders for the MRP controller
PP Confirm	CO13	Cancel confirmation of production order
PP Confirm	CO14 and CO15	Display and enter production order confirmations
PP Distribution	DRPS	Calculate safety stock
PP Distribution	DRP9	Maintain plant categories

Enterprise Asset Management (Plant Maintenance) Module

The Enterprise Asset Management module (formerly Plant Maintenance, though the older term is still often used) comprises activities intended to keep expensive capital equipment running well. Key functional capabilities include

- ▶ Planning for and performing inspections
- ▶ Scheduling labor and other services
- ▶ Scheduling materials necessary to perform services

▶ Planning for downtime and other outages

▶ Performing proactive preventive maintenance

▶ Performing reactive repairs

Businesses rely on hundreds of various EAM/PM transactions to run their enterprise asset management functions. Table 11.6 shows sampling of EAM/PM transaction codes.

TABLE 11.6 Sample EAM/PM T-Codes

Functionality	T-Code	Description
EAM Maintenance	IW31 and IW32	Create and display work orders
EAM Maintenance	IW38 and IW39	Change and display work order list editing
EAM Maintenance	IW40	Display multi-level work orders
EAM History	IW13	Material where-used list
EAM Tasks Lists	IP02 and IP03	Display and change maintenance plans
EAM Maintenance	IP42	Create strategy maintenance plan
EAM Maintenance	IP30	Deadline monitoring
EAM Maintenance	IP11 and IP12	Change and display maintenance strategy
EAM Measuring	IK11 and IK12	Create and change measurement documents
EAM Measuring	IA03	Display equipment task list
EAM Equipment	IE01 and IE02	Create and change equipment
EAM Equipment	IQ01 and IQ02	Create and change serial numbers
EAM Confirmations	IW41	Enter order confirmation

Materials Management Module

SAP's Materials Management module includes some of the most common functionality deployed for ERP. It supports functions such as

▶ Creating and processing purchase requisitions (PRs)

▶ Working through purchase orders (POs)

▶ Goods receipts

▶ Accounts payable

▶ Inventory management

- Bills of material (BOMs)
- Managing materials from master raw to finished goods

Beyond being popular, SAP MM is also perhaps the most comprehensive and far-reaching module of SAP ERP (as it touches nearly everything else). Table 11.7 shows a very small sampling of common MM transaction codes.

TABLE 11.7 Sample MM T-Codes

Functionality	T-Code	Description
MM Logistics	MM02 and MM03	Change and display materials
MM Logistics	MMBE	Stock overview
MM Logistics	MMI1	Create operating supplies
MM Logistics	MMS1	Create service
MM Purchasing	ME21N	Create purchase order
MM Purchasing	ME51N and ME52N	Create and change purchase requisitions
MM Purchasing	ME5A	Purchase requisitions: List display
MM Purchasing	ME54	Release purchase requisitions
MM Purchasing	ME59	Automatic generation of POs
MM Inventory	MB21 and MB22	Create and change reservations
MM Inventory	MB1B	Transfer posting
MM Inventory	MB1C	Other goods receipts
MM Inventory	MI01 and MI02	Create and change physical inventory document
MM Inventory	MI21	Print physical inventory document
MM Inventory	MI05 and MI06	Change and display inventory count
MM Inventory	MI07	Process list of differences
MM External	ML81	Create service entry sheet

Quality Management Module

The Quality Management module provides functionality that is useful in several contexts (it plugs in to several other components to provide quality management functions in the context of those components). SAP QM serves the following purposes:

- Quality planning
- Quality inspection

▶ Quality control

▶ Quality certificates

▶ Quality notifications

Organizations use the QM module to manage quality related to materials, vendors, partners, and manufacturers. This includes goods inventory inspections, monitoring of production batch shelf-life, inspection cadence management, quality inspection facilitation, highlighting and addressing of production issues via notifications and task assignments, and processing of customer complaints. QM can be further subdivided into several submodules:

▶ QM-CA Quality Certificates

▶ QM-CA-MD Basic Data for Certificates

▶ QM-IM Quality Inspection

▶ QM-IM-RR Results Recording

▶ QM-IM-SM Sample Management

▶ QM-IM-UD Inspection Lot Completion

▶ QM-PT-BD Basic Data

▶ QM-PT-BD-CAT Catalog

▶ QM-PT-BD-ICH Inspection Characteristic

▶ QM-PT-BD-SPL Samples and SPC

▶ QM-PT-CP Control Plan

▶ QM-PT-FA Failure Mode and Effects Analysis

▶ QM-PT-IP Inspection Planning

▶ QM-PT-RP-PRC QM Control in Procurement

▶ QM-PT-RP-SD QM Control in Sales and Distribution

▶ QM-QC-AQC Active Quality Control

▶ QM-QC-IS Information System

▶ QM-QN Quality Notifications

▶ QM-QN-NM-8D QM 8D-Report Automotive

Table 11.8 shows a sampling of common QM transaction codes.

TABLE 11.8   Sample QM T-Codes

Functionality	T-Code	Description
QM Certificates	QC52 and QC53	Change and display certificate in procurement
QM Certificates	QC55	Worklist certificates: procurement
QM Certificates	QCE2 and QCE3	Change and display communication support
QM Certificates	QCMS	Certificate for inspection lot
QM Inspection	QST08	Display testing schedule items
QM Inspection	QST10	Display planning module
QM Control	QDP3	Change sampling scheme
QM Control	QDL1 and QCL2	Create and change quality levels
QM Notifications	QMW1	Create quality notification
QM Notifications	QM50	Time line display quality notifications
QM Management	OQB8	Define QM systems

SAP ERP Human Capital Management

The third principal SAP business scenario, SAP ERP HCM, includes the traditional HR module, which is used for recruiting, benefits, time management, payroll, training, career management, succession planning, and several other related functions. Historically, SAP divided HR into Personnel Administration (PA), Training/Event Management (PE), Personnel Time Management (PT), and Payroll (PY). Table 11.9 shows a sampling of HR transaction codes.

TABLE 11.9   Sample HR (HCM) T-Codes

Functionality	T-Code	Description
PA Benefits	PZ07	Participation overview
PA Benefits	PZ43	Retirement benefits
PA Compensation	PA97 and PA98	Compensation administration
PA Staffing	OORW	Work scheduling: Rule values
PA Staffing	OOPD	HR master data
PA Staffing	OOSO	Create requirements profile
PA Staffing	OODY	Shift planning: Time types/balances
PA Admin	PA00	Initial PA master data menu

Functionality	T-Code	Description
PT Admin	PTMW and PTME	Time manager's workplace
PT Attendance	CAT4	CATS time sheets: Approve data
PT Attendance	CAPS	Approve times: Master data
PE Events	PVH1	Create/change instructor
PE Events	PVB2	Display business event budget
PE Events	PVO2	Pre-book attendance
PT Time Events	PTCOR	Clock-in/Clock-out corrections: Test
PY General	PA03	Maintain personnel control record
PY General	PU98	Assign wage types to groups
PY Tax	PU19	Tax reporter

SAP ERP Corporate Services

The fourth and final principal SAP business area, ERP Corporate Services, is built atop yet another set of modules: SAP Asset Management (AM), QM (previously discussed), Real Estate (RE), and the SAP Transportation (TM) submodule of logistics. RE and TM functionality are outlined in more detail next.

SAP RE Module

The SAP Real Estate module helps an organization manage its facilities and properties. Because of all the legal, geographic, and regulatory concerns around property management, SAP RE consists of many submodules, ranging from real estate controlling, accounting, and contracting to rent adjustments, taxes, land use management, service charge management, and various sales-related processes. Table 11.10 shows a sampling of RE transaction codes.

TABLE 11.10 Sample RE T-Codes

Functionality	T-Code	Description
RE Sales	FOUBN	Display sales settlement history
RE Sales	FOU3N	Display sales reports
RE Sales	FOJUNS	Enter sales with condition types
RE Taxes	REITDS	Input tax distribution
RE Taxes	REITZA	Maintain option rate methods
RE Management	FOMG	Repeat run invoice printout

Functionality	T-Code	Description
RE Contracts	REGC0001	Applications
RE Contracts	REGC0102	Authorization types
RE Management	FOB1	Lease-out one-time postings
RE Management	FO35	Create a building
RE Management	FO8K	Carry out real estate accrual/deferral

SAP TM Submodule

The SAP Transportation submodule includes logistics activities intended to move goods from one place to another. It lets you create forwarding orders, transfer orders, and deliveries; create freight bookings; plan methods of transport; choose transportation carriers; dispatch and monitor the transportation process; and more. Table 11.11 shows a sampling of TM transaction codes.

TABLE 11.11   Sample TM T-Codes

Functionality	T-Code	Description
Logistics Transportation	VT01N	Create shipment
Logistics Transportation	VT11	Select shipments: Materials planning
Logistics Transportation	VT12	Select shipments: Transportation processing
Logistics Transportation	VT70	Output for shipments
Logistics Freight	TK11	Create condition (shipment costs)
Logistics Freight	VI01	Create shipment costs
Logistics Freight	VI12	List shipment costs: Settlement

Other Popular Business Transactions

Beyond the transactions identified by core ERP area, many others are important in conducting regular business. Two of the most important and most popular are cross-application transactions and another set of transactions related to environmental and workplace safety. These are outlined next.

Cross-Application Components Module

Many business processes and technical functions are required to operate "across" functional areas. SAP calls these cross-application components, and they represent more than 10,000 unique transactions. Popular Cross-Application (CA) business functionality includes:

▶ Audit management

▶ Banks

▶ Employee self-service

▶ Master data management

▶ Project risk management

Technically oriented cross-application functionality is even more prevalent, including functionality that is used by IT teams to manage and maintain SAP:

▶ Archiving and Document Management

▶ Application Link Enabling (ALE)

▶ Digital Signature Services

▶ General Application Functions

▶ Data Transfer and Retention

▶ Scripting Services

▶ Print Workbench

▶ Schedule Manager

▶ Messages

▶ Development Workbench

Table 11.12 shows a small sampling of cross-application transaction codes.

TABLE 11.12   Sample CA T-Codes

Functionality	T-Code	Description
CA Doc Mgmt	OD07	Document management frontend
CA Doc Mgmt	CVI2	Change recipient list
CA Digital Signatures	CJ00	Find digital signatures
CA Digital Signatures	DSAL	Digital signature logs

Functionality	T-Code	Description
CA ESS	HRUSER	Setup and maintain ESS users
CA ESS	PZ00	ESS start menu
CA ESS	PZ01	Who's who
CA ESS	PZ30	My photo
CA Print	EFCM	Print workbench form class processing
CA Print	EFTP	Print workbench mass processing
CA Scheduler	SCMA	Schedule manager: Scheduler
CA Scheduler	SCMO	Schedule manager: Monitor
CA General Status	BS02 and BS03	Maintain and display status profiles
CA General Status	BS22 and BS23	Maintain and display system status

Environment, Health, and Safety Module

The Environment, Health, and Safety (EH&S) module helps organizations manage and monitor areas such as food safety, compliance with environmental regulations, employee and product safety track records, occupational health matters, waste management compliance, dangerous goods movements, and more. Table 11.13 shows a sampling of EH&S transaction codes.

TABLE 11.13   Sample EH&S T-Codes

Functionality	T-Code	Description
EH&S DG	DGC4	Dangerous goods: Define DG classes
EH&S DG	DGC5	Dangerous goods: Define water pollution classes
EH&S DG	DGC6	Dangerous goods: Specify danger labels
EH&S DG	HMCC	Dangerous goods: Hazard identification numbers
EH&S Product Safety	CG02	Substance workbench
EH&S Product Safety	CGE2	Packaging workbench
EH&S Waste	WAM01 and WAM02	Create and edit disposal documents
EH&S Waste	WAM04	Find disposal documents

SAP's EH&S functionality continues to expand in response to organizational and community pressure to create a safer workplace, sustainable processes, and a cleaner environment.

Summary

In this hour, we explored what it means to work with SAP ERP as a business end user. We explored a number of common business functions and a sampling of specific transaction codes executed by end users to support the four core SAP ERP business scenarios. We also explored other important functional areas and related transaction codes. By providing a sampling of the detailed business transactions used to run a business, this hour should have cemented what it really means to use SAP ERP to do your job.

Case Study: Hour 11

Review the following case study, which reflects a business user interested in better understanding MNC's SAP ERP environment. You can find answers to the questions related to this case study in Appendix A, "Case Study Answers."

Situation

As MNC continues to deploy SAP Enterprise Resource Planning (ERP), it's focused on augmenting the existing staff with new employees experienced with what SAP calls the four core business scenarios. You are a prospective new hire with both materials management and real estate management experience. One of MNC's hiring managers has asked you to do a phone interview.

Questions

1. What are the four core SAP business scenarios?

2. Which scenario is most related to your materials management experience?

3. Which scenario is most related to your real estate management experience?

4. The interviewer is especially interested in your SAP MM purchasing experience. What kinds of transactions should you mention to demonstrate this experience?

5. The interviewer asks about the SAP RE submodules you know best. What are the kinds of subareas you might discuss to demonstrate your experience?

Using Other SAP Business Suite Applications

What You'll Learn in This Hour:

▶ SAP SRM common business transactions
▶ SAP CRM modules and common business transactions
▶ SAP SCM functions and common business transactions
▶ SAP PLM common business transactions and system limitations

The previous hour explored how to use SAP ERP to do your job. In this hour, we go beyond ERP and look into the four other classic SAP Business Suite applications and how to use them to do your job.

Using SAP SRM

SAP Supplier Relationship Management (SRM) is one of SAP's first applications outside ERP and business intelligence/data warehousing. It's a mature offering with a robust set of capabilities for managing the procurement and support of the goods and services a company uses internally to run day in and day out. SAP SRM helps to optimize and manage the relationship between a company and its suppliers, much the way that SAP CRM helps organizations manage relationships with customers. Key functionality for SAP SRM includes self-service procurement (classic shopping cart functionality), strategic sourcing, master data management (formerly catalog content management), spend analysis, and supplier evaluation. Table 12.1 shows common transaction codes (T-codes) used in SAP SRM.

TABLE 12.1 Sample SAP SRM T-Codes

Functionality	T-Code	Description
SRM	BBPSC01	Shopping cart - Full functionality
SRM	BBPSC02	Shopping cart - wizard
SRM	BBPSC03	Shopping cart - Limited functions
SRM	BBPSC04	Shopping cart status
SRM	BBPSC05	Public template (Create)
SRM	BBPSC06	Public template (Change)
SRM	BBPSC07	Manager inbox
SRM	BBPSC08	Employee inbox
SRM	BBPSC09	Administrator cockpit
SRM	BBPSC10	Reviewer inbox
SRM	BBPSC11	Shopping cart display item overview
SRM	BBPSC12	Shopping cart display item details
SRM	BBPCF01	GR/SE for vendor
SRM	BBPCF02	GR/SE for desktop user
SRM	BBPCF03	Goods receipts/services for professional users
SRM	BBPCF04	Confirmation approval
SRM	BBPCF05	Carry out review for confirmation
SRM	BBPCF07	External confirmation display
SRM	PPOCA_BBP	Create attributes
SRM	PPOCV_BBP	Create vendor groups
SRM	PPOMA_BBP	Change attributes
SRM	PPOMV_BBP	Change vendor groups
SRM	PPOSA_BBP	Display attributes
SRM	PPOSV_BBP	Display vendor groups
SRM	BBP_PD	Document display (EBP) SRM - Enterprise buyer
SRM	BBPGETVD	Transfer vendor master SRM - Enterprise buyer

Using SAP CRM

As discussed in Hour 5, "Overview of SAP Applications and Components," SAP CRM provides processes for customer interactions. This includes fundamentally critical customer-related functions such as marketing, sales, service, and support—functions that have only increased in importance, which explains why the entire CRM market has grown faster than any other major business application—and also explains in part why SAP CRM deployments account for much of SAP's growth over the past few years. Another reason is the acquisition of hybris, which added a multichannel e-commerce and product content management (PCM) solution to SAP's mature CRM platform. Today, important functions or modules in SAP CRM include

▶ Sales

▶ Marketing

▶ Service

▶ Pricing

▶ Analytics

▶ Interaction Center (IC)

▶ SAP hybris PCM capabilities (multichannel capabilities, formerly delivered via SAP's Web Channel)

SAP provides more than 400 CRM transaction codes. Some of the most useful and popular ones are listed in Table 12.2.

TABLE 12.2 Sample SAP CRM T-Codes

Functionality	T-Code	Description
CRM General	CRMD_ORDER	CRM transaction processing
CRM General	CRMD_BUS2000111	Maintain opportunities
CRM General	CRMD_BUS2000112	Maintain service contracts
CRM General	CRMD_BUS2000120	Process complaints
CRM General	CRMD_BUS2000121	Maintain sales contracts
CRM General	CRMD_BUS2000108	Maintain leads
CRM General	CRMD_BUS2000115	Maintain sales transactions
CRM Pricing	CTFC_CRM	CRM field catalog
CRM Pricing	PRC_CONDTYPE_CRM	Maintain pricing conditions type
CRM General	CRMBS02	Maintain status profiles

Functionality	T-Code	Description
CRM General	CRM_DNO_MONITOR	Transaction Monitor
CRM Investigation	CRM_MI	Display documents in investigation
CRM Activity	CRMCACTARC	Archiving control CRM activity
CRM Activity	CRMC_ACTIVITY_H	Customizing maintenance activity
CRM Activity	CRMC_ACT_SURVEY	Customer maintenance activity questionnaire
CRM IC	CRMC_IC_CLMPROF	Call list profile maintenance
CRM Marketing	CRM_MKTPL	Marketing planner
CRM Events	CRMV_EVENT	Customizing event handler
CRM Email	CRMD_EMAIL	Maintain mail form
CRM Email	E2C	Email to CRM
CRM Cross-App	CRM_UI	Start CRM web client
CRM Cross-App	CRMM_BUPA_MAP	Business partner data exchange
CRM Cross-App	CRMC_UI_PROFILE	Define business roles

Using SAP SCM

Because it's one of SAP's oldest applications, SAP SCM is mature, capable, and, frankly, complex. Organizations use SAP SCM to streamline and optimize their supply chains and production schedules while minimizing costs. The core component of SCM is the SAP Advanced Planner and Optimizer (APO), which includes

▶ Requirements forecasting on the basis of historical data held in Demand Planning (DP)

▶ Cross-plant distribution of orders onto the available transport and production capacities by Supply Network Planning (SNP)

▶ Production Planning–Detailed Scheduling (PP-DS)

▶ Transportation Planning–Vehicle Scheduling (TP-VS)

▶ Vendor-Managed Inventory (VMI)

▶ Availability-to-Promise (ATP) functionality, providing multilevel availability checks that can be carried out against material stocks, production, warehouse and transport capacities, costs across plants, and more.

Beyond SAP APO, other components of SAP SCM include the following:

▸ SAP Event Management (EM), which provides functions for managing deviations between planning and reality

▸ SAP Inventory Collaboration Hub, which supports cross-enterprise integration for supplier-managed inventories (SMI) or vendor-managed inventories (VMI).

▸ The SAP Auto-ID Infrastructure (AII), which provides connectivity between RFID scanners and SAP SCM

Business transactions include those focused on the following functionality:

▸ Supply chain planning system

▸ Supply value chain system

▸ Supply chain execution system

▸ Supply chain visibility system

▸ SCM inventory management system

▸ SCM transportation and logistics management system

▸ Supply chain network design system

▸ Supply chain event management system

▸ SCM proof of delivery system

▸ SCM forecasting system

▸ SCM asset management system

▸ Supply chain reporting system

Table 12.3 shows a sampling of common Supply Chain Management transaction codes.

TABLE 12.3 Sample SAP SCM T-Codes

Functionality	T-Code	Description
SCM APO	AMON1	Alert monitor
SCM APO	RRP3	APO product view
SCM APO	MSDP_ADMIN	SNP and DP administration
SCM APO	CSNP	Cost maintenance: SNP
SCM APO	SDP94	Supply and demand planner: Initial screen

Functionality	T-Code	Description
SCM APO	SDP8B	Define planning book
SCM APO	OM17	Data reconciliation
SCM APO	SCC_TL1	Transportation lanes
SCM APO	OM13	Analyze liveCache and LCA builds
SCM APO	OM16	Data viewer
SCM APO	RLCDEL	Delete orders from liveCache
SCM APO	MC90	Release to supply network planning
SCM APO	MAT1	Products
SCM APO	MC62	Maintain characteristic values
SCM APO	MVM	Model planning version
SCM APO	RES01	Change resources
SCM Basis	CIF	APO core interface
SCM Basis	CFM1	Create integration models
SCM Basis	CFM4	Display integration models
SCM Basis	CFM7	Delete integration models

Using SAP PLM

SAP Product Lifecycle Management (PLM) is reasonably self-explanatory: It helps organizations manage their products over each product's lifecycle. PLM includes functionality such as product and process modeling, process routing, product design and assembly, structure management and synchronization, recipe management, built-in analytics (via the Business Content Viewer tool), and more. Table 12.4 lists a sampling of native and common Product Lifecycle Management transaction codes.

TABLE 12.4 Sample SAP PLM T-Codes

Functionality	T-Code	Description
PLM Management	WPS1	Revision planning
PLM Management	WPS2	Create order as report
PLM Recipe	RMWB	Start recipe workbench
PLM Recipe	MRTRSC02	Master recipe generation
PLM Logbook	CLIST	Configuration control: Component list

Functionality	T-Code	Description
PLM Logbook	LBK1	Logbook application
PLM Replication	CRWBD	Replication workbench
PLM Replication	UPSREP01_CM	Create replication table from baselines
PLM Recipe	FRML02	Edit formula
PLM Recipe	FRML03	Display formula
PLM Recipe	FRML04	Formula information system
PLM Recipe	FRMLC07	Customize: Substance types per view
PLM Recipe	FRMLC49	Roles for events
PLM Recipe	FRMLC52	Set parameters for formula view
PLM Transformation	RMXM_BOM_CMP	Compare bills of material (BOMs)

Because SAP PLM is tightly integrated with procurement management processes, material master data, engineering and document management functionality, safety and maintenance processes, and tools such as ECM/OCM, AutoCAD, Inventor, Pro-E, Solidworks, and others, it's difficult to provide a comprehensive list of native-only PLM transactions. However, Table 12.4 should nonetheless provide some insight into what it means to use SAP PLM to manage a product lifecycle.

Summary

This hour explored, at a high level, how to use four common SAP Business Suite applications. With your new insight into how to use SAP SRM, CRM, SCM, and PLM, combined with your insight into how to use SAP ERP to do your job (Hour 11, "Using SAP ERP to Do Your Job"), we can now turn our attention in the next hour to using several of SAP's reporting applications and tools.

Case Study: Hour 12

Review the following case study, focused on how to use SAP SRM, CRM, SCM, and PLM. You can find answers to the questions related to this case study in Appendix A, "Case Study Answers."

Situation

MNC is seeking moderately experienced business application end users to support its upcoming SAP Business Suite implementation. You've been asked to perform phone screens with MNC internal candidates who have a lot of passion and a certain amount of experience with the legacy applications to be replaced by SAP SRM, CRM, SCM, and PLM. Your goal is to identify high-potential candidates and get them involved in career development tasks that will prepare them for SAP.

Questions

1. What kinds of business transactions or functional experience would show you that a candidate has reasonably good experience with customer relationship management applications?

2. One of your phone screen candidates spent 20 minutes talking intelligently about configuring shopping cart functionality, managing multi-vendor catalogs, and evaluating suppliers. Which SAP Business Suite module might be a good fit for her?

3. Another phone screen candidate discussed his experience with demand planning, production planning, transportation planning, and vehicle scheduling. Which SAP Business Suite component might he learn most quickly?

4. Many of MNC's current PLM end users never learned about recipe management despite the fact that the old system was fully capable of delivering such functionality. What kinds of transactions should you expect to hear about from a PLM end user experienced in this area?

5. Your last candidate seemed quite experienced in product lifecycle management tasks but was adamant that PLM was self-contained and required no other modules or systems for functionality. How true is his position with regard to SAP PLM, and would he be an ideal candidate in the short term?

Using SAP for Reporting

What You'll Learn in This Hour:

- ▶ Types of reporting users and systems
- ▶ New SAP reporting solutions
- ▶ Overview of several of the tools in the SAP BusinessObjects family
- ▶ Overview of BW, BWA, SAP BW Powered by HANA, and the Business Explorer
- ▶ Native SAP ERP reporting options
- ▶ Other legacy operational reporting options

Business applications mean little without the ability to create operational reports, analyze data, visualize trends, and ultimately make smarter decisions. This hour covers reporting methods ranging from legacy ERP reporting tools and approaches still used today to SAP's most recent products and applications. Throughout this hour, we discuss which tools to use for enterprise-level reporting, operational reporting, ad-hoc queries, ad-hoc exploration, dashboards or visualizations, and so on. But first, we need to set the stage by explaining the types of reporting users, along with the systems or tools that serve as the source of their report needs.

Types of SAP Reporting Users

SAP applications support and manage a firm's business processes and underlying data. Although this data is stored in the SAP system and can be presented on SAP screens, you might still want to produce printed or custom output from the system or present your findings through visualizations or dashboards. In the most general sense, these outputs are called *reports*. Business users, managers, executives, and others use reports to understand their business and make smarter decisions.

Although there are many classes of report users, we often see three types of users, based on purpose: lightweight dashboard users, decision makers (including dedicated "BI users"), and operational reporting users:

▶ **Lightweight dashboard users (executives and occasional "light" users):** Consume highly aggregated and summarized data sitting in cubes and typically presented via a prestocked dashboard or via simple phone apps and other applications hosted on laptops, smartphones, tablets, and similar devices. Self-service users often fall into this "light user" category, too. Response time requirements are closer to those for transactional users (for example, less than 1 second). Executives, self-service users (such as those required to perform time entry or interested in viewing pay stubs), and others in need of simple status or data entry screens fall into this class of light users.

▶ **Decision makers, including dedicated business intelligence (BI) users:** Analyze vast amounts of data, perhaps months or years of detailed and summary transactional data hosted in cubes, to identify trends or relationships between the data over time, by region/ geography, by product line, and so on. These users are sometimes characterized as data miners because they query data in an ad-hoc manner to discover information that could dramatically impact the how the business is run. For example, BI users might explore details surrounding customers in a particular geography, what they purchase or lease, what other items are also typically purchased or leased in the next period, how these are all financed and serviced, and therefore what are the most profitable anticipated assembly-line, warehousing, and distribution methods that might be employed to maximize a store's sales during a single trip or during the life of the product or customer. Thus, BI users are less predictable in terms of data or system resource requirements.

▶ **Operational reporting users:** Analyze relatively small amounts of targeted data, looking for trends based on quantities (for example, number of a particular set of products sold in a region, sorted by sales rep, sorted by largest customer orders, and so on). Operational reporting users often execute a repetitive set of queries on a weekly or monthly basis in the course of doing their jobs, and they are fairly predictable in terms of overall data and system resource requirements. Operational reporting and dashboard users together make up perhaps 70–90% of all reporting users.

Figure 13.1 shows these three broad types of users and the systems or tools they might use for SAP reporting.

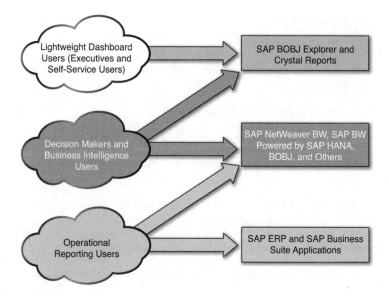

FIGURE 13.1
SAP reporting users vary in terms of their perspectives and therefore the systems or tools they need.

To address these different reporting user types, several new and many legacy SAP reporting methods and tools are available, including the following:

▸ SAP Business Objects Explorer and Crystal Reports for discovery, exploration, and enterprise reporting

▸ Xcelcius for creating dashboards and visualizations

▸ SAP NetWeaver BW, BWA, BW on HANA, SAP Business Explorer (BEx) Analyzer, and SAP BOBJ Enterprise for BI/analytics

▸ Web Intelligence, SAP Report Painter, ABAP List Processing (ABAP programming), ABAP Query Reporting, and Ad Hoc Query Reporting for SAP ERP operational reporting

▸ Older SAP reporting options including Structural Graphics Reporting, Executive Information Systems, and SAP Information System (report trees)

Several of these methods and tools are explored next.

SAP Business Objects

Acquired by SAP in 2007, SAP Business Objects (BO or BOBJ) is arguably one of SAP's most important acquisitions. Acquiring BOBJ gave SAP the ability to provide a greater, more tightly integrated, or deeper level of the following:

▶ Foundational services necessary to deploy and manage its BI toolset

▶ Tools needed to address lightweight self-service reporting, queries, and analysis

▶ Enterprise reporting capabilities its customers were already accustomed to using (in particular Crystal Reports)

▶ Data visualization capabilities accessible from different client platforms and manipulated by common front-end user applications such as Microsoft Excel

▶ Additional plug-in capabilities for those same front-end applications

▶ Ability to create abstracted end-user views ("universes") of the data otherwise trapped in different SAP and non-SAP databases

▶ A stronger enterprise information management (EIM) framework to lay the groundwork for ETL-based queries and analyses

BOBJ brought much more to SAP's suite of reporting capabilities as well. Several important applications and tools are outlined next.

SAP BO Explorer

One of SAP's simplest and most effective reporting tools is the SAP BO Explorer. Executives and other light users use it in the same way you use a search engine to mine through corporate data that's been dumped into what SAP calls "information spaces." After SAP BO Explorer finds the data, it allows the user to view it in simple charts, tables, and other visualization methods (see Figure 13.2) or dumped yet again into Microsoft Excel for further analysis.

Before you can use BO Explorer, someone in your organization needs to create and populate the information spaces. Doing so requires authorization to access the data. In addition, the information spaces need to be regularly re-indexed; users search through the indexes, after all, in the same way that most search engines do.

Fortunately, once the information spaces are set up, it's easy to install and actually use the SAP BusinessObjects Explore front end. You can load it in the same way you do any other application on a laptop or desktop (for the richest and most powerful experience) or use the mobile app available on iPhones and iPads.

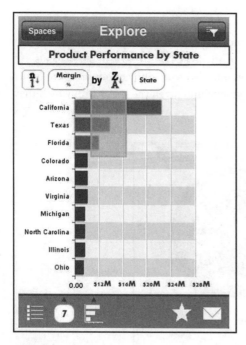

FIGURE 13.2
A sample SAP BusinessObjects Explorer screen, accessed via a smartphone app.

SAP BO Crystal Reports

SAP acquired Crystal Reports with its Business Objects acquisition in 2007 (BOBJ in turn had acquired Crystal Solutions from Seagate Software in 2003) to augment its capabilities around operational and enterprise reporting. Though it's been known by many names, including Crystal Decisions and Crystal Services, Crystal Reports in one form or another has been an industry reporting standard for over two decades. Benefits include

▶ Fast and easy setup, including templates and wizards for creating canned reports

▶ Usefulness in building a wide breadth of reports, from standardized financials and other business reports to legal reports

▶ Formatting flexibility, from multipage reports to those built on multiple queries

▶ Ease of including graphics and basic visualizations

▶ Ability to securely distribute reports over the web

Crystal Reports has been so successful over the years that it's now the de facto reporting solution for not only thousands of companies, but more than 500 ISVs, too.

SAP BO Xcelcius Enterprise

When it comes to designing and deploying personalized dashboards or secure visualizations via portals, through reports, Microsoft Office documents, or Adobe PDFs, turn to SAP BO Xcelcius Enterprise. It's easy to use, it's powerful, and it lets you quickly create and communicate output. Its professional dashboard capabilities are especially compelling given the speed with which they can be created (see Figure 13.3).

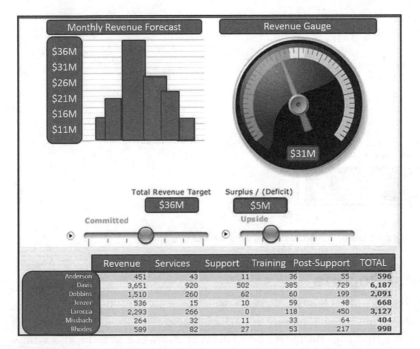

FIGURE 13.3
A useful SAP BusinessObjects Xcelcius dashboard can be created in about 15 minutes.

Reports can be designed to operate offline or to provide up-to-the-minute real-time status. SAP BO Xcelcius is powerful, too, in that it supports detailed drill-down, what-if analysis, and the ability to easily embed sliders, gauges, selectors, and other controls directly into dashboards and other forms of reports. SAP BO Xcelcius also comes with prebuilt report "skins," along with standardized charts and maps. It's arguably one the most useful visualization tools in any vendor's reporting suite of products.

SAP BO Web Intelligence

Formerly branded as "Interactive Analysis," SAP BO Web Intelligence goes beyond simple reporting to give business intelligence users and decision makers a robust platform for business analysis. Use it to perform deep analysis against your existing reports and to merge other data sources into the mix, just as you would a self-service BI mashup tool. The key is that the data sources have to be defined in BO "universes," which are simply organized sets of data pulled from any number of sources, such as BEx queries (against one or more SAP BI Info Cubes), HANA systems, Microsoft Excel CSV files, data accessed through web services, and more.

Similar to its reporting brethren, it supports multiple sources and multiple queries, and it works in both real-time and offline modes. Once you've determined that you'd like to see a certain set of analyzed data on a regular basis, use SAP BO Web Intelligence's web-based interface to create new self-service reports from scratch. Alternatively, you can use existing reports as templates for new ones. Mine and analyze your new and existing data, too, incorporating calculations, filtering, ranking, and sorting capabilities into your self-service analysis work.

The front end can be launched from the SAP BI Launch Pad as a Java applet (a "rich Internet application") or as a Web Intelligence rich client. There's a more limited HTML web interface available, too. Look to the SAP BO Web Intelligence user guide for the trade-offs and benefits of each front end.

SAP NetWeaver BW Family

Long before SAP acquired BOBJ, it already had developed a suite of reasonably capable reporting assets. The original SAP Business Information Warehouse (BIW) was SAP's second major application after R/3 and its first attempt to provide real (though limited) business intelligence. Renamed several times throughout the years—now called Business Warehouse (BW)—the tool was actually developed to offload reporting from SAP R/3. By pulling users off of R/3 and redirecting them to run their reports and queries on BW, precious R/3 resources were granted additional bandwidth to host more R/3 users or preserve fast online user response times. Read more about SAP NetWeaver BW in Hour 5, "Overview of SAP Applications and Components," and Hour 6, "SAP NetWeaver and HANA."

SAP NetWeaver BWA

Just as SAP NetWeaver Business Warehouse returned processing bandwidth back to R/3 and subsequent SAP ERP systems, so too did SAP's Business Warehouse Accelerator grant additional bandwidth back to SAP NetWeaver BW systems. This was SAP's first in-memory hardware/software solution applied to reporting, and while quite successful several years ago, it has been largely replaced by SAP BW powered by SAP HANA.

SAP BW Powered by SAP HANA

As discussed in Hour 6, BW is supported by SAP's latest in-memory database. From a user's perspective, when moving from SAP BW to SAP BW powered by SAP HANA, not a lot changes other than the real-time nature of the reports they can access. With SAP BW powered by SAP HANA, users benefit from faster financial planning, customer insight, sales data, metrics reporting, data loads, query performance, and so on. The IT department benefits from lower database maintenance, simplified administration, and the like, too. Only the CFO and her bean counters are negatively impacted—but only if they're short-sighted and consider costs more important than the benefits and other value achieved through faster and smarter business intelligence.

SAP Business Explorer

SAP Business Explorer, sometimes incorrectly called the BEx Analyzer, is the lightweight reporting tool that SAP has long provided to work with SAP BW Info Cube data sources. The SAP Business Explorer initially became popular as an alternative for slow wide area network (WAN)–connected sites; the BEx web-based user interface, called the BEx browser, was much more efficient than dumping data from Info Cubes located in a company data center to a desktop on the other side of the world.

Today, BEx is in maintenance mode. It grew more powerful over the years, eventually offering robust report formatting and ad-hoc analysis capabilities. By April 2013, though, it simply could not compete with the higher-end SAP BO reporting options previously described. SAP Business Explorer is still a mainstay for many organizations uninterested in retooling their reporting methods, though, which is why we included it here.

SAP ERP Operational Reporting Tools

SAP has developed or acquired numerous tools over the years to meet an organization's operational reporting requirements. Some of these include Web Intelligence (outlined previously), SAP Report Painter, ABAP List Processing (ABAP programming), ABAP Query Reporting, and Ad Hoc Query Reporting. The following sections discuss some of these.

SAP Report Painter

Popular for many years, SAP Report Painter was an upgrade to the old SAP Report Writer that shipped with SAP R/3. It helped fill the gap when SAP's standard FI and CO reports proved inadequate for a business user. Its graphical front end and ability to quickly create simple reports made it useful in a time when such reports required dedicated programmers and weeks or months of development and testing time. SAP Report Painter required predefined reporting structures, but once those were set up, it was possible to create groups of reports, call up other data sources (including other reports or via ABAP queries or master data queries), apply custom headings, create custom (though limited) graphics, and more. Still used in some cases, SAP Report Painter has been largely replaced by SAP BO Crystal Reports, SAP BO Xcelcius Enterprise, and other more modern alternatives.

ABAP List Processing

Custom reports can be created in SAP by writing ABAP code to generate lists. This method is called list processing. Using list processing, ABAP programmers write statements in the ABAP Editor to query the database and generate reports. Writing reports using ABAP list processing is therefore rather technical in nature and subsequently relegated most often to the post-go-live technical team.

This option becomes viable when you require information that the canned reports cannot provide. This option is also used for creating interface files or files that provide input to (and thus feed) external systems. For example, if you need your SAP system to connect to an external enterprise system such as an outside third-party bolt-on product, you might consider using the ABAP list processing method to write a report and then have the output transmitted to the external system.

Legacy SAP Reporting Options

We debated whether to include some of SAP's oldest built-in reporting options and decided we should provide at least a bit of insight into long-time products that often still play a role in an organization's overall reporting framework. These products include Structural Graphics, Executive Information System, SAP Information System (or Report Trees). General Report Selection, the ABAP Query and SAP Query, and SAP QuickViewer, which are described next.

Structural Graphics

Structural Graphics is an additional human resources tool used in the Organizational Management application component. This method enables you to display and edit the structures and objects in your organizational plan and to select reports directly from the graphical structure for an object.

Executive Information System

The Executive Information System (EIS) is just what it sounds like: a reporting tool tailored for high-level decision making. EIS is old but useful for users who require quick access to real-time information found in SAP ERP (and do not want to spend the time and expense necessary to deploy a full-fledged data warehouse, analytics and reporting system, or SAP BusinessObjects reporting solutions). Using the EIS report portfolio, you call up a hierarchy graphic defined for access to your own report portfolio. You can also use the report selection, in which you call up either the general report tree of drill-down reports or your own custom tree. Or you can use the Report Portfolio report, in which you enter the name of an individual report portfolio and then display it.

SAP Information System (Report Trees)

Most of the reports you need are available within each module. That is, each module contains its own information system that houses reports specific to that module. In earlier hours, you reviewed some of these module-specific information systems. One example is the SAP ERP Human Resources information system. Note that you can access all canned SAP reports via the general SAP information system.

General Report Selection

SAP has many tools within SAP ERP and other components that you can use to extract and then present data in the form of reports. In the past, basic reporting capabilities were afforded through the transaction code SART or by navigating via the menu path Information Systems, General Report Selection. In newer SAP releases, SART is not available directly; instead, you use SARP to access report trees.

Executing Reports

You can execute reports directly from the General Report Selection screen. Depending on the modules currently installed on your SAP system, different reports are available. Double-clicking a report icon launches the selection screen for the report. Selection screens are used by most SAP reports to enable an end user to clarify the output desired by entering precise input data (such as a payroll period, personnel number, reason for running a particular payroll cycle, and so on).

Once the input data is provided, execute the report by clicking the Execute button on the toolbar (or pressing the F8 key). The report executes, and output appears on the screen. This output can be viewed, saved electronically in Microsoft Word RTF format or Microsoft Excel XLS format by executing %pc in the transaction dialog box, or printed.

Searching for Reports

The general selection tree has a search function in which you can enter search criteria and search for a report based on its name. From any starting point in the tree, use the menu path Edit, Find, Nodes. You are presented with an SAP Find dialog box. Enter your search criteria (for this example, enter the word ledger).

After you type your search criteria in the Find box and click the Find button, a new Find window displays the results of your search. The new window includes hot keys (sometimes referred to as hypertext in SAP documentation) that link the text to the corresponding reports so that you can jump directly to the report. If no reports matched your search criteria, you receive a message box indicating that the search has been unsuccessful.

Selection Screens

Selection screens are presented when you execute an SAP report. The selection screens are useful in delimiting precisely which output you seek (to avoid huge reports). For example, to generate a list of all open purchase orders, execute a report listing your company's purchase orders and indicate on the selection screen that you want to display only orders with the status Open. In some cases, though, each time you execute a report, you are looking for the same specific data. In such a case, you need to fill in the selection fields on the screen for the data you desire. To assist you in this task, SAP makes use of a concept called variants.

Output Lists

After generating a report in SAP, you can save the output as a list. On all report output screens, list options are available that enable you to save the file in Office, a report tree, or to an external file (such as Microsoft Word or Excel). Save the list using the menu path List, Export, and then choose Word Processing, Spreadsheet, Local File, or XML.

Note the distinction between a report and a list. A *report* generated at any time in the system contains real-time data at the time of generation. A *list* is saved output from a previously generated list and does not reflect the real-time data in your SAP ERP system. In other words, lists are static, whereas reports are dynamic.

SAP's Earliest Reporting Tools

In the earliest versions of SAP, two tools were delivered for end-user reporting within the SAP ERP system itself. ABAP Query (now called the SAP Query) was designed for all modules, and Ad Hoc Query was designed exclusively for the Human Capital Management module. You can still create custom reports in SAP ERP by creating queries using the ABAP Query tool. ABAP queries are based on logical databases, functional areas, and user groups. Similarly, Ad Hoc Query is a reporting tool that was created to be used with the original SAP R/3 Human Resources (HR, later called HCM). Like the ABAP Query tool, it was initially based on logical databases, functional areas, and user groups: As the name implied, it enabled queries used in an ad-hoc manner to query the SAP database. The output from such a query could then be formatted into a report.

Today's SAP Query and its features have been enhanced. In addition, the Ad Hoc Query tool can now be used with all modules in SAP, under the name InfoSet Query (although in the Human Capital Management module, SAP still refers to it as Ad Hoc Query). Both reporting tools enable you to create reports within your SAP environment, and neither requires any technical skills.

SAP also introduced another tool, the QuickViewer. These legacy query tools (SAP Query, InfoSet/Ad Hoc Query, and QuickViewer) are built on three main components:

- ▶ Query groups (/nSQ03)

- ▶ InfoSets (/nSQ02)

- ▶ Administrative decisions (company specific)

Each component permits a user with no technical programming skills to create custom reports. Custom reporting in SAP 20 years ago meant having a programmer sit down at a terminal and type lines and lines of ABAP code to pull data from the SAP database to create a report. The programmer would have to account for security access, output, formatting, and so on. The purpose of the newer SAP-delivered query tools is that all the work is done behind the scenes, without the need of a programmer. The use of the three main components holds it all together, as outlined next.

Query Groups

A *query group* is a collection of SAP users who are grouped together. A user's assignment to a user group determines which queries he or she can execute or maintain. In addition, it designates which InfoSets (data sources) the user can access. Basically, query groups permit users to create, modify, and execute reports in a certain area within SAP ERP. For example, you can create a query group for the Finance department that includes your financial users; similarly, you can create a query group for the Human Resources department that contains reports specific to Human Resources. Using query groups is an easy way to group and segregate your reports.

Query groups are often maintained by the system administrator and are created on the Maintain Query Groups screen, which you can access by running transaction code /nSQ03. Users can belong to multiple query groups and might, under certain circumstances, copy and execute queries from other query groups (only if the permissions are the same). Any user within a user group has authority to execute queries that are assigned to that group, but only users with the appropriate authorization can modify queries or define new ones. Users cannot modify queries from other query groups. Although maintaining query groups is usually a task for a system administrator, we show how to create a sample user group later in this section.

InfoSets

InfoSets (known as *functional areas* in the early days of SAP) are the second component of SAP reporting. InfoSets are created on the Maintain InfoSets screen, which you can access by running transaction code /nSQ02. InfoSets are areas that provide special views of logical databases and determine which fields of a logical database or data source can be evaluated in queries. Basically, an InfoSet is the data source; it's where you get the data to use in your reports. InfoSets can be built on a variety of sources, but the most common is the use of what is known as a logical database. Recall that writing reports without query tools requires a programmer to write code that goes into the main SAP ERP database and retrieves the records it needs. This is no easy skill. SAP's answer to this issue is the logical database.

Logical databases are rational prearranged groupings of data from multiple related tables that are indexed. In lay terms, logical databases place all the fields you want to report on in an easy container from which you simply select the fields you need to include in your report. Although maintaining InfoSets is usually a task for a system administrator, you'll learn how to create a sample InfoSet later in this section.

Administrative Decisions

Creating query groups and InfoSets is an easy task. Before you begin, you must first review the following administrative decisions to see which best applies to your organization:

▶ What is your client/transport strategy?

▶ Will you use the standard or global query area?

With regard to your client transport strategy and custom-coded ABAP reports written by programmers, the traditional methodology for report creation is as follows: A programmer accesses a development environment where the first draft of the custom report is coded. The report is then transported to a testing client where it is tested. If it passes testing, the report then moves on to your production environment for use. This methodology differs from the strategy often used with the query family of reporting tools. The addition of the query tools to SAP enables end users with no technical skills to create reports in real time. It is with this in mind that your organization has to make a decision regarding its transport strategy.

The creation of query objects can be performed in any client. However, you should follow some best practices. For starters, end users who will be using the query tools often only have user IDs in the live production environment. Therefore, many companies maintain query groups live in the production client.

Depending on your SAP authorization privileges, you might need to request assistance from your system administrator in creating a test query group, functional area, and query. It is also possible, if you are working with a newly installed SAP system, that you will receive a message saying you must convert objects first. If you receive this message, contact your system administrator. He or she will be required to perform a standard administration function to convert the objects before you can proceed.

Similarly, InfoSets can be created in any client; however, best practice dictates that InfoSets be treated consistently with normal programming methodology. It's best to create InfoSets in a development environment and then transport them to a test client, where they are tested and then moved on to production for use. InfoSets are treated differently because a trained user has the capability to add special coding or programs to InfoSets (which is beyond the scope of this book) that can have an impact on system resources or functioning, and testing them is required in those cases. That leaves the reports (queries) themselves. Unlike custom-coded ABAP reports, query reports are designed to be made in real time, in an ad-hoc fashion, so the best practice is to create your queries live in your production environment.

After determining your client/transport strategy, the second administrative decision you need to make is to choose a query area. SAP supports two:

▶ **Standard query areas, which are client-specific and available only within the client in which they were created:** For example, if you created a standard query in the production client, it exists only in the production client. You can transport query objects created in the standard area between multiple clients on the same application server via the Transport Truck function on the main InfoSets screen (SQ02). This bypasses the customary Workbench Organizer.

▶ **Global query areas, which are used throughout the entire system and are client-independent:** SAP delivers many of its standard reports in the SAP global query area. These queries are also intended for transport into other systems and are connected to the ABAP Workbench. A common best practice is to allow SAP to continue to deliver reports via the global area and for end users to use the standard query area to create query-related reports. With your administrative decisions completed, you are ready to begin the configuration.

SAP Query

Create and maintain SAP queries through the Maintain Queries screen in SAP ERP, accessible via transaction code SQ01. Unlike query groups and InfoSets, which are often maintained by system administrators, SAP queries are primarily maintained by trained end users (after the configuration steps are complete) and power users.

Only users with the appropriate authorizations can modify queries or create new ones. Security for managing query reporting is available on a couple different levels. Besides the user group segregation, there are also authorization group specifications. Security configurations are very customer specific; contact your systems administrator to learn more about your company's security configuration.

InfoSet (Ad Hoc) Query

Unlike SAP Query, InfoSet Query is designed for basic users to retrieve simple single-use lists of data from an SAP ERP database. Using this tool, all query information (including the selection criteria) is available on a single screen. Since version SAP R/3 4.6, the Human Capital Management module reporting tool, called Ad Hoc Query, was combined with the technology of SAP Query and made available for all modules. It's now called InfoSet Query (although it is still referred to as Ad Hoc Query when executed for HR reporting). This section refers to it as InfoSet (Ad Hoc) Query; the functionality is the same regardless of its name.

You can use InfoSet (Ad Hoc) Query to quickly answer simple questions, such as how many employees received stock options last year, or to create a comprehensive report for printing or downloading to your PC. InfoSet (Ad Hoc) Query is designed so that users can pose questions to the SAP system and receive real-time answers. Other sample questions you might pose using an Ad Hoc Query include

- How many employees are over the age of 48?

- Which invoices are charged to cost center 851118?

- How many widgets were available for delivery on July 29, 2015?

InfoSet (Ad Hoc) Query is a helpful tool that your functional users can use to retrieve important, comprehensive information quickly and easily. When the one-time configuration is completed, creating an InfoSet query is a relatively elementary task.

SAP QuickViewer

The SAP QuickViewer tool is one of the earliest "what-you-see-is-what-you-get" (WYSIWYG) visualization utilities for quickly collecting data from your SAP ERP system. To define a report with QuickViewer, you simply enter text (titles) and then select the fields and options that define your QuickView. Just as SAP Query creates queries, QuickViewer creates QuickViews. QuickViews are not as handy as queries, however; they cannot be exchanged among users. The good news is that they can be converted to queries to be used with the SAP Query. Use QuickViewer to quickly answer simple questions. Like SAP queries, InfoSet (Ad Hoc) queries are built on the foundation of query areas, query groups, and InfoSets.

When the one-time configuration is complete, creating a QuickView is also a relatively elementary task. As with the SAP queries discussed earlier, QuickViews can be run in Basis or Layout (Graphical) mode. In Basis mode, the system automatically renders the report from parameters. In Graphical mode, a user can tweak the report's interface via a visual tool.

Summary

The reporting knowledge learned in this hour might be the most meaningful end-user takeaway from this book because it makes it possible to truly use SAP to run a business. Keep in mind that trial and error is required for becoming accustomed to working with SAP's reporting options. Finally, although it would be nice to depend on SAP's latest reporting solutions and tools acquired through BusinessObjects and other acquisitions, in the real world, many companies still rely on SAP's breadth of legacy tools, many of which are described in this hour.

Case Study: Hour 13

Consider this case study and the questions that follow. You can find answers to the questions related to this case study in Appendix A, "Case Study Answers."

Situation

MNC just hired a new director of finance who is also an SAP novice. She has asked for someone on the MNC Enterprise Reporting team to help her review the reporting options within SAP ERP Finance. Lucky you, your Enterprise Reporting Manager assigned you to the job! Help your new director get up to speed.

Questions

1. What are the three types of reporting users outlined this hour?

2. Name at least two examples of visualization tools outlined this hour.

3. Which SAP BO tool provides the ability to pull true business intelligence insight from existing reports or serve as a BI mashup tool?

4. Which SAP reporting options are associated with SAP NetWeaver Business Warehouse?

5. With which SAP application are most of SAP's legacy reporting options associated?

Using Simplified Finance and Office Integration

What You'll Learn in This Hour:

▶ What SAP Simple Finance actually simplifies

▶ SAP Simple Finance's capabilities and features

▶ Integrating SAP with Office applications

▶ SAP with Microsoft SharePoint

▶ Using archiving and forms with SAP

We start this hour with Simple Finance (sFin), SAP's newest incarnation of enterprise book-keeping, enabled by HANA technology. We demonstrate how sFin significantly eases the job of financial accountants and controllers by eliminating the pain-in-the-neck job of manual reconciliation at month-end closings. Also, because most corporate work is still done on "the desktop," the second half of this hour provides guidance around how to download data from SAP systems, easily import that data into Microsoft Excel, create form letters in Microsoft Word with addresses from SAP CRM or HCM, import SAP data into Microsoft Access, and integrate SAP with Microsoft SharePoint. We close the hour with an overview of common forms management and archiving solutions.

SAP Simple Finance Add-On

SAP Simple Finance, or the SAP Simple Finance add-on for SAP Business Suite powered by SAP HANA (as SAP officially refers to it[1]), resulted from a redesign of FI/CO initiated by Hasso Plattner to leverage the power of HANA. As a replacement for the classic SAP Finance (FI) module, Simple Finance (sFin)[2] uses SAP HANA calculation views to run trial balance sheets, profit and loss statements, and cash flow analyses on-demand, any time of the day and any day of the quarter.

---

[1] See http://help.sap.com/saphelp_sfin100/helpdata/en/cb/f6d652b072ff25e10000000a4450e5/frameset.htm.

[2] See http://scn.sap.com/docs/DOC-59882

The main difference between the classic ERP 6.x Finance module and sFin add-on is the evolution from a system with separate datasets for external finance (FI) and internal controlling (CO) transactions into a system with a single dataset where finance and controlling data are matched into a joint database. This way, a "single source of truth" is presumably established for internal and external accounting, down to the single line item. Through this single document process, there is no longer a need for tedious financial reconciliations.[3]

In Hours 3, "SAP Technology Basics," and 5, "Overview of SAP Applications and Components," we discussed how the HANA architecture enables the processing of millions of database records in mere milliseconds. This amazing performance is best put to use in modules that handle very large quantities of detailed transactions, such as the Finance (FI) and Controlling (CO) modules of SAP's Enterprise Core Component (ECC), the foundation of SAP ERP.

The FI and CO modules have been notorious over the years for requiring complex customizations to process the volumes of transactions they drive; FI and CO developers have spent the past few decades trying to optimize these modules by using aggregates based on time, header/line item, hierarchies, indexes, and archives. It's finally possible to start tossing out these expensive customizations.

The Old ERP World

In a traditional ERP environment such as SAP ECC, accountants handle incoming documents on a daily basis and record them in the system. If a document is related to Primary Costs, for instance, both the line item table (COEP) and the totals table (COSP) in the SAP ERP database will be updated (see Figure 14.1).

Frequently, managers run reports, read the aggregates or index tables to analyze these primary costs, and then drill down to the line items for details. In this case, users need access to both tables. This architecture accesses less data at a time and therefore is better suited for an environment where the database is a bottleneck.

The Ideal World

Given the performance potential of HANA, we can easily identify redundancies. Imagine now a perfect environment in which the performance of the database is not limited, and totals can be calculated on the fly. In this case, the aggregate table wouldn't be needed. The view shown in Figure 14.2 looks much cleaner, right? This can easily be achieved by extending the line-item tables with all the fields from the header table. This eliminates the need for all the redundant aggregate tables and index tables. With HANA's column store architecture, the line items can be

---

[3] Content of this section provided by Julien Delvat; see his blog post to comment http://scn.sap.com/community/epm/financial-excellence/blog/2014/09/18/implementing-sap-simple-finance.

retrieved quickly and aggregated on the fly. Imagine how your database could be slimmed down by removing all totals and indices, and the potential performance gains in both the data entry and analysis tasks!

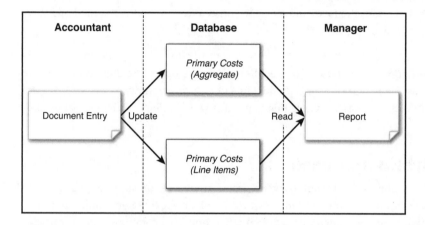

FIGURE 14.1
Reports and database access in a traditional ERP environment.

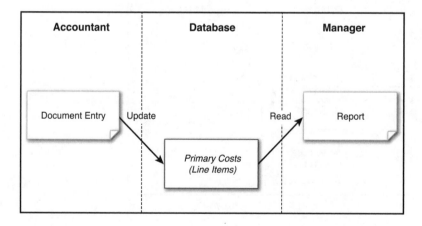

FIGURE 14.2
Reports and database access in an ideal ERP environment.

Unfortunately, this ideal world has some limitations. First, all the reports and programs would have to be rewritten to select from line-item tables instead of aggregates, which, in SAP's case, could easily take years. Second, some information cannot be stored as a line item but requires a summary level.

For instance, imagine a customer requiring a purchase order for 1,000 widgets to be shipped in boxes containing 100 widgets each month. Every month, the manager needs to know how many were sent (a simple summary of shipment line items) and how many are left to be shipped. If only the line item table exists, the following questions arise: Where shall the required quantity be stored? Where can it be decremented?

These may sound like exceptions, but they are, in fact, common for all planning scenarios or setting targets usually done in some form of aggregation. Common aggregate dimensions include a cost center group, cost element group, or a product line or customer family, as well as WIP (work in progress) transactions. For these, a single line-item table wouldn't be sufficient; a better solution is needed.

sFin: The Hybrid Approach

In order to solve the double issue of redoing the programs and values on summary data, the SAP development team came up with a hybrid architecture, in which the line-item values and the summary-specific values are separated into different tables and then combined into a consolidated view (as shown in Figure 14.3).

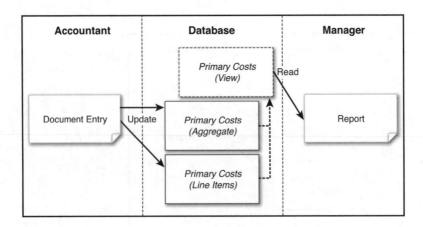

FIGURE 14.3
Reports and database access in sFin.

It is important to understand that these new views (technically called CDS views) are automatically generated by sFin during installation and guarantee the continuity of all existing programs, standard (variance, assessments, settlement, etc.) or custom, while reducing the database footprint and boosting the overall performance. As Hasso Plattner himself said in his blog, "It is the by far the biggest improvement in the history of SAP's enterprise systems."[4]

Reduce Reconciliation Efforts

As discussed earlier this hour, removing the totals tables speeds up all financial process, and the critical period-end close is no exception. But the redesign of the core didn't stop there. Indeed, accountants spend a lot of time during the short period-end window reconciling FI and CO.

A typical case is the rework needed when corrections are done in the ledger and subsequent cost allocations have to be reverted and reprocessed. In order to avoid this situation, the FI and CO documents have been merged 1:1 at the line-item level into a "logical document." With this new architecture in place, the internal and external reporting is harmonized, and the reporting and analysis can be performed with more flexibility, given the smooth link between FI and CO (see Figure 14.4).

Unified Financial and Management Accounting

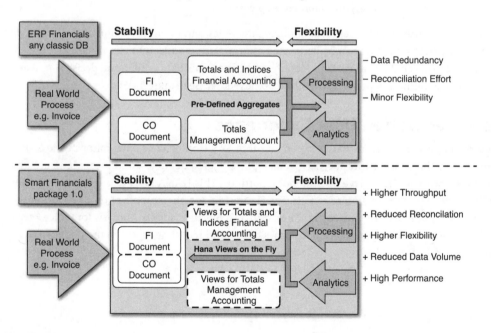

FIGURE 14.4
Consolidation of separate FI and CO documents to a unified logical document (courtesy of SAP).

---

[4] See https://blogs.saphana.com/2013/11/03/massive-simplification-case-of-sap-financials-on-hana/.

For instance, every company running account-based CO-PA needs to collect FI documents at the end of the period and use them to perform managerial accounting activities like top-down distribution. Financial accountants spend huge amounts of time reconciling between CO-PA and FI-GL. Thanks to the logical document introduced with sFin, the account-based CO-PA integration mechanisms can be used in real time; there is no need for reconciliation anymore, and several steps can be skipped at each month's end. However, be aware that sFin does not yet support costing-based CO-PA.

Eliminating Financial Closings Bottlenecks

The financial close is complex because of the sheer number of processes to run, as well as their interdependencies. From a high level, the financial ledger needs to be closed, then all orders need to be settled and their WIP calculated. Finally, the cost allocations need to be performed in order to calculate customer/product/corporate profitability before data can be exported to the data warehouse for reporting and analysis. That has to happen for all entities before moving to the corporate level. Only after this long process (which leads to the publication of reports) can any error or discrepancy be found. Potentially, several of the batch programs might need to be reverted and rerun until everything matches up correctly.

With SAP sFin, thanks to the removal of aggregate tables and the introduction of the logical document, the period-end close can be performed on a recurring basis, and reports can be published in real time. This enables analysts to identify and correct mistakes earlier and decision makers to correct course during the period rather than 30 days later (see Figure 14.5).

Next-Generation User Experience

FI users will also enjoy the new user experience that SAP Fiori delivers once connected to SAP sFin. The key difference is that the CDS views replace aggregate tables, and these views are also integrated into SAP HANA Live operational reporting.[5] This HANA layer acts as a content publication service for the creation of reports. See Figure 14.6 for an example of an SAP Fiori dashboard. With new tools like Lumira, Explorer, and SAP BusinessObjects Analysis for Office,[6] users can easily discover and analyze large volumes of data, in real time, down to the line item, as demonstrated in Figure 14.7.

---

[5] See http://scn.sap.com/docs/DOC-59928.

[6] See http://www.sap.com/pc/analytics/business-intelligence/software/data-analysis-microsoft/index.html.

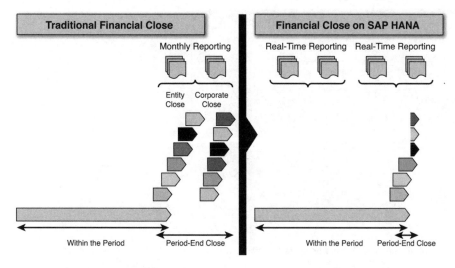

FIGURE 14.5
Traditional financial close versus financial close using SAP HANA (courtesy of SAP).

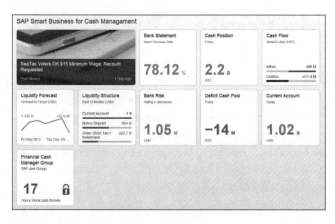

FIGURE 14.6
SAP Fiori dashboard in SAP Smart Business.

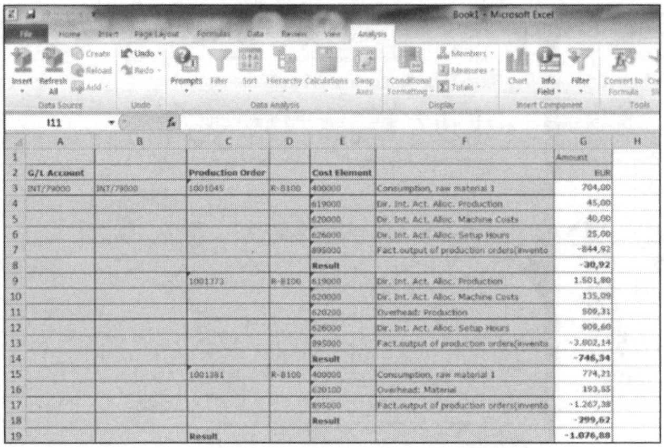

FIGURE 14.7
WIP analysis with SAP BusinessObjects Analysis for Office.

Now that you understand the value that SAP sFin can provide to your organization, the biggest hurdle that lies ahead is how to migrate from your current FI/CO environment to SAP sFin. Two options are available:

▶ Using sFin as a central ledger

▶ Moving from Business Suite to HANA and implement the sFin add-in

sFin as a Central Ledger

Many large organizations maintain more than a single ERP. This situation is usually the result of performance trade-offs (smaller ERP systems based on region, for example), history (the result of mergers or acquisitions), or legal requirements (such as the strict laws in some countries forbidding sensitive data to be stored out-of-country). In order to achieve an overall company-wide view of such a spread-out organization where operations have been essentially localized, financial data must be collected and centralized for reporting.

However, this process is very slow, doesn't allow real-time decisions at a high level, and presents a disconnection between the aggregated results in the central repository and the line items stored in decentralized locations. SAP sFin can help solve this dilemma because it can collect all of the financial information from the various decentralized source ERP systems in real time.

This non-disruptive solution can be deployed in the cloud or on-premise, too, giving organizations the flexibility to deploy sFin quickly or in line with their standard SAP deployment practices (see Figure 14.8).

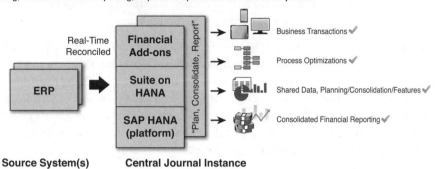

FIGURE 14.8
SAP sFin as a central journal (courtesy of SAP).

From Business Suite to sFin Add-in

If your organization is maintaining a single ERP environment, or only a few ERP instances, a better solution could be to migrate from traditional SAP ERP Business Suite to HANA and add sFin. To do this, you would have to perform a migration of your underlying database to SAP HANA before installing the sFin add-in. Check the documentation for more details on the requirements (see Figure 14.9).

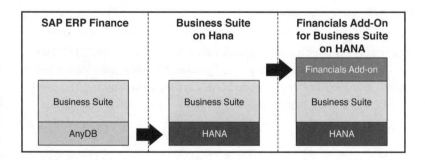

FIGURE 14.9
Migrating from traditional Business Suite to sFin.

Integrating SAP with Desktop Applications

For many years, familiar applications such as Microsoft Excel, Word, Access, and so on have been able to connect to SAP and download SAP data using a simple technology called object linking and embedding (OLE, pronounced "oh el ee" or "oh lay").

Microsoft SharePoint, Exchange, Outlook, Visio, various database sources, and more have been added to the list of Microsoft products that can integrate with SAP. Using OLE, you can take data out of a SAP system and place it into another system, all the while maintaining the format and integrity of the data. For example, you can view data residing in any number of SAP database tables as a series of columns and rows in Microsoft Excel; this provides an easy way to view and manipulate data otherwise trapped in the SAP database as a difficult-to-decipher collection of numbers and words. This is accomplished through the SAP Assistant.

The SAP Assistant

The SAP Assistant is an OLE interface used for calling SAP functions and transactions from non-SAP applications. The SAP Assistant exposes both ActiveX controls and OLE object classes, for logging in to SAP, managing data and tables, calling functions and transactions, and more. Beyond the Microsoft Office suite of OLE-compatible applications, the SAP Assistant also supports

▶ Google Docs and Spreadsheets

▶ Corel Office, including Paradox

▶ Star Office

▶ Lotus SmartSuite

▶ Various web server development environments

Actually, all modern application development languages in use today support OLE. This includes the old-school C++ programming language, the latest and greatest Microsoft .NET Visual Basic offerings, IBM's WebSphere Information Integrator, and SAP's Sybase PowerBuilder. The developer of almost any non-SAP application can create objects capable of accessing information in SAP.

Using %pc to Download Data

Another easy method of pulling data out of SAP involves executing %pc in the SAPGUI's transaction dialog box; simply type in the characters %pc in the transaction dialog box (see Figure 14.10) and then press Enter. A pop-up menu appears, giving you a choice of several file formats and a Clipboard option (see Figure 14.11). Choose the format most appropriate for your immediate needs, press Enter, browse to the desired directory path, type the name of the output file you want to create, and then click Save to save the list data to the filename you specified. We take a closer look at several of these file formats next.

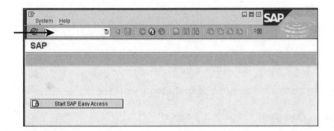

FIGURE 14.10
The box at the top of the SAP display is called the transaction dialog box; this is where you enter commands such as %pc.

FIGURE 14.11
List to select the file format you want to convert your SAP data into.

Exporting SAP Data to Microsoft Excel

There are several ways to get your SAP data into Microsoft Excel. The most basic method
involves the System List function, which enables you to save lists displayed on your SAP screen.
To use the System List function to export SAP lists to Microsoft Excel, follow these steps:

1. Navigate to the SAP screen containing the list you want to output.

2. Select System, List, Save, Local File.

3. Use the possible entries help button to change the location and filename of your new file.

4. Click the Transfer button.

5. Launch Microsoft Excel and open the file.

To output SAP Query reports to Microsoft Excel, follow these steps:

1. Execute the SAP Query report that contains the data to include in your report.

2. Select the Display as Table option and then execute the report.

3. Select List, Download to File.

4. Use the possible entries help button to change the location and filename of your new file.

5. Click the Transfer button.

6. Launch Microsoft Excel and open the file.

You can also use the SAP Query tool to export data to Microsoft Excel, as follows:

1. Execute an SAP query. The options listed on the selection screen enable you to designate
   the type of output you want for your report.

2. For a basic transfer to a Microsoft Excel spreadsheet, select the Display as Table radio
   button.

3. Select List, Save, Local File to download this table into Microsoft Excel. A Save As box
   appears, enabling you to select the download file format. Be sure to select the spreadsheet
   option.

4. After the download is complete, start Microsoft Excel and open the data you have
   just saved.

5. Return to the SAP Query output screen displaying your table (see Figure 14.12).

You can use the same method to download reports or perform other ad-hoc queries.

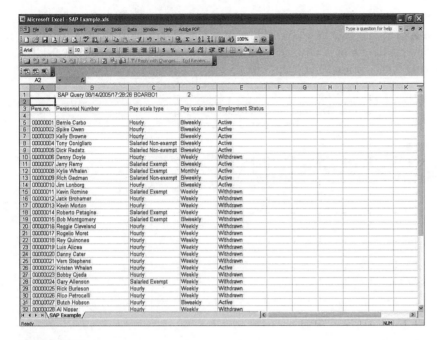

FIGURE 14.12
A Microsoft Excel spreadsheet containing SAP Query data looks the same as the data in your original query output.

Creating SAP Form Letters in Microsoft Word

SAP features a great interface for creating form letters and other documents using Microsoft Word. Let's say that you need to output SAP HCM employee data into Word so that you can create a form letter to all employees. Follow these steps:

1. Select a query to execute.

2. From the selection screen, select the Display as Table option and then execute your report.

3. When the output appears, rather than save this file to Microsoft Excel, click the Word Processing button at the top of your query output screen. Doing so opens the Word Processor Settings dialog box.

4. Press Enter to continue. The dialog box that is displayed presents you with a number of options. You can designate whether you want to create a new Word document, use a current Word document (one that is currently "open" on your system), or use an existing Word document (one that is saved on your computer).

5. Click the green check mark to begin the merge between SAP and Microsoft Word. Upon execution, SAP opens Microsoft Word (see Figure 14.13). Note that your Microsoft Word application now contains a new mail merge toolbar that enables you to insert SAP fields into your Microsoft Word form letter.

The mail merge toolbar containing
a link to your SAP fields

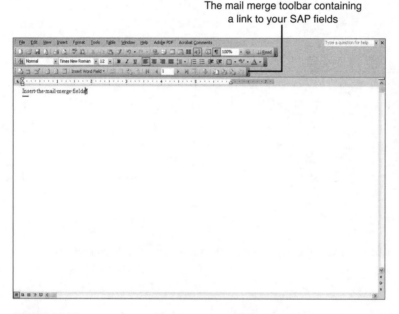

FIGURE 14.13
A Microsoft Word application launches with a new document.

6. In Microsoft Word, press the Enter key to begin at a new line and then click the Insert Merge Field button on the toolbar. In the drop-down list, you see all the SAP fields contained in your original SAP query.

7. As appropriate for your needs, select one of your SAP fields. It then appears in brackets in your Microsoft Word document. Press Enter and insert another SAP field. Type into your Microsoft Word document and then insert another SAP field.

8. To preview the output of your form letter, click the ABC (View Merged Data) button on the mail merge toolbar.

9. Use the record selector (forward and backward) buttons on the mail merge toolbar to view the various records.

As you have seen, exporting SAP data to Microsoft Excel and Word is useful when it comes to performing further offline manipulation of your data, for creating reports and graphs, or for drafting form letters. Exporting data to a Microsoft Access database is quite useful, too, especially when it comes to general reporting.

NOTE

Save and Repeat

You can save your Microsoft Word merge document for repeated use. The next time you want to use the same form letter (but with the latest data from SAP), you need to reopen the SAP query that serves as the source of the document, select List, Word Processing, and then select the Existing Word Document radio button. You are then prompted to enter the name of your Word document where you saved the file. Microsoft Word will launch, displaying your existing form letter, containing the latest data from your SAP system.

Importing SAP Data into Microsoft Access

When a Microsoft Excel XLS file resides on your local system or an accessible file share, you can import this file into Microsoft Access, as follows:

1. Launch Microsoft Access on your system.

2. On the initial window, select the Blank Database option and click OK. You are prompted to create a name and to select a location for your database. For this example, select the C:\My Documents directory and name the database mySAP.mdb.

3. Click the Create button. You then see the main Microsoft Access window.

4. To bring the SAP data into Microsoft Access, in Access select File, Get External Data, Import, and input the location and filename of the output file you saved earlier. By default, the Files of Type box lists Microsoft Access (*.mdb). You have to change this to Microsoft Excel (*.xls).

5. Click Import. Just as in the Microsoft Excel import, in Access you are presented with the Import Spreadsheet Wizard.

6. On the first screen of the wizard, click the Next button to continue. The second screen asks whether you want to create a new table or add the data to an existing table. To create a new Access database table containing your SAP data, click Next. The next window gives you an opportunity to name each of your fields.

7. Use your mouse to select each column and then type a field name for each. After you name all your fields, click Next.

8. On the following screen, assign a unique identifying number for each of your records and then click the Next button to continue.

9. On the last screen, which asks you to provide a name for your table, type something and click Finish. Microsoft Access then presents you with a confirmation window.

10. Click OK in the final Import Spreadsheet Wizard confirmation window, and you are returned to the Microsoft Access main window, where your new table is now listed under the Table tab.

11. To look at your table, select it and then click the Open button. Your SAP list now appears as a Microsoft Access table; it also includes an additional primary key field.

This process takes longer than exporting SAP data into Microsoft Excel. However, Microsoft Access is a sound reporting tool that many SAP customers use as their primary reporting tool—especially when other applications or tools—such as SAP NetWeaver Business Warehouse (BW), SAP Business Objects, SAP Crystal Solutions, Microsoft's business intelligence tools, or IBM's Cognos analytics tools—are unavailable.

Microsoft Access Report Wizard

Creating reports in Microsoft Access is easy when you use a tool called the Microsoft Access Report Wizard. This wizard simplifies the layout process of your fields by visually stepping you through a series of questions about the type of report you want to create. The wizard walks you through the step-by-step creation of a report, while behind the scenes Access is formatting, grouping, and sorting your report based on the selections you make.

To use this wizard, perform the following steps:

1. Close any open Access databases by selecting File, Close.

2. In the main Microsoft Access database window, click Reports.

3. Click the New button to launch the Microsoft Access Report Wizard (or choose the option to create a report in Design view).

4. If you are running the Report Wizard, select the Report Wizard option in the top box and your table name in the second box. Click OK to proceed.

NOTE

Comparing Sources

Exporting to Microsoft Access is helpful when you want to compare data among multiple systems. For example, if your company stores your vendor master data in SAP and also stores this vendor master data in a non-SAP application (implying that you have not implemented SAP NetWeaver Process Integration with Master Data Management), you can use Microsoft Access as a tool to quickly compare the two sources for overall data consistency.

5. In the field selection screen, select which fields to output to your report. Select a field by highlighting it with your mouse and then click the Next button to include it in the report. In Figure 14.14, the Employment Status field has been selected.

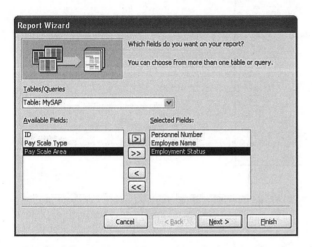

FIGURE 14.14
The Microsoft Access Report Wizard field selection window enables you to specify which fields you want to include in your report output.

6. When the Report Wizard asks whether you want to add any grouping levels to your report, select them if you are creating a report where you might want to group and subtotal portions of the output. Otherwise, click the Next button to continue.

7. Identify your sort order criteria, such as Employee Name (see Figure 14.15).

8. Specify formatting criteria, such as the orientation of the report (portrait or landscape) and the layout of the report (columnar, tabular, or justified), and click Next.

9. Choose from a selection of predefined formats for your report and then click Next.

10. Type a name for your report and click Finish to complete the creation of your report.

For users with minimal report-creation skills, Microsoft Access is a great reporting tool. Using Access, you can also include graphics in your reports, or you can create graphs and charts of your SAP data.

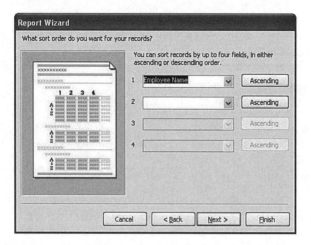

FIGURE 14.15
The Microsoft Access Report Wizard enables you to select multiple sorting criteria.

NOTE

Using Macros

If you are an advanced Access user, consider writing a macro that automatically retrieves the latest SAP download file and imports it into your existing Microsoft Access table—replacing the old data and thus automating the Microsoft Access import process. For more information about this function, search the Microsoft Access help for "automate importing." In the same way, advanced ABAP or Java programmers can write a program that automatically generates a file used by the download portion of this process, thus automating the entire SAP-to-Access reporting process.

Integrating SAP with Microsoft SharePoint

Microsoft Office SharePoint Server is often used to build a company's intranet portals and websites. There are several ways to integrate SAP data within SharePoint. This is especially useful because it enables occasional users to access data like invoices without using the SAPGUI. Though not exhaustive, this list provides a high-level understanding of what is possible:

> ▶ **Using SAP Business Server Pages (BSP) and SAP Web Dynpro:** A SharePoint developer can match the look and feel of your SharePoint site so that the output visually appears seamless to the end user. The ABAP Development Workbench (transaction SE80) allows browsing of the available BSP applications. Accessing SAP using BSP and Web Dynpro requires that single sign-on (SSO) be established between SAP and SharePoint, using a technology called SPNego (which is briefly outlined from a technical perspective in Hour 18, "SAP Installation and Implementation").

▶ **Using SAP Web Services with SharePoint Business Connectivity Services (BCS):** ABAP developers can expose data, and SharePoint administrators can pull data into SharePoint so that it acts as an information hub for a team. The list of available web services you can choose from is available in the SAP Enterprise Services Repository.

▶ **Deploying SAP Portal iViews as a SharePoint Web Part:** When you view an SAP portal page and see a table or something that resembles a spreadsheet, this is actually an iView. SharePoint supports bidirectional communications; not only can you display data from SharePoint, but you can update SAP data from SharePoint, as well. As with BSP and Web Dynpro, this functionality also requires that SSO be set up.

In addition, support for Microsoft's interactive programming language Silverlight can be used to build dynamic and intuitive business applications. Using Silverlight controls, a SharePoint site can enable Microsoft Office users to intuitively drill down into sales data from SAP ERP by quarter, region, product line, business area, and more—all without a lot of back-end technical coding or programming.

Integrating Microsoft Directory with SAP

Although this functionality is enabled at a technical and administrative level and therefore does not align to the "business user" nature of this hour, Active Directory (AD) integration is remarkably useful to SAP users. Microsoft AD provides a single security context for all users and servers. Through this mechanism, SAP servers register as objects into the directory, which in turn are search enabled. It's through this feature that SAPGUI users can automatically populate their SAP Logon Pads and quickly connect to SAP systems. AD also plays a key role in facilitating SSO. AD integration makes an SAP end user's life remarkably easier. Work with your SAP Basis team and Windows AD team to encourage this fundamental level of SAP and Microsoft integration.

OpenText Archiving for SAP

Despite the company's name, OpenText is not an open source text processor at all. Instead, OpenText Corporation provides four different archiving solutions certified for SAP:

▶ **OpenText Data Archiving for SAP:** Provides the ability to archive data from SAP to optical disc storage, fulfilling federal and other regulatory requirements regarding data storage and retention. This data can still be accessed directly within SAP, retrieving it from the optical media takes a few seconds. Many companies keep data only one or two years in the SAP database to keep system performance steady.

▶ **OpenText Archiving for SAP:** Sold by SAP as SAP Archiving by OpenText, this solution focuses on scanned documents linked to structured transactions. For example, invoices, orders, and employee documents are moved out of the SAP database to save storage space and preserve system performance; they are placed in less-expensive but still readily accessible storage.

▶ **OpenText Document Access for SAP:** Adds a federated view to all documents and data stored in SAP or another application via the SAPGUI and SAP NetWeaver Portal.

▶ **OpenText Extended ECM for SAP:** Tracks and maintains enterprise-wide data spread across multiple applications, like emails, contracts, electronic forms, various reports and spreadsheets, and so on through using SAP's standard user interfaces. This solution's ability to capture, manage, store, preserve, and deliver data on behalf of one or more customer owners within SAP makes it tremendously useful.

SAP and Adobe Forms

SAP Interactive Forms by Adobe enables the use of the ubiquitous PDF forms within SAP business processes. The two-way data communication allows users to prepopulate a form as in a Microsoft Word form letter, and feed back the input provided by the user to SAP. Adobe's interactive forms also provide the ability to apply business logic to a process and feature the ability to gather electronic signatures and apply them to the appropriate documents.

The familiar forms are simple for an SAP end user to use and complete. SAP delivers more than 2,300 (print and interactive) standard forms through different SAP solutions, like SAP HCM, SAP Financials, SAP SRM, SAP CRM, and more. SAP's customers can import these forms and customize them to adapt them to their own business processes, or they can create new forms from scratch.

Print forms are completely free of cost, regardless of how and to what extent the customers customize them or create new ones from scratch. Interactive forms delivered by SAP can also be adapted or customized cosmetically without having to be licensed. Adding, deleting, or changing the color or position of static graphic elements or of boilerplate text and deleting a form field is considered cosmetic. Non-cosmetic customizations include:

▶ Adding an interactive field on a form

▶ Copying a field from one form design to another form design

▶ Changing the position of a field on the form

▶ Adding a new image field (which calls data from the SAP application) and submitting the image location via URL in the form data

▶ Adding a new image field (which calls data from the SAP application) and submitting the image data in the form data

Forms are considered modified and are licensable if they are brought into productive use. Interactive forms created from scratch and deployed on a productive system are also licensable.

Summary

sFin is the first example of the next generation of SAP Business Suite solutions based on HANA technology. SAP says that more simplified logistics are to come. In this hour we demonstrated how significantly sFin simplifies processes for financial accountants and controllers, especially at month-end closings, by eliminating the need for manual reconciliation.

The second part of the hour provided insight into how to integrate SAP with common office applications like Microsoft Excel, Word, Access, and SharePoint. A quick look at OpenText's solutions for SAP, Adobe's Interactive Forms, and other such solutions concluded this hour.

Case Study: Hour 14

Consider this case study and the questions that follow. You can find answers to the questions related to this case study in Appendix A, "Case Study Answers."

Situation

MNC runs SAP Business Suite and Microsoft Office, and due to mergers, several ERP systems are in use. The financial department is unhappy about the overtime the accountants have to spend on weekends for reconciliation during month-end closings. The marketing department complains about the effort to generate form letters with customer addresses from SAP CRM. The customer support department looks for an easy way to let customers fill forms for complaints, and all departments are in urgent need of a document management and archiving system. As usual, the IT budget is limited.

Questions

1. How can MNC's financial department reduce the effort required for data reconciliation between FI and CO documents and help eliminate financial closing bottlenecks?

2. What are the options and preconditions for enabling simplified finance processes?

3. How can MNC's end users quickly download data into Microsoft Word or Excel, for example, without having to install additional software tools?

4. How can MNC's marketing department capture customer addresses from CRM used to generate a Word forms letter?

5. How can forms be populated with data from SAP, and how can entries made by customers in this form be fed into SAP?

6. What functionality does the OpenText ECM suite provide for SAP solutions?

PART IV

SAP for IT Professionals

An SAP Project Manager's Perspective

What You'll Learn in This Hour:

▶ SAP's ASAP 8 implementation methodology and its evolution

▶ The role and makeup of the SAP project team and its subteams

▶ How the necessary SAP leadership entities work together

▶ Other SAP project management methods

▶ Successful project team characteristics

▶ Tools and project closeout

As we found in Hour 2, "SAP Business Basics," Hour 3, "SAP Technology Basics," and Hour 4, "SAP Project Basics," there are business, technical, and project management perspectives related to implementing SAP. The project management perspective is important because it wraps up the business and technology perspectives into a single overarching plan intended to help a company ultimately realize the value of SAP's software. In this hour, we explore the project management perspective in more depth.

The SAP Implementation Methodology

SAP found long ago that without a sound implementation roadmap, its customers would typically underachieve or outright fail to realize their SAP-derived business process reengineering goals. To explain their failure, they would often blame SAP's complex software. Truth be told, SAP's software is indeed complex and surely time-consuming to implement. But the reasons for this complexity are largely beyond SAP's control. SAP is difficult to implement because

▶ Running a large business is innately complex, especially when that business involves multiple lines of business and countries.

▶ Global realities (languages, currencies, regulatory bodies, and so on) dramatically complicate matters.

▶ Business users are rarely interested in changing how they work; new business processes, applications, user interfaces, and the like seem like they will require the business users to learn more and stay at work longer.

▶ Executives and other business leaders are not inclined to naturally endorse the kinds of changes and business risks embodied by change-enablers such as SAP. They need good business reasons, excellent risk mitigation strategies, and some kind of quantifiable return on investment (ROI).

▶ Calculating an SAP project's true ROI is often subjective, if not impossible.

▶ Until recently, IT computing platforms artificially limited innovation or failed to provide the necessary technical agility needed by an organization's business applications to in turn enable greater business agility.

▶ SAP implementation teams often lack the required program management, change management, and business transformation skills necessary to pull off a successful project.

▶ The application implementation process itself is cumbersome, subject to unexpected additional iterations, and therefore expensive—perhaps double or more what was originally budgeted.

To help ensure that its software lived up to its customers' expectations, SAP had to provide a predictable methodology. As we briefly mentioned previously, that methodology was Accelerated SAP (ASAP). As of this writing, ASAP version 8 is available from the SAP Service Marketplace at https://service.sap.com/asap.

Complex projects such as SAP ERP have a significantly greater chance of failure under weak change management processes. To remedy this, initiate your project with strong alignment and commitment among all stakeholders as to how changes will be controlled, managed, and enforced throughout the project. This not only facilitates project success but also helps maintain focus on the project's value and the business problems the project was initiated to resolve.

Introduction to ASAP

Originally envisioned for smaller SAP projects (because larger projects necessitated systems integrators who typically brought with them their own methodologies), ASAP eventually became the de facto standard for describing an SAP implementation roadmap from a project management perspective. It helped organizations get their arms around what it meant to reengineer their current operating environments, organizational structures, and operational systems and processes (from both business and IT perspectives). Today, ASAP is especially focused on delivering value quickly (through new and updated accelerators, prescriptive guidance, and tools) and incrementally (rather than waiting until the end of a project to deliver all the value).

Nearly two decades after being developed, ASAP continues to be used by small and large systems integrators alike to create SAP implementation roadmaps. ASAP helps steer a project team through "quality gates" to optimize the time, people, and other resources necessary to implement SAP. Throughout its phases, ASAP provides reusable templates, tools, and training. ASAP accomplishes all this through a number of workstreams that weave their way throughout the methodology's phases. Similar to focus areas, these workstreams include

► Project management

► Organizational change management

► Training

► Data migration

► Data archiving

► Value management

► Business process management

► Technical solution management

► Application lifecycle management

► Test management

► Cutover management

Each workstream includes the latest in SAP accelerators, prescriptive guidance, and support for ASAP's different project deployment strategies, including the ability to run an SAP project as an iterative "agile" project.

A bit of modification to SAP's methodology was required to allow ASAP to deliver value faster and more predictably. Today, ASAP's phases include the following:

► Phase 1: Project preparation

► Phase 2: Business blueprint

► Phase 3: Realization

► Phase 4: Final preparation

► Phase 5: Go-live and support

► Phase 6: Operate (also called Run)

ASAP 8 has been broadly updated compared to its predecessors. The inclusion of agile and the addition of new content covering organizational change management, blueprinting, testing, training, cutover planning, updated project management tasks, and more makes version 8 adoption worthwhile. Figure 15.1 provides a view of the ASAP 8 roadmap and the time typically spent executing each phase (although, of course, the idea of running SAP post-go-live actually represents years and years). Each phase is described next.

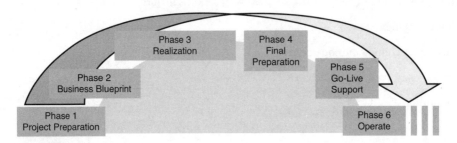

FIGURE 15.1
The ASAP roadmap helps frame an SAP implementation from start to finish.

Phase 1: Project Preparation

Phase 1 consists of the steps necessary to start a project. During this phase, the project management team is initially structured and assembled. This team then begins the process of identifying, collecting, developing, and managing all the resources and tools necessary to execute and manage an SAP project implementation. Several important milestones occur in in this phase:

▶ Obtaining senior-level management/stakeholder support

▶ Identifying clear project objectives

▶ Developing an efficient decision-making process

▶ Creating a working environment suitable for change and reengineering

▶ Building a qualified and capable project team

Phase 2: Business Blueprint

The intent of the business blueprinting phase is to help extract pertinent information about the organization seeking to implement SAP and then map the existing organization's business processes to SAP's industry best practices. The blueprinting information is collected via templates, which are essentially questionnaires designed to probe for business-specific data describing how a company currently conducts business (or how it should be conducting business). These questionnaires also serve to document the essence of the implementation. Each business blueprint document outlines business requirements and thus the groundwork for future reengineered business processes. The kinds of questions asked are germane to many different business functions and reflect data points such as the specific information necessary to complete a purchase requisition or pull together information for a particular financial report.

Tools such as the Question and Answer Database (QAdb) were originally used to facilitate business blueprint creation and maintenance; the QAdb housed all the data and thus acted as the heart of the blueprint. Systems integrators have married their own methodologies and tools to supplant the QAdb, but the process and ideas remain the same. The same holds true for the SAP Issues Database, another tool used in the blueprinting process. This database and its successors store open concerns and pending issues that relate to the implementation. Centrally storing this information assists in gathering and then managing issues to resolution, so that important matters do not fall through the cracks. The database makes it possible to easily search through, assign, and update tasks.

Today's SAP implementation teams use SAP Solution Manager (SolMan) to house the business blueprint—the primary outcome of Phase 2. Much more robust and capable than most other alternatives, SolMan provides great visibility, auditing ability, and supportability to contemporary implementations.

Phase 3: Realization

Phase 3 is about making the business blueprint a reality. This is done in two steps or work packages; 80% of the work is completed as part of the "baseline configuration," and the remaining work is completed in what's called "final configuration."

As the realization phase begins winding down, be sure that all data and rationale regarding how business processes were configured are documented; don't let all your business process knowledge walk out the door when the lead systems integrator and other partners conclude their work. This is also a good time to start thinking about how and when the company's end users tasked with actually using the system for day-to-day business purposes will be trained.

Phase 3 consumes most of a project's resources and time. After the business blueprint has been wrapped up, business function experts (called *functional experts*) can begin prototyping and configuring SAP, essentially modeling the business processes outlined during blueprinting. This phase comprises two work packages:

▶ **Baseline configuration:** The SAP consulting team configures a basic functioning system, which acts as a baseline system to later be refined (configured in more detail).

▶ **Fine-tuning configuration:** Once a baseline system is established, the implementation project team further configures the system to reflect the blueprint's remaining (typically very industry- or company-specific or complex) business process requirements.

The initial configuration completed during the baseline configuration is based on the information provided in the blueprinting documents. This configuration represents something like 80% of the system's ultimate capabilities. The remaining 20% of the configuration not tackled during the baseline configuration is completed during the fine-tuning configuration. Fine-tuning takes care of the exceptions and final tweaking necessary to meet the business's needs. As this phase transitions into the next, you should find yourself not only in the midst of SAP training but also at the tail end of what should have been rigorous functional testing, integration testing, and overall solution performance testing and stress testing.

Phase 4: Final Preparation

Phase 4 includes the necessary final preparation and fine-tuning of the computing platforms and SAP applications prior to go-live. This phase also includes migrating the last of your data from the old legacy system or systems to SAP. Be sure to complete the remaining functional, integration, and stress testing. The teams are under tremendous pressure as last-minute issues are uncovered and functionality is found to be lacking. Save any real rework for after go-live; there will be plenty of time to introduce new functionality in subsequent releases or change waves. Now is the time to ensure that the SAP system delivers the core business functionality needed to run the business.

Also take this time to perform any final preventive maintenance on the platform. Validate that the overall system performs adequately if not optimally; the system's online response time performance and the performance of critical batch jobs and reports are hugely important to end-user perceptions about whether the project is a success or a failure.

Finally, give yourself plenty of time to plan and document your go-live support strategy. Outside of typical computer operations and IT maintenance tasks, preparing for go-live needs to include preparing for your end users' inevitable questions as they start to actively work on the new SAP system. Be sure that the SAP help desk is properly staffed and adequately trained to support the new system, for example.

Phase 5: Go-Live Support

The go-live milestone itself is just a point in time: With a flip of a switch, users have access to the new system. Orchestrating a smooth and uneventful go-live is another matter altogether, though. Preparation is the key, including attention to what-if scenarios related not only to the individual business processes deployed but also to how the technology underpinning these business processes performs. Business processes need to be proactively monitored for performance. Similarly, the technology stack layers need to be monitored relative to how well each layer and the computing platform overall enables the SAP application to meet the business's service level agreements (SLAs).

Don't forget to nail down maintenance contracts and post-go-live consulting agreements. Also don't forget to document all operational processes and procedures. Fortunately, with literally thousands of successful go-live "nonevents" to their name, the support professionals at SAP and in the SAP partner community have a wealth of information to share. Additional resources are available, too, ranging from blogs, wikis, and whitepapers, to conferences, SAP publications, SAP's own online support site, and more. Turn to Hour 24, "Other Resources and Closing Thoughts," for details.

Phase 6: Operate (Run)

The operate phase (still often referred to as the run phase) is the final phase in the ASAP methodology. The goal of this phase is to ensure that the system continues to operate and perform well post-go-live. SAP helps IT organizations deliver a highly available and well-performing system through several tools, the most important of which is SAP Solution Manager.

SAP Program and Project Leadership

A typical project leadership structure for SAP implementations consists of an executive steering committee or project board headed by a project sponsor. The overall SAP project leader, also called the SAP program manager (PgM) or sometimes the SAP project director, is answerable to this committee. In turn, the core project team is headed by the overall SAP project manager (PjM). For midsize and smaller projects, the PgM and PjM roles are held by a single person.

The program and project managers are supported by a number of "bundle," or project, leads called business process analysts (BPAs). The BPAs lead specific SAP workstreams, or "rows." Examples of rows include the Order Management row, Purchasing row, and Warehouse Inventory row. As you might have noticed, a row equates to a functional business area. Row BPAs are therefore the core functional team leaders responsible for delivering a specific set of business processes via SAP's business functionality.

The Executive Steering Committee

The executive steering committee (sometimes called the project board) consists of the SAP project's key stakeholders, executive decision makers, senior business and IT leaders, and other stakeholders who have a keen interest in seeing the SAP implementation deliver value. It is this committee's ability to steer the project, given the inevitable changes both inside and external to the project, that makes it vital. The project sponsor is a key member of the committee who, along with the overall SAP project manager, provides the bulk of the project's leadership. Other committee members include the following:

▶ The committee chair, who if not the project's sponsor is probably a senior company executive with a vested interest in making SAP a reality.

▶ The leader of the organization's project management office (PMO).

▶ Key functional area or row leaders, each of whom is a high-level representative of his or her respective business area (such as finance, manufacturing, logistics, worldwide sales, and so on).

▶ The organization's chief information officer (CIO) or another senior IT representative who has the final say in IT-related matters.

▶ The director of applications or enterprise computing (or someone with similar responsibility and authority). This person is usually responsible for the legacy business systems that are currently used by the organization—several of which in all likelihood will be retired when SAP is up and running.

▶ A representative from SAP SE who aids in communications and stakeholder management and helps navigate implementation roadblocks. This person is often SAP SE's appointed program or project manager.

▶ An executive-level chief architect (who may also be SAP SE's appointed program or project manager). This person acts as the SAP technical liaison to the steering committee and is responsible for setting strategic technical direction and to some extent driving IT-related decisions.

The steering committee meets weekly or more often to review status, to quickly work through issues, and to publish decisions, recommendations, and overall opinions. Tasks crucial to the steering committee include the following:

▶ Identifying and approving the scope of the project, including inevitable scope changes

▶ Prioritizing the project among all corporate projects

▶ Providing the necessary funding and resources from the business to ensure project success

▶ Setting priorities when resource or scheduling conflicts arise

▶ Settling disputes

▶ Committing resources to the project

▶ Monitoring the progress and impact of the implementation

▶ Empowering the team to make decisions

The importance of upper management's buy-in and influence cannot be underestimated; they have a direct impact on the success of the implementation. Historically, many failed SAP projects have had unclear or divided upper-management support.

Project Sponsor

At this point, certain senior-level executives have already been convinced that implementing SAP is right for the company and its stakeholders. Other executives might still be on the fence, unconvinced that the business units are on the right track or that the investment in SAP is warranted and in the organization's long-term best interests. The project sponsor plays a key role in getting everyone on the same page. The project sponsor builds momentum, gains buy-in, and helps communicate and publicize the benefits of the project throughout the company. The project sponsor has the following responsibilities:

▶ Providing the business leadership required for ensuring that the project is carried through

▶ Leading the project board in resolving issues

▶ Acting as the champion of the board, linking end-user organizations and their functional areas to the SAP project and linking the SAP project to the firm's executive management team

▶ Helping drive much of the initial decision making regarding who the firm will partner with to implement and oversee SAP

The project sponsor is also typically involved in selecting the candidate within the organization who will lead the SAP implementation on behalf of the firm—the company-internal project leader, discussed next.

The Overall SAP Program or Project Manager

Arguably the most critical role in an SAP implementation is the overall SAP program or project manager role. This position is usually held by an employee of the systems integrator representing the company implementing SAP. The overall leader works closely with company and partner leaders to drive the SAP implementation forward. This role is critical in that this person:

▶ Sets the tone of the project in terms of leadership, accountability, role model, and more

▶ Chairs and manages the project within the company's PMO structure

▶ Acts as a single point of accountability and contact in the project board

▶ Typically holds a seat on the steering committee

▶ Controls and oversees the project from a resource and staffing perspective

▶ Oversees costs, schedule, quality, and other key project matters across the various functional areas and teams

▶ Acts as the point of escalation when business needs and IT limitations fail to mesh

▶ Maintains and communicates the pulse of the project with regard to risk and issues management, escalating quality issues, and communicating overall project milestones and status

During project execution, this leader also spends a great amount of time managing and influencing others who are responsible for blueprints, test plans and testing, training plans and delivery, and production support. This person also spends a lot of time developing the cut-over plan, which is used to methodically transition from the legacy system to the new SAP system.

The Project Management Office

An organizational structure with executive power and extensive business/IT relationships needs to provide the overall SAP implementation's project management. Often labeled the project management office (PMO), this team is responsible for developing and coordinating a cooperative environment among all the different team members so that together the team will succeed. An SAP project would likely be only one of several in flight and being managed by the PMO, but the SAP project will likely have the most attention. The PMO's leader typically reports to an executive within the business as well as an executive running the organization's IT function (such as the CIO) and would therefore be intimately familiar with the inner workings and politics of the organization for which SAP is being implemented. The PMO leader might designate a senior project manager over the triumvirate of PMs responsible for the SAP project (representing the company, the primary SAP systems integration partner, and SAP SE), or in smaller organizations fulfill that role personally. Key PMO tasks include the following:

▶ Managing scope and resource planning and validating and aligning resources and budgets to the project's goals and objectives

▶ Developing and maintaining the overall project plan and scheduling tasks

▶ Maximizing project quality, which might include escalating issues to the stakeholder committee or project board as necessary

▶ Managing communications, including monitoring and improving upon the project's progress via regular reporting and stage-wise or phase-specific scheduled meetings

▶ Managing risks and contingencies and providing direction to the project team when priorities and leaders conflict

Each of these responsibilities is explored next. In the end, the PMO provides the resources and methods necessary to help ensure a successful SAP implementation.

Scope Management

Managing scope is particularly important for the PMO. Allowing a "the sky is the limit" mentality neither serves the company introducing SAP nor the project delivery team. Without an agreed-on scope, there's just no hope that anyone will walk away happy at the conclusion of the project (if indeed a conclusion can be arrived at, given the ongoing scope creep implied by "the sky is the limit"). Scope will inevitably change, to be sure. It needs to be actively managed to ensure that scope changes are vetted properly and their impact considered broadly.

Scheduling

Effective and efficient projects are founded on accurate task duration estimates, balanced by controls, and steered by active and flexible management. Schedules created at the project's onset will change. Therefore, it's imperative that stakeholders from across the project team meet regularly to discuss what-ifs and potential schedule issues. Maintaining a well-thought-out and regularly updated schedule gives stakeholders an idea of what to expect throughout the project's execution.

The schedule communicates milestones, critical path activities, and the relative importance of resource commitments. The effects of project constraints and other potential issues give further weight to scheduling's importance. Remember that effective time scheduling requires risk assessment; buffer time needs to be allocated to tasks, for example, where the risk of an overrun significantly impacts the project's cost, schedule, quality, or risks. A daily review of the schedule is therefore probably warranted.

Quality Planning

Planning for (rather than hoping for) quality helps ensure that various project tasks and the overall project achieve their intended results. Note the difference between quality assurance (QA) and quality control (QC). QA speaks to the processes used by the PMO to ensure that the project's tasks are wrapped in quality planning and systematic evaluation activities. Conversely, QC determines how well the project's results align to known quality standards. This alignment is accomplished through regular process-monitoring activities. Together, QA and QC help ensure that problems with quality may be addressed early on by the project's leaders.

Communications Planning

In any project, the PM needs to regularly communicate the project's progress and activities to a set of stakeholders. In the same way, every member of the team needs to communicate in some form or fashion to other members and to external stakeholders, partners, and so on. Especially in the case of complex, multi-phased, and collaborative projects like SAP, good communications planning and processes are critical.

Risk and Contingency Planning

Risks are inherent in every project. Changes in scope, timing, staffing, executive support, and so on will affect the project's schedule, dependencies, costs, quality, task completion, and more. Therefore, it's incumbent upon the PM to identify key risks and other issues as soon as possible (by tracking them in a risk and issues log, for example). In this way, contingencies can be weighed and developed prior to any real emergencies.

The Project Team's Subteams

With the high-level project methodology and PMO details behind us, let's turn our attention to the SAP project team and its subteams. The design, makeup, and skillsets embodied in the SAP project team are critical to an implementation's success. Team buy-in and participation needs to encompass executive management support, underlying IT support, and especially all the firm's various business units transitioning to SAP. When structuring the overall project team, consider the following:

▶ Assess all the business areas that will be affected by the SAP installation (such as the finance department, accounting team, warehousing group, plant maintenance organization, an executive decision-making body, and so on).

▶ Identify the skills required of each team member, from managerial and leadership to professional and technical skills.

▶ Assess the members of the company's IT organization specifically tasked with supporting SAP (sometimes called the SAP support team or SAP virtual team).

The company's project team needs to include key individuals from the business groups who will be impacted by the SAP implementation and IT organizations who will support the implementation prior to and after go-live. Executive-level management support is absolutely required. Throughout the project team, members must be focused on day-to-day tactics, even as they keep central the company's long-term vision. Figure 15.2 illustrates a sample project team and subteam structure.

With a sense of the roles and tasks that need to be performed, it's now possible to organize the overall project team into the specific business and technology teams chartered with looking after their respective areas.

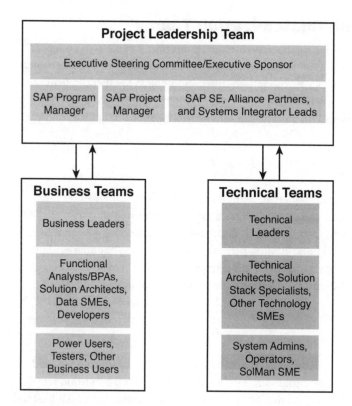

Project Leadership Team

Executive Steering Committee/Executive Sponsor

| SAP Program Manager | SAP Project Manager | SAP SE, Alliance Partners, and Systems Integrator Leads |

Business Teams

Business Leaders

Functional Analysts/BPAs, Solution Architects, Data SMEs, Developers

Power Users, Testers, Other Business Users

Technical Teams

Technical Leaders

Technical Architects, Solution Stack Specialists, Other Technology SMEs

System Admins, Operators, SolMan SME

FIGURE 15.2
With a SAP project team, business teams and technical teams should report to a central leadership body.

The Business Configuration Teams

Business process analysts (BPAs) make up various business configuration teams that are critical to implementing SAP. The number of BPAs depends on the scope of the project (that is, the applications being deployed and the specific modules or functionality being implemented). Business teams might be organized by mega process (such as order-to-cash) or by functional modules (such as SAP ERP Sales and Distribution, SAP ERP Materials Management, and so on). During the first part of realization, the business teams work on prototyping each of the business processes or scenarios described in the blueprint. One or more business sandboxes are typically used for each of these efforts. After several weeks to months, after the prototyping has been completed and the business processes modeled well (or well enough), these teams begin configuration (that is, actually configuring the SAP business processes in the SAP development environment).

The Development and Customization Teams

Developers are responsible for customizing the system to do things that it can't be "configured" to do out-of-the-box. A development team is thus employed to fill in the gaps where SAP is lacking. These developers create custom code or specialized integration points to other applications using ABAP, Java, Microsoft .NET, or other software programs and programming languages. Some of this custom configuration will go quickly, but other customizations might take many months to develop, test, and refine.

The Integration Team

The integration team is another business-oriented team focused on integrating business functionality across different applications and modules. This is critical to ensuring that the new SAP system's business processes work well across applications, modules, and technologies that, if overlooked or poorly managed, could inadvertently become like do-not-cross boundaries. This effort takes place in the test or QA environments and begins as soon as the configuration teams complete their first round of configuration. Integration testing occurs throughout the rest of the realization phase.

The Test Teams

The test teams are responsible for identifying issues with SAP functionality, performance, and capabilities. Their goal is to help create a high-quality solution. They either use existing templates or create new "use cases" that reflect each of the to-be business scenarios. As each business scenario is tested, the team discovers areas where things don't work as expected. Perhaps a certain type of customer will be unable to place a particular type of order, or a certain business unit will lack access to key information. The kinds of issues are countless and often complex, making the testing team and the process it employs one of the project's most critical. On a regular basis, the testing team reports its findings back to the development and configuration teams, where the broken configurations, customizations, and integrations are fixed (and retested).

The Data Team

While all this SAP configuration, development, and testing is in progress, another team of people focuses on data. Sometimes referred to as data architecture or information architecture, this team works to understand how data flows between business processes, systems, and stakeholders. The data specialists figure out how much of the old system's data needs to be kept, where, and for how long. They determine what needs to be moved into the new SAP system, too, including how to get it there. For example, the company might need to move a large subset of the legacy system's most recent transactional data into the new SAP system and maintain other data in a reference system to meet legal or regulatory requirements. Other data might need to be staged in a data warehouse to make it possible to view old orders, invoices, or purchase requisitions.

Still other data, such as master customer data, reference data, warehouse inventories, financial balances, and the like will need to be transformed and migrated into the new SAP system.

The Application and Platform Security Teams

A team focused on end-user roles, authorizations, and overall security will work with all the other business teams to help establish and enforce who can see, create, and change data. Similarly, a subset of the technical team works to ensure that the SAP platforms and systems are physically secured, protected from viruses, and otherwise safeguarded. Like the business team members, these security specialists get to work as soon as realization commences, and they continue to work throughout the project.

The Technical Teams

A great number of technical experts representing many different SAP technical teams also work throughout the realization phase. Many of these experts work for the SAP technology team (historically labeled the SAP Basis team). Because the number of SAP applications has expanded so greatly over the past five years, the number of requisite system landscapes has been growing every year, too. The SAP technology team plans for, installs, and manages the SAP application layer. From Ariba to Business Objects, Business Warehouse to hybris, Customer Relationship Management to Supplier Relationship Management, Solution Manager to SuccessFactors, and so on, the SAP technology team has its hands full throughout a project. Implementing any one of these applications constitutes a project in its own right, after all; technical specialists are required throughout blueprinting and design, realization, testing, go-live, operations, administration, and so on.

There's another need, too: the need to manage and navigate the fuzzy area between technology and functionality. The techno-functional team handles this, and its architects and consultants are especially important once blueprinting starts. They help the business teams communicate and work effectively with the technology teams and vice versa. While deep in neither business nor technology, they act as the bridge between the two disciplines.

The infrastructure team is another critical technical team. For in-house environments, this team is responsible for setting up the necessary servers, operating systems, disk subsystems, databases, and private cloud resources required to run an SAP application. These team members install and patch both the computing platform infrastructure and the SAP applications, starting with the business and technical sandboxes. Later, they do the same for the development systems, test/QA systems, production systems, and so on, and they carefully move and synchronize configuration updates between these systems.

Other technical teams operate the computers and other infrastructure, while still others will manage, maintain, and administer all these systems.

Many other technical teams also play important roles in the realization phase. For example, training teams prepare end users for the day when they will use the new system. Teams focused on user experience (UX) might create easy-to-use Microsoft SharePoint-based or Adobe Forms–based front ends. Other UX developers might develop apps enabling iPhone, Windows Phone, or Android-based smartphones to access SAP. Still other technologists might install remote access services so end users in low-bandwidth parts of the world can access SAP using Citrix or Microsoft Remote Desktop Services (RDS).

Project Team Member Characteristics

Regardless of the specific role a member of an SAP project team might hold, there are five key characteristics the team overall (and individuals, where it makes sense) should embody:

▶ The aptitude to assess how the new system will enable or affect individual and collective business processes company-wide

▶ The ability to identify the impact on current business processes

▶ The ability to comprehend the requirements for reengineering the specific business processes that will be handled by SAP software

▶ The knowledge to design and complete the integration of the SAP structure, hierarchies, and business process configuration across the enterprise

▶ The ability to efficiently share their knowledge throughout the implementation and serve as a willing and available body of knowledge long after go-live

With the right team assembled and ready to go, the SAP project is positioned well for realization.

Project Tools and Other Methodologies

Because ASAP has proven itself effective, most SAP implementation partners continue to use the ASAP framework or a customized version of it, if not the tools. Many years ago, ASAP evolved into GlobalSAP and later ValueSAP. ASAP was intended to be limited in terms of rigid phases; the fact that implementation phases in the real world often overlapped, or that businesses found themselves in the midst of multiple ASAP phases as a result of a geographically phased rollout, was contrary to ASAP. The newer SAP deployment methodologies therefore added evaluation and continuous business improvement to their core focus on implementation. These changes helped overcome some of the previous shortfalls.

SAP SE released an improved delivery vehicle—SAP Solution Manager (SolMan)—many years after ASAP was introduced. Today SolMan has matured considerably, offering not only multiple roadmaps to implementation but also improved content. This content includes sample documents, new templates, a repository for canned business processes, and excellent project management tools. SolMan is no longer optional, either. It's a necessary implementation-enabling tool.

SAP SolMan has built on ASAP's groundwork. Robust project monitoring and reporting capabilities have been recently augmented with Learning Maps, which are role-specific Internet-enabled training tools featuring online tutoring and virtual classrooms. With Learning Maps, the project team can more quickly get up to speed. With training and related support of the ASAP and ValueSAP methodologies replaced by SolMan, project teams do well to transition from ASAP-based and other methodologies to those facilitated by SAP SolMan.

It's important to remember, though, that at the end of the day, these approaches all amount to little more than frameworks or methodologies with supporting templates. Even SolMan facilitates only an implementation; much real work still needs to be done. However, if you are seeking to deploy well-known and mature SAP functionality and are focused on avoiding too much custom development, SolMan is a necessary component of your implementation arsenal.

Project Closeout

Eventually, every successful SAP project comes to the point where the new system is turned on, the old legacy applications and processes are retired, and the work of the project team winds down. After production cut-over and go-live, it is important for the overall project or program manager to complete or "closeout" the project. Closeout demands capturing lessons learned and documenting key project outcomes such as

- The project's objectives, including to what extent they were achieved
- Actual delivered quality of the project versus the level of quality requested
- The status and final outcomes surrounding project issues

It's also important to answer questions such as the following:

- **Project documentation:** Have all project documents been accepted and signed off by the responsible customer party?
- **Financial health of the project:** Have all payments been made or negotiated?
- **Financial outcome:** Has a final report been developed and shared with the project's stakeholders, reflecting final budget numbers and other such financials?
- **Project team evaluation:** Has an evaluation for each project team member been written and delivered?

It is also important to capture what the team learned as the project progressed. Project issues and resolutions, the status of change orders, installation and configuration checklists, and so on provide useful insight and knowledge. In addition, be sure to track and return all assets used by the project team, file or dispose of confidential or restricted materials, and close out other remaining housekeeping matters.

Finally, we have found after project closeout that companies underestimate post-go-live "maintenance mode." Soon after an SAP project is completed, it's time to upgrade, kick off a support pack cycle, or kick off sub-projects for items that did not make the core go-live. One could argue that you are never out of project mode with SAP. Be careful not to too quickly roll off resources before the necessary processes and procedures are in place to deal with ongoing SAP maintenance and support (explored in Hour 21, "SAP Enhancements, Upgrades, and More").

Summary

In this hour, we looked at SAP's updated project implementation methodology ASAP, developed by SAP to manage SAP implementations in a repeatable manner. We also outlined the structure and development of key leadership positions, SAP project teams and subteams, project management focus areas, and more. Matters of project execution and control, followed by the project closeout process, concluded the hour.

Case Study: Hour 15

Read the case study situation and address the questions that follow. You can find answers to the questions related to this case study in Appendix A, "Case Study Answers."

Situation

MNC is seeking to transition its aging human resources management system with SAP ERP HCM. Given your 20 years of project management and business experience, and your deep network of business and IT relationships across MNC, you have been selected as the SAP program manager. You need to make a brief presentation to the steering committee regarding the project's chances of success. A quick assessment before your presentation reveals the following:

- ▶ Executive leadership has no appetite for projects that last more than a year.
- ▶ MNC has a strong and proactive PMO but no available project managers.
- ▶ MNC has no available senior technical leaders or architects.
- ▶ The vice president of human resources has personal history with a failed SAP implementation at another company, and she openly shares her distaste for SAP projects.

Questions

1. How might SAP's updated ASAP methodology be useful in helping the project go live in less than a year?

2. With your IT team's lack of technical leadership regarding SAP, where should you turn for help?

3. How will MNC's PMO work toward the project's advantage?

4. What challenges do you face, given the VP of HR's past history with SAP?

5. Considering the whole situation, what initial recommendation should you make to the steering committee regarding this project?

A Technology Professional's Perspective on SAP

What You'll Learn in This Hour:

▶ Mapping business priorities to technical implementation realities

▶ Understanding the relationship between system response times and CPU load

▶ How to use the SAP Quicksizer and read SAP Early Watch reports

▶ General technical aspects of SAP system availability and security

▶ SAP Basis team staffing and working considerations

With the project manager's SAP perspective behind us, it makes sense to now look at the SAP technology professional's perspective. As a tall tower needs a stable basis, a SAP solution stack and its technical team need to provide a similarly strong foundation. After all, it's the SAP technology, or "Basis," team that will make the most impactful contributions in the near term and set the stage for the developers and configurators to ultimately create an SAP business solution. These company-internal SAP technology professionals and their hired-gun consulting counterparts are responsible for planning, delivering, and maintaining the technical infrastructure necessary to run SAP. From strategic technical architecture decisions to tactical choices related to operating the system, the SAP technology professional's job is as broad as it is essential.

Shifting Focus: From Business to Technology

After the business blueprinting and project management tasks have been addressed, the next phase in conducting an SAP deployment involves the technical infrastructure underpinning SAP's components and products. SAP Basis and other technology professionals need to identify and design the necessary SAP components to be deployed based on the business requirements outlined earlier in the project. The SAP Basis team temporarily changes the SAP project's attention from a business focus to a technology focus. Blueprinting and design work give way to questions about how to integrate the various SAP and third-party applications, the specific development and testing methodology to be put into place, and the evaluation and selection of the SAP computing platform—a combination of hardware, operating systems, and database software for starters. Many of these steps are detailed in SAP's Installation Master Guides, discussed in the next section.

Installation Master Guides and SAP Notes

Even for long-time SAP specialists, preparing to install SAP—not to mention understanding the actual installation process—is confusing. The best place to start is SAP's Master Guides. They are component specific and essential to success. Use them.

You need more than the Master Guides, though. You also need to read the many installation-specific notes (SAP Notes) related to the technical scenario you're implementing. Obtaining the guides and notes is easy. Point your browser to http://service.sap.com/instguides and then to http://service.sap.com/notes (the latter of which requires an SAP Service Marketplace user ID). To catch up with all the relevant notes is a cumbersome task because there are plenty of references to other SAP Notes. In addition, relevant information can be hidden in the SAP developer network (SDN),[1] SAP Community Network (SCN),[2] and various blogs; an Internet search can uncover astonishing helpful hints.

Take the time to read through the guides and hints to determine whether you're indeed ready to continue. Are you missing a particular piece of software? Do you have all the latest patches and updates recommended by the installation guides? Are your server and disk platform standards up to the task? These and other questions need to be addressed before moving on.

Setting the Stage: The SAP Landscape

A typical SAP environment consists of multiple SAP instances (or installations) in a landscape. Due to the fact that SAP applications are among the most "mission critical" in any company, there are good reasons to test new customizations, code, and patches thoroughly before they are implemented on the productive system. This is why a development system and a quality assurance or test system should complement any production system. Many IT organizations add a user training system and technical sandbox to this list. No SAP licenses are necessary for such non-productive systems, and the ones who don't keep sensitive data can be moved to the cloud.

Once the breadth of the landscape for each component is defined, it is important to take a critical look at how each of these various systems are architected, or "sized," as discussed next.

---

[1] See https://www.sdn.sap.com/.

[2] See http://scn.sap.com/welcome.

Understanding SAP Sizing

Before an SAP installation is performed, someone must plan for, or "architect," the SAP environment. This process gives way to designing the system, a process called *sizing*. Sizing is a balancing act between what the business wants the new system to do and the investment in resources the system needs to perform. In short, sizing is the process to find the smallest possible system to survive the highest expected load.

It is your task to translate business demand into technical parameters. Even you can use tools like the SAP Quicksizer or simply ask the experts of the SAP competency center of your preferred hardware vendor, but you have to accept that the result is bound to the adage "garbage in, garbage out." In the case of sizing, the garbage relates to the estimation of the expected load. Therefore, having a basic understanding of the principles of sizing would be helpful to avoid an over or undersized system landscape. An oversized SAP system reflects poor TCO; an undersized system can slow down business significantly, particularly when the system is needed (being used) most.

The performance of an SAP system depends on the ratio of the available resources to the actual load. An SAP user's productivity is essentially determined by the response time of the system. From the user's point of view, the response time is the period during which the user must wait after having pressed the Enter key until a system response is displayed onscreen. During this period, the user usually cannot perform any other tasks. Therefore, short response times are the ultimate objective of every SAP system. Average response times below one second are generally perceived as good, while anything longer is generally regarded as disruptive for the workflow. Good response times can only be achieved after the system starts up and the buffers are filled— that is, when the system has "warmed up." So performance is usually perceived as being slow after a reboot.

From the SAP Quicksizer and hardware vendor viewpoint, response time is the average length of time required to process a transaction. This refers to the time from the arrival of a processing request at the application server until the moment when the response from the application server is transferred to the network.[3] From the point of view of the user, response time also includes the round-trip time on the network infrastructure and the processing on the end device.

From the business departments' point of view, it is usually only the performance of production systems that matters because these systems directly influence the productivity of the enterprise. However, the performance of the development and test systems matters as well because these systems indirectly influence the project costs via the productivity of the developers.

---

[3] The CCMS transaction DINOGUI displays the execution time of the dialog step on the servers. The time displayed as DIALOG also includes the runtimes on the network up to the SAPGUI.

NOTE

In theory, your controller's dream of a resource utilization of 100% could be achieved easily if all users were forced to send their requests in regular intervals, like the load generators in a benchmark. In reality, with an average CPU load of almost 100%, the response times will be unacceptable.

Predicting an SAP System's Load

The real challenge occurs when an SAP solution is implemented for the very first time, called a Greenfield Project. Usually not much of the information necessary for a sizing is available in such projects, so most of the parameters have to be estimated based on experience and best practices.

At least the number of users and which functionality they will use should be known. The fact that the numbers of transactions to be processed scales with the number of users, can be used to make a coarse estimate of a system's necessary resources. However, we have to distinguish between several types of users:

▶ The number of licensed or named users is irrelevant for sizing because it is unlikely that all named users are active in the system at the same time.

▶ The number of simultaneously logged-on users is essential for sizing of main memory because the SAP system allocates memory for the context of each user.

▶ The number of simultaneously active users (concurrent users) is the most relevant because these users execute business processes that in turn require CPU resources, generate IO operations, and write data to disk.

NOTE

First Rule of Thumb for SAP Sizing

30%–50% of the named users are logged on simultaneously; 30%–50% of them are concurrently active.

The various SAP transactions generate very different loads because of their complexity, interaction with other modules, and particularly in the number of database tables that must be accessed. These differences are considered by load factors specifically for every solution. For sizing, users need to be assigned to the solutions they use most. ·

Not all users strain the system to the same extent (that is, create the same kind of system "load"). By their degrees of activity, the concurrent users can be classified into three categories:

▶ **Low-activity users:** Execute at least one interaction step every 5 or 6 minutes. An example is a manager whose main activity is to analyze information.

▶ **Medium-activity users:** Execute an interaction step every 30 seconds. This is the most common active user profile in the SAP ERP system.

▶ **High-activity users:** Execute an interaction step every 10 seconds. Such a high degree of activity is at the limit of human capability and occurs only in the case of users who are entering mass data.

NOTE
___

Second Rule of Thumb for SAP Sizing

A good starting point is to assume that 40% of users are low, 50% are medium, and only 10% represent high activity. (However, in SAP retail environments, these defaults are 10% low, 60% medium, and 30% high.)
___

Although for a classic ERP system, the number of employees in an enterprise represents a natural upper limit for the number of users (for example, in Employee Self-Services), this does not necessarily apply to a web shop. During a successful marketing campaign, dramatic peak loads can occur that must be processed by the CRM and ERP system before customers change to another site due to excessively long wait times.

Besides user-initiated online transactions, the sizing also has to consider the batch jobs. The general assumption is that batch jobs require fewer system resources than online transactions because they are not critical in terms of the response time. However, this assumption may not apply in all cases.

In certain scenarios, the nightly batch load can actually be much bigger than the maximum load caused by online users during office hours, and their total runtime is critical for the business. A typical example is the SAP solution for the retail industry (IS-Retail), in which the nightly replenishment-planning run absolutely must finish in time so that the trucks can be loaded and depart early in the morning. Other examples are the invoice runs in the SAP solutions for utility companies (IS-Utility), banks (IS-Banking), or insurance companies (IS-Insurance). In all these cases, the transaction load of the nighttime batch jobs is several times bigger than that of the online users. Heavy batches happening in all industries are payment runs, dunning, and financial closings. Given the fact that even smaller businesses today have subsidiaries all over the world, the night hours at the datacenter's location may be working hours on the other side of the globe.

In addition, the system design must consider the uneven distribution of the system load over time. A realistic activity pattern contains typical daily and yearly maximums. In most enterprises, there is a load peak at the beginning of lunchtime, which quickly decreases throughout the early afternoon. Managers who start a large report shortly before they leave for lunch, hoping that they will find the result upon their return, cause this peak.

Depending on the industry in question, there also might be seasonal peak loads. Examples are ice cream manufacturers, whose peak season is summer, and gift item manufacturers, whose busiest time of the year is at Christmas. Considerably more important to the system-design process than the indication of how many million orders are entered per year is the maximum number of orders that must be processed by the system during a specified window.

NOTE

Be Aware of Peaks! Averages Are Futile!

Keep in mind that the average speed of your car is less than the speed of a snail if you average your car's speed over 24 hours—considering the time the car is sitting at zero miles per hour waiting for your return at the parking lot or in your garage. However, the car manufacturer has to design the engine, transmission, suspension, and brakes for top speeds. The same is true for SAP systems. Therefore, the system sizing must consider the uneven distribution of the system's load over time. In contrast to the synthetically generated load in a benchmark, real SAP end users do not perform their transactions steadily during the day or year. So remember that averages can be manipulated to the point of being useless; focus instead on business-specific and seasonal peaks.

Be aware that several SAP solutions cannot be unilaterally sized by user numbers in principle, either because they do not have online users (such as SAP NetWeaver Process Integration) or because a single user can generate unpredictably high resource consumption (such as users running transactions against SAP's analytical solutions, including SAP BW, APO, and HANA).

Understanding the SAP Quicksizer

After all the business-relevant information has been collected, it has to be transformed into hardware architecture. The SAP Quicksizer[4] online tool is available to every SAP customer and partner to calculate the minimal necessary SAPS, memory, disk space, and I/O throughput numbers based on the input given:

▶ Every SAP application has its own requirements and therefore its own section in a Quicksizer project.

---

[4] See service.sap.com/quicksizing, SAPS user credentials are necessary to access the tool.

▶ Quicksizer does both user-based and transaction-based sizing. (The greater of the two has to be used to determine the hardware requirements.)

▶ Quicksizer assumes a moderately customized system (less than 20% customer code).

▶ Quicksizer results include a 40% security margin for uncertainties.

▶ The output considers productive systems only; estimates need to be made to size development, quality assurance, test, training, sandbox, and other non-production systems.

▶ Quicksizer does not consider resource demand of operating systems and hypervisors!

▶ Like many other software tools, Quicksizer is subject to the "garbage in, garbage out" concept; there is no check against nonsense entries.

For more details, take a look at the SAP Quicksizer Guidelines at the SAP Service Marketplace.[5] There is also a special version for SAP HANA[6] with hints and SAP Notes for various HANA scenarios.

Like the SAP solutions portfolio, the SAP Quicksizer is continuously extended and adapted based on practical experience from customer situations. To ensure that old versions are not used unintentionally, there is no offline version of Quicksizer.

NOTE
_____

Questionnaires Are a Waste of Time (Mostly)

Usually the information mentioned above is collected offline with questionnaires and later fed into the Quicksizer tool by a sizing expert from the hardware vendors. A customer requesting offerings from multiple hardware vendors has to enter the same data into practically identical questionnaires, resulting in the same data keyed into the Quicksizer several times and multiplying the work for a result that must be identical, if no typing errors happen.

The most efficient way for a customer to get comparable offerings is to enter the data themselves into the Quicksizer and select the "send also to" boxes in the results section of the Quicksizer to send the data to all the vendors considered. This ensures that an "apples to apples" comparison is done.
_____

_____

[5] Select SAP Service Marketplace, Products, Performance and Scalability, Sizing, Sizing Guidelines.

[6] See https://websmp107.sap-ag.de/hanaqs.

Beyond the Quicksizer: Measurement-Based Sizing

Fortunately, the majority of enterprises use the complete SAP suite for many years in-house or at a classic outsourcer. In this case the individual resource demand can be derived from measurement rather than fiddling around with estimations. For obvious reasons, a measurement-based sizing is by far more accurate than a Greenfield sizing because it considers all individual parameters of a company.

As part of a maintenance contract, SAP customers receive two Early Watch Reports per year or, alternatively, an Early Watch Alert on demand after a major system change. The reports focuses on the health status of the system and also shows information about the platform and utilization figures that can be used to determine the actual resource consumption of the SAP solution.

From the title page of the Early Watch report you can derive the type of SAP solution and database as well as the SAP release. From the section Performance Indicators (mostly on page 3), you get the following:

▶ Number of active users as "measured in the system"

▶ Maximum number of dialog steps per hour

▶ Actual database size

▶ Last-month database growth

Unfortunately, the number of users measured in the system has nothing to do with the concurrently logged-on or concurrently active users necessary for sizing. Actually, the numbers are calculated from the numbers of dialog steps measured and are therefore a kind of hypothetical equivalent to a standard user. Depending on the number of dialog steps per week, the users (identified by usernames) are sorted into categories: low (< 400 dialog steps per week), medium (400–4,800 dialog steps per week), and high (> 4,800 dialog steps per week). The number of active users in the Performance Indicators table is only the sum of the high and medium users. Low users are neglected. If the number of low users is very high compared to medium and high users, ten low users will be counted as one medium user.

Of much better use in determining resource consumption is the section "Hardware Capacity Check." From "Hardware Configuration," you can derive the hardware manufacturer and model of the database and application servers, the number of cores, and the amount of memory installed. The most essential section, however, provides the maximum CPU load and memory utilization derived from each server by the SAPOSCOL agent.

Together with the SAPS rating of the individual server, it is easy to calculate the maximum SAPS consumption at each server and add up the total number of SAPS the system "draws" under peak load—actually exactly the number we tried to estimate with cumbersome best practices in a Greenfield sizing.

In an ideal world, you should know the SAPS ratings of all the servers in your current SAP landscape. If you don't, they have to be derived from SAP benchmarks. In any case, however, you have to consider the effect of the SAP release dependency of SAPS numbers, as discussed in Hour 3, "SAP Technology Basics."

In addition, take the following facts into account when deriving sizing-relevant information from Early Watch Reports:

▶ The averages for response times, users, and transaction/time profiles are derived from a full week (from Monday to Sunday).

▶ The maximum CPU load is the highest average over a full hour, and the relatively small load peaks that usually cause the most trouble are ironed out.

▶ The numbers can be totally misleading in virtualized environments if an older version of the SAPOSCOL agent is used, not capable of distinguishing between multiple SAP systems running on the same server

▶ The report covers only three weeks. If a high load-generating activity like a year-end closing is not within these weeks, you miss the real peak.

Performance analysis tools from different vendors like IBM and HP have the same shortcomings because they derive their information from the same source as Early Watch Reports.

Unfortunately, the Early Watch Reports do not provide any information about the storage input/output operations per second (IOPS) generated by the system.

Be aware that the rule of thumb used by the SAP Quicksizer (0.6 IOPS per SAPS) is based on an elder scientific study supervised by one of the authors with only a few datasets of a now-outdated R/3 release. New studies in cooperation with the Hasso Plattner Institute of the University of Potsdam analyzing several million measurements from several SAP solutions show no general correlation between SAPS and IOPS. Therefore, the IOPS have to be measured for each individual SAP system using OS-level commands such as sar or tools like glance.

Can Performance Be Guaranteed?

Every business department expects the IT department to guarantee the level of performance defined in the SLAs at all times. As shown above, however, the response time is a dependent variable that results from the ratio between transaction load and available resources. Therefore, it is generally impossible to guarantee a constant response time if the system load is not constant either.

The situation of the IT department (or cloud service provider) is comparable to a shipping company that can guarantee the horsepower of its trucks but not how quickly they will get from A to B if the payload, slopes, weather, road conditions, and traffic situation are unknown. In the same way, IT can guarantee the number of SAPS available but cannot guarantee the response time of the system if transaction load and user behavior is unknown. Guaranteed response times over the Internet are completely unrealistic, as we cannot even know the route the data packets will take.

Furthermore, the unpredictability of the capacity requirements of business processes has a much greater effect than the above-mentioned technical conditions. The sizing process is based on measurements of the performance requirements for transactions, which cover only a tiny part of the whole functionality used in an SAP system.

Adding extra, generalized estimates to the main calculated estimate is the only way to allow for the influence of customizing, reports, batch jobs, and hot spots. These generalized estimates are average values for systems with average reports. Experience shows that systems with an above-average level of customization to specific requirements can differ greatly from these values.

Further, the response times for almost all transactions inevitably increases together with the size of the database. Examples are operations such as online availability checks and price determination. To return to our truck metaphor, this is the same as an increase of the load during a journey. The condition and incline of the road are equivalent to the number of users and transactions in the system. Customer-written code then corresponds to potholes, and user exits to detours.

Understanding SAP Availability

SAP systems are usually among the most mission-critical systems in an enterprise. Just as modern life depends on the availability of electricity, enterprises are dependent on the availability of their SAP solutions.

SAP application servers are normally made highly available through a combination of redundancy in the form of multiple application servers and the use of SAP logon groups. For the database server, a variety of proven high-availability (HA) solutions exist, like Oracle Real Application Clusters (RAC), Microsoft SQL Server database mirroring and availability groups, or SAP HANA system replication.

However, it is not sufficient to take care of only the hardware parts of the infrastructure to guarantee the necessary stability of a business-critical system. You also have to include IT services such as data backup, file and print services, directory services for managing users, deployment services for the installation and update of operating systems, and network services such as DNS or DHCP.

As the old adage says, the weakest link determines the stability of the entire process chain. For example, an SAP transaction can be canceled because a name resolution via the DNS service does not work or because access to a file system has failed due to 100% data volume utilization.

The example demonstrates that the stability of an SAP system is affected not only by technical deficiencies that can be solved but also by a lack of knowledge and care regarding the monitoring and maintenance of the systems.

In real life, it is often a misconfiguration that causes the DNS service to fail, and an extension not done in time is the reason a volume is used up to 100%.

How to Define Availability?

In many cases, system availability is expressed in terms of a percentage over one year. Such a percentage, however, defines only the total downtime aggregated over the year but does not reveal anything about the frequency of system downtimes. A system that loses network connectivity twice a month for 10 minutes will not make users very happy despite having an average availability of 99.9% per year. The alternative measure of mean time between failures (MTBF), however, is not totally helpful either if it takes several days to restore operational availability if an incident does happen.

A more meaningful measurement for system availability is therefore the relationship between MTBF and the time required to repair the system. Availability is thus defined by the mean time to repair (MTTR) divided by the mean time between failures:

Availability = 1 − MTTR / MTBF

Each of the many components of an IT infrastructure has its own level of availability. The overall system availability is then calculated by multiplying the availability of the individual components. The availability of a system is therefore the product of the availabilities of its individual components in a mathematical sense as well as in a practical one.

The result is that the total system availability is always lower than that of the individual components. For example, two serial components with an availability of 99% each have an availability of only about 98% (99% × 99%), which is more than a week of downtime per year.

On the other hand, by redundantly merging two components with an individual availability of 99% each, you obtain a total availability of 99.99%. This is the reason why in a Cisco UCS system, all network components are implemented redundantly by default.

The availability is then calculated as the combined probability of both components failing at the same time—that is, the product of the two probabilities of failure:

$$A_{total} = (1 - A_1) \times (1 - A_2)$$

For this we assume, however, that an individual component is still able to operate the system when all other components have failed. Therefore, several redundant power supplies do not ensure an increased availability if the power of all of them is necessary to cover the power requirements when the server is fully utilized.

The book *SAP Hardware Solutions*[7] introduces various methods that can be used to implement completely redundant infrastructures, down to the cabling level.

How Much Stability Is Required?

The terms *availability* and *stability* are often confused, but they are two different things. While availability indicates that sufficient capacity is available, stability indicates whether the business processes also run as required. Stability is something an application service provider has to cater for in addition to availability.

In service oriented architectures, the interfaces between the interconnected systems have become critical key points for the stability of cross-system business processes. Another problem with distributed but tightly coupled business systems arises if one of the involved systems must be reset after a fatal error of its database to the state before the system failure occurred, causing inconsistencies within the business process chain.

With the vision of one single HANA in-memory database as the single data repository for all SAP solutions, the consistency problem is solved at the root, at least for SAP-only implementations.

Planning for Downtime

You will inevitably need to ensure sufficient time windows for maintenance when defining SLAs. In particular, you need to take care that the time intervals between maintenance windows do not become too long. For example, if you have only one maintenance window per quarter in a 24/7 operation, this means that errors identified by the manufacturer cannot be eliminated for three months via patches, bug fixes, or corrections. Just such an error can cause unplanned downtime.

Having too few maintenance windows and windows that are too short are therefore counterproductive for total availability. The times for maintenance, like times when availability does not need to be ensured, are counted as achieved availability.

Considering Disaster Recoverability

After SAP is deployed, it is likely that the business will depend on the new system's availability for the firm's very existence. With all the firm's revenue flowing through the system and all the

---

[7] Missbach, Michael, and Uwe M. Hoffman. *SAP Hardware Solutions*, Prentice Hall, 2001.

books of record maintained in one place, it's simply not acceptable to just have some kind of plan in case of a disaster. In conjunction with business interruption or business continuity planning, a disaster recovery (DR) plan is necessary; it marries the business side of DR with technical requirements.

SAP and its hardware and software partners support many different DR approaches and solutions. Some of these are hardware specific and therefore demand attention during the sizing and architecture phases. Other "bolt-on" DR solutions can be incorporated into an SAP architecture later. Common disaster recovery solutions include the following:

► Basic backup/restore from tape or disk (an essential part of any disaster recovery plan, which may or may not include the options that follow)

► Database log shipping (configured at the database layer)

► Solutions involving storage replication technologies (for example, via your EMC, NetApp, or IBM storage systems, or directly through a database such as HANA or SQL Server, or through a special utility specifically designed to provide this capability to cloud or on-premise assets)

Well before you ever think about purchasing a DR system, spend time talking with colleagues or peers at other firms who have already implemented a similar solution. You will probably be surprised at how complex a DR solution can become once all the business requirements and technology constraints are brought to light. And turn to your technology partners for real-world lessons learned and other takeaways.

How Many Resources in Case of a Disaster?

Even if datacenters for mission-critical applications feature fully redundant infrastructures, if a disaster strikes, having a single datacenter is like having none. In case the power has to be switched off because a datacenter's raised floor has been flooded, the emergency power supply is not much use.

To reduce investments, many disaster recovery (DR) concepts stipulate that reduced resources are acceptable for a limited period in case of an emergency, as long as the system is available at all.

However, you must understand the consequences of such a reduction of resources. Having half of the CPU and main memory resources does not mean a doubling of the response time but rather that only half the number of users can still work with the system in case of an emergency.

One reason is the nonlinear relationship between CPU usage and response time, as described above. Also, a system that has only 50% of main memory left but that is used for logging in 100% of users is forced to perform massive paging, which renders the response time totally unacceptable.

The good news, however, is that the investment in the infrastructure of a second datacenter that replicates the resources in the primary datacenter by 100% can be used for all the non-productive parts of the SAP system landscape. Only a test system of the same size as the productive system can grant that the results of the stress tests replicate the behavior of the productive system. So using such a system as the target for fail-over in case of a disaster is a best practice.

Consider that investments in high availability (HA) and disaster recovery (DR) are like taking measures against fire and accidents: You accept a considerable amount of expenditure for insurance that protects against an event that you hope will never happen.

When evaluating the different solutions available in cloud architectures, you shouldn't think in terms of how much availability the company can afford but rather how much downtime it can survive.

The same is true in regard to fire drills. Just as a fire extinguisher is useless if nobody knows how to use it, a backup is useless if nobody knows how to rebuild the system from it. Doing regular test rebuilds helps ensure that a backup is usable in case it is needed.

Security Considerations

As business and IT models change, information security has gotten tougher. Traditional security strategies have relied on passwords and simple network perimeter defenses. However, with the adoption of cloud services, bring-your-own-device (BYOD) initiatives like SAP Afaria and any-time, anyplace access to sensitive information, IT infrastructure has become a porous, borderless environment. In such an environment, there is really no such thing as a network perimeter.

Attackers often exploit multiple points of entry to gain privileged access to SAP resources and steal data or disrupt systems. This is further exacerbated by the growing use of cloud services and mobile devices that, on one hand, improve productivity and cost efficiency but on the other increase an organization's vulnerability to damaging attacks.

Security must be implemented using a defense-in-depth strategy that spans internal controls and segregation of duties, points of user access, network infrastructure, and cloud data centers—all the way up the application stack.

Simply implementing firewalls between access boundaries is no longer sufficient. Modern cyber-threats often target end-user devices through spear phishing and malware campaigns designed to hijack user access to SAP resources and thus completely skirt traditional perimeter controls. Only comprehensive architecture based on threat-focused, continuous security capabilities can adequately defend SAP applications against modern cyberthreats.

Beyond external attackers, organizations must also cope with significant insider threats. The case of Edward Snowden illustrates, perhaps, the most widely known example, but incidents of insider attacks happen frequently and often go unreported. For example, in 2008, a computer technician working at a bank in Lichtenstein sold a CD with incriminating information to the tax authorities of a number of countries. Investigations into the tax evasions resulted in millions of dollars of fines for thousands of bank customers and even the resignation of the chief executive of one of the largest German enterprises.

Although the motives of an insider may vary, the challenge for IT professionals rests in discriminating which activities constitute unauthorized use or malicious intent, and which activities are legitimate. Techniques for mitigating insider threats stem from good security policy and practice, including background checks, security training and awareness, access enforcement and monitoring, and anomaly detection.[8]

While it's fair to say that no one would design a security architecture exclusively to defend one particular system or application, any SAP deployment without a proper and complete security architecture is at risk. Though it is not the intent of this book to provide instruction on building a comprehensive information security program and architecture, the guidance in this section can help identify gaps and opportunities for improvement.

You may argue that the security and network departments have to be in charge of security; however, security is everyone's responsibility. While not everyone plays the same role, everyone plays a part. Therefore, a SAP Basis professional will spend a good amount of time not only working to ensure that the SAP application layer performs well and is available but also working to ensure that it is secure. Such activities include general tasks like hardening the OS and database to repel viruses, Trojans, and similar threats. There are also SAP-specific activities such as implementing Secure Network Communications (SNC) to interface with an external security provider. Finally, the Basis team needs to be involved in safeguarding a system's physical servers and disk infrastructure from internal *and* external attacks.

Hardening the SAP Environment

In organizations where the SAP Basis team "owns" the servers and databases used for SAP, they also own the responsibility for hardening the operating system and the application.

Microsoft, for example, provides hardening guidance in the form of whitepapers[9] that document best practices for reducing the attack surface of Windows. Tools like Windows Update Server and Windows Security Configuration Wizard help administrators uniformly deploy and enforce security settings and patch levels.

---

[8]   U.S. CERT, *Insider Best Practices*; see https://www.cert.org/insider-threat/best-practices/.

[9]   See http://blogs.msdn.com/b/saponsqlserver/archive/2012/05/28/sap-on-sql-server-security-whitepaper-released.aspx.

Data Execution Prevention (DEP) is a function of Windows designed to help prevent (malicious) software from being executed in protected areas of main memory. DEP can be used to ward off some buffer overflow attacks caused by code injection (for example, MSBlaster). This setting is activated by default. However, an Active Directory service must be implemented and hardened correctly to allow these functions to apply the necessary security.

Microsoft's Active Directory (AD) can be used to centrally control and enforce security policies and configuration for both SAP and all access management requirements across an organization's IT environment. Placing SAP systems in a dedicated Active Directory container allows an administrator responsible for security to implement specific security settings on the SAP servers in a controlled manner.

The Windows Security Configuration Wizard (SCW) can create an XML policy file that contains security hardening settings. The policy can then be uniformly applied to the entire SAP cloud environment. The SCW XML file can also be converted to an Active Directory policy, allowing the configuration to be applied to individual servers or groups of servers. After uploading the standard Cloud XML security configuration policy to Active Directory, the Group Policy Editor can be used to further harden the Windows operating system. Using the Group Policy Editor Tool, check the system audit policy and adjust as required.

An AD administrator can delegate limited control of the SAP organizational unit (OU). This also allows the SAP administrator to create the <SID>adm and SAPService<SID> accounts prior to running the SAP installation program. This eliminates the need to install SAP using a domain administrator account or to install SAP using local service accounts, which is not recommended.[10]

If a SAP administrator is familiar with Active Directory, the AD team may delegate authority to reset passwords or create new accounts to the SAP administrator. In this case, the SAP administrator will only have permissions to change accounts inside the SAP OU. To prevent other policies from "undoing" SAP-specific policies, it is recommended to activate the policy block setting on the SAP container.

TIP
_____

Use a Single Policy for All SAP Containers

Use a single policy for sandbox, test, and production containers to ensure consistent behavior across all SAP systems. Extra care must be taken when extending security policies in cloud environments as they must still be unique, regardless of how wide the SAP container may scale out (and even further for hybrid cloud environments).

_____

[10] See http://technet.microsoft.com/en-us/library/cc732524.aspx.

Cloning virtual machines and then adding them to the initial pool is a common practice in cloud environments. Some properties of the new cloned VMs might need to be changed to reflect uniqueness in the SAP landscape. This requires that all previous security policies follow and cover the new VM and its users.

Many security vulnerabilities require a web browser to run malicious code on a server. As a matter of practice, there is no valid reason to have any web browser on an SAP server. Internet Explorer can be removed completely from Windows Server 2012. However, it is not sufficient to simply delete the IE directory because the code is tightly integrated with Windows. Therefore, you must follow the steps in SAP Note 2055981—Removing Internet Explorer & Remotely Managing Windows Servers.[11] With Internet Explorer removed from the Windows guest OS, you can safely ignore security patches addressing the IE issues in Microsoft's monthly security bulletin.[12]

Never Touch a Running System?

All commercially available operating systems require patching. Constant improvements to software systems and elimination of known security weak spots require the controlled implementation of patches in production systems.

Microsoft, for example, releases security patches on the second Tuesday of each month. However, it is not recommended to blindly apply all patches that are released. Each patch must be individually assessed to determine whether it is relevant. Only patches relevant for an SAP system should be implemented in production—and only after adequate testing. If patches are clearly not relevant for an SAP system, their installation can be delayed until the next planned downtime. Alternatively, the patch can be delayed until Microsoft releases the next Windows Service Pack, which will include a "rollup" of all previous security patches.

Finally, if unused components are disabled or blocked, there is no immediate requirement to patch these components. The system administrator may decide to patch during the next planned outage some months after the security bulletin is released. Often the system administrator patches unused or disabled functionality for consistency rather than security reasons. Some customers have requirements that all Windows servers be patched to a consistent level, even if the functionality is completely disabled. In such cases, the security solution may alleviate the need for immediate emergency outages even on adequately secured SAP servers.

Last, but not least, the hypervisor should not been forgotten. There are "Hypervisor hardening" guides from hypervisor vendors like VMware[13] and Microsoft[14] are worth reviewing before any

---

[11] See http://service.sap.com/sap/support/notes/2055981.

[12] See www.microsoft.com/technet/security/current.aspx.

[13] See www.vmware.com/support/support-resources/hardening-guides.html.

[14] See www.technet.microsoft.com/en-us/library/dd569113.aspx.

major private cloud implementation. These guides also provide a better understanding of the expectations for hypervisor security in a public cloud offering.

Also pay attention to SAP archiving and backup/restore. If these functions are misconfigured, the infrastructure necessary to perform these functions can be used to improperly access data. Utilities that use table-level auditing to verify by whom and when data may have been read, changed, or created can be become quite handy for security audits. Setting up and enforcing database-specific roles (such as who can access and back up the data, update database executables or binaries, or act as a database operator) are also important.

With all this is mind, take the time to establish an excellent working relationship with the organization's IT security team. Large enterprises have dedicated SAP security teams to support role and authorization management, user provisioning, power user monitoring, and user-centric segregation of duties.

In general, you have to ensure that SAP Basis professionals, computer operators, and database administrators practice the same kind of segregation of duties used to minimize end-user-derived fraud. Good checks and balances help keep honest people honest and secured systems secure.

Network Considerations

Cloud computing, global hosting providers, and end users working around the world have come together to reflect an environment where business applications like SAP depend on the network more than ever.

You may wonder why the network topic has not been discussed already together with the other technical infrastructure topics like servers and storage. You may even think that networking is not a topic for the SAP Basis team at all. And you are right: With today's 10 and 100 GB Ethernet in the datacenter and plenty of bandwidth on the Internet, network sizing is not a topic anymore. However, with SAP systems connected to the Internet, the network has become an essential part of security strategy.

From Secure Network Communication (SNC) to Public Key Infrastructure (PKI, which enables users to securely move data across unsecured networks), to single sign-on (SSO, which brings multiple applications together from a logon perspective), access to SAP is becoming easier.

The easier this front-end or end-user access, though, the more complex the back end becomes. Shared routers and switches need to be physically protected; dedicated network links connecting SAP application, web, database, and other servers together need to be secured; and the entire end-to-end network infrastructure needs to be monitored for unauthorized intrusion and managed in terms of capacity and performance. The SAP Basis team needs to work closely with an organization's IT network architecture and support teams to ensure that access, security, provisioning, and a host of other network services are performed.

The availability of SAP components through the Internet must also be addressed. The goal of all this is to provide a secure environment for the SAP servers without impacting the application's ultimate functionality. Depending on the specific situation, the network might need special firewalls or proxy servers or other such devices targeted to provide a more secure environment for SAP. On all these components, access control lists (ACLs) have to be maintained.

Within each system of an SAP system landscape, it is further possible—and often desired—to create separate network segments. Some of these might be dedicated to end-user access, whereas others might serve only the intense database-to-application server traffic, or traffic dedicated to network-based server backups. A fourth network segment might even be designated for systems management and monitoring traffic. HANA scale-out implementations demand the configuration of up to seven VLANs.

Until recently, all this configurations had to be done on a box-by-box basis, which results in configurations that are difficult to maintain and audit. It is a quite tedious and error-prone job to reconfigure IP addresses and VLANs and decipher ACLs whenever the application landscape changes.

It is mandatory to close all the open ports on hundreds of network devices when, for example, an SAP development system with access over the Internet for external consultants is retired after the project has been finished. But this work often has low priority. If it is not down, however, it will leave the backdoor wide open for potential intruders.

Technologies like Cisco Application Centric Infrastructure (ACI) are revolutionizing this process by introducing the ability to create an *application network profile*, which is a configuration template that expresses relationships between compute segments. ACI translates those relationships into networking constructs that routers and switches can implement (like VLANs, IP addresses, and so on).

The Cisco ACI fabric consists of discrete components that operate as routers and switches but are provisioned and monitored as a single entity. The operation is like a distributed switch and router configuration that provides advanced traffic optimization, security, and telemetry functions, stitching together virtual and physical workloads.

ACI provides not only the ability to instantiate new network configurations almost instantaneously but also to remove them just as quickly. ACI makes sure that all network "doors" opened for the external developers are consistently closed after the SAP system has gone live.

Tools such as Cisco UCS Director (UCSD) orchestrate the ACI services together with compute provisioning (such as via Cisco UCS, VMware vCenter, or OpenStack) to provide a fast provisioning service for the entire infrastructure.

Operational Considerations

Beyond helping to architect the technical systems and deploy the components that make up an SAP system, an SAP Basis professional also has to consider how the Basis team should be staffed to operate and maintain the systems once they're in place.

SAP Basis Team Staffing

One of the most valuable resources in an SAP implementation, the SAP technology or Basis team directly impacts how well the SAP production system will perform its intended function to support the company's business processes. A good team needs to have the experience and ability to do everything from correctly install the system to maintain steady-state operations, minimize downtime via smartly applied change management practices, calculate the impact of growing workloads down the road, spearhead business-aligned IT projects, plan for and complete SAP functional enhancements and upgrades, and more.

Many SAP Basis teams are composed of two subteams: a project team and a run (or steady-state or "base load") team. Further, it's common for SAP Basis teams to be made up of a mix of company employees, hosting partner resources, and contractors possessing specialized skills or experience.

NOTE

Only a well-structured and completely staffed SAP Basis organization can pull off a new implementation, much less maintain an SAP production system over many years. Although the list of teams provided here might seem extensive, this is only the beginning. Work with the project's prime systems integrator, hardware and hosting partners, SAP, and your IT department to determine the best mix of teams and people for your unique SAP system landscape and project constraints.

Although the SAP Basis team often takes the lead in matters related to SAP, it cannot do so alone. Other IT teams that the SAP Basis team needs to collaborate with include

▶ **IT project management office (PMO) team:** Consisting of project management professionals experienced in managing large-scale and complex IT/business projects.

▶ **Server infrastructure team:** Tasked with racking and building out servers, orchestrating operating systems, and generally preparing and maintaining the various database, application, Internet, and other servers for the specific roles they will play in the SAP landscape.

▶ **Storage infrastructure team:** Responsible for SAN design, deployment, performance, and maintenance oversight. The SAN/disk team plays a critical role given that the lifeblood of the system—the data—sits squarely within its area of responsibility.

▶ **Security and network teams:** Tasked with managing physical security and SAP-specific end-user roles and authorizations.

▶ **Database team:** Responsible for deployment and ongoing administration. In many cases, the SAP Basis team also takes care of its databases, especially in case of HANA.

▶ **Backups team:** Tasked with ensuring that backup and restore, systems monitoring, and basic availability tasks are regularly and proactively addressed (covered in more detail in the next section).

Beyond properly staffing the SAP Basis team and working with other teams, there's another broad collection of tasks that consume the SAP Basis professional's time: proactively performing the necessary operations, administration, and management tasks necessary to keep the SAP system running well. Several of these tasks are outlined next.

Operations, Administration, and Management

Among others, an organization's computer operations team will assist the SAP Basis team in taking care of SAP after go-live. This is a really big job, though, spanning not only the entire SAP technology stack but also multiple business applications and perhaps serving several different end-user communities. Because maintaining SAP is very complex, we gave it a full hour. Check out Hour 20, "SAP System Administration and Management," for more information about how to

▶ Proactively monitor SAP's business processes

▶ Review the SAP system's logs

▶ Manage the system's computing platform and other infrastructure

▶ Verify and fine-tune workload distribution

▶ Perform database administration

▶ Manage printed output

▶ Manage batch jobs (also called background processing)

▶ Conduct performance management

▶ Address day-to-day operations

With your foundation in the SAP technology professional's perspective, let's shift gears and take a closer look at the final critical cog in an SAP IT implementation or production system: the role and perspective of the SAP developer. Afterward, we'll look at technical matters related to installing, maintaining, and enhancing SAP.

Summary

In this hour, we reviewed the priorities and perspectives of SAP technology professionals. We covered what it means to mesh business requirements with the various technologies and technical considerations underpinning an SAP implementation. After addressing which components to plan for, along with architecture and sizing, we also reviewed basic network, storage, server, application, and end-user access matters that need to be addressed well before SAP is installed. A brief introduction to the SAP-related IT teams necessary to deploy and maintain SAP concluded this hour.

Case Study: Hour 16

Consider this SAP Basis professional case study and questions that follow. You can find answers to the questions related to this case study in Appendix A, "Case Study Answers."

Situation

As a new senior Basis lead for MNC's upcoming SAP Enterprise Resource Planning (ERP) implementation, you have been asked to review the current state of affairs and make recommendations. In your review, you note that MNC has excellent computer operations, server, and database administration teams but that there seems to be poor alignment between the company's current mainframe computing standards and the proposed SAP ERP Human Capital Management (HCM) environment (which is being built atop a Microsoft Windows/SQL Server platform). The company is also used to supporting mission-critical computing applications with development, test, and preproduction staging environments, but the company seems to have little formal experience with disaster recovery.

Questions

1. What are your thoughts about the readiness of the current technical teams to help you support SAP?

2. As outlined in this hour's introduction, what are the three broad areas that the SAP technology or Basis team is responsible for performing?

3. Where will you point the team to begin preparing for installation planning?

4. Would you recommend that MNC maintain its current system landscape strategy?

5. Though lacking formal disaster recovery expertise, MNC is quite familiar and comfortable with performing regular tape backups and restores. What are two other types of DR solutions you might look into?

An SAP Developer's Perspective

What You'll Learn in This Hour:

► How developers differ from configuration specialists

► Overview of legacy and newer programming tools

► Review of implementation options

► How Solution Manager facilitates development

► Viewing the SAP procedure model

► Implementation Guide basics

Much has changed in the world of SAP development since the previous edition of this book was released. Like business users, IT project managers, and SAP technology professionals, SAP developers have a unique perspective when it comes to SAP's business applications. Developers and their configuration colleagues create the solutions that help business users run the business. This hour looks at how the world of SAP development has changed and how those changes affect SAP implementation and support. A review of the tools and methodologies used to create or customize SAP functionality concludes this hour.

The term *development tool* is often used generically to refer to a number of utilities provided by SAP to create or enhance SAP systems, code, and configuration. These can be categorized into two specific groups—programming tools and configuration tools, covered next—alongside developer methodologies.

Programming Tools

SAP programming tools were introduced in Hour 6, "SAP NetWeaver and HANA." This included a look at SAP NetWeaver Composition tools used to develop, monitor, and manage business processes spanning potentially many different applications and technologies. As a reminder, these include the following:

▶ SAP NetWeaver Composition Environment (CE)

▶ SAP NetWeaver Developer Studio

▶ SAP NetWeaver Visual Composer

These tools can be further divided into three major areas, based on the underlying SAP platform: ABAP, Java, and the SAP NetWeaver Composition Environment.

Developers use programming tools to customize an SAP system beyond the system's basic capabilities. Such customization enables gaps in an SAP application's standard functionality to be filled in. Customizing can also be useful for

▶ Developing enhancements (new functionality) unavailable in the standard SAP programs

▶ Creating special reports requested by business leaders to help run the business

▶ Creating special forms needed to bring new data into the system (in such a way that most of the risks related to human data entry errors are avoided)

▶ Connecting or interfacing SAP with other systems

▶ Developing special conversion programs capable of transferring data from one system into another (typically from a legacy system to a new SAP system)

Several of the tools used to carry out customization are covered next.

SAP Business Process Management

SAP NetWeaver Business Process Management (BPM) is essentially a subset of the SAP NetWeaver Composition Environment. As discussed previously, it lets you model, execute, and monitor an organization's business processes, based on a common process model. You compose and define process steps, set up business rules and exceptions, model your process flows, and then set up user interfaces or interactive forms as required. All this functionality is performed using three tools:

▶ **Process Composer:** Used by architects and developers to create and test business process models

▶ **Process Server:** Used to execute the process models

▶ **Process Desk:** Used by process users to perform their jobs

SAP Mobile Application Development Platform

The latest release of the SAP Mobile Platform includes a SAP mobile application development platform (MADP). It provides a Java gateway and a Java-based version of SAP Process Integration (PI) for data integration from various different systems. Perhaps more importantly, it provides authentication, connectivity, and administrative services that together enable SAP to be extended to support mobile documents, content management, expense management, and more (built into SAP Afaria).

ABAP and SE80

SAP's Advanced Business Application Programming (ABAP, pronounced "ah bop") dates back to the 1980s. Despite newer alternatives, ABAP remains the primary tool for SAP programming. At the heart of ABAP programming is the ABAP Development Workbench, available via transaction SE80. This workbench offers a rich set of functions developers can use to create and modify SAP programs. Its primary functions include the following:

- ▶ Object Navigator
- ▶ Package Builder
- ▶ Object Navigator
- ▶ Web Application Builder for ITS (Internet Transaction Server) Services
- ▶ Web Application Builder for BSP (Business Server Pages)
- ▶ Web Services
- ▶ ABAP Dictionary
- ▶ ABAP Editor
- ▶ Class Builder and Function Builder
- ▶ Screen Painter and Menu Painter
- ▶ Web Dynpro

The last tool in the list, Web Dynpro for ABAP, is especially important because it replaced the older SAPGUI-based screen painter tools.

Java and NWDS

Java development for SAP's NetWeaver application server is based on the current Java EE 5 standard. Java was adopted by SAP as a platform-independent open source development framework to allow customers to leverage existing non-SAP development resources. At one point in time, it was thought that ABAP development would be replaced by Java development. With archenemy Oracle's acquisition of Sun Microsystems (and therefore Java) in 2010, however, SAP's priorities have likely changed; if anything, expect to see Java's role diminish.

To develop in Java, SAP provides the SAP NetWeaver Developer Studio (NWDS). Often shortened to Developer Studio, this tool is based on the open source Eclipse software development framework and includes the following features:

- ▶ Built-in Java EE 5 design-time support

- ▶ Web services support

- ▶ On-the-fly application debugging

- ▶ Hot deployment

- ▶ Wizards and graphical tools to speed up development

SAP offers several options for distributing Java changes through the SAP landscape. Although Java objects can still be deployed locally via manual processes, SAP's NetWeaver Development Infrastructure (NWDI) allows customers to manage Java development with a capable change management tool modeled after SAP's ABAP-oriented Transport Management System (TMS).

Composition Environment

The SAP NetWeaver Composition Environment (CE) provides a service oriented and standards-based development environment where SAP developers can model and develop composite applications called *composites*. Composites are solutions developed by combining readily available functions, datasets, or existing solutions. Using "reusable" SAP and third-party components in this way accelerates business process innovation.

The ABAP Development Workbench, Java NWDS, and the SAP CE provide the core toolsets for SAP development. However, the real work of creating a usable SAP application is accomplished through SAP's various configuration tools, covered later this hour. For now, let's turn our attention to methodologies used by SAP developers.

Developer and SAP Methodologies

The latest Accelerated SAP (ASAP) methodology and Solution Manager tools include new sample documents, new development templates, a repository for canned business processes, and better project-management tools than their predecessors. How these assets align with the latest ASAP 8 methodology is outlined next.

NOTE

ASAP Methodology Limitations

Although SAP's Accelerated SAP methodology has matured considerably over the years, it's important to remember that it only provides a step-wise framework for the high-level tasks necessary to implement SAP. Detailed development assets and the kind of prescriptive guidance necessary to determine what to use and how to use it necessarily exists outside the methodology. For example, many SAP implementation partners will bring with them their own detailed methodologies, frameworks, tools, and other materials.

Implementation Development Phases

As shown in Figure 17.1, SAP implementation represents a four-phased process which is essentially a shortened version of the original ASAP methodology.

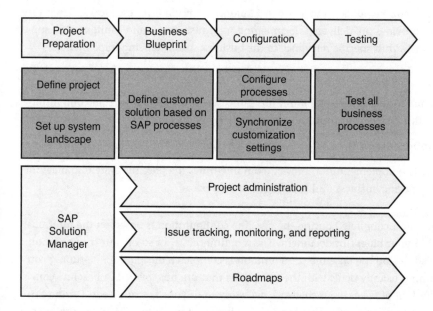

FIGURE 17.1
The four core SAP implementation phases.

Project Preparation

Project preparation starts with retrieving information and resources. It is an important time to assemble the necessary components for the implementation. Some important milestones that need to be accomplished during this time include the following:

▶ Obtain senior-level management/stakeholder support.

▶ Identify clear project objectives.

▶ Architect an efficient decision-making process.

▶ Create an environment suitable for change and reengineering.

▶ Build a qualified and capable project team.

Business Blueprint

SAP has defined a business blueprint phase to help extract pertinent information about your company that is necessary for the implementation. Business blueprinting also essentially documents the implementation, outlining your future business processes and business requirements.

To further assist with this process, SAP offers implementation content on a variety of products and scenarios, which can be pulled in to Solution Manager from the Business Process Repository (BPR). This content provides pre-delivered documentation, transactions, and configuration support to assist customers with specific relevance to the business scenario being implemented.

Configuration

With the completion of the business blueprint, the "functional" experts may begin configuring SAP. The configuration phase is broken into two underlying phases:

▶ **Baseline configuration:** The SAP consulting team configures the baseline system.

▶ **Fine-tuning:** The implementation project team fine-tunes the baseline system to meet the SAP project's specific business and process requirements.

The initial configuration completed during the baseline configuration is based on the information you provided in your blueprint document. The remaining 20% or so of your configuration that was not tackled during the baseline configuration is completed during the fine-tuning configuration. Fine-tuning usually deals with the exceptions that are not covered in baseline configuration. This final bit of tweaking is the work necessary to fit your special needs. During this phase, you also work through configuring the SAP Implementation Guide (IMG), the tool used to actually configure SAP in a step-by-step manner.

Testing, Final Preparation, and Go-Live

From a tool's perspective, final preparation and go-live equates to testing. Workload testing (including peak volume, daily load, and other forms of stress testing) and integration or functional testing should be performed to ensure the accuracy of your data and the stability of your SAP system. Now is an important time to also perform preventive maintenance checks to ensure optimal performance of your SAP system. Preparing for go-live means preparing for the inevitable end-user questions—such as those they'll ask as they start actively working on the new SAP system.

Preparation is the key to a successful go-live, including attention to what-if scenarios related not only to the individual business processes deployed but also to the functioning of the technology underpinning these business processes. And preparation for ongoing support, including mainte-nance contracts and documented processes and procedures, is essential. Fortunately, a wealth of information and additional resources are available.

Run SAP and Other Roadmaps

The Run SAP roadmaps provide a methodology to help organizations achieve operational effi-ciencies. These include how-to and best-practice documentation for management and adminis-tration tasks. SAP continues to grow its number of product-specific roadmaps as new applications and components are developed. A few of the Run SAP roadmaps available today include

- ASAP Implementation Roadmap for SAP NetWeaver Enterprise Portal

- Solution Management Roadmap

- Global Template Roadmap

- Upgrade Roadmap

- Methodology for Accelerated Transformation to Enterprise SOA

It is important to remember that at the end of the day, these approaches all amount to little more than frameworks or methods for organizing development work through supporting tem-plates. Even Solution Manager only facilitates an SAP implementation. The real work still needs to be done through the SAP Implementation Guide, described next.

Configuration and the SAP IMG

If you return to the configuration phase, you will remember that the Implementation Guide (IMG) plays a central role in assisting you with configuring SAP. The IMG is essentially a large tree structure diagram that lists all actions required for implementing SAP, guiding you through each of the steps in all the different SAP areas that require configuration. For each business application, the SAP IMG

- Explains the steps in the implementation process

- Communicates the SAP standard (default) settings

- Describes system configuration work (tasks or activities)

The guide begins with basic settings such as "What country are you in?" It eventually drills down into specific matters such as "What number do you want your purchase orders to begin with?" It is nearly impossible to complete an SAP implementation without being familiar with the SAP IMG. To begin, execute transaction code /nSPRO or select Tools, Customizing, IMG, Execute Project. The main screen appears, and it should look similar to the one in Figure 17.2.

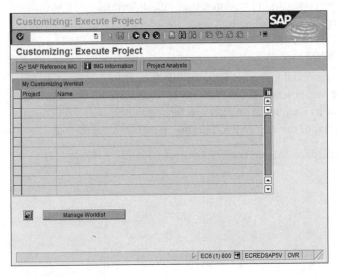

FIGURE 17.2
The Implementation Guide main screen varies in appearance depending on your SAP component and installation, as well as the amount of configuration that has been completed.

Different Views of the IMG

Developers use the SAP IMG in several different ways, taking advantage of different views. Different views provide different information and priorities. You can also create your own custom views of the IMG. There are four levels of the SAP IMG, which are explored next:

- ▶ SAP Reference IMG
- ▶ SAP Enterprise IMG
- ▶ SAP Project IMGs
- ▶ SAP Upgrade Customizing IMGs

SAP Reference IMG

The SAP Reference IMG (accessed by clicking the button by the same name illustrated previously Figure 17.2) contains documentation on all the SAP business application components supplied by SAP. It serves as a single source for all configuration data (see Figure 17.3).

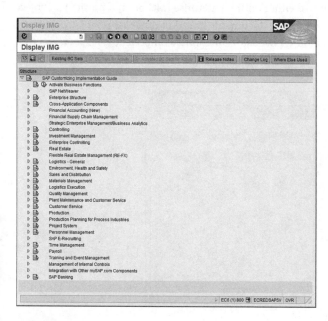

FIGURE 17.3
Using the SAP Reference IMG, you can customize your entire classic SAP ERP or Business Suite application from a single console.

SAP Enterprise IMG

The SAP Enterprise IMG is a subset of the SAP Reference IMG, containing documentation only for the components being implemented. It appears the same as the Reference IMG but lists only the configuration steps necessary for your company's implementation. For example, if you are implementing only logistics within SAP Enterprise Resource Planning (ERP), your IMG will contain only logistics-related information; other information, such as information related to configuring HR payroll, would not be present.

SAP Project IMGs

SAP Project IMGs are Enterprise IMG subsets that contain only the documentation for the Enterprise IMG components you are implementing (such as a Customizing project). For example, if you are implementing SAP ECC Logistics exclusively but have divided the implementation into two projects—one for Sales and Distribution and a second for Materials Management—you can set up two different projects. This can make the projects easier to manage and configure.

SAP Upgrade Customizing IMGs

SAP Upgrade Customizing IMGs are based either on the Enterprise IMG or on a particular Project IMG. The IMG view in Figure 17.4 shows all the documents linked to a release note for a given release upgrade. To read a release note for a particular functional component, click its respective square icon.

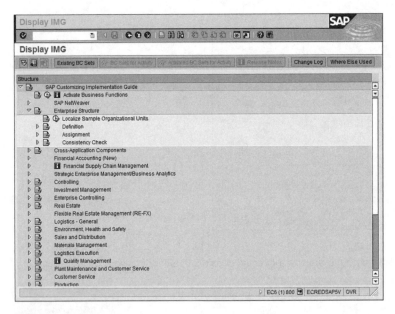

FIGURE 17.4
An SAP Upgrade Customizing IMG enables you to specify a configuration based on specific SAP releases.

Integration with Solution Manager

With the latest features of SAP Solution Manager (SolMan), you can now create projects within SolMan and link them to one or multiple IMG projects in component systems. This enables you to navigate configuration for one or more projects from a central location and provide a single configuration repository within SAP SolMan.

Additional IMG Fundamentals

With the transaction code SPRO, the initial view of an IMG structure is always a tree diagram with symbols shown to the left. You can use the plus (+) sign to the left of each item (for older SAP releases) or the triangle (for newer SAP releases) in the tree structure to expand a branch of the tree to view its substructure. You can also expand a branch by placing your cursor on a line item and then selecting Edit, Expand/Collapse or by placing your cursor on a line item and pressing the F5 key on your keyboard. To expand all possible branches, place your cursor on the highest level and select Edit, All Subnodes.

IMG Help

It is important to learn how to retrieve help for any individual line item in the IMG. By looking at the description of each line item, it is not always clear exactly what the configuration of that item entails. You can access selection-specific help by double-clicking any activity (line item) in the IMG. This brings you detailed help on the configuration activity you have selected. In some cases, you get a small window describing the reasons for the activity and what it entails, including actual examples of what the activity is used to configure. In other instances, you might get the SAP Help application, which enables you to search for more information. Help is also available after you execute a line item in the IMG. Most activities in the IMG bring you to a screen where you need to add or modify values in a table to configure your SAP system.

The field descriptions and selection-specific help might not provide all the information necessary for you to understand what to do. Placing your cursor in any field and then pressing the F1 key on your keyboard from any IMG activity screen launches field-level selection-specific help. The Help file is presented as a small window describing the possible values for entry in that field. Using Help in the IMG is essential to obtaining additional information about the activities required to configure your SAP system.

IMG Documentation

The IMG is typically your main source for configuration. That is essentially why, along with Solution Manager, it is the ideal location for documenting your configuration. Use the Status Information icon to navigate to the Memo tab of the Status Information screen. From there, record your comments, notes, or configuration information about the appropriate configuration step provided in the IMG. Alternatively, use your cursor to select the documentation symbol, and your screen launches a screen like the one shown in Figure 17.5.

For each line item in the IMG, you can enter text in this way and, in doing so, document the system as you go along. This is therefore a very helpful tool, not to mention a great reference to use after your implementation is complete or during SAP upgrades and changes. You can type configuration notes into the space provided in the Memo tab and save them with that line item in the IMG. You can then use the Read Note symbol to review any of these notes at a later time.

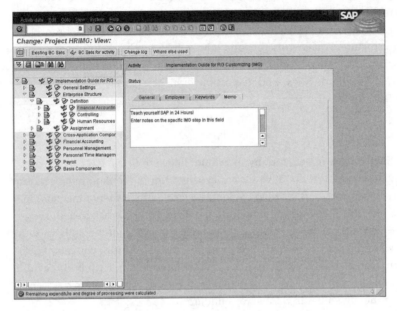

FIGURE 17.5
Use the IMG's Memo feature to write configuration notes documenting particular activities.

Status Information

Selecting the Status Information symbol brings you to the General tab, as shown in Figure 17.6. This tab allows you to record the status and progress of your configuration for a particular line item, including planned versus actual start and end dates and more.

One purpose of the Status Information screen is to maintain a record of your configuration to date and to track your implementation progress. It is also a good place to see who is working on what. One of the first things you need to assign on this screen is the Status field. Status types include the following:

- ▶ In Process
- ▶ In Q/A Testing
- ▶ Complete

You set up the different status levels as determined by your company's specifications. This status designation segregates your configuration tasks into different completion categories.

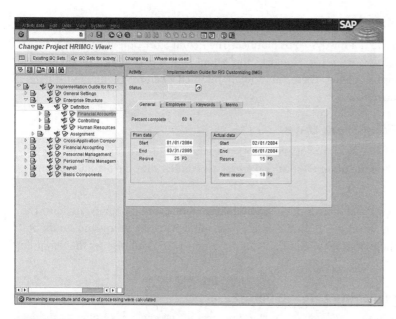

FIGURE 17.6
The Status Information screen records the status of the item, planned versus actual start and stop dates, the percentage completed, and more.

Percent Complete

The Percent Complete field is used to display a processing status for an activity, expressed as a percentage. Sample percent completed values include 25%, 50%, 75%, 100%, and so on. At one time, determining these values was up to the individual. In newer releases of SAP, though, the percent complete is actually calculated by SAP.

Plan Start and End Dates

The Plan Start Date field is where you record the initial projected date on which this particular activity should commence. Click the Possible Entries Help button on this field to display a calendar that enables you to select the date (so that you do not have to enter it directly). The date is selected using the calendar control by selecting the month, date, and year and then double-clicking or by selecting the green check mark. The Plan End Date field is where you record the projected completion date for this particular activity. The SAP calendar is also available on this field.

Plan Work Days

The Plan Work Days field records the planned duration of an activity in days. The planned expenditure can be maintained manually. If neither actual expenditure nor processing status is maintained, the remaining expenditure is calculated.

Actual Start and End Dates

In the real world, things do not always go as planned. The Actual Start Date field records the actual date that an activity was started. Similarly, the Actual End Date field records the actual date that an activity was completed. These fields are maintained when the planned start date and the actual start date differ.

Actual and Remaining Work Days

The Actual Work Days field records the actual duration, in days, of an activity. This field is usually maintained only when the planned start and end dates conflict with the actual start and end dates.

The Remaining Work Days field records the remaining expenditure for an activity, in days. The remaining expenditure is calculated from the actual expenditure and the processing status, or from the planned expenditure, if these fields are not maintained. You can also set the remaining expenditure manually.

Employee Tab for Resource Assignments

For each particular task in the IMG, you can assign resources (or people) responsible for that task. Use the Employee tab in the Status Information screen to denote these resource assignments. By using the Possible Entries Help button in the resource field, you can select the resources responsible for performing an activity. As the multiple resources boxes show, you can assign multiple resources to a single task.

Release Notes

Release notes contain specific relevant information about changes to the SAP system since the last release. They contain functionality and screen changes, as well as menu path and table structure changes. Release notes are helpful when developers are supporting an upgrade from one SAP version to another. They are also a good tool for retrieving additional information explaining how a particular piece of functionality works in the SAP system. To see whether release notes are available in your case, turn on an indicator in your IMG that displays a marker next to each activity.

Summary

Decisions concerning the development tools and implementation strategy affect the time, cost, and path you follow in your SAP implementation. SAP rapid deployment options are effective and efficient solutions that might not be the best fit for your company. Because no two companies are alike, you should discuss your company's individual needs with your SAP representative before deciding what tools and methodologies you should employ, and take it from there.

When an "empty" shell of SAP is installed, the IMG is the tool you use to assist in customizing and implementing your SAP system. The IMG is designed to pinpoint the configuration activities you are required to perform for your SAP implementation to be a success. It also enables you to tweak your SAP system to ideally suit your company's individual needs through custom configuration.

Case Study: Hour 17

Review the following developer-specific case study and the questions that follow. You can find answers to the questions related to this case study in Appendix A, "Case Study Answers."

Situation

You recently attended a team meeting hosted by MNC's developers and configuration specialists. Upon returning to your business unit, you were asked several questions from junior colleagues anxious to understand more.

Questions

1. What is the transaction code to launch the ABAP Development Workbench?

2. What is the name of the development environment for creating SAP Java applications?

3. What are the three primary toolsets used for SAP development?

4. The ASAP Implementation Roadmap for SAP NetWeaver Enterprise Portal is an example of what?

5. Which view of the IMG contains only the relevant documentation for the SAP components your company is implementing?

HOUR 18
SAP Installation and Implementation

What You'll Learn in This Hour:

▶ The SAP technical installation phases
▶ The planning and preplanning phases of an installation
▶ Acquiring and installing a trial version of SAP
▶ Installing HANA on Amazon's cloud
▶ Introducing the SAP Cloud Application Library
▶ Setting up single sign-on

We've come a long way on our path toward implementing SAP, and we've finally reached the point of performing the actual technical installation in preparation for configuring and developing the actual business system. To make this hour more relevant to all the readers who do not actually have access to SAP software, we walk through installing one of the trial versions of SAP as well as walking through a real (abbreviated) SAP on-premise installation. With so much focus today on the cloud, we conclude this hour by describing the installation of a HANA system on Amazon's AWS cloud, and we introduce the SAP Cloud Application library.

First Steps

Before any technical installation can commence, SAP Solution Manager must be installed. You need the SAP Solution Manager (SolMan) to generate SAP's license keys and send escalations to SAP support for any other SAP solution anyway. SolMan is also used for patching, performing transports, and monitoring the overall SAP system landscape.

It is important to understand the installation process at a high level. Installing SAP can be broken down into four phases: planning, pre-installation steps, performing the actual installation itself, and performing post-installation tasks. Careful attention to planning and all the pre-installation tasks will generally result in a smooth installation. In the same way, careful attention to the post-installation tasks ensures the SAP system will actually be usable.

NOTE

In almost every new SAP implementation, the first SAP technical installation is some kind of technical sandbox or "crash and burn" system. The idea is for the technical team to become accustomed to the installation procedure before installing a system that will actually be used as a development, test, training, production, or other system.

SAP Installation Preparation

The first phase in an SAP installation is planning, which entails research and reading. Locate and download the installation guides from the SAP Service Marketplace[1] and carefully read all SAP Notes[2] listed in the guides (and the SAP Notes they are referring to as well as the SAP Notes mentioned in the referred notes...) to avoid showstoppers. To put these steps in perspective, keep in mind that SAP publishes updates regularly; the SAP Notes can change monthly or even weekly.

You need an SAP Service Marketplace ID to access this system. To get such an ID, you have to be an SAP customer or partner. The SAP Service Marketplace (see Figure 18.1) is like a real marketplace cluttered with marketing verbiage, so it can be quite cumbersome to actually locate the guides.

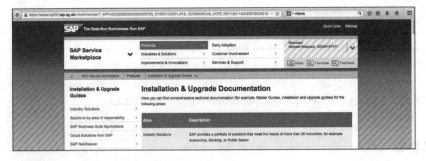

FIGURE 18.1
The SAP Service Marketplace.

Locating and Downloading the Installation Guide

Navigating the SAP Service Marketplace and Software Download Center can be confusing. Therefore, this section provides a step-by-step description of how to locate the necessary guides and files. If you are already familiar with this process, you can go directly to the next section.

---

[1] See http://service.sap.com/instguides.

[2] See http://service.sap.com/notes.

At first you may not be able to find a link to the software you want to install. The trick is to scroll down until you see the alphabetical index (as shown in Figure 18.2).

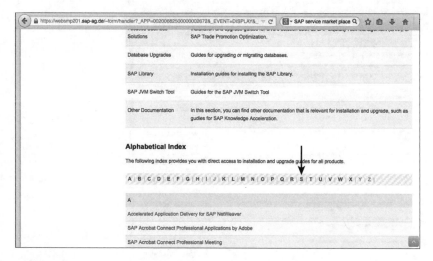

FIGURE 18.2
The installation guide index of the SAP Service Marketplace.

To obtain the SAP Solution Manager Installation Guide, click the letter S or scroll down until you reach the selection shown in Figure 18.3.

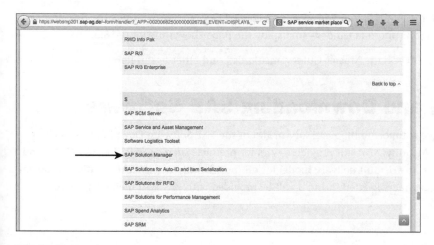

FIGURE 18.3
The link to the SAP SolMan installation guide on SAP Service Marketplace.

Click this link to reach another page cluttered with marketing verbiage (see Figure 18.4).

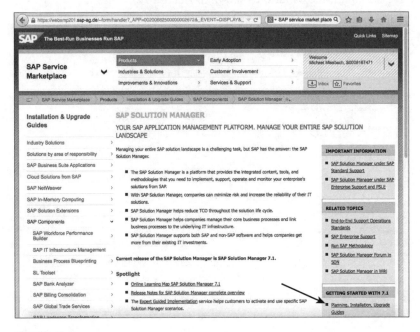

FIGURE 18.4
SolMan at the SAP Service Marketplace.

If your screen is large enough, you will see a box labeled Getting Started. Click the first item—Planning, Installation, Upgrade Guides—to display the page shown in Figure 18.5.

From here, you can access the Master Guides, media list, and other useful items.

Locating and Downloading SAP Software

The next challenge is to locate the necessary media at the SAP Software Download Center[3] (see Figure 18.6). Actually, SAP still provides DVDs for products such as SAP ERP, SAP CRM, and SAP SRM. However, the default delivery model for all (particularly newer) SAP solutions is download only. Only customers located in India will be provided with physical media by default.

---

[3] See https://support.sap.com/swdc.

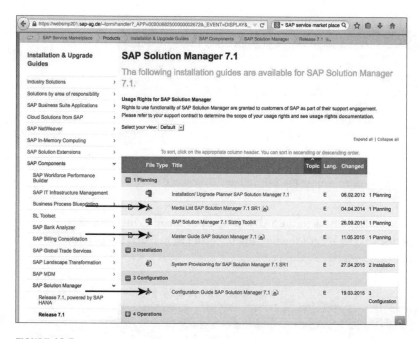

FIGURE 18.5
The SAP SolMan download page.

FIGURE 18.6
The SAP Software Download Center.

Start with the download of the database by directing your mouse to the field labeled Files for Your Database or type in the following link: https://support.sap.com/software/databases.html (see Figure 18.7).

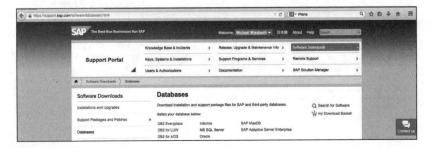

FIGURE 18.7
The database installation files, as seen through the SAP Software Download Center.

To obtain the application code, go back to the SAP Software Download Center and click Installations and Upgrades and then click the tile Alphabetical List to reach the application index, where you click the letter S (see Figure 18.8).

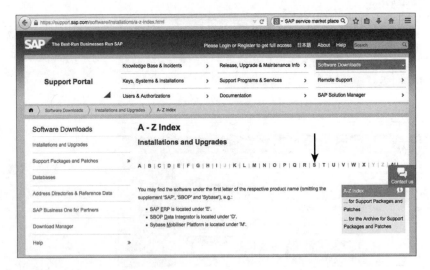

FIGURE 18.8
The download index of the SAP Service Marketplace.

Many SAP solutions start with an S, so when you click S in the application index, you get a long list (see Figure 18.9). Scroll down halfway until you locate the link to the SAP Solution Manager software download (in the right column). (Note that you won't see SAP HANA displayed in this list. SAP's in-memory database is hidden under the letter H at the applications index.)

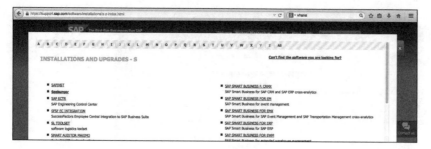

FIGURE 18.9
The list of solutions starting with an **S** on the SAP Service Marketplace.

The next page has only one link to click (see Figure 18.10).

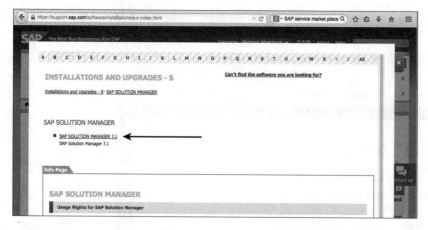

FIGURE 18.10
SAP SolMan download on the SAP Service Marketplace.

Now you have reached your target; just click Installation to get to the screen shown in Figure 18.11.

Select the Media for Solution Manager on Windows with Oracle as database we need in this example. Maybe you are confused why obviously nothing happens after you clicked on the selected combination of operating system and database. Actually you need to scroll down one last time to get a screen similar to the one displayed in Figure 18.12, which was generated by your click.

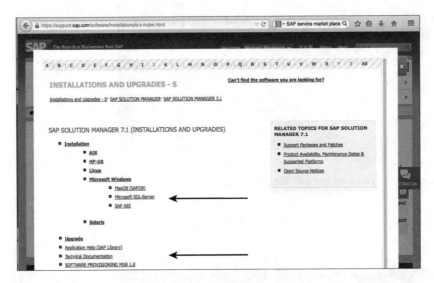

FIGURE 18.11
The SAP Solution Manager download on the SAP Service Marketplace.

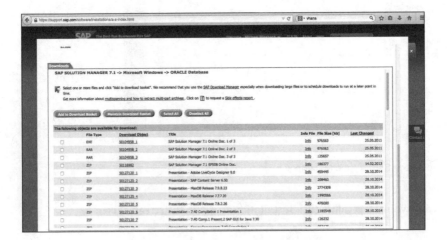

FIGURE 18.12
The SAP SolMan download site on the SAP Service Marketplace.

Under Technical Documentation, you will also find a shortcut to the installation guide. Note that HANA is not mentioned, despite SAP SolMan being supported on SAP's in-memory database.

Now you can select the installation files for all the databases (despite your collection above) and also the database code, nicely compressed as .zip, .rar, and .exe files. You can download them one after another by clicking the Download Object number or put them into your SAP download basket by clicking on the rectangular boxes on the left side. In this case, however, you have to have the SAP Download Manager installed. You can download the Download Manager also from the Service Marketplace (or you can click the highlighted word SAP Download Manager in the top line of the page). Figure 18.13 displays the download basket filled with the files for SAP SolMan.

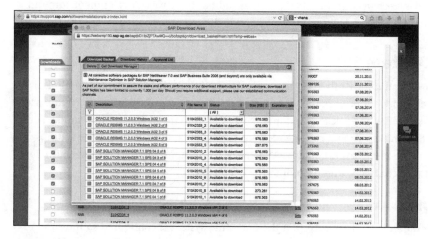

FIGURE 18.13
The download basket filled with the files for SAP SolMan.

Copy the media to a central location. You will eventually need these files again to install your development, test, quality assurance, training, and other non-production systems as well as the production system.

Infrastructure Readiness

After you have downloaded all the necessary guides and software/code, you have to prepare the server, network, and operating infrastructure, as discussed next.

Server

For a sandbox, any server certified for SAP with at least two cores, 6 GB RAM, 200–250 GB for SAP system files, and the necessary temporary disk space for installation media should do the job. Recommended are four cores and 16 GB RAM; as more buffers fit into the physical memory, the better the performance.

Network

All you need for your SAP sandbox in regard to the network is a valid IP address. But things are not this simple for your network team when it comes to the implementation of a complete productive system landscape connected to users and partners over the Internet. Like the details of the storage subsystems, the network architecture is beyond the scope of this book. If you would like to dig deeper (perhaps you are a member of the network team), turn to our book *SAP on the Cloud*,[4] which provides deep insights into this topic, including the newest developments around cloud computing, the Internet of Things (IoT), and application-centric infrastructure (ACI).

Operating System

The OS installation is similar any other application installation. Basic OS recommendations include using standard drive mount points or letters and using standard file allocation unit sizes. For Linux systems, swap file and package requirements are found in the installation guide. For Windows systems, SAP makes some recommendations for the page file size and a few settings to optimize performance in the install guide. SAP expects the customer to take responsibility for licensing, maintenance contracts, and obtaining the OS media.

Prerequisite Checklist

Using a checklist is a great way to ensure that the operating system is configured so that it is repeatable and ready for SAP to be installed. The following is an example of such a checklist for SAP on SUSE Linux with Oracle:

- ► Check network teaming and other network interface properties.

- ► Install the Java Runtime Environment (JRE).

- ► Verify that the appropriate Linux rpms have been installed.

- ► Select Message Digest 5 (MD5) algorithm password encryption as the default encryption method used.

- ► Verify that enough swap space is available. (Check your SAP Notes for minimum requirements.)

- ► Read SAP Note 1915299 on troubleshooting the installation of Oracle Database 12c Release 1

---

4 Missbach, Michael, et al. *SAP on the Cloud 2nd Edition*, Heidelberg: Springer, 2015.

NOTE

A Linux RPM actually refers to several different entities. It may refer to the RPM Package Manager, the rpm program (used to manage installed software), or the file format used for such files (the rpm file format). In the last case, the rpm file format is used for distributing software in a "packaged" format, either as a precompiled binary or in its source code format.

Database Server Installation

The database installation process depends on the SAP software release and the database software. SAP supports several database platforms, including its own HANA, ASE and IQ, and MaxDB, and the two most popular options—Microsoft SQL Server and Oracle—are explored in the following sections.

Microsoft SQL Server Software

Microsoft SQL Server is installed "outside" the SAP installation procedure. SAP provides installation instructions for SQL Server, too, although for the most part, the installation process reflects a standard SQL Server database installation. Like nearly all of Microsoft's software installation processes, it's also quick and fairly pain free. SAP supports only the Enterprise Edition of SQL Server (though the 180-day Evaluation Edition version of SQL Server is functionally equivalent to the Enterprise Edition and will also work). With its high-availability features and outstanding real-world performance, SQL Server has been increasing its market share for SAP, as well as the average size of SAP systems that rely on it for business-critical and mission-critical computing.

Note that SAP SE has published a SQL Server installation DVD image that can be downloaded. The image contains a script that installs SQL Server with all the correct collation and other settings.[5]

Oracle Database Software

Although Oracle's market share has steadily declined over the years, Oracle databases are still commonly found in SAP environments, especially the largest and oldest systems. After all, despite its expense, Oracle is a capable and mature database product. The installation of the database software is normally accomplished by running a batch file provided by SAP that contains answers to all the configuration questions asked by the Oracle installer. In more recent releases of SAP, the Oracle Server software comes in SAR files, which are unzipped during the SAP installation process. Interestingly, the SAP installation process still stops and requires the installer to complete the Oracle installation before proceeding by running RUNINSTALLER. After the Oracle installation completes, the current Oracle patch set must be installed. Oracle Enterprise Edition is required.

---

[5] See SAP Note 1970448: https://websmp130.sap-ag.de/sap/support/notes/1970448.

SAP Software Installation

From this point on, you can just follow the official SAP installation guide or instructions on blogs such as http://www.thusjanthan.com/guide-installing-sap-netweaver-7-31-suse-using-oracle-11g/. Given all the steps involved, you certainly by now appreciate the complexity of an SAP installation.

Post-Installation Tasks

The installation of SAP is almost complete, but you still need to carry out the following tasks before the system is ready to use:

1. Stop and start the system using stopsap and startsap, respectively.

2. Log on to the system (user SAP* or DDIC in client 000, 001, or 066 [the latter of which can only be accessed by user SAP*]). The default passwords for SAP* and DDIC are no longer 19920706 and 06071992, as in days past. For new systems, use the passwords you provided during the installation.

3. Install the permanent SAP license. The temporary license key, which is valid for 90 days, is created during the installation. You can obtain a permanent license key for the installation from http://service.sap.com/licensekeys.

4. Apply the latest kernel and support packages. After the installation, apply the most current support package stack available for download from the SAP Software Distribution Center (http://service.sap.com/swdc).

5. Create a client copy (just in case you need to fall back later to a pristine client or create a new pristine client to be modified by the development team).

6. Modify the SAP profiles based on recommendations from SAP Notes and from recommendations from your Basis team. For example, you'll want to change the default number and mix of SAP work processes, memory configuration and buffer parameters, and so on.

This concludes our installation of an SAP Solution Manager 4.0 system. With all the complexity of a real-world SAP installation behind us, let's turn our attention to the much simpler process of installing the trial version of SAP.

Installing the SAP Trial Version

Initiated by the Solution Developer Network, SAP also offers trial versions on the SAP Store.[6] Just go the SAP Store and enter either trial or SCN in the search line to get the page shown in Figure 18.14.

---

[6] See https://store.sap.com.

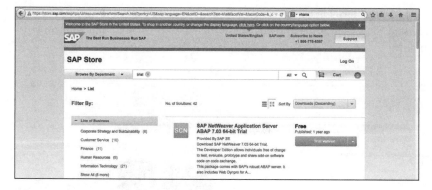

FIGURE 18.14
The trial versions of SAP available from the SAP Store.

You have to scroll down quite a bit to select from the available trial versions. Be aware that at the very bottom of the page you can select many more. After you provide your name, email address, and company name, confirm that you agree to the terms and conditions and then click on the Submit button. You then receive an email with a link that is valid for 48 hours only to get a nice collection of software components. Figure 18.15 shows an example of the link for SAP NetWeaver Application Server ABAP 7.03.

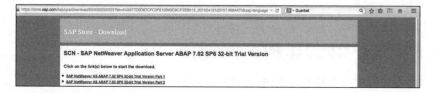

FIGURE 18.15
The download page for NetWeaver trial version.

Part 1 contains nearly 4 GB, so it can take 30 minutes to download; luckily Part 2 is only 103 MB. Extract the RAR files, click on the file welcome.htm, and follow the steps on the right side of the welcome screen (see Figure 18.16).

Though it's much less complex than a real-world SAP installation, you must still prepare the necessary infrastructure. If you install on a laptop, make sure that the resources meet the system requirements mentioned.

Then log on to your PC with administrator privileges and start the installer. The remainder of the installation process typically takes hours (depending on the infrastructure)—perhaps as many as six or more for thinly provisioned hardware. Be patient! Ours took three hours. The SAP installation process is disk intensive and therefore pretty slow for a desktop or laptop. If your machine's hard disk light is furiously flashing away, you are probably in good shape. SAP is also offering short-term hosted trials,[7] but some of them are restricted to three days, and you can't load even your own data.

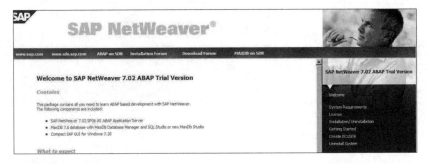

FIGURE 18.16
The installation page for the NetWeaver trial version.

To log on to SAP, install the SAPGUI. After the SAP trial version is extracted, the SAPGUI directory is created. Inside the directory is a file, SapGuiSetup.exe. We suggest you remove other SAPGUI installations before you install the trial version of the SAPGUI (and run the included tool to clean the OS registry). When you're ready, run the SapGuiSetup.exe program and follow the prompts.

HANA on Public Cloud Platforms

As an alternative to the on-premise installation of SAP Solution Manager instances, let's now look at how to provision a "ready to load your data" HANA instance on Amazon AWS. For details, take a look at the latest Amazon Quick Start reference.[8] Note that while SAP HANA is available on both Amazon and Microsoft Azure,[9] at this writing, Microsoft Azure does not yet support running SAP applications on HANA; therefore, Amazon is discussed in detail here.

As author Karthik Krishnan says,[10] "Implementing SAP HANA in the AWS cloud is an advanced topic. If you are new to AWS, see the Getting Started section of the AWS documentation. In

---

[7] See http://www.sap.com/software-free-trials/index.html.

[8] See https://s3.amazonaws.com/quickstart-reference/sap/hana/latest/doc/SAP+HANA+Quick+Start. pdf.

[9] See http://azure.microsoft.com/blog/2014/07/22/step-by-step-guide-for-deployment-of-sap-hana-developer-edition-on-microsoft-azure/.

[10] See https://s3.amazonaws.com/sap-hana-aws/v1.0/doc/SAP+HANA+Quick+Start.pdf.

addition familiarity with the following technologies is recommended: Amazon EC2[11]; Amazon VPC[12] and AWS CloudFormation.[13]"

Single-node or multi-node SAP HANA virtual appliances with a memory footprint between 60 and 244 GB are automatically configured according to SAP best practices. While HANA runs on Linux, a Windows Server instance is deployed for downloading SAP HANA media as well as for hosting the SAP HANA Studio application.

HANA Database Size and Timing Limitations

Only HANA instances with a maximum size of 244 GB are officially supported by SAP for production use on AWS. For SAP Business One on HANA, the limit is 60 GB for production usage. Remember that the maximum size of the compressed dataset is only approximately 60% of the physical (and licensed) memory footprint of a HANA database.

To run a proof of concept (PoC) with a larger dataset, you have to ask one of the hardware vendors certified for HANA to lend a unit or use their try-and-buy offerings. Be aware that the PoC has to be finished within 90 days (the "grace period" of the HANA license); after this, the installation will expire. There is no way to prolong this time other than to complete a new installation or buy a regular license from SAP.

Amazon leverages a bring-your-own-license (BYOL) model for SAP software. In this case, you must already own a HANA license and download the SAP HANA Platform Edition from the SAP Software Download Center before you can start.

Don't forget that the cloud is not free; resources costs money. Depending of the memory footprint chosen, the cost Amazon charges for the infrastructure of a single SAP HANA node ranges from approximately $1.78 per hour (for 60 GB) to $4.35 per hour (for 244 GB) at this writing. Other factors that influence the cost include billing options and the geography or region in which the AWS resources are hosted.

The HANA Four-Step Deployment Process

The setup of a deployment that includes building the Amazon VPC, subnets, and so on involves four steps:

1. Sign up for an AWS account, choose the Amazon EC2 region where you want to deploy HANA, prepare the EC2 instance and EBS volumes to deploy HANA, and generate a key pair. Part of the signup process involves receiving a phone call and entering a PIN using the phone keypad.

---

[11] See http://aws.amazon.com/documentation/ec2/.

[12] See https://aws.amazon.com/documentation/vpc/.

[13] See https://aws.amazon.com/documentation/cloudformation/.

2. Set up the Amazon Virtual Private Cloud (VPC), deploy a Windows server for the SAP software download and HANA Studio, deploy a NAT instance, and configure secure access to and from resources located within the Amazon VPC. Fortunately, all you have to do is launch an AWS CloudFormation template that configures the virtual network that provides the base AWS infrastructure for your deployment. The only mandatory input expected by the template is KeyName, which is the name of the key pair you created during step 1.

3. Download HANA media from the SAP Software Download Center to an EBS volume on the Windows server provisioned in step 2. To connect to the RDP instance, get the password to the RDP instance by clicking the Connect button and using the key pair file used during launch. Connect to the RDP instance with the password decrypted and then IP into the system via Remote Desktop (see Figures 18.17 and 18.18).

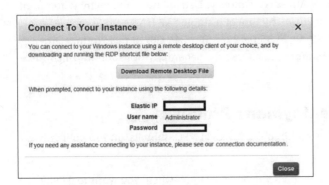

FIGURE 18.17
NAT and the RDP instance.

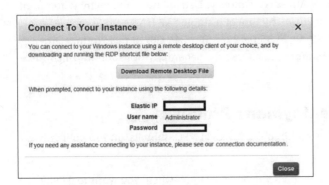

FIGURE 18.18
Connecting to the RDP instance.

The RDP instance includes a 16 GB Amazon EBS volume mounted as D:\, as illustrated in Figure 18.19.

FIGURE 18.19
Windows Server Volume Layout.

Now you can download the SAP HANA Platform Edition media to D:\ from the SAP Software Download Center:

1. Go to https://support.sap.com/swdc and log in.

2. Select Installation and Upgrades in the left navigation pane and then select A–Z index.

3. Select H and then select SAP HANA Platform Edition from the list.

4. Click SAP HANA Platform Edit 1.0 on top of the page (don't get confused by the info page below) and then click Installation.

5. In the Downloads windows, find the revision you want to download and download each file directly to the D:\ drive. The first file of the set is packaged to extract the contents of all the files pertaining to the revision you have downloaded.

6. Double-click the first file to start the extraction process and make sure that the contents are extracted into drive D:\.

4. Finally, launch several AWS CloudFormation and PowerShell scripts to initiate the SAP HANA deployment on AWS. Have the system ID, master password, instance type, and number of HANA nodes ready for this step. The scripts will perform the following tasks:

1. Create an Amazon EBS snapshot of the SAP media volume

2. Provision Amazon EC2 instance(s) for SAP HANA deployment

3. Provision Amazon EBS storage using general-purpose (SSD) volumes for HANA servers

4. Perform operating system–level tasks in support of SAP HANA installation

5. Perform SAP HANA installation and post-configuration steps

A typical single-node SAP HANA deployment takes about 25 minutes, and multi-node deployment takes 35 to 60 minutes. In a multi-node scenario, the master node is deployed first and then worker nodes are deployed concurrently. To deploy HANA into an existing Amazon VPC, just manually download the HANA installation media from the SAP Software Download Center to an Amazon EBS volume, extract the media, and create a snapshot of the volume. In the second step, use an AWS CloudFormation template to deploy SAP HANA nodes and enter Amazon VPC parameters and other details manually.

Accessing Your New HANA System

To access the SAP HANA nodes, you can use a Remote Desktop client, connect to the Windows instance where SAP HANA Studio has been preloaded, or provision an encrypted IPsec hardware VPN connection between your corporate datacenter and your Amazon VPC to connect directly to the HANA systems from a corporate network.

You can also set up AWS Direct Connect between your data center and AWS to gain direct access to your AWS resources. See the Amazon Direct Connect web pages for details.

The SAP Cloud Appliance Library

Several cloud providers offer to orchestrate the necessary hardware infrastructure for an SAP solution in less than half an hour. However, as you have seen this hour, a significant amount of time and effort goes into the download, installation, and configuration of the required SAP software.

To shorten the time for SAP customers who just want to evaluate new functionality or just to test a minor upgrade of a component, SAP provides a collection of applications called Cloud Appliance Libraries (CAL). The libraries started life inside SAP SE as an internal project called "Titanium," with the goal of providing SAP employees on-demand access to preconfigured, instantly available SAP applications to use for development and demonstration purposes. Recently SAP also made this "library" available for customers in order to provide faster ways to provision sandboxes, test, and development environments (see Figure 18.20).

SAP customers can pick and choose from a library of machine images, containing many different SAP software components or combinations of specific configurations. SAP provides and manages the actual content of the offering, whereas the infrastructure for this service is placed in public IaaS clouds. Today, Microsoft Azure and AWS provide access to SAP's CAL.

For SAP, the sweet spot of the CAL is that new customers can take advantage of fast try-and-buy offerings. Thanks to the integration of SAP Landscape Virtualization Management (LVM) connector to CAL, customer on-premise infrastructure can be connected with the public cloud in a unified and transparent way (see Figure 18.21).

Be aware that CAL, by its very nature, can provide Greenfield installations only. However, there is not much help with CAL for the lifecycle management of an existing customized SAP system landscape.

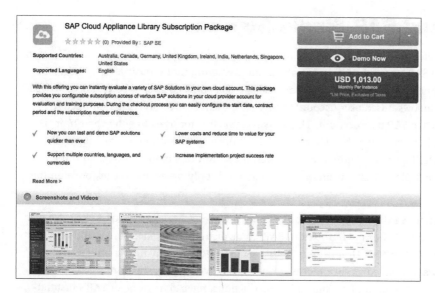

FIGURE 18.20
SAP Cloud Application Library subscription page.[14]

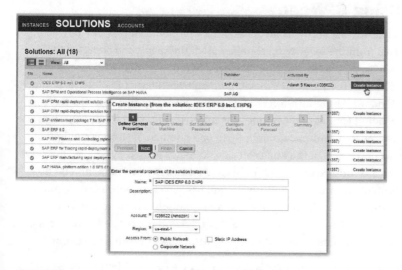

FIGURE 18.21
Creating an ERP development system with IDES[15] data via the Cloud Application Library.

---

[14] See https://cal.sap.com.

[15] International Demonstration and Evaluation System, SAP's model company.

Introducing SAP Single Sign-on

It's time to leave the trial version of SAP behind and cover one more important installation step. Once a real-world SAP system has been installed, and assuming that a basic level of Microsoft Active Directory integration has been performed, *single sign-on* (SSO) should be enabled. SAP SSO allows a user's Windows-based user account (assigned in Active Directory) to be mapped to the same user's respective SAP user account. This makes it possible for users to enter their user IDs and passwords only once (when they log on to their Windows workstation, for example); they do not have to enter logon information again when they want to log on to SAP. And if the user has accounts in multiple SAP clients on an SAP system, it is only necessary to click once on the desired client.

Basic SSO integration is rather simple. It requires only a Generic Security Service API v2 *dynamic link library* (DLL) (which is free of charge from SAP) to be distributed to each server and end-user computer participating in SSO. Unfortunately, this SSO technology is available only in a pure Microsoft environment; mixed environments cannot take advantage of this simple integration method. For SSO installation and configuration instructions, refer to any one of SAP's installation guides for Microsoft Windows-based systems.

Enabling SSO Using SPNego

An alternative way to enable SAP SSO is by using SPNego (best pronounced "ess pea nay go"). The name SPNego is derived from the security mechanism used: the *simple and protected GSS API negotiation mechanism*. SPNego is used to authenticate a client application with a remote server. This capability was first introduced by Microsoft long ago via Internet Explorer 5.1, and it was called Integrated Windows Authentication. Today, SPNego is integrated with the most popular web browsers, including Firefox and Chrome. The authentication is handled through Kerberos, which allows systems to communicate securely to one another. SPNego is configured both on Microsoft Windows and SAP. On the Microsoft side, Kerberos is used by Active Directory to validate the user. On the SAP side, Kerberos communicates with SAP to validate an end user and determine that user's ability to access SAP. Within Windows Server, a service user account (Windows user account) must be created, and then some configuration is done to relate the SAP system with this service account. Then within SAP, the SPNego Wizard is executed to define the Windows server and the service account. The user mapping within SAP must also be defined.

When everything is configured, the logon process is actually quite elegant. When users log on to their computers using their network accounts through Active Directory, they receive *ticket-generating tickets* (TGTs). When a user attempts to retrieve data from SAP, SAP sends a request to the user's system to negotiate security. The user's system retrieves its TGT and then sends the ticket to SAP. This ticket contains the user's account information and other data. SAP then takes that ticket and determines whether the user is mapped to an SAP account. If so, the user's access is further validated to ensure that permission exists to access the requested data. In the old days, you needed a Java system in the middle doing the SPNego. With state-of-the-art ABAP support packs, this need has become obsolete.

SPNego is often used to link SAP and Microsoft Office SharePoint Server 2010 and higher. In addition to SPNego, however, SharePoint Server can use yet another SSO method: Security Assertion Markup Language, covered next.

Enabling SSO Through SAML

Security Assertion Markup Language (SAML, pronounced "sam-el") is an open and powerful standard for exchanging authentication and authorization data between different security domains. This means that a user with Company A may request and obtain data from an application running within Company B. Because it is an open standard, SAML is not tied to a particular technology. SAML was created by the OASIS Security Services Technical Committee for the purpose of resolving web browser SSO issues in complex, real-world business scenarios.

SAML is new to both SAP and Microsoft. Microsoft has begun to roll out SAML support with its Active Directory products, but where you will see the most impact of SAML is between SAP and Microsoft Office SharePoint Server 2010. SAML is also used for authentication and authorization within Duet Enterprise.

SAML relies on an identity provider to authenticate users. SharePoint Server and other trusted resources can act as SAML identity providers. If the authentication proves successful, the user is issued a token. This token is then used when the user tries to access another system; it presents its token containing the user's assertions. Assertions contain information describing and validating a user (essentially consisting of a packet of security data). If a target system "recognizes" a user, the user is granted access.

Summary

This hour outlined the steps necessary for a successful technical installation. We walked through the steps necessary to install an actual installation of SAP on the Linux/Oracle platform. Finishing the post-installation phase marks the end of the technical implementation; the functional team may step in next. Afterward, we walked through obtaining and installing SAP's trial version. The hour concluded with a discussion of SAP's technical integration with Microsoft's Active Directory and SSO, including the roles of SPNego and SAML.

Case Study: Hour 18

Consider this SAP installation case study and the questions that follow. You can find answers to the questions related to this case study in Appendix A, "Case Study Answers."

Situation

MNC has standardized on Windows/SQL Server and needs to implement SAP Solution Manager in preparation for further SAP installations, including HANA in the cloud and a technical sandbox for the team. You have worked with your implementation partners to architect and size the solutions. With all the necessary planning behind you, you are ready to begin the installation processes, keeping in mind that the team also wishes to perform a proof-of-concept (PoC) test running against 200 GB of compressed data on HANA.

Questions

1. What should you do first?

2. What kind of SAP landscape environment should be installed first?

3. Where can you go to download SAP media?

4. Can you run the HANA PoC on Amazon?

5. In what timeframe does the HANA PoC need to be finished?

6. MNC is looking for ways to cut IT support costs. Currently, MNC's IT help desk spends an inordinate amount of time changing and resetting passwords. What low-cost technology can be implemented that will immediately provide relief to the IT help desk?

HOUR 19
SAP and the Cloud

What You'll Learn in This Hour:

▶ What cloud fits to what SAP solution
▶ A brief history of cloud and other computing delivery models
▶ How virtualization helps you to onboard SAP to the cloud
▶ Exit strategies from the cloud
▶ OpenStack and Monsoon
▶ Integrating ERP with SuccessFactors, Ariba, and hybris

This hour provides a deeper look into cloud computing with SAP, including how different clouds appeal to different types of consumers and providers. It then outlines several classes of cloud providers. An evolution of computing platforms from legacy to client/server, web-based, and finally the cloud helps set the stage for a closer look at how SAP is already using the cloud today. This hour also describes how customers can utilize the offerings of Amazon AWS, Microsoft Azure, and other cloud providers. We introduce Monsoon, SAP's internal OpenStack cloud implementation for development, and discuss exit strategies to mitigate risks of such approaches. This hour closes with some hints about integrating the SaaS solutions SAP has acquired during the past few years into an existing SAP solution landscape.

Forecast: Fairly Cloudy

The information technology industry has a funny way of reinventing itself every decade or two. We were doing virtualization back in the heyday of the IBM mainframe, and today we're all making a big deal of virtualization as if it's something new. We redistributed the power of IT from centralized mainframe computing to every desktop through client/server computing, and today we're busy recentralizing IT through the architectural equivalent of mainframe computing in the sky. After all, what are clouds but simply a new paradigm for delivering a service from some faraway computer?

But cloud computing isn't really all that new either. If you've ever used Microsoft's Live Hotmail product, you've been using the cloud. It is widely considered the first cloud computing application, and Hotmail was launched in 1996, well before people started labeling everything with "as-a-service"!

Amazon, interested in putting to use its vast collection of computing resources (otherwise sitting idly by until the occasional seasonal or viral purchasing peak put more of it to use) is probably the quintessential model of early cloud innovation. That an online bookseller would all but define the Infrastructure-as-a-Service (IaaS) computing model has got to give the big IT providers like CSC, HP, and IBM pause. Amazon pioneered not only the idea that inexpensive barebones servers could be tied together with a set of contemporary principles to create a computing fabric but also the revolutionary concept of buying the resources before the first tenants sign up so they don't have to wait months until the service can be delivered and have sign up for years like in a classical hosting model at the big IT providers.

So again, cloud computing is really nothing entirely new. It's just the reinvention of a computing delivery model that (again!) makes sense to a group of consumers seeking a more complete set of services delivered more effectively.

Hour 8, "SAP on the Cloud and New SAP Solutions," provided an overview of the different flavors of clouds. Although there's a lot more to it, the simplest way to define "the cloud" is to elaborate how it differs from classical hosting. Other than in a hosted environment where the customers still have their "own" equipment (sometimes "protected" by barbed-wire fences within the data-center), the resources in a cloud are shared among all tenants, and the provider decides on the infrastructure components used. IaaS is offered as a self-service model with automatic provisioning of the infrastructure; however, the customer still has to install and maintain the application and take care of software licenses and maintenance contracts. With several exceptions, billing is based on the time resources allocated rather than consumption.

Aside from the points just mentioned, there are not many differences in the technologies used between cloud solutions and on-premise infrastructure. Even better, the technologies developed for automatic provisioning of the infrastructure can be also used on-premise to host sensitive data and processes. Hybrid cloud is gaining significance as organizations realize that they need public cloud agility combined with the control and security associated with private clouds.

Just as cloud computing can vary based on its targeted consumer or user community (business end users, application developers, and IT professionals), cloud computing also varies or can be differentiated based on the entity that hosts the computers and other resources employed to deliver the cloud services. Where these computers are physically located represents still another dimension. The industry generally recognizes several variations of cloud service providers that use traditional IT, unmanaged private cloud, outsourced private cloud, and the public cloud (see Figure 19.1) to develop one or more of the following clouds hosting models:

- Internal private cloud

- Hosted private cloud

- Public cloud

- Hybrid cloud

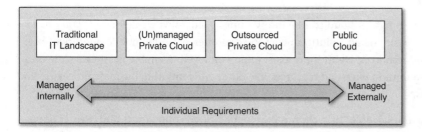

FIGURE 19.1
Sourcing options for SAP.

Private Cloud

There are still many good reasons for a company to keep its mission-critical applications together with the necessary infrastructure on its own premises. Most of the reasons are related to risk, security, or government regulations. However, a company can leverage the architectures and tools developed for cloud computing (and described in the following sections). In this way, the same scalable, highly elastic, and above all resilient infrastructure will be available, but all resources are kept under its own tight control.

Key characteristics of private clouds in general include

- A high level of control and security

- The ability to comply with regulatory requirements

- Fewer integration or performance issues than with public counterparts

- Arguably lower cost than traditional-computing-platform counterparts

Public Cloud

The public cloud is as diverse as it is broad; the vast majority of cloud offerings today are public. Anybody who offers infrastructure or software over the Internet can claim to be a public cloud provider. However, just acquiring a hangar (or an old bunker) and filling it with several thousand cheap blades does not make a cloud service. The key is how the service is managed and maintained.

For companies using cloud services for critical business processes, well-negotiated, financially incentivized *service level agreements* (*SLAs*) can mean the difference between an application that meets a business's needs and one that fails miserably. So don't let the price cloud your judgment.

Hybrid Cloud

By its very description, a hybrid cloud can be many things. Generally, we define a *hybrid cloud service* as any extended, or "tiered," platform composed of interconnected public and private or on-premise and cloud resources. Hybrids are most often employed to enable front-end scale and resiliency while safeguarding back-end resources like data, differentiating business processes, and other sensitive assets.

With fewer (or more manageable) risks than a pure public cloud counterpart and greater opportunities to introduce business-enabling innovation than its traditional computing counterpart, the hybrid cloud represents, for many consumers, the most reasonable and realistic first step into the cloud (see Figure 19.2).

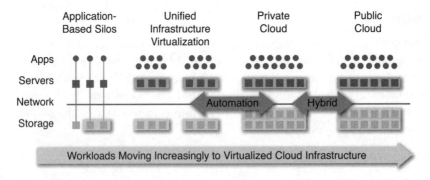

FIGURE 19.2
Transition from virtualization to cloud computing.

Bringing Together SAP and the Cloud

Like many other software providers that can point to long-time cloud attributes, SAP is no exception. SAP's core transactional systems, even dating back to R/2, have long supported the idea of multi-tenancy. SAP's client model—where company A can run alongside company B on the same application instance, using the same underlying computing platform—is one of the earliest examples of multi-tenant software. In the next few pages, we explore other real-world intersections between SAP and cloud computing.

SAP's Web Application Server

SAP didn't make the switch between client/server and more contemporary computing models in one great leap. Web-based computing platforms helped propel the SAP application platform's evolution. Although not originally envisioned, SAP's Web Application Server (WebAS) evolved into a formidable web-enabled technical platform.

WebAS provided enhanced support for Extensible Markup Language (XML) and web services technologies, including early support for Simple Object Access Protocol (SOAP) and Web Services Description Language (WSDL). With support for Unicode offered as of WebAS 6.30, the capability to standardize on a particular companywide technology platform relative to matters as diverse as language support also made a compelling argument for deploying what ultimately morphed into the platform undergirding NetWeaver.

SAP and SaaS

When the fourth edition of this book was written, SAP's only production-ready cloud-based SaaS solution was the midmarket offering Business ByDesign (BBD). Even today, none of SAP's other "traditional" applications can be delivered in this way simply because they haven't been architected from the ground up as SaaS applications. SAP's CRM-on-demand is pretty close, and you could argue that it supports the basic tenets of a SaaS model. In the meantime, SAP has expanded its SaaS portfolio significantly with the acquisition of SuccessFactors, Ariba, Fieldglass, and Concur. The functionality of these solutions was already described in Hour 12, "Using Other SAP Business Suite Applications." The challenges involved in implementing them in a complete enterprise application framework will be discussed in the last section of this hour.

SAP and PaaS

With regard to SAP and PaaS, SAP's composition environment could be PaaS enabled. More specifically, it could be hosted in such a way that the hardware, virtualization layer, operating system, database, and middleware layers are managed by a "cloud" provider. This aligns with the idea that PaaS offerings support developers as their primary consumers.

But what about using a PaaS platform to support existing SAP systems? Is there a scenario where PaaS might make sense? Perhaps, but SAP's vision is unclear. Some years ago, SAP purchased a PaaS provider, Coghead, which layered an Adobe development environment atop Amazon's IaaS offering, EC2. However, not much was heard about this.

The HANA Enterprise Cloud (HEC) on the other side resembles more of a genuine hosting offering than a contemporary cloud solution.

SAP and IaaS

At this writing, Amazon and Azure dominate in regard to SAP IaaS on public clouds. Despite the fact that neither Amazon nor Azure uses certified servers or shows up on the list of certified hardware for HANA, Amazon can even provide SAP licenses (see SAP Note 1656099 for the SAP applications supported). SAP provides special benchmarks for compute images for Amazon and Azure.[1]

SAP-certified cloud providers[2] like Atos, CapGemini, CSC, Deloitte, Freudenberg-IT, NNIT, NTT, T-Systems, Verizon, and Virtustream provide infrastructures fully certified for SAP and HANA and also offer the patching and maintenance of the SAP solutions in addition to the basic IaaS.

Virtualization Is Not Cloud Computing

Keep in mind that although virtualization might help enable cloud computing, the terms *virtualization* and *cloud computing* are not interchangeable, despite the advertising of some virtualization vendors. In fact, virtualization is not even a necessary ingredient for the cloud; elasticity, flexibility, automated provisioning, and pay-as-you-go pricing models can all be accommodated by software-enabled bare metal (physical hardware), too, as the Cisco UCS–based HANA cloud reference architecture demonstrates. This is actually good news because many client/server applications or HANA were never designed with virtualization in mind. Some applications work quite well virtualized, whereas others might require or perform best with direct access to server and disk hardware. Fortunately, the benefits of cloud computing can be harnessed in either scenario.

Moving SAP Systems to the Cloud

Even if virtualization alone is not cloud computing, virtualization can be helpful for onboarding existing SAP systems to the cloud. Remember that the HANA on Amazon and SAP Cloud Application Library (CAL) installations in Hour 18, "SAP Installation and Implementation," were Greenfield installations without any customization or data load. Moving an existing, customized environment, including the data, is a different story.

A benefit of virtualization is obviously that it enables us to copy a server on a logical level (as a flat file), including all SAP applications and configuration items within the virtual machine.

Although virtualization is one of the main pillars of cloud computing, cloud providers can use different types of hypervisor technology or virtual machine containers for their IaaS service. Depending on the compatibility of each provider's technology, there are three different scenarios for moving virtual machines from one cloud provider to another:

---

[1] See http://global.sap.com/campaigns/benchmark/appbm_cloud.epx.

[2] See http://global.sap.com/community/ebook/2012_Partner_Guide/partner-list.html.

- ▶ **Online transitioning of VMs:** If the incumbent and new service providers' cloud platforms are based on the same standard (such as OpenStack), it is technically possible to move the virtual machines that host the SAP applications online or with a near-online procedure. Obviously, a secure, high-bandwidth, and low-latency network between the old and new service providers is a prerequisite. If such a network is not available, the VM images can still be easily copied as flat files started at the new provider with a minimum of change to the configuration.

- ▶ **Exporting/importing of VMs:** If one or both service providers use a proprietary cloud platform, the procedure requires more effort. At the incumbent cloud service provider, the virtual machines in which SAP applications run need to be halted, exported, and converted to a generally accepted format, such as VMware ESX VMDK images, Citrix Xen VHD images, or Microsoft Hyper-V VHD. The images will need to be transported to the new cloud provider's datacenter either via a private network or a physical storage device. Subsequently, the VM image needs to be imported and, if required, converted to the new service provider's cloud platform technology.

- ▶ **Lifting and shifting application data and configuration:** Obviously, this is the worst-case scenario for public cloud providers who do not offer an export/import functionality for virtual machines. Moving from one cloud service provider to another requires pretty much the same effort and costs as moving today from one traditional hosted infrastructure solution to another. In the best case, only flat files such as SAP database or NetWeaver configuration files need to be copied. If different operating systems or databases are used, though, SAP data needs to be migrated (via an SAP heterogeneous system copy using R3load) to the target operating system or database before the new systems can be set up at the new service provider.

SAP as a Service?

SAP marketing is pushing the mantra "SAP as a Service." What does this statement mean? Potential customers looking for an SAP-as-a-Service offering probably envision a pay-as-you-go model for accessing SAP's classic ERP or Business Suite business applications.

For many years, service providers have hosted both the SAP application and the underlying virtualized SAP infrastructure; owned and managed the IT operations and administration staff; and worked out the back-end OS, database, and SAP licensing details for each business application's technology stack. A well-staffed hosting provider might even own the development and customization resources necessary to keep the application's capabilities and the customer's changing business needs in sync. In the end, the customer would ideally cut a monthly check based on the number of SAP end users who accessed the system. Isn't this cloud computing?

Close, but no! Is it a compelling way to deliver SAP nonetheless? Perhaps. But this scenario has simply been shoe-horned into a description that at first glance *sounds* like cloud computing. In reality, it's an interesting single-customer outsourcing model at best. The scenario provides no automated provisioning, no resource elasticity based on changing workloads, nothing akin to support for multi-tenancy, and no automated patch management or platform maintenance. Everything seemingly "cloud-like" is actually handled in a manual fashion, and with these manual processes come the requisite downtime windows, inability to dynamically scale up and down, and so on. SAP's architectural limitations combined with traditional technology platform architectures preclude creating a true SAP-as-a-Service model. Since outsourcing the infrastructure and operation to IBM Softlayer, SAP just sells the service on their paper. The private cloud IaaS solutions outlined previously will move us closer to a SAP-as-a-Service model.

Nonproduction SAP Systems in the Cloud

We might hear a lot about 3-system SAP landscapes in books and at conferences, but in the real world of SAP, many more systems are deployed over time. We tend to see anywhere from 2 to 10 or more "behind-the-scenes" nonproduction systems deployed for every production system. Common ones include staging (or preproduction) systems, multi-tiered quality-assurance systems (to better support parallel functional integration and regression testing) and development systems, several types of training systems (supporting different end-user communities), and specialized technical sandboxes (to help the IT team work through quarterly enhancement cycles). Additional technical sandboxes might be in place, too, to learn to use the latest products, to test data migration and load processes, or to pilot a pending functional upgrade. And the business teams might ask for a number of last-minute business sandboxes to pilot new SAP functionality or full-blown applications as they seek to develop new business capabilities. Even when we remove the various development and test/QA systems from this list (which can complicate matters related to the promote-to-production process), we are conservatively counting up a large number of small, nonproduction systems that could more flexibly and less expensively be hosted in an IaaS or a PaaS cloud.

Along these same lines, systems described as "standalone" may be easily transitioned to IaaS clouds, too. Reference systems maintained for historical purposes (and seldom used in reality) are excellent candidates. Pilot and *proof-of-concept* (POC) systems are, too. Many of these systems are small and need minimal computing resources. Many are transitional or short-lived in nature (here today, gone tomorrow). Still others support highly flexible user communities with low utilization and less-than-critical availability expectations. In other words, these systems are excellent candidates for the cloud!

Tomorrow: Completely Cloudy, No Chance of Sun

What does the future hold for SAP cloud computing? To be clear, we have no proprietary knowledge beyond what SAP has publicized and what many of its customers are clamoring for. So it's hard to pinpoint much besides the fact that the cloud will continue to change how SAP systems and platforms are delivered and managed. We expect, however, that many of the changes over the next few years will be driven by SAP's mission-critical *customers*. SAP's customers will continue to demand both a new round of innovation-enabling platforms and applications and the same or better levels of platform and application maturity necessary to move their businesses to the next level. They'll require that this innovation and maturity be delivered at minimal risk—if any. For example

▶ Customers will continue to demand from cloud providers the kind of stringent SLAs that align with mission-critical systems—high reliability, great availability, markedly less planned downtime, and greater resiliency in the wake of inevitable platform and data failures.

▶ Security, safeguards, and control of critical corporate data in the cloud, as well as how privacy issues are managed and enforced, will continue to drive cloud maturity.

▶ A renewed focus by cloud providers intent on helping their customers avoid vendor lock-in will actually encourage *more* customers to move to the cloud (comfortable in the knowledge that if their decision doesn't pan out as well as they like, they can presumably pick up their data, business processes, and portable applications and drop them into another SAP-supported cloud).

▶ The most forward-thinking cloud vendors are on the way to creating policy engines that allow customers to specify where data can and cannot reside, spell out their key performance indicators, and precisely address their real-time performance needs, critical batch processing do-not-exceed windows, availability requirements, workload bursting policies, service management requirements, tiered storage policies, data backup/retention policies, disaster recovery and business continuity considerations, operational priorities, and so on. In this way, a company hosted on such a cloud could be sure that its government, risk, and compliance associated with ITAR, FDA, HIPAA, and so many others and strategic concerns are properly and proactively addressed.

The key areas SAP should and will likely focus on are related to their cloud strategy. With greater application maturity and support for cloud-enabled workloads, combined with the ability to burst workloads into the public cloud to address unplanned peaks or seasonal workloads, SAP will be better positioned to keep its cash cow customers happy. So expect to see SAP's relationship with the big IaaS and PaaS providers continue to grow, its Landscape Virtualization Management (LVM) and cloud management products continue to mature, and its application architecture to slowly evolve until talk of a full-blown rewrite is actually unnecessary.

Cloud Transition and Exit Strategies

Technologies like Cisco Intercloud (see Figure 19.3) enable the extension of on-premise, private clouds by public cloud resource without the hassle of reconfiguring IP addresses. This concept also makes it easy to change the provider and avoid vendor lock-in in case of IaaS and PaaS.

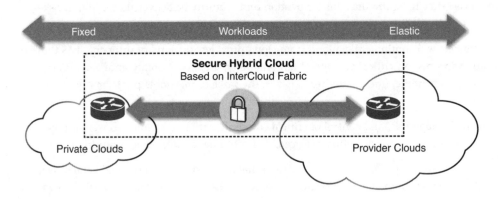

FIGURE 19.3
The Cisco Intercloud fabric extends IP addresses from private into public clouds.

But changing a SaaS provider involves some special challenges. The SaaS model works well as long you are happy with the services provided, but there are still concepts missing for "the day after."

For sure, you get your data back as an RTF or CSV file, but how can you make the ERP bookings several years back available to a tax auditor without owning the software? As long you run on-premise or use an IaaS or a PaaS model, you can keep an old system "sleeping on disk" without paying maintenance fees for the software.

Similar "exit" related topics have to be considered if you transform your SAP licenses into an SAP cloud license. As long you follow the "bring your own license" approach, you can move freely between cloud providers and even decide to go back to on-premise. In case of SAP as a Service, it would be wise to discuss an exit strategy with SAP before signing a contract to transform your SAP licenses.

Project Monsoon

Let's look into SAP's own in-house cloud deployment in the hopes that we can apply their learnings. Despite all the commitment to the cloud, SAP's own productive transactional and analytical SAP systems run in a rather traditional on-premise approach, even on HANA. Like many other enterprises, SAP adopted the cloud approach for its own development activities. Over the years, SAP's own internal clouds have evolved into massive but quite heterogeneous infrastructures boasting an army of physical and virtual machines with more than 2,000 TB of RAM and 50 PB of storage.

New functional requirements, changes in technology, and a number of mergers and acquisitions resulted in various technology silos, thus greatly complicating any migration efforts. The upgrades are manual, semi-automated, or automated, depending on the age of the cloud implementation. New highly diverse technology approaches and a mix of VMware and XEN/KVM distributed over several datacenters worldwide led to increasingly high complexity for SAP's infrastructure operations and maintenance team.

In addition, SAP rented massive resources from Amazon and Rackspace. This unstructured environment is not a problem specific to SAP but represents the reality in large-scale enterprises cloud deployments whose growth has not been controlled over the years. Even if SAP is in good company with the challenge, this situation leads to vast disadvantages both for internal users and cloud management teams:

▶ Despite the cloud paradigm, the time developers spend waiting for new infrastructure is too long because operations governance demands management approvals for resource allocation.

▶ Only entire releases can be rolled out, and this stumbling block results in higher expenditures in the upgrade/update process.

▶ A variety of individual solutions make a largely standardized infrastructure landscape impossible, which leads to poor scalability.

▶ Technology silos cause the necessary knowledge to be distributed across too many people, exacerbating the usual difficulties in collaborating during tense troubleshooting.

To resolve these issues and improve the situation for its in-house developers, SAP started the Monsoon project. The goal of this project is to implement a homogeneous cloud architecture with uniform IaaS management as well as an automated end-to-end application lifecycle management that can be extended to all of SAP's datacenters worldwide. In addition, SAP wants to return the resources rented from AWS and Rackspace to its own on-premise datacenters.

DevOps

Monsoon is implemented in DevOps mode so that development and operations of Monsoon is split into two teams expected to work hand-in-hand to enable "continuous delivery." This means that parts of Monsoon have already been implemented and used actively in production, while other parts are still in development. After passing through development and testing, components are being directly transferred into the production environment without wait time for a separate release cycle.

Open Source

In general, the Monsoon project makes intensive use of open source technologies. The open source automation solution Chef[3] is the cornerstone of Monsoon's self-service portal, enabling SAP's developers to deploy and automatically configure the needed infrastructure resources themselves. This also applies to self-developed applications. In addition to the hypervisors XEN and KVM, solutions like the container virtualization technology Docker[4] and the Cloud Foundry[5] foundation are being utilized.

OpenStack

The anchor of Monsoon's software-defined infrastructure is OpenStack. This open source project is focused on the orchestration and management of cloud environments. As with other open source initiatives, a community of developers provides contributions to the project, and a con- glomerate of vendors stand behind OpenStack, trying to position their own services built on OpenStack prominently in the market. A broad range of service providers and software vendors have developed services and solutions compatible with the OpenStack APIs. OpenStack has con- tinuously evolved into an industry standard and is destined to become the de facto standard for cloud infrastructure.

Among other things, OpenStack is also responsible for authentication, metering, and billing. At the cloud service broker and cloud integration layer, SAP Monsoon uses OpenStack Nova as a cloud computing fabric controller,[6] Cinder to provide "block storage as a service,"[7] Neutron to provide "networking as a service" between interface devices (for example, virtual NICs),[8] and Ironic to provision bare-metal machines by leveraging common technologies such as PXE boot and IPMI.[9] In addition, external APIs like Amazon EC2 can be exploited in order to distribute workloads over several cloud infrastructures (multi-cloud).

The Risks of OpenStack

In view of the complexity associated with Monsoon, the project rather deserves the name Mammoth. OpenStack is the biggest open source project the Industry has ever seen with plenty

---

[3] See https://www.chef.io/chef/.

[4] See https://www.docker.com.

[5] See http://www.cloudfoundry.org/index.html.

[6] See http://docs.openstack.org/developer/nova/.

[7] See http://docs.openstack.org/developer/cinder/.

[8] See http://docs.openstack.org/developer/neutron/.

[9] See http://docs.openstack.org/developer/ironic/.

of components developed by different communities that must work flawlessly together. The stability of the entire project depends on the stability of each component, and this can be problematic, as practical experiences demonstrate.[10]

A community of developers and vendors participates with further add-ons and source code for maintenance purposes and other improvements. Therefore, in using OpenStack, we have to consider the complexity of mixing up several independent projects.

Also, utilizing "open" products are not so "free" as the concept of free licenses promises; they need professional support. Specialized knowledge is necessary not only to build and develop open source cloud infrastructure but also to ensure proper infrastructure operations, and extensive skills in solution administration and maintenance are required. All this depends on proper documentation. Knowing that most developers don't like to write documentation even when they are paid for it, you can imagine what they do in a volunteer project.[11]

Also, OpenStack is still in development mode, which means there is not much experienced skill available on the market yet. The present supply of trained, skilled, and experienced OpenStack administrators, architects, and cloud service brokers is negligible. This market is still in the nascent stage, and big IT vendors are currently training and improving their staff knowledge.

IT organizations that attempt to deal with this complexity on their own by integrating all components from scratch tend to expose themselves to the risks involved in creating their own unmanageable cloud solution instead of using an industry-compliant standard. The customization of OpenStack to an individual company's requirements can easily lead to an OpenStack environment that is incompatible with external OpenStack-based cloud infrastructure. Thus, the connection of internal and external cloud infrastructure in a hybrid scenario becomes quite tricky.

After all, CIOs should immediately plan how to build basic skill levels for OpenStack within their IT organizations. Even if specialized service contractors can help during the implementation and operation of OpenStack-based clouds, IT architects and managers should still have the main responsibility and know what is happening. OpenStack is not an instant meal that just needs to be warmed up but rather a complex technology platform composed of several individual components whose configuration is somewhat like the preparation of a multi-course gourmet dinner. Skills and passion are on the most-wanted list.

Integrating SAP SaaS Solutions

It is quite unlikely that a SaaS business solution can be used in a standalone fashion. In an enterprise using cloud-based solutions, there is always a need to integrate them with existing

---

[10] See http://www.theregister.co.uk/2014/05/13/openstack_neutron_explainer/.

[11] See http://www.theregister.co.uk/2014/10/30/todo_opensource_lessons/.

on-premise systems or other cloud-based solutions. Synchronizing the data used or created in a process between two systems is a complex activity, and the effort to implement, test, and maintain such integration should be not be underestimated.

SAP announced prepackaged integration for S/4HANA with existing SaaS solutions. The initial example includes a rapid deployment kit for integration between SuccessFactors and S/4HANA in HCM. For those not already running S/4HANA, the following section introduces the integration of SuccessFactors, Ariba, and hybris for SAP ERP systems.

SuccessFactors

A genuine SaaS solution, SuccessFactors is architected as a multi-tenant system that provides an isolated application instance for each customer. All tenants share the same database schema, but tenant data is segmented at the database level to prevent customer data from mixing. This cloud solution was developed on a Cisco UCS infrastructure.

SuccessFactors needs to be integrated with ERP. Transferring a compensation increase from SuccessFactors to SAP payroll provides just one example. Keeping SAP HCM as the system of record or replacing it with SuccessFactors Employee Central in a model that SAP calls a "Talent Hybrid" impacts the integration design significantly and influences the selection of the middleware platform.

Different types of integration are available with SAP on-premise systems and SuccessFactors. The integration add-on 2.0 for SAP HCM and SuccessFactors Business Execution (BizX) supports NetWeaver Process Integration (PI), HANA Cloud, and flat file download. To implement the add-on, you need some knowledge of ABAP to modify the mapping of BizX fields to SAP ERP fields and of PI to transfer customer-specific fields from SAP to BizX or vice versa.

To use NetWeaver PI, you need to install the proper Enterprise Service Repository (ESR) content. To utilize SAP HANA Cloud integration (HCI), you need to run through the onboarding process with SAP. To do so, contact SAP Cloud Managed Services. While PI is included in a base NetWeaver license and only requires the cost for the implementation of PI, HCI costs 7.5% of a SuccessFactors subscription to use. This can add up when multiple applications are used.

If you implement only integration scenarios for employee data and evaluation data and use only the file download for the integration, you do not need NetWeaver PI or SAP HCI. In that case, you can use the SuccessFactors FTP site or your own FTP server. PGP encryption is supported for the integration add-on for SAP HCM and SuccessFactors BizX and saves data in files located in the file system. If you run the extraction reports for employee data using the file download option or one of the evaluation reports, SAP generates a .csv or .txt file with the physical filename that you assigned to the logical filename and stores the files under the physical file path that you assigned to the logical file path in Customizing.

For Employee Central, the Boomi AtomSphere[12] middleware platform comes bundled with the Employee Central subscription, although this solution can be expensive to use for a Talent Hybrid scenario.

SAP plans to offer the same predefined Employee Central integration content on both PI and HCI, although PI cannot be used to integrate Employee Central with third-party cloud applications such as Kronos or WorkForce Software EmpCenter. HCI does have this capability and may become bundled with an Employee Central subscription at some point in the future.

Communication with SuccessFactors BizX uses HTTPS and SOAP messages. SOAP connections are protected with web services security. For more information, Google the Security Guide for SAP NetWeaver and choose Web Services Security.[13]

A customer who is used to the degree traditional SAP solutions being customized to adapt to his individual processes might be frustrated that with SaaS his users have to adapt to the processes set by SuccessFactors. This transition requires a change in mindset about how a service is delivered. We recommend that you bring someone onto the project who is strong in change management; otherwise, the blame for a failed project will go to whoever defined the inadequate strategies. As always, remember that an implementation is about supporting customer services, not about implementing technology.

Ariba

Many customers combine an on-premises SAP SRM system with Ariba in a hybrid model. In this case, Ariba needs to be integrated into the application workflow of the existing SAP application stack. To ensure that all goods and services procured is are correctly accounted for in the finance and incoming goods departments, Ariba has to be integrated into the SAP ERP system (see Figure 19.4).

Don't underestimate the effort required to change the existing application logic (see SAP Note 1991088). The Ariba Network Integration for SAP Business Suite Administrator's Guide[14] describes the integration of Ariba to the SAP ERP systems of buyers and contains non-modifying add-ons that enables an SAP system to exchange messages in cXML[15] format, which Ariba supports.

---

[12] See http://www.boomi.com.

[13] See https://help.sap.com/saphelp_nw73ehp1/helpdata/en/f3/780118b9cd48c7a668c60c3f8c4030/frameset.htm.

[14] See http://service.sap.com/~sapidb/011000358700000993782013E.

[15] See the cXML user's guide, available at cxml.org.

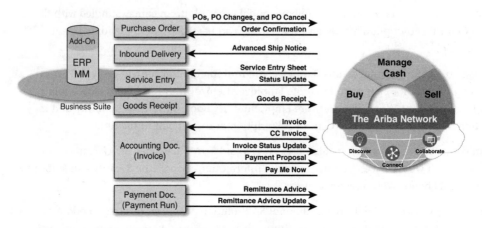

FIGURE 19.4
Message flow between SAP ERP and Ariba (courtesy of SAP).

A similar guide is available for the integration of the SAP ERP systems of vendors.[16] Among the manifold tasks within an integration is the mapping of tax categories and tax rates used in Ariba to the country-specific tax codes in your ERP system. You also need to decide which invoice document type is to be created when an invoice or a credit memo from Ariba arrives, and you need to set control parameters to decide how to proceed if a document cannot be processed because of warnings or errors.

SAP ERP systems in private or public clouds can be either connected directly to the Ariba network or "mediated" through SAP PI; a mixture is not recommended.[17] In case you decide to use PI, you can utilize the Content Package delivered together with the Ariba network adapter for SAP NetWeaver.[18] All messages are exchanged in cXML format via web services. The document output is triggered using message output control. To enable the transfer of purchase orders between SAP ERP and the Ariba network, you therefore have to customize the message output control.

Incoming *Ship Notice Requests* create inbound delivery documents in SAP ERP and update the purchase orders accordingly. An incoming *Service Entry Request* creates a service entry sheet in SAP ERP and updates the purchase order accordingly. The approval or rejection of the service entry sheet triggers a *Status Update Request* message that transfers the status to the Ariba network.

---

[16]   See help.sap.com/se4aribanet10.

[17]   See scn.sap.com/docs/DOC-51873.

[18]   Log in to Ariba Connect and select Software Online, Download Software, Ariba Adapter for SAP.

At this writing, the following restrictions for the integration of invoices exist:

▶ In Ariba, suppliers can change the unit of measure of invoice items so that it differs from the corresponding purchase order items. SAP does not tolerate different units of measure in invoice items and the referenced purchase order items.

▶ Ariba and the cXML definition support different currencies for different amounts within an invoice. An SAP invoice supports a single currency for all amounts.

▶ Ariba allows multiple taxes per invoice item. If in SAP the country of the receiving company code does not have a tax jurisdiction system, multiple taxes at the invoice item level are not supported. If multiple taxes are provided at the invoice header level, the item tax code in SAP has to be determined using a BAdI implementation.

▶ Ariba allows several additional amounts in one invoice, such as special handling and shipping. The SAP invoice supports only "unplanned delivery costs" for additional costs. Ariba Integration 1.0 for SAP sums up special handling and the shipping amount of the Ariba invoice as unplanned delivery costs.

▶ If unplanned delivery costs are posted as a separate G/L line in an SAP invoice, the tax category in cXML can be mapped to ERP tax codes for unplanned delivery costs only if the shipping amount and the special handling amount in cXML have the same tax category and the same tax rate. If they differ, the invoice generally cannot be processed in SAP ERP.

▶ Ariba supports allowances and charges both at the invoice header and item levels. However, allowances and charges at the header level cannot be transferred to the SAP invoice since the *Unplanned Delivery Costs* field is already used to represent shipping and special handling costs. Therefore, allowances and charges at the header level are not supported if you integrate Ariba with SAP. Allowances and charges at the item level are supported and are handled according to the standard invoice verification process.

For the integration of Ariba Discount Management with ERP, the SAP system can transfer payment proposals based on accounting documents for incoming invoices to Ariba. The default option is to pay within the grace period to take advantage of the cash discount terms. The option to pay after the due date, without receiving any discount, needs to be enabled by implementing a BAdI method.

SAP sends an updated payment proposal if data relevant for payments is changed. For example, if payment terms or discount amounts are changed in accounting, the system assigns a credit memo and thus reduces the payment amount by a partial payment. When invoices are completely paid, the corresponding payment proposals are sent to Ariba with the operation *delete* to ensure that the corresponding scheduled payments are deleted.

hybris

As an exception to SAP's acquisition policy, hybris is not a SaaS solution. The architecture is based on the Spring[19] open source framework. The hybris Platform uses Java EE servlet containers like Tomcat[20] or VMware vFabric tcServer[21] for execution either in a private cloud (on-premise) or hosted by a public cloud provider. Services are implemented in the form of Spring beans.

The system consists of web and application servers and a database used as the persistence layer (where data can physically reside without the need for the power to remain on). The web server provides static content and redirects requests for dynamic content to the application server where the hybris suite is installed and all business processes are running. Using Java and JVM, the containers are able to run on Microsoft Windows, Apple Mac OS X Server, or various UNIX operating systems.

Since the release of 5.1, SAP HANA and MongoDB are supported as the persistence layer, in addition to Oracle, MySQL, and Microsoft SQL Server.

Summary

This hour introduced cloud computing, including information about the ideas of cloud consumers and providers. We reviewed the evolution of the cloud and looked at how SAP uses the cloud internally and how it might continue to evolve from a cloud-enablement perspective. We also gave a short overview of how some of the recent SAP acquisitions can be integrated into Business Suite to conclude this hour.

Case Study: Hour 19

Consider this SAP cloud case study and the questions that follow. You can find answers to the questions related to this case study in Appendix A, "Case Study Answers."

Situation

With pressures to reduce costs and increase business agility, MNC's entire IT organization has been tasked with reviewing opportunities to leverage cloud computing. Your SAP technical team has been scheduled to work with the CIO's new cloud steering committee, and you have been tasked with building awareness regarding the cloud and what it really means in the context of SAP. Assist the committee by answering their questions.

---

[19] See http://www.springsource.org/about.

[20] See http://tomcat.apache.org.

[21] See http://www.vmware.com/products/vfabric-tcserver/.

Questions

1. Who are the consumers of SaaS, PaaS, and IaaS?

2. Of the outlined cloud provider models, which represents the most reasonable or realistic first step toward cloud computing?

3. What kind of SAP applications are delivered through SaaS?

4. Of the cloud applications and systems outlined this hour, which ones might be most applicable to the SAP team today or soon?

5. How might SAP's Monsoon help us?

HOUR 20
SAP System Administration and Management

What You'll Learn in This Hour:

- ▶ Proactive system monitoring
- ▶ Introduction to SAP CCMS and the SAP Solution Manager for administration
- ▶ Introduction to the SAP Landscape Virtualization Manager
- ▶ Introduction to Nagios
- ▶ Day-to-day monitoring and management

Administration, maintenance, and management of the ongoing operations of SAP systems are crucial for good performance and avoiding surprises. This includes monitoring for availability; performing user administration and basic authorizations; patching of operating systems, the hypervisor, and applications; and other fundamental technical administrative functions. Management, on the other hand, is akin to controlling the system. This hour covers both SAP administration and management.

Management Tools

There are plenty of system management tools around, but only SAP tools give you insight into the SAP application itself; all the third-party tools that claim to provide insight into the application derive their data by using the basic monitoring features of SAP (described in the next section).

One of the factors most appreciated about SAP systems is how manageable they are, even without the benefit of third-party tools. No other large-scale business application even comes close. SAP put a lot of thought into making its applications manageable out of the box, incorporating key technology stack coverage like operating system and database support alongside application-layer support. In the next few pages, we'll go through some of the built-in and other monitoring utilities and solutions you should evaluate.[1]

---

[1] See http://wiki.scn.sap.com/wiki/display/TechOps/Home?original_fqdn=wiki.sdn.sap.com.

Computing Center Management System

SAP was one of the first software vendors to provide an integrated tool to manage its applications. Its Computing Center Management System (CCMS) is part of the SAP application instance itself and does not require additional installation effort. Besides managing the SAP application, CCMS also monitors the database and the operating system hosting the SAP system.

The tool allow SAP administrators to monitor and manage SAP's overall health, application and database server utilization, user and batch job performance, print jobs, and so on in real time as well as from a historical perspective.

To gather data from the server hardware, a daemon called SAPOSCOL has to be started before the database and the SAP application itself are started. The CPU, memory and disk utilization, swapping/paging activity, LAN statistics, file system status, top CPU consumers, and hardware information collected by SAPOSCOL will be also used for the go-live reports and Early Watch Reports described later in this hour. The analysis for the server is missing from these reports when the SAPOSCOL daemon has not been started.

Using CCMS is simple. There are hundreds of shortcut transaction codes (T-codes) to pull performance and availability data out of CCMS. For example, T-codes like ST06 and DB02 provide OS- and database-specific data, respectively. ST03 and ST04 give information related to system-level performance. ST07, SM04, and AL08 provide end-user–focused data, such as the number of users logged in to a particular functional area or application server or executing specific functional transactions. And ST30 enables you to drill down into an SAP performance analysis.

Because CCMS is unable to manage Java-based solutions such as the SAP Enterprise Portal, SAP added agents like Wily Introscope[2] and the ability to use SNMP traps for the successor of CCMS, the SAP Solution Manager (SolMan).

SAP Solution Manager

As an SAP system landscape typically includes a large number of installed SAP systems, each with its own CCMS, it would be quite cumbersome to manage the landscape using individual CCMSs. The SAP Solution Manager enables the central management of a complete SAP system landscape. SolMan is also used to forward tickets to SAP support if you run into trouble. SolMan is provided to SAP customers as part of their license agreement, with no additional license fees necessary, but SolMan needs an infrastructure on its own, and it has to be implemented, hosted, patched, and managed.

---

[2] Now owned by CA. A read-only version is bundled with SAP Solution Manager; however, the Right to View (RTV) is restricted.

Figure 20.1 shows the agents and connections between a managed system with both ABAP and Java stack, SolMan, the Introscope host, and the SAP NetWeaver Landscape Directory (SLD).

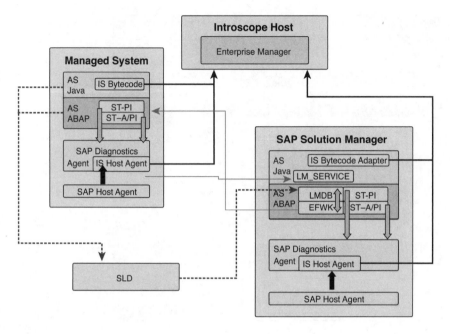

FIGURE 20.1
Communication between a managed system, SolMan, SLD, and Introscope.

SolMan provides end-to-end monitoring for SAP system landscapes of any size from a single centralized management console or "single pane of glass." This includes the application and job monitoring of complex components like SRM and CRM, PI, and APO. It also includes the ability to monitor status of other SAP products, such as ITS, SAPRouter, Business Connector, and more.

RFC connectivity between SAP systems can be checked, too, along with the status of XML, Java, and ABAP technology components within Web AS. However, the basis is still the CCMS Monitoring Infrastructure and SAPOSCOL. Mobile apps for Solution Manager are available for business process analytics, incident management, change approval, job monitoring, etc. on iPads and Android tablets.

SolMan Technical Monitoring

SolMan contains a large number of scenarios, such as technical monitoring. In the opening window for this scenario in Figure 20.2, you can see a well-done system hierarchy to the left: technical systems, database instance, technical instance, and guests. The list is fully interactive and allows navigation between systems and their metrics, divided into availability, performance, configuration, and exceptions. System monitoring allows monitoring of metrics for each system.

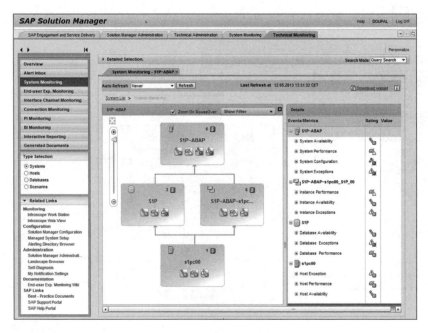

FIGURE 20.2
The SolMan Workcenter window for technical monitoring.

On the right side of Figure 20.2, you can see the system monitoring interface overview. Here, you can specify one of the most fundamental metrics: the number of connected users.

The system monitor is set to the technical system and is displayed in the system performance section. Actual data is color coded either gray (undefined), green (good), yellow (warning), or red (undesirable). For example, there would be a red rating when more users are connected than the SAP license allows. The corresponding thresholds, ratings, and alerts can be individually set, and you can connect notifications to them. See Figure 20.3 for an example of a system overview.

In addition to the current status and rating, you can also display statistics on historical data. By clicking the graph icon, you open the metric monitoring window (another part of the technical monitoring scenario), where data is displayed in an interactive graph form.

In this window, you can filter by period, change the display threshold, and display certain value when you click on a point in the curve. In addition, you can view metric trend and data source table. If you need to track your own metrics, it's easy to set them up. Perhaps best of all, you can use system monitoring even from your smartphone.

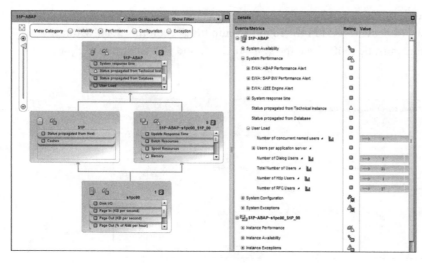

FIGURE 20.3
SolMan overview for a managed system (in this example, SP1).

SolMan Dashboards

SolMan includes numerous dashboards that overview each SAP system landscape (see Figure 20.4).

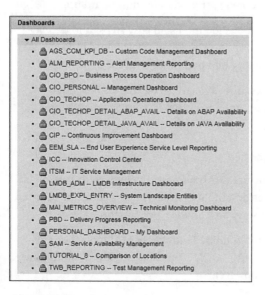

FIGURE 20.4
SolMan dashboards.

To enable the dashboards, some functionality must be activated, such as Service Availability Management (SAM). To activate SAM in the solman_setup transaction the global settings and the infrastructure must be configured, the scope defined, and SAP reporting set up (see Figure 20.5).

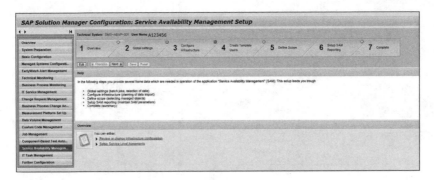

FIGURE 20.5
SolMan Service Availability Management (SAM) setup.

The dashboards can be used only if the appropriate scenario is active. This means there is no Customer Code Management dashboard when the Customer Code Management option is not configured and active. Also keep in mind that the user needs special rights to call the dashboards. To make this easier, SAP provides preconfigured user profiles for dashboard use.

In addition, every user can configure his or her own dashboard, using easy steps, and decide which metrics to see. For example, the SolMan Application Operations Dashboard in Figure 20.6 is configured to provide an overview of the availability and performance of the system.

More systems can be configured if the monitoring is already active. You can also display which kinds of systems are connected to the SolMan and the entries in your SAP Landscape Management Database (LMDB).

Monitoring and Alerting Infrastructure

The end-to-end Monitoring and Alerting Infrastructure (MAI) became available with SolMan 7.2 SP12. It provides advanced analysis tools for error handling and business process monitoring. However, MAI is primarily intended for internal use by SAP and for SAP Support.

In the role SAP_SM_TECH_MON_TOOL, you can run a limited number of MAI tools that are available for customers by calling the transaction MAI_TOOLS. The tools displayed by choosing Expert Mode are reserved for use by SAP Support, however.[3]

---

[3] See http://help.sap.com/saphelp_sm71_sp10/helpdata/en/d4/5d8afe9f104fd98bb4fbb4b8cb4c2f/content.htm.

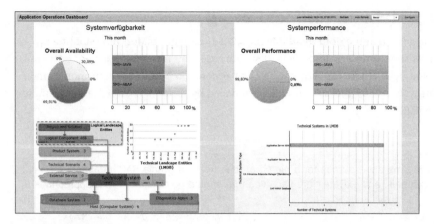

FIGURE 20.6
The SolMan Application Operation Dashboard.

SAP Landscape Virtualization Manager

SAP Landscape Virtualization Manager (LVM)[4] is a Java application that runs as an add-on to SAP NetWeaver Application Server Java. Like its predecessor Adaptive Computing Controller (ACC), LVM depends on agents running on the OS to collect the status and performance of a machine and its interfaces to virtualization managers and storage arrays to perform its tasks. The SAP host agents can be downloaded from the SAP Service Marketplace; the agents for the storage have to be provided by the storage vendors.

LVM lets you deploy SAP systems by dragging and dropping them onto available hardware resources. This feature is actually enabled by mounting the logical storage volumes (LUNs) on an external storage device where all the data, code, and configuration files of an SAP system are stored on a server. LVM can also be used to deploy virtual machines, and it supports the relocation of SAP instances between physical and virtual machines as well.

Non-productive systems can be "sent to sleep" simply by shutting them down and waking them up on demand to save energy. Additional application server instances can be invoked unattended if workload exceeds predefined limits. The SAP system and database still have to be installed the "traditional way" for obvious reasons, however.

For an additional license fee LVM can also generate automatically complete SAP test, training, and QA instances, utilizing the various cloning features available from enterprise storage vendors. This feature includes the necessary pre- and post-processing steps.

---

4   Not to be confused with logical volume management, a method of transparently storing computer data spread over several partitions.

Using Your Database for Monitoring

There may be occasions when the data available in CCMS (RZ20) or SolMan may not line up with your business or monitoring requirements. It such a case, you may leverage your database to query the data you need. There are many ways to incorporate a query into your monitoring/ management strategy. See Examples 20.1 and 20.2 provided by secure-24. Ultimately, the implementation is up to you.

EXAMPLE 20.1

The following query returns short dumps for a period of time from an Oracle SAP database (the bold items like +dbo+, +xTime+, and +xDate+ are variables that should be populated with appropriate values):

```
select datum Shortdump_Date , uzeit Time, to_char(AHOST) Host,UNAME UserName,
MANDT Client,
to_char(substr(FLIST||FLIST02,6, to_number(substr(FLIST||FLIST02,3,3))))
 ShortDump ,decode (substr(FLIST||FLIST02,substr(FLIST||FLIST02,3,3) , 2 ),
 'XC',
 to_char(substr(FLIST||FLIST02,to_number(substr(FLIST||FLIST02,3,3))+11,
 to_number((substr(FLIST||FLIST02,
 to_number(substr(FLIST||FLIST02,3,3))+8,3))) )), '' ) Exception,
 to_char( substr(FLIST||FLIST02,instr(FLIST||FLIST02,'AP0')+5,
 to_number(substr(FLIST||FLIST02,instr(FLIST||FLIST02,'AP0')+2,3))))
 Report from '+dbo+'.SNAP where SEQNO=\'000\' and
 DATUM >= '+ xDate +' and uzeit >= '+ xTime +''Exception,    to_char( substr(FLIST|
 |FLIST02,instr(FLIST||FLIST02,'AP0')+5, to_number(substr(FLIST||FLIST02,instr(FLIST
 ||FLIST02,'AP0')+2,3))))
   Report from '+dbo+'.SNAP where SEQNO=\'000\'
                           and DATUM >= '+ xDate +' and uzeit >= '+ xTime +''
```

EXAMPLE 20.2

The following query will return aborted job information from an Oracle-based SAP database (the bold items like +dbo+, +xTime+, +xDate+, and +jobName+ are variables that should be populated with appropriate values):

```
SELECT JOBNAME,STRTDATE,STRTTIME,ENDDATE,ENDTIME,STATUS from
'+dbo+'.TBTCO where ENDDATE >= '+ xDate +' and
ENDTIME >= '+ xTime +' and (JOBNAME like '+jobName+')
```

Nagios

Nagios is an example of an open source monitoring system that can be used to manage SAP systems together with networks and infrastructure. Nagios offers monitoring and alerting services for servers, switches, applications, and services. It alerts users when something goes wrong and alerts them a second time when the problem has been resolved. Nagios is licensed under the GNU GPL v2.

The actual checking is done by plug-ins that Nagios schedules on a regular basis. These plug-ins can be any kind of script or binary program; they simply have to follow certain conventions when presenting their check results. There are lots of plug-ins available to monitor the whole stack, including the system hardware, the operating system, the database, and applications.

Nagios plug-ins for monitoring SAP provide an interface to the SAP CCMS infrastructure and display the results in Nagios, check backups and archives on Oracle instances, check SAP application availability and response time (packet round-trip time), and so on.

check_sap_health is a new plug-in written in Perl.[5] Out of the box, it can be used to monitor the following aspects of an SAP system:

▶ **Connectivity and logins to an instance:** It also measures the response time, which can be used to draw a graph showing the behavior over a long time.

▶ **CCMS metrics:** Everything available from transaction RZ20 can be monitored—end nodes in the tree as well as subtrees as a whole. If a monitoring tree element has a numerical value, it will be used to draw a graph.

▶ **Failed updates:** By querying the VBHDR table, check_sap_health can alert when the number of failed updates is above a defined limit.

▶ **Shortdumps:** The plug-in checks whether shortdumps occurred during the last n minutes, and it alerts if there were more than a certain threshold. It is possible to check for short-dumps of specific programs/users only. In this way, you can create separate Nagios services for systems and applications.

▶ **Background jobs:** In this mode, the plug-in alerts if jobs have a bad exit status and/or if the runtime exceeded a defined limit. Again, it is possible to check on a global basis or to select only specific programs/users.

It also provides an API that can be used to dynamically extend the plug-in with self-written Perl snippets. This allows you to implement custom RFC/BAPI calls in a few lines of code so that monitoring of business logic and enterprise-specific functions is a breeze. Examples for existing use cases are

▶ Measuring and graphing the runtimes of specific functions for capacity planning

▶ Measuring the runtimes of specific functions from several distant locations to identify network connectivity and performance problems

▶ Reading end times of nightly UC4-jobs and checking whether SLAs have been violated

---

[5] See http://labs.consol.de/nagios/check_sap_health/ by gerhard.lausser@consol.de.

Day-to-Day SAP Monitoring

Because a complete implementation of LVM is a rather complex project, the spread of LVM and Nagios is somewhat limited. Fortunately, basic SolMan installation is easily done for most SAP landscapes. While a complete description of all functions of the SolMan is beyond the scope of this book, we explain in the following sections how to use SolMan to fulfill the most common monitoring and maintenance tasks. Detailed instructions can be found in several publications.[6]

System Status

The Alert Overview (see Figure 20.7), displays all alerts for all Solution Manager–connected systems. You can create an overview to see the alerts of a single system or a special kind of systems.

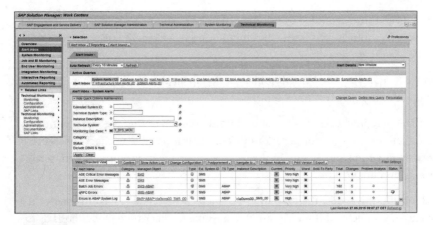

FIGURE 20.7
SolMan – Technical Monitoring – alert inbox.

If you want to check the systems and have a trusted connection, you can drill directly into the systems. SolMan provides a configurable self-monitoring capability that can be configured for this purpose (see Figure 20.8).

To set up special application monitoring like job monitoring, BI monitoring, PI monitoring, or integration monitoring, you need specific parameter values and the necessary thresholds from your application team. The setup has to be done in solman_setup (see Figure 20.9).

---

[6] For example, see Lars Teuber, Corina Weidmann, and Liane Will's *Monitoring and Operations with SAP Solution Manager*.

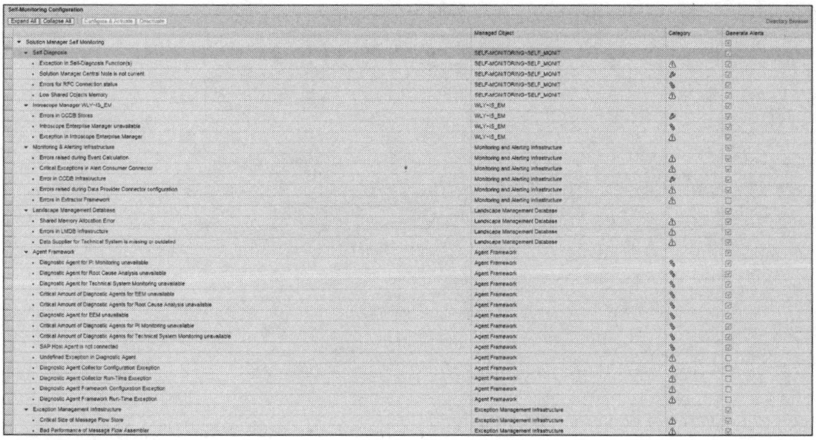

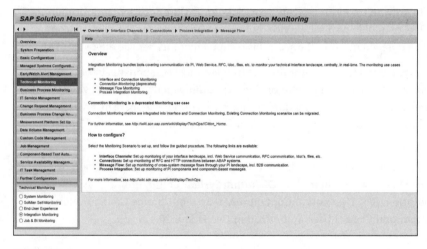

FIGURE 20.8
Solution Manager's self-monitoring screen.

FIGURE 20.9
SolMan – solman_setup, Technical Monitoring, Integration Monitoring.

System Recommendations

Searching the SAP Service Marketplace every day for notes that could be relevant for your system would be a cumbersome task. With system recommendations, you can pretty easily check whether there are new security notes, HotNews, performance notes, legal change notes, or correction notes. Components can be filtered to enable applications owners to check for their specific applications (see Figure 20.10).

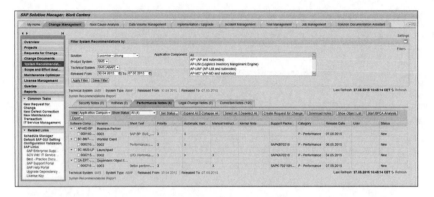

FIGURE 20.10
SolMan, Change Management, System Recommendations.

Configuration Validation Check

Security continues to grow in importance every year. SolMan feature Security Optimization Service (SOS), which is available as a self-service and as a remote service. The first is incorporated into SAP license agreements, and the second is a supplementary service offered by SAP.

The most effective way, however, to monitor the security of critical components in an SAP system is to use Configuration Validation as part of Change Management. The check validates the managed system configuration against standard or reference configurations. The SAP extractor framework automatically extracts all required data for the validation from the connected systems.

You can configure validation checking for the following areas: Software Configuration, ABAP Instance Parameters, Database Configuration, Operating System Configuration, Business Warehouse Configuration, RFC Destination Configuration, System Change Configuration, Security Configuration, and Critical User Authorization (see Figure 20.11).

Solution Manager Self-Services

In addition to SOS, plenty of other self-services can be executed with SolMan, either by you or remotely by SAP SE personnel. SAP Note 1609155 provides a comprehensive overview of available self-services (see Figure 20.12).

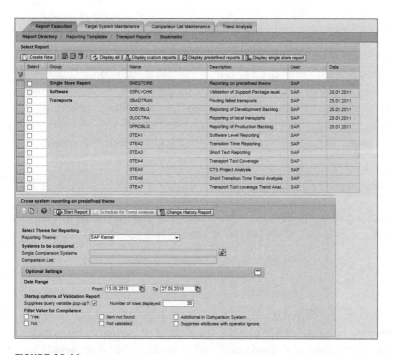

FIGURE 20.11
SolMan, Configuration Validation Check.

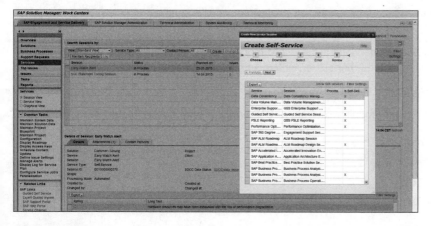

FIGURE 20.12
Solution Manager's self-services.

Summary

Proactive SAP system administration and management are key to maintaining a highly available and well-performing system. System administration in the broadest sense cannot exist in a vacuum; it must be tied to tools and approaches that facilitate proactive maintenance and management by exception. SAP SolMan, CCMS, and LVM are still tools system administrators use most to do their management tasks. This hour provided insight into only a few of the many tools and techniques used by SAP IT professionals to administrator and manage their SAP systems.

Case Study: Hour 20

Consider this SAP system administration and management case study and the questions that follow. You can find answers to the questions related to this case study in Appendix A, "Case Study Answers."

Situation

MNC's SAP environment has been growing and consists now of about 50 different SAP instances. Part of your team's responsibility is to proactively monitor the entire SAP environment, particularly the SAP ERP ECC, CRM, Enterprise Portal (Java only), and dual-stack PI environment.

Questions

1. Which SolMan dashboard enables you to view end-user experience from a service level perspective?

2. Which SAP CCMS transactions allow you to monitor end-user data such as the number of users per functional area, per server, or executing specific functional transactions?

3. What does SAP LVM let you do?

4. How can you centrally monitor your entire SAP environment, including multiple landscapes?

SAP Enhancements, Upgrades, and More

What You'll Learn in This Hour:

▶ The three most common types of SAP application updates

▶ The significance of enhancements

▶ Upgrade and enhancement terminology

▶ Differences between technical and functional upgrades

▶ Avoiding confusing upgrades and migrations

▶ Upgrading project requirements

Despite how well an SAP system might be running, the ever-changing demands of business, legal obligations, and components of the software stack running out of support make updates of the SAP system landscape mandatory. After they've finally gone "live," most SAP installations are updated monthly or quarterly in one way or another. These updates come in the form of what SAP terms application *enhancements*, *upgrades*, and *technology stack updates*, topics we cover this hour.

The widespread use of the adage "never touch a running system" is evidence that every change brings with it a risk in an increasingly complex system landscape. Practical experience shows that insufficiently prepared changes are the main cause of malfunction. Therefore, good change management practices have particular significance as a central quality assurance instrument, regardless of the types of application changes.

Setting the Stage: Making Changes to SAP

In the world of SAP, systems are updated fairly regularly. The nature of these updates can vary tremendously. The SAP and infrastructure technical teams update the technology stack on a fairly regular basis. The following are some examples:

▶ Operating system software requires patches and other updates in response to bug fixes or to protect against viruses and other potential threats.

▶ Database software requires patches and other updates in response to bug fixes or to protect against viruses and other potential threats.

▶ Server system boards and disk controllers require firmware updates every now and then to fix bugs or support new hardware options.

▶ New and faster network cards, disk controllers, disk drives, and so on are updated every few years.

Beyond technology updates, the various business teams put in requests to change or add business functionality:

▶ **Release updates:** The finance team might need updates made in SAP Enterprise Resource Planning's Finance module to adhere to a new accounting principle or to help close the monthly books faster.

▶ **Legal patches:** In response to new federal and state regulations, the logistics team might request updates in how international trade is conducted or accounted for.

▶ **Functional changes and business process changes:** These changes range from updates in a transaction's screen layout to a complete rebuild of the business processes of a department.

The word *update* is used in other specific ways, making its generic use pretty confusing. To make matters worse, people toss around many other words that also imply changing SAP. In the case of non-ERP SAP components and applications, major business updates come in the form of upgrades, for example. In the case of SAP Enterprise Resource Planning (ERP), business updates are delivered more incrementally through SAP's enhancement packages (EHPs). And in other cases, systems and data are migrated. How to correctly use these terms and what they mean are discussed in this hour.

Enhancement and Upgrade Terminology

A discussion of terminology is in order before we go further. There are many similar and therefore confusing terms related to making changes to a live SAP environment, especially when it comes to changing SAP. The terms *migration* and *upgrade* are often misused, while the general term *enhancement* is simply misunderstood. Let's turn to enhancements first.

Enhancements Explained

In general, SAP enhancements are modifications or updates to existing SAP systems; they modify or extend current functionality. After your organization has gone live with SAP, you might be inclined to think that all the real work in terms of developing and maintaining functionality has been done and little follow-on work remains. To some extent, this is true for the IT team; the stress of implementation and late-into-the-night testing will be replaced with steady-state maintenance, occasional technology stack patches, and so on.

For the business analysts and development teams tasked with representing the business and its needs, however, much work remains to be done well after go-live. After all, the business will continue to evolve, and new functional needs will come to light in the wake of changes. Even more common, bug fixes and other updates to existing business processes need to be tested and introduced. This is where enhancement planning pays great dividends for the organization.

Enhancements can be SAP driven (such as those done through SAP support packages) or customer driven (meaning they are developed in-house and transported through the SAP landscape). Enhancements in many cases can represent a combination of updates, too. For instance, to enhance a current financial business process, an organization might need to update the system's SAP WebApp server to a required support package level and then make subsequent custom modifications to adapt the new functionality to an SAP system's specific business process.

Enhancements can also be delivered through specific SAP EHPs. EHPs are prepackaged collections of business functionality that act as "mini upgrades" to the core SAP system's functionality. EHPs differ from support packages in that they add functionality on top of the SAP application stack instead of providing it through modifying existing functionality. Surprisingly, SAP makes it possible to install EHPs without impacting the system; no downtime is required to actually implement them. However, to actually make enhancements or changes to the system, they must be activated in the SAP Implementation Guide (IMG). (Refer to Hour 17, "An SAP Developer's Perspective," for a discussion of the IMG.) In this way, through EHPs, SAP customers have the ability to modularly upgrade functionality. Although EHPs can extend the product lifecycle for a season (for SAP ERP systems), there will come a time when an upgrade will indeed be necessary, which leads us to our next discussion.

Don't stay too much behind. Many SAP implementations stay on older releases unless regulatory and compliance purposes enforce an update. This might seems like a good strategy for avoiding the effort of ongoing "housekeeping"; however, this strategy can end up in a situation where additional functionality delivered by SAP EHPs cannot be applied when the business needs them.

Upgrade Terminology

The term *upgrade* is confusing because it is used so generally. The key is to ask what is actually being changed, or "upgraded." Are we talking about an SAP server hardware upgrade, an operating system (OS) upgrade, an Oracle or a SQL Server database upgrade, an SAP kernel upgrade, an SAP support pack upgrade, or a full-blown SAP functional release or version upgrade? As you learned earlier, most of these examples fall under the realm of "technology updates" and have nothing to do with upgrading SAP. When using the term *upgrade*, be as specific and detailed as possible to avoid confusion. When upgrading non-SAP components in the SAP landscape, it is okay to say, "We are upgrading our SAP servers" or "We are upgrading the database to SQL Server 2014." However, it's preferable to talk of updating rather than upgrading these technology stack components.

Talk of doing an SAP upgrade really means upgrading SAP itself. This might mean you're upgrading the functionality of the SAP system—performing an SAP functional upgrade. Such a change is a major undertaking, nearly akin to doing a new implementation. On the other hand, the technical team might speak of performing an SAP *technical* upgrade. As mentioned, this is an upgrade to the Basis layer underpinning the SAP application; no functionality is changed or even touched in an SAP technical upgrade. Technical upgrades equate to updating the SAP kernel (replacing old files with new ones) along with perhaps some other updates to the technology stack (necessary for support reasons because not every SAP Basis release is supported by every operating system version or hardware platform, for example). Suffice it to say here, therefore, that it is important to communicate properly about the scope and magnitude of an SAP upgrade, if only to keep everyone on the same page.

Upgrades Are Not Migrations

The term *migration* is often thrown about interchangeably with the term *upgrade*, and it's necessary to differentiate between the two because they mean completely different things in the world of SAP. Even longtime SAP customers talk inaccurately about "migrating" their SAP ERP systems to SAP ERP 6.0 or "migrating" SAP Customer Relationship Management (CRM) to the latest functional release. These statements are incorrect. Figure 21.1 properly aligns these terms.

To add to the confusion, SAP released a tool called Test Data Migration Server (TDMS) several years ago; this tool has nothing to do with traditional migrations but rather is more aligned with copy functionality. TDMS allows SAP customers to essentially copy a portion of an SAP database and build a new system around the smaller, condensed database, thus enabling rapid prototyping for new projects. With TDMS, the term *migration* takes on yet another meaning. TDMS enables *data migration*, such as helping to move data from a non-SAP system, such as Oracle PeopleSoft, into an SAP system. TDMS also facilitates moving data between SAP systems in the form of partial or full client copies. These types of projects are labeled SAP data migrations.

It is for all these reasons that we find it necessary to differentiate between different types of migrations. In SAP vernacular, *migration* is most correctly associated with technology platform changes. These are properly labeled as OS/DB (operating system/database) migrations. An OS/DB migration is required when a customer's IT department decides to move the SAP computing platform from one operating system or database platform to a different operating system or database platform. Such a move is a complex endeavor that requires the services of a properly certified OS/DB migration specialist. And such migrations have nothing to do with upgrades. In fact, in a migration, the functional release level remains static; it's not even an option to perform an upgrade concurrently with an OS/DB migration.

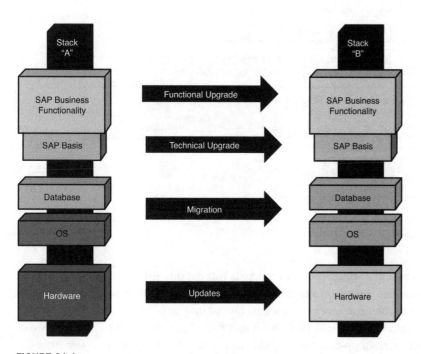

FIGURE 21.1
In the world of SAP, the terms *upgrade*, *migration*, and *update* are not interchangeable.

SAP OS/DB Migrations

An SAP OS/DB migration may be conducted to change platforms between different flavors of UNIX, Linux, and Windows. It is also conducted to move between different database platforms, such as from Oracle, DB2, or SQL Server to HANA. The problem an OS/DB migration solves is that databases are not "binary compatible" with one another on different operating systems. Therefore the SAP system's database data files cannot just be copied from one platform to a new platform. Similarly, a change of database vendors requires reloading the SAP data into the new database; you can't move data files recognized by IBM DB2 to a system running Microsoft SQL Server or HANA without unloading the data into a generic format and then reloading it into the new database's format.

Sometimes you'll hear the term *heterogeneous system copy* also used to describe an OS/DB migration, as opposed to its cousin the *homogenous system copy*, where the OS or DB platform does not change (see Figure 21.2).

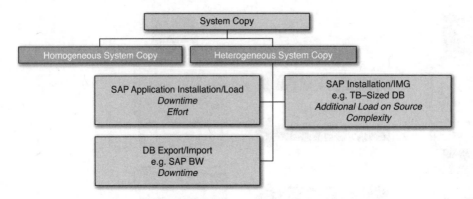

FIGURE 21.2
SAP system copy/migration methodologies.

While a migration from a RISC-based platform to x86 is without any risk if you have an experienced and certified SAP migration consultant, it is still a major project that has to be carefully prepared. The migration itself consumes the smallest part of the consulting hours; the major part is the ridiculous amount of testing required for each and every interface to *other* systems, down to simple printer interfaces. An up-and-running SAP Supply Chain Management system after an OS/DB migration is useless if the delivery papers can't be printed because the printer queues are not configured correctly for the new platform. Figure 21.3 shows the four phases of an SAP OS/DB migration, and Figure 21.4 illustrates a typical project plan.

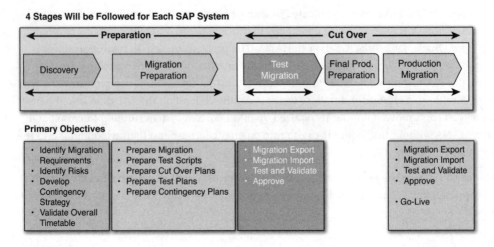

FIGURE 21.3
The phases of an SAP OS/DB migration.

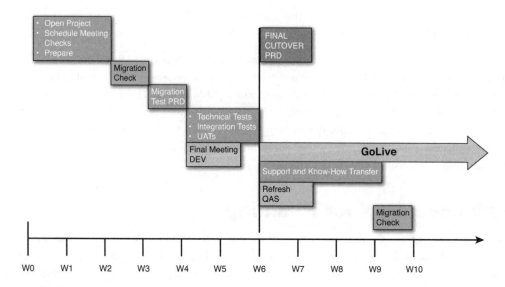

FIGURE 21.4
A typical high-level SAP OS/DB migration plan.

The good news is that this migration work applies only to the database; changing the platform of the SAP application server is quite easy because both ABAP and Java code are platform independent. You just need to install the proper version of the SAP WebApp Server and connect it to the database instance. Mixing and matching application servers running on different platforms is possible, but it's uncommon because of the maintenance effort required.

Migrating to SAP HANA During an Upgrade

If you are planning to change the database platform to SAP HANA, this is considered a heterogeneous migration. However, if you're doing an upgrade at the same time, you can leverage the Database Migration Option (DMO), using the Software Update Manager (SUM) tool. DMO is an option in SUM for a combined update and migration for ABAP-based systems. SAP Note 1813548 describes the prerequisites for BW and Business Suite systems, as well as restrictions. At a high level, this process allows you to run the prepare and uptime phases on the source database and then switch the database connection to the target HANA database for the downtime phases of migrating the application data and data conversion along with the finalization of the upgrade.

More on SAP Upgrades

As stated earlier this hour, *upgrade* refers to installing a major version change of SAP, such as moving from SAP R/3 Enterprise to SAP ERP 6.0. In a technical upgrade, the upgrade project is about changing the SAP Basis layer's version and not about adding the new functionality of that new version. In a functional upgrade, on the other hand, the goal is to move to the new functionality provided by the new SAP system.

Many times, adding functionality requires individual components of the SAP system to be upgraded. For instance, an SAP add-on or a number of support packages might need to be installed in the system (using either the SAP transaction SPAM or SAINT). And the SAP Basis layer typically needs to be upgraded, as well. Upgrade projects are complex and confusing, with different project team member requirements depending on what is being upgraded or changed. The entire process is planning intensive, which brings us to the topic of the next section: high-level planning for upgrades and enhancements.

High-Level Project Planning

Planning for upgrades and enhancements is critical due to the magnitude of change and therefore the magnitude of risk. Remember, SAP systems are used to run the company business; when the SAP system is down, the business is down. So the idea of managing and minimizing the risk of this downtime is nearly always the most important matter in any kind of pending change, whether it's a hardware update, an OS/DB migration, or a functional upgrade. Said another way, changes of such great consequence to mission-critical SAP systems deserve nothing less than careful planning. Planning work should help the IT team avoid unplanned outages and unsatisfied unproductive users.

Project Planning for Enhancements

Enhancements are often implemented in quarterly "waves," or phases, comprising multiple SAP user groups and therefore multiple functional areas and business processes. Complicating matters further, each wave typically takes one to two quarters to plan for and test. And beyond the functional updates, technology changes might be required to support the new functionality. Quarterly enhancements might also include one or even all of the following updates, as well:

- ▶ Server, disk subsystem, or other infrastructure refreshes
- ▶ Database patches, updates, and "upgrades"
- ▶ Operating system updates, security patches, and "upgrades"
- ▶ SAP kernel updates
- ▶ SAP support package stack (ABAP and Java) updates
- ▶ SAP modification transports
- ▶ Customer transports

As you can imagine, this scope of changes can require significant team coordination and project management expertise. In some cases, the better part of an IT department can be absorbed while implementing a wave of SAP enhancements, especially when you consider that these changes have to be moved through multiple environments as part of the SAP landscape (development, quality assurance, production, and so on).

After these changes have been implemented, one or more testing cycles have to be performed to ensure that all the changes do not break any existing processes and to ensure that the changes are ready for the move to production. This is usually performed by a combination of SAP experts and business users who (either manually or via automated scripts) test at minimum the core pieces of changed SAP functionality to ensure that they still work properly.

As errors are encountered in testing, fixes have to be developed that are then applied after the enhancements to subsequent environments. For example, it might be discovered in testing that an SAP support package caused a particular SAP business transaction to abort, also called a shortdump (because an SAP shortdump is created in the process of aborting). During the trouble-shooting process, the tester might find a relevant SAP Note that has been released by SAP that resolves the problem. This note is then downloaded into the development environment, and a corresponding transport is created. In the next phase of testing, it is confirmed that this fix indeed resolves the problem with the SAP transaction. This transport is then added to the post-enhancement transport list scheduled for production and eventually moved into production.

Project Planning for SAP Upgrades

Technical upgrades are more common than functional upgrades and certainly more common than migrations. Nonetheless, they are still pretty infrequent, occurring every six months to perhaps two years. Interestingly, an SAP technical upgrade is similar in nature and duration to a migration; they take three to six months of planning and require the same SAP infrastructure support folks and SAP Basis professionals. It is also necessary to add ABAP programmers, SAP functional analysts, and power users (to do the necessary business process testing after each test wave) to the list of project resources. A functional upgrade takes this complexity one step further and requires functional (business) specialists, as well.

During the planning stages of an SAP upgrade, it is wise to evaluate whether the existing database should be already converted to HANA with a heterogeneous migration. Due to the fact that HANA requires a new underlying infrastructure, it's becoming more common to find combination OS/DB migration and SAP technical upgrade projects.

When the new SAP infrastructure is in place, a system copy must occur from one of the source SAP systems to the new environment. Typically, a copy of the productive system is used as the source for the first test upgrade. It's the biggest system, after all, and naturally represents all the current system's functionality that will eventually be upgraded (and then need to be tested). Some customers prefer to start with an upgrade of the development environment, but this choice complicates things. Why? Because any changes put into the real development and promoted through the system to production on the source environment must also be pushed and promoted through the upgraded environment. This "dual path to production" keeps the environments functionally synchronized but adds a lot of work. Smart IT organizations will forgo upgrading development as long as they can.

Upgrade Tools

The SAP technical or Basis team will use two SAP tools—PREPARE and the Upgrade Assistant—to perform the technical upgrade. The PREPARE tool performs a thorough evaluation of the SAP system and recommends changes, fixes, and service packs that must be applied to the system before the upgrade can actually begin (preparing the system for upgrade). After the changes have made and running again PREPARE shows that no more preparation steps are required, the upgrade can begin.

One critical prepare phase involves binding support packages and add-ins to the upgrade process. In many cases, a certain support package level is required to be bound to the upgrade. In most cases, it makes sense to put in all the latest support packages during the upgrade instead of waiting until the upgrade completes to apply them. The reason a certain support package level may be required has to do with the level of the support packs on the source system. If the source system is at a support package level that introduced functionality that was not included in the base target system but was included for the target version as a support package, the upgrade must apply the same level of functionality through support packages. Otherwise, data will be lost.

The Upgrade Assistant tool graphically displays the upgrade process. It is menu driven, allowing the Basis team to choose one of several options for how to proceed with the upgrade. Options such as Downtime Minimized and Resource Minimized help determine how long the upgrade will take and at what point in the upgrade the system must be shut down. The Downtime Minimized option enables the team to do much of the upgrade work while the system is still up and running, thus reducing the overall system outage (downtime) required to finish the upgrade. The Resource Minimized option forces the system to go offline at an earlier phase. However, it reduces the overall time it takes to actually execute the upgrade process.

Upgrade Testing and Remediation

After the first development upgrade, the system needs to be handed over to the functional and ABAP teams for remediation and testing. SAP tracks problems to upgraded objects with transactions /nSPAU for repository objects and /nSPDD for dictionary objects. SPAU and SPDD enable a developer to look at objects affected by the upgrade and gives options for how to proceed with remediation. Once the objects are repaired, the changes are saved to a transport and can be used to quickly repair the problems as they appear in the upgrades to the quality and production systems. Optionally, the Reset to Original option with SPAU or SPDD allows a developer to revert to the standard SAP code applied by the last upgrade or support pack. Version control is handled in SPAU and SPDD so that the developer can call up previous versions of the object in question.

ABAP code remediation efforts depend on the amount of customization done to an SAP system. Most customers spend about 30% of an upgrade project testing and fixing their custom code. Many IT consulting companies have developed tools that analyze an SAP system before an upgrade to accurately estimate the effort required for code remediation. Such an investment is an excellent idea for all but the most vanilla of installations.

Summary

SAP enhancements, migrations, and upgrades are significant project undertakings, requiring specialized skillsets. With your understanding of the correct definitions and terminologies for each, in conjunction with knowledge of how each project is pursued to completion, you should be well prepared to consider these options as they naturally arise in the SAP deployment and maintenance lifecycle.

Case Study: Hour 21

Review and address the enhancement case study questions posed here. You can find answers to the questions related to this case study in Appendix A, "Case Study Answers."

Situation

Today, MNC runs SAP ERP as its core application for Financials and Human Capital Management. The system is hosted by a provider, and ongoing support costs are astronomical. In addition, the SAP system runs on an out-of-support version of UNIX and Oracle. MNC is planning an upgrade to the latest release of SAP ERP on HANA.

Questions

1. What is the most important factor that needs to be managed and minimized regarding this very critical change?

2. MNC Global has employed a recruiter to help hire a project manager for this SAP project. The online advertisement reads, "Project Manager with migration skills, requires experience migrating from legacy SAP ERP to SAP ERP on HANA." Is this ad technically accurate? How should it read?

3. From a platform perspective, how can MNC Global potentially lower the ongoing support costs for the SAP system or increase the ability to innovate after the upgrade project?

4. In general, what's the difference between updates, upgrades, and migrations?

5. Is it feasible to combine this SAP upgrade project with an OS/DB migration?

PART V

SAP Careers

SAP Careers for the Business User

SAP SE and its partners and customers create an ecosystem representing more than a million jobs worldwide, in a variety of disciplines. Many of these jobs are business related in whole or in part, too, including end users, power users, business process analysts, testers, project managers, and more. While working with SAP can be a challenging and rewarding career path, finding the right job is just plain hard work, especially if you have little experience or direction. In this hour, we provide much-needed direction and shed light on the art of finding and developing a career in some kind of SAP-related business capacity. For those of you interested in developing a technical career, turn your attention to Hour 23, "SAP Careers for the IT Professional."

Types of Business Jobs

SAP business professionals and their business-oriented careers vary tremendously. A decade ago, such a career might have been narrowly defined as an end user or super user working at a customer site. Business configurators, testers, and project managers working on behalf of SAP or one of SAP's partners are considered business professionals, too, though. Today the term *business professional* is more broadly applied. SAP business professionals also work in areas such as

▸ Presales, helping prospective customers understand SAP's business functionality and various components and products from a business perspective

▸ Business development, inside sales, account management, and similar "sales" roles

▸ Quality, testing, and risk management experts

- Education roles, ranging from selling to actually developing and delivering end-user or other functional/business-related training

- Quasi business/technical roles such as workflow and security (each of which has a business component as well as a technology component)

- Project management, which consists of project and program managers (at many levels of seniority, with many different skillsets and backgrounds), project specialists, resource management specialists, and so on

- Recruiting, including recruiters and other HR/career development specialists

Let's turn our attention to some of the first steps in identifying and landing a business role.

First Steps: Experience, Training, Networking, and Certifications

Over the years, we've provided guidance to many wannabe SAPlings and others interested in breaking into the SAP job market. When it comes to first steps, consider the following:

- Think about your current experience, what you already can do, what you already know, and how you might potentially use all of this to add value to an SAP project or in-place SAP system. The idea is to insert yourself as-is. Because this kind of play is all about leveraging your current (lack of SAP) knowledge, you will need to get a break from someone. An SAP business role is predicated on some kind of business experience. Maybe you could shadow a friend or colleague who is already in a business role? Perhaps you could intern or volunteer to help on weekends or after hours with regression testing? What about using your specific business experience in warehousing or accounts payable to work with an SAP functional consultant or business process analyst in the midst of a maintenance cycle or upgrade who just needs another pair of arms and eyes?

- Consider your "fringe" experience. Maybe you've got experience creating business forms and reports—experience that fortunately can easily be applied to an SAP environment. Perhaps you've actually worked in the past with some of the reporting tools that SAP has since acquired, including Crystal Reports or Business Objects. Or maybe you've got experience with or an understanding of web-based business intelligence tools, Microsoft Excel, PowerBI, and more. Explore how you can put these fringe skills to use.

- Attend training. Yes, classic SAP training is expensive. Look for alternatives but don't focus on purely online methods at the expense of formal face-to-face training classes. You need to focus as much on meeting new people as on learning new skills, so figure out how to strike a balance.

► Consider that SAP classes are filled with both new and veteran SAP users. Push yourself and make new contacts and friends. Connect and network and make your job aspirations known. Many universities and SAP-certified training partners offer various classes, too, often at lower cost than the traditional SAP-sponsored courses. Look into these venues and find ways to learn SAP that help you go beyond simply learning. You need networking opportunities.

► Speaking of networking, join the local SAP Users Group chapter. In the Americas, it's called ASUG, or the America's SAP Users' Group. ASUG meets regularly and across numerous cities. Look for other user groups, too; large companies and consulting organizations hold SAP social events. Seek out invitations and get connected.

► Think about the future. As SAP's solutions evolve and the needs of business changes, we all need to learn things to keep us current. Be first! Race to learn what your more experienced colleagues don't know yet—the new stuff. For business professionals, this might include learning about new cloud-based SAP solutions, other new SAP solutions, new solution functionality, how to upgrade SAP's legacy applications to include this new functionality, benefits and trade-offs of this new functionality, gaps in functionality that are addressed by SAP's partners or independent software vendors (ISVs), new training tools, new reporting methods and tools, and so on.

► Finally, if you're a business-domain project manager, get certified as a Project Management Institute (PMI) Project Management Professional (PMP) or Program Management Professional (PgMP), as an SAP project manager, and in SAP's latest ASAP methodology and SAP Solution Manager application.

While you're preparing from an education and exposure perspective, keep working to get plugged into an SAP environment. End-user organizations, consulting organizations, hosting providers, training providers, and others need people who are hungry and willing to do the work to stay relevant. Make sure they know you're that person.

The first question you might ask yourself when seeking a career in SAP is, "Where do I look?" The Internet is a valuable resource, and we outline popular SAP resources and job websites in Hour 24, "Other Resources and Closing Thoughts." However, such resources give only a glimpse into where SAP career opportunities actually exist. In this section, let's take a closer look at some of those in detail.

Right Where You Are

The first obvious choice when searching for a career in SAP is to look right at home, at your current employer. Seek out your company's strategic business and IT plans and search your employer's own job boards. Search popular websites using your company's name as your search criteria, too. If your company is an SAP customer or has plans to become an SAP customer soon, the potential advantage you have as a current employee can make this an ideal method for uncovering an upcoming SAP opportunity.

Of course, your "opportunity" depends on a number of factors. Are you well regarded? Do you work well across organizational boundaries and with other teams and people? Do you get results? Can you be freed from your current assignment?

Even in the absence of an at-home opportunity, use what you've learned from your online job searches to begin focusing on what's hot and how you stack up against the current marketplace for those hot jobs. If the job boards are full of positions requiring SAP hybris, SuccessFactors, and ERP experience, think about how your own business experience maps to those applications. Do you need more experience? Would you benefit from specific training or exposure? Can you use what you know and who you know to wedge yourself in?

On the other hand, if you are certain that no SAP opportunities are available at your current company, it might be time to take a look outside. Be sure to do some due diligence before assuming that your company does not use SAP, though. At large companies, certain divisions might have implemented SAP and others not, especially in the wake of mergers and acquisitions. Also, if your company is a supplier or vendor of an SAP customer, you might be interfacing with an SAP system and not even know it, missing an opportunity to pick up valuable SAP experience in the process. Once you're sure your current employer isn't an option, consider the options outlined next.

SAP SE

When looking for a business-user career in SAP, starting right at the source with SAP itself is not a bad idea. With thousands of employees around the globe, SAP SE and its worldwide subsidiaries represent a long list of job prospects on their own. As of this writing, a quick search on SAP's career site (see Figure 22.1, or navigate to www.sap.com/careers and click something akin to the Find Me My Dream Job button) reveals more than 1,700 jobs around the world. Use the keyword and location searches to narrow down your list to business-specific or fringe-business roles.

Business-oriented careers at SAP SE include areas as diverse as the following:

- ▶ Business-user specialists and consultants (with an emphasis on different industries and languages)
- ▶ Solution and product managers and directors
- ▶ Presales managers and directors
- ▶ Business development managers
- ▶ Inside sales specialists
- ▶ Channel development managers

▶ Account executives

▶ Industry advisors and other specialists

▶ Various line-of-business (LOB) specialists

▶ Various business process, functional, and SAP component specialists (from interns to entry-level college graduates to senior specialists)

▶ Quality management experts

▶ Functional education and training delivery and sales specialists

▶ Project management analysts

▶ Risk specialists

▶ Recruiters and other HR/career development specialists

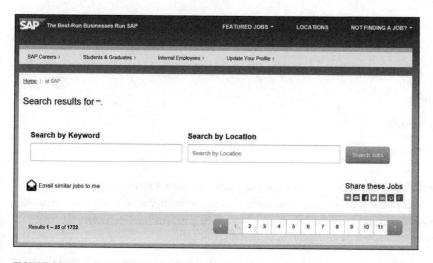

FIGURE 22.1
Use SAP's career site to identify available positions around the world.

With so many opportunities across such a breadth of careers, it should be easy to identify several prospective opportunities. Update your resume to reflect your relevant experience and training, along with what differentiates you from the crowd. This is where your deep experience in a specific area, or breadth of exposure to a broad cross-section of business, can help you land a phone screen.

SAP Partners

Beyond working at SAP SE itself, your next option may be to pursue an SAP job at one of the many SAP partners that provide software and services for SAP's applications and customers. These partners include the full gambit, from large multibillion-dollar corporations such as SAP that employ thousands of workers, to outsourcing and cloud providers such as Accenture, ATOS Origin, Cognizant, CSC, HCL, Hexaware HP, IBM, QMS, Secure 24, T-Systems, Velocity, Virtustream, and Wipro, or to smaller specialty companies that provide more discrete services. SAP has broadened its partner categories into the following:

- ► Integration partners

- ► SME channel partners (broken down by SAP's offerings)

- ► Content partners

- ► Education partners

- ► Hosting partners

- ► SAP BusinessObjects partners (further divided into several specialties)

- ► RunSAP Operations partners

- ► Services partners

- ► Technology partners

- ► Software solution partners

These different partners, along with SAP and the SAP customer base, form what SAP calls its eco-system. To get an idea of the SAP partners available, execute a partner search at www.sap.com/ecosystem/customers/directories/SearchPartner.epx. Note that you will have to enter one set of criteria, such as name, country, or category, to return a set of results.

Within this partner network are also the elite groups of global services partners that provide SAP consulting opportunities across business sectors. Combined, these companies employ thousands of SAP professionals worldwide and help support the growing SAP customer base. The current list of global services consulting partners continues to change and most recently includes the following:

- ► Accenture
- ► All for One Steeb AG
- ► ATOS
- ► Bluefin
- ► Capgemini

- ► Cognizant
- ► CSC
- ► Deloitte
- ► Ernst &Young LLP
- ► Fujitsu

- ▶ The Hackett Group
- ▶ HCL
- ▶ Hitachi, Ltd.
- ▶ HP
- ▶ HRIZONS LLC
- ▶ IBM
- ▶ Infosys Technologies Ltd.

- ▶ InEight Inc.
- ▶ itelligence AG
- ▶ Logica
- ▶ OpenText
- ▶ Siemens IT Solutions and Services
- ▶ Tata Consultancy Services
- ▶ T-Systems

See www.sap.com/ecosystem/customers/directories/services.epx to browse this list and read more. As you can see, these global partners are SAP's "Who's Who?" for global SAP consulting openings. They offer prime career opportunities for the serious SAP professional. Whether you are looking for a position in business process management at one of the global services partners such as Capgemini or IBM or seeking an SAP financial auditing position at Deloitte or Accenture, these partners offer well-developed SAP career paths.

SAP Customers

Although many SAP career options have been presented, another likely alternative is that you will find an opportunity working with one of SAP's many customers. Located around the globe, they offer a similar breadth of opportunities as SAP SE and its partners. One key is to find an employer that aligns with your own industry expertise (if you're deep in a particular area).

Alternatively, find an employer who needs your breadth of experience. If you're broad across many different areas or are experienced in "horizontal" disciplines such as project management, testing, auditing, or risk management, you have something special to position.

Other Ideas

As you've seen by now, SAP opportunities for the business professional are everywhere. Whether a company is planning an SAP implementation or maintaining an existing SAP landscape, a team of business professionals is required to keep the systems in a state where the requirements of the business may be met. In this section, we review several types of opportunities in more detail.

Business and Functional Positions

On any SAP implementation or in any SAP environment, individuals are needed who can bridge the gap between an organization's business requirements and business processes and the technology necessary to support the business. From functional analysts, super users, and more, there are a variety of positions for the prospective business professional. Although the actual job titles for these positions can vary greatly, we discuss a few of them here.

On the business side of the house, every SAP implementation needs personnel who can champion SAP business solutions for their team. For this reason, and rightly so, they are often called *super users*. They are usually the IT-savvy business-knowledgeable folks within their respective departments who can communicate well and have the ability to bring along those who are challenged by new technology. Super users are often the first trained on a given SAP project, and they work most closely with their SAP functional configuration counterparts to resolve issues. This puts super users in a prime position to gain priceless SAP knowledge.

In the SAP technology arena, we have functional analysts, often called configuration leads, business analysts, or business process owners. We also have technical analysts, who can be referred to as functional developers or configuration experts. All of these roles are generally aligned with a particular SAP module or modules, such as FI, HR, MM, and so on. These individuals have to work with their business-side counterparts to make the company SAP vision a reality. This is important to note because the more SAP modules a company has implemented, the more people they will require to fill these areas of expertise.

For example, a functional analyst may work with a team leader or super user to gather business requirements for an enhancement to the SAP system. The functional analyst will then work with the technical analyst and potentially other members of the technical team to have SAP configuration activated or modified to meet the business requirements.

As you can see, business and functional roles can be very involved and require tremendous coordination and expertise. All of these roles are vital to an SAP implementation and require motivated, competent individuals to be successful.

Functional Project and Program Management

As you can imagine, bringing together all the functional and technical roles, tasks, and dependencies necessary to pull off a large-scale SAP project is challenging. Many companies and consulting organizations have established project management offices (PMOs) to coordinate their project managers. And as you have read previously, it is not uncommon for an SAP project or broader program to require a number of project managers to direct a set of SAP initiatives or represent different stakeholder bodies. Again, this provides a prime opportunity for those looking to break into the SAP arena as a PjM or PgM.

Program and project managers are always in high demand. PMI certification, relevant "big project" experience, and good timing could land you the perfect SAP opportunity. As a PM, you can pick up SAP functional design, technical architecture, and development experience as you work with project team members, and you will be even more valuable in the future.

Functional Trainers and Testers

Although they do not receive the same recognition as other SAP positions, SAP trainers and testers are noteworthy and critical to the success of SAP implementations and projects. As companies learn to carry out their business processes on SAP, trainers take on the difficult challenge of carrying out the new vision to end users who may or may not be completely on board with the new changes. Talented trainers and training leads are needed to develop training classes, organize students, and deliver a variety of training modules to an enterprise perhaps unwilling to change.

Likewise, the SAP testing process is a never-ending cycle. Whether it is project-related enhancements to the system or quarterly patches and updates, SAP systems have to be tested to ensure that changes are ready for production. This requires people who can create and exercise test scripts either manually or via automated testing tools. Although a tester might not always be the most high profile of positions, in this role you can gain valuable experience on SAP configuration and SAP business processes that can lead to other rewarding positions.

Preparing for a Business Career in SAP

Now that you know where SAP positions are available and have an idea what types of jobs are out there, how do you get one? The key is to drive your own career. Don't be passive and assume that others will do this for you. Your manager may be helpful, for example, but then again your manager might not. Think about how often your managers have failed to make it through the latest round of layoffs, have retired, have moved on to other positions, or have simply done a less-than-stellar job thinking about people other than themselves. In this section, we look at how to prepare for a business-oriented career in SAP.

Again, Right Where You Are

As discussed in the first section this hour, if your current employer is planning an SAP implementation or currently runs SAP, there is probably no better place to look than right where you are. Generally, companies that commence a new SAP project are looking for volunteers from the business willing to take on the new challenge and champion the project. If your company does have an SAP initiative planned, there is no time like the present to put your name in the hat as an interested party. New projects are also ideal because a variety of positions are needed, and there's very little in-house expertise. This means a motivated individual can take advantage of the situation and take the opportunity to develop a new career path.

Although it can be more challenging to move from a non-SAP job to an SAP role at a company already running SAP, you should pursue it as diligently as you possibly can. Leverage your current experience and knowledge of your company to put your potential move in a positive light. Also, if your dream SAP career position is not yet available, do not be afraid to tackle less-appealing SAP positions. They can serve as stepping-stones to a more rewarding position later.

Of course, if your current company does not use SAP, has no plans to use SAP, or refuses to give you an opportunity, you need to search elsewhere.

Leverage Existing Business Experience

As mentioned in the preceding section, SAP creates many positions built around business modules and business processes. Just as it is important to know how to configure business processes in SAP, it is equally important to understand the detailed inner workings of the business process itself. If you have that kind of knowledge, you can be a valuable asset to the SAP team. In fact, it is very common for business process experts to become SAP configuration experts and vice versa.

If you have significant experience in a particular business area but your company does not use SAP, do not be discouraged. This kind of expertise often translates within your industry. For instance, if you worked in the materials management area in the chemicals industry for 15 years, you might be able to leverage that experience to find a job at another chemicals company with a similar business model that uses SAP. This concept applies to all SAP modules across industry segments. Simply identify your role, find a company using SAP, and then pursue that role at the new company!

Similarly, if you pick up new business solutions or applications quickly, think about becoming an SAP super user or taking on stretch assignments to become the "go-to" person in your business area for all things SAP. Alternatively, consider using your in-depth knowledge to become a trainer! Use your business experience to quickly learn how your business processes run on SAP. Then teach others in your department or elsewhere to become proficient end users of the system. With a bit of luck and a good measure of positive feedback from your students, one of these interim training roles can open doors to other SAP career opportunities, perhaps one you really want down the road.

Focus on the Fringe

There are many other "fringe" business functions you may use to break into the SAP market. As discussed earlier, SAP integrates with almost every area of IT, so you have the prospect of working your way into SAP over time. The area of workflow management is a good example; it requires a special combination of business and technical skills to plan, build, and maintain workflows.

Change management is another example. One of our peers started out as an IT change management analyst and handled change management documentation for her company's SAP team. She eventually took on the job of managing and sending SAP transports throughout the system landscapes and today works as an SAP Basis technician (yes, she chose technology over a business career!) at a large corporation. By being a team player, making the most of her opportunities, and taking advantage of her experiences, she advanced her skillset and career.

Similar prospects exist in other areas where business and IT functions converge. An SAP bolt-on or complementary product may end up integrating with your business area of expertise and open a window of opportunity. So pay attention and be ready to take advantage of your skills and experience when the opportunity presents itself. Better yet, pursue those opportunities while carefully and purposefully building your skills and experience.

Work On the Intangibles

Although skillsets and expertise are necessary in your pursuit of an SAP career, do not underestimate the multitude of soft skills and other intangibles that make the difference between getting hired and forever being an interview candidate. As we wrap up this hour, let's focus on several of the little things that make a big difference.

Your Ability to Network

Despite all of your business acumen, experience, and know-how, if you cannot show how you've successfully networked to get the job done, you are in trouble. Today's business world is complex, and the days of the Lone Ranger are gone. Getting things done really requires working well with others, especially with those you cannot directly influence (such as co-workers and peers and partners in sister organizations).

So be prepared to help your prospective employers understand how you have worked as part of a team to make things happen. Be sure to highlight your individual contributions (including personal leadership and your focus on delivery excellence) but give credit to the team for making its deadlines. Show off your professional network and describe how you will extend that network in your new environment if you're given the chance to work there. By covering this base in an interview, you are telling prospective employers that you understand you can't do it all by yourself. They will not only appreciate your selfless perspective but gain some real insight into how you'll fit into their team.

Get Educated!

SAP professionals are just that—professionals—and as such, SAP jobs reflect minimum qualifications, similar to other professional positions. Many of the positions you see posted at SAP, its partners, and customers require at least a bachelor's degree. Often, an MBA or other master's degree is desirable if not mandatory. This is not to say that a certain number of years of experience will not get you the job, but advanced education certainly helps plant you at the head of the pack (or nearer to the top of a résumé stack).

Likewise, SAP certification can give you a great advantage as you search for your SAP career. Although it is expensive and might not be as accessible as some certifications, for these same reasons, it offers you more exclusivity and regard in SAP circles. SAP training is reflected in various levels of proficiency, such as associate level, professional level, master level, and so on. Do your homework and read more at www.sap.com/services/education/certification/index.epx. Any of these certifications can put you well on your way to an SAP career, and the Professional and Master certifications really put you in another class of demand. Take care to take training classes that reinforce or augment your experience, however; careening off into a completely different industry or functional specialty can result in an expensive dead end for those seeking initial SAP employment.

If you are not in a financial position to advance your degree or pay for SAP training classes, keep striving. In Hour 24, you will learn about a host of helpful sources. Most of these are available on the Internet, where you can pick up a wealth of information on SAP and its products. Though you still have to find the right opportunity, do not miss out because you are not prepared and knowledgeable. Terminology, architecture, and standards in easy-to-consume presentations, PDFs, YouTube, and other video-based training are easily accessible. Use these resources to fill in as many gaps as you can in your education and knowledge and trust that you will be given the opportunity to put to good use the time you invested in learning on your own. In the right interviewing circumstances, this kind of proactive self-education can help differentiate you from your less self-motivated colleagues, too.

Professional Presentation

As we discuss the intangibles, it is worth mentioning that how you present yourself is as important as ever. You may have heard the line, "Dress for the job you want, not the job you have." Sure, much of the world is more casual than ever before—especially in light of work-at-home and other remote-office accommodations. But when you're interviewing, and later when you actually show up at company meetings and other get-togethers, consider your wardrobe. In most corporations running SAP or selling SAP services, especially the more conservative brands, the idea of business professionalism is very much alive. After all, these are companies that can afford SAP. They are generally not running the business on a shoestring, and they expect their people to properly reflect the company's position and success.

Besides, SAP business-oriented positions invariably interact at all levels of management and with all manner of business and IT professionals. As a senior SAP Financials expert or SAP upgrade project manager, you may be called upon to give a presentation to a group of business leaders, the CIO or COO, or another group of stakeholders. You don't want to walk in looking unprofessional and have people wonder if a mistake was made in the hiring process. If you are serious about advancing your career, invest in your wardrobe and soft skills so that you can separate yourself from your less-professional peers.

Next, improve your communication skills. Study the culture and primary language reflected by your employer and work not only to fit in but to excel in communication. Your communication skills ultimately reflect who you are more than anything else, including your wardrobe. Many senior-level SAP professionals are not where they are necessarily because they are the most knowledgeable business process expert or masterful business development leader but rather because they are able to communicate well across business and technology departments. Simply broadening your vocabulary, improving your pronunciation, and clearly articulating your words is a big help.

Thinking before speaking is an even bigger help. Live by the mantra "only the facts." Speak the truth and avoid anything outside the truth. If you're not 100% sure that what you are saying is accurate, keep your mouth shut. Don't be a person who is quick with an answer that turns out to be incorrect. When you open your mouth to speak, you want people to edge in a little closer to you because they know what you're going to say is accurate, truthful, and worth their time. This little tip alone can boost your career advancement quickly and continuously.

Don't stop at verbal skills, though. Make sure you're professional when it comes to presentations, email, and other written communications—including blogs and other "informal" communications. Re-familiarize yourself with how to create an effective Microsoft PowerPoint presentation. There are plenty of poor examples in the world. Don't create another one. Know your audience and know your material. Stick with three or four bullet points per slide and use graphs and figures to communicate data trends and complex relationships, respectively. The ability to deliver a succinct and effective presentation says a lot on its own because it shows that you understand what it means to communicate to a specific audience. The ability to share business matters in this way, with accuracy and confidence, is a skill both rare and sought after.

A Word on Ethics

In an effort to run their businesses with accuracy and transparency, SAP customers spend millions of dollars on their SAP systems. Themes such as system availability, compliance, and data integrity are paramount in these organizations. In the same way, these attributes need to be reflected by the people tasked with managing and supporting these systems.

Companies today know more than ever that they can train the right candidates. If you are a bit weak in a particular technology, business concept, application, or soft skill, a good hiring manager knows those specific gaps can be filled through training and a certain amount of mentoring. Instead of waiting to find absolutely the perfect fit, these people are instead often looking for the right kind of people to hire. The basic experience, talent, and education prerequisites need to be in place, sure. But companies know they can't really teach ethics and responsibility (despite all the time many of us spend annually in corporate compliance training and similar initiatives, which are fine in themselves as a way to educate but certainly do little to change innate behavior). It is precisely this kind of ethical and responsible behavior that smart companies are seeking more than ever today. So in whatever you do, strive for integrity. Showcase your strong character and ethical foundation during the interview process. And at work make every decision as if it will be publicly broadcast around the world. People notice the choices you make, and one day good choices will pay off, maybe with just the career change you are hoping for. We believe it happens frequently, actually.

Summary

Now that we have looked at the what, the where, and the how of discovering a career in SAP, the rest is up to you. There are a slew of challenging and rewarding opportunities available to the willing and able. If you are serious about making a career change and becoming an SAP business professional, follow the simple advice in this hour and get to work. Make every effort to achieve your goal by managing your own career rather than letting others drive for you. Markets change, and companies rise and fall, but SAP professionals are generally in high demand regardless of the economy. Work on your skills—business, technical, and soft skills— while you continue to pursue the avenues outlined this hour. We wish you all the best in your endeavors and hope to call you an esteemed SAP colleague and peer someday soon.

Case Study: Hour 22

Consider this business-user career development case study and the questions that follow. You can find answers to the questions related to this case study in Appendix A, "Case Study Answers."

Situation

After 10 years in various banking-related business roles at DeadEnd Company, you are ready for a change. You have heard about a new SAP ERP implementation down the road at MNC's banking affiliate, and through several job boards, you are aware that the firm is actively hiring. Answer the following questions as you research what opportunities are available and how you might work your way into a new SAP business career at MNC.

Questions

1. You have heard that MNC is relying on a number of consulting firms to assist with its implementation. Where might you be able to find information about these SAP partners?

2. As a banking conglomerate, which one of the three major industry categories might MNC fall into, and why might that prove important in your job search?

3. With a background in accounting and your ability to pick up technology quickly, what might be a good fit for you in the business/functional arena?

4. In your time at your current employer, you have managed a number of high-profile projects. What type of certification might you pursue to enhance your education and improve your chances of obtaining an SAP project management position at MNC?

5. You have shown a strong ability to act as a liaison between the business teams and the IT organization at your current employer. What intangible soft skills do you think you might possess that you could highlight in your interviews at MNC?

SAP Careers for the IT Professional

What You'll Learn in This Hour:

▶ Where to find technical SAP career opportunities
▶ The breadth of technical roles in the SAP market
▶ Important attributes of a technical professional
▶ Ways to prepare for a technical career in SAP

In the same way that SAP has created an ecosystem of opportunities for business professionals, a tremendous variety of opportunities for technical professionals exists as well. In this hour, we walk through these opportunities. As in the previous hour, keep one thought central: It's *your* career. Manage it proactively and intentionally.

SAP, Its Partners, and Its Customers

As with developing a business career in SAP, if you're interested in developing a technical career, you'll probably follow a similar path and work for SAP, one of its partners, or one of SAP's customers. Each of these potential avenues is covered next.

SAP SE

SAP SE offers outstanding opportunities to develop a technical career in SAP consulting and support. Point your browser to SAP's home page at www.sap.com and click the Careers link (or navigate directly to www.careersatsap.com).

From the Careers page, you can search for open jobs posted in SAP's Online Career Center. Choose your region and language (English, German, French, or Japanese), and you're presented with SAP's Job Search screen. At this writing, hundreds and hundreds of technical jobs are available around the world. Some of the more interesting ones are

- ► IT technology consultants with skills in server management, system administration, and SAP Basis

- ► C/C++ developers for SAP Kernel and SAP HANA performance optimization

- ► Cloud automation and management experts, including OpenStack evangelists

- ► HEC integration managers and Hadoop developers for the SAP HANA R&D team

- ► C++ database engineer for SAP HANA performance optimization

- ► Technical writers, support engineers, and technical trainers, along with hundreds of other SAP industry-specific and component-specific technical positions

- ► HANA partner engineers and Internet of Things (IoT) consultants

In addition, SAP SE offers plenty of student internships (called *working students*, from the German word "Werkstudent").

Other attractive technical positions abound. By setting up a profile, you can add yourself to SAP's talent community and either receive updates and information on SAP program work or notifications of great opportunities that match your interests. If you have applied for a job, you will receive additional information about your application process in a separate email.

SAP Partners

In addition to working at SAP, another option might be to pursue an SAP job at one of the many SAP partners that provide software and services for SAP and SAP customers. These partners include everything from large multibillion-dollar corporations such as Accenture, Cisco, CSC, Deloitte, HP, Freudenberg IT, and IBM; to software partners such as BMC, Microsoft, Open Text Corporation, Winshuttle, Red Hat, and nearly 600 others; to small specialty firms that provide discrete consulting or support services. Check out Hour 22, "SAP Careers for the Business User," for additional partners and quasi-technical roles. Combined with SAP SE and its customer base, these partners form what is called the *SAP ecosystem*.

SAP Customers

Although many SAP career settings have been presented, perhaps the most likely alternative is that you will find an opportunity with one of SAP's more than 291,000 customers in more than 180 countries.[1] What types of customers, you may ask? The SAP customer base spans numerous industry segments, as outlined in Hour 1, "SAP Explained." As a refresher, remember that SAP

---

[1] See http://www.sap.com/bin/sapcom/en_us/downloadasset.2015-04-apr-21-01.sap-fact-sheet-en-pdf.html.

breaks these industry segments into several major categories, each of which comprises many specific industries, ranging from banking, healthcare, and the public sector to automotive, chemicals, oil and gas, media, retail, and utilities. These are just a small subset of the industry segments available. Chances are that no matter where you live, you are not very far from a company that runs SAP. In Hour 24, "Other Resources and Closing Thoughts," you find information on popular job search engines where SAP's customers and recruiting partners post thousands of employment opportunities.

Types of Available Opportunities

As you may recall, SAP projects create a variety of roles and job functions both in the technical and business arenas. Whether a company is planning an SAP implementation or maintaining an existing SAP landscape, a support team is required to keep the systems technically running, functioning well, and in a state where the requirements of the business are met. In this section, we look at the types of opportunities available in more detail.

Technical Positions

Similar to the business and functional positions, a wide variety of technical positions are required to keep an SAP landscape running effectively. Hour 6, "SAP NetWeaver and HANA," outlined technical NetWeaver and other expert roles serving as SAP system administrators. Experienced or senior technical personnel often take on team lead or architect roles and are responsible for designing the overall SAP technical strategy for their enterprise. SAP security, which is also a technical or Basis component, has become specialized enough that it now stands as its own job function in the majority of companies. SAP security experts work closely with the functional teams to make sure end users can do their jobs while at the same time maintaining the system's business process integrity.

In addition to system administration roles, a team of developers and programmers are required to manage SAP configuration and code. At one time, these individuals were known as ABAPers (pronounced "ah-bop-ers") when there was only a simple Basis layer with which to contend. Today, with so many other development options and platforms, this term has broadened. Development can now include ABAP, Java, SAP NetWeaver Composition Environment, .NET, and many other cloud-centric development niches in or around the core SAP Enterprise Resource Planning (ERP) environment.

With the array of SAP products available, technical positions are becoming more and more specialized. SAP Basis jack-of-all-trades system administrators can grow into SAP Process Integration or SAP NetWeaver Portal experts, for example. Similarly, ABAP programmers are adding HANA studio and other skills to keep up with changing technology. All of these role-expanding trends bode well for those looking to find not just a job in SAP but a career.

Technical Project Management

Good technical project and program managers (technical PMs), especially those with experience on SAP projects, are in high demand. With new SAP product releases, upgrades, cloud and HANA migrations, hardware refreshes, and other technology projects occurring every day, the demand for capable project managers continues to grow. Many companies and consulting organizations have established project management offices (PMOs) to coordinate groups of project managers working across disciplines. As you have read previously, it is not uncommon for an SAP project to require a number of project managers—technical, functional, and so on—to direct a set of SAP initiatives or represent different stakeholder bodies.

This need for seasoned project managers provides a prime opportunity for those looking to break into the SAP arena as a technical PM. Certification from the Project Management Institute (PMI) and the right timing could land you just the SAP opportunity for which you are searching. As a technical PM, you are exposed to several dimensions of an SAP project, from functional design to technical architecture, sizing, development, testing processes, and more. As you work with your project team members, any number of doors might be opened, possibly leading to a career change.

Technical Trainers

Like their business counterparts, technical trainers play an essential if unrecognized role in SAP implementations, upgrades, and similarly complex projects. Technical trainers help ensure that technical teams are educated to perform their roles. Many trainers work for small SAP-authorized training companies, delivering SAP's training classes. Others work for SAP itself, delivering training on behalf of the company. Still others work for or contract on behalf of SAP to develop these training materials. Finally, large companies that have deployed SAP sometimes create their own training organizations as part of a larger SAP Center of Excellence or company-wide training organization.

SAP Testers

Much like training, the SAP testing process is a never-ending cycle. Whether it is to test project-related enhancements to a system or confirm that quarterly patches and updates have not broken any existing functionality, SAP systems have to be tested to ensure that changes are ready for production. This requires people who can create and exercise test scripts either manually or via automated testing tools. Although testers may not always hold the highest-profile positions, they can gain valuable experience on SAP configuration, SAP business processes, and the important area of technical change management—any of which might lead to other rewarding positions.

Preparing for a Career in SAP

Now that you know where SAP positions are available and have an idea of what types of jobs are out there, how do you get one? This section focuses on just that, as we explore how to develop a technical career in SAP.

Right Where You Are

If your current employer is planning an SAP implementation or currently runs SAP, there is probably no better place to look than right where you are. Generally, companies that kick off a new SAP project are looking for volunteers from the business who are willing to take on a new technical challenge and champion the project. If your company has an SAP initiative planned, there is no time like the present to put your name in the hat as an interested party. New projects are also ideal because a variety of positions are needed, and there's little in-house expertise. This means a motivated individual can take advantage of the situation and take the opportunity to develop a new career path. Crossing over from the business to a role that requires a combination of business and technology acumen is rare. Technical gaps can often be filled more easily than business gaps, however (especially since business experience is generally required). Use this to your advantage.

Leverage your current experience and knowledge of your company to paint your potential move in a positive light. In the end, SAP is all about business processes—you know the company and the business processes, which are two huge advantages!

Finally, if your dream SAP career position is not available yet, do not be afraid to tackle less-appealing SAP positions. They can serve as stepping-stones to a more rewarding position later. Of course, if your current company does not use SAP, has no plans to use SAP, or refuses to give you an opportunity, you will need to search elsewhere.

Leverage Existing Technical Experience

As mentioned in the preceding section, SAP creates many positions built around business modules and business processes. Just as it is important to know how to configure business processes in SAP, it is equally important to understand how the business processes interface with other systems and how they operate on a computing platform (comprised of hardware, operating systems, databases, SAP application technology, and more). If you have *any* of this kind of knowledge, you can be a valuable asset to the SAP team.

Similarly, if you've got a business background but pick up new technologies quickly, think about becoming the "go-to" person in your technical group for all things related to SAP from a business perspective. Every team needs these kinds of liaisons. Similarly, as outlined in

Hour 22, consider using your specialized knowledge and excellent communications skills to become a trainer. Leverage your technical savvy and a desire to share what you know with others and teach your junior or SAP-aspiring colleagues how to install, upgrade, maintain, or in some other way support the technical underpinnings of an SAP system.

Using Your Existing Technical Expertise

If you are currently a successful IT professional, but SAP technology is all "Greek" to you, do not worry. SAP technology touches nearly every facet of the IT industry. In the past, many technical SAP professionals got their starts in other areas of IT and transitioned in time to more SAP-focused roles. Look for those opportunities, then, regardless of where you might be employed today. We have seen computer operators, self-taught programmers, SAN specialists, network administrators, and desktop support specialists work their way into senior architecture, project management, IT director, and other interesting and valuable positions.[2] Years and many SAP projects later, these people are seasoned SAP professionals with impressive careers. With this in mind, let us now look at various IT positions and how they line up with potential careers in SAP.

Hardware and Infrastructure Specialists

If you currently support server hardware and understand enterprise computing topics such as storage area networks, high availability and clustering, or virtualization, you might be in a good position to add SAP experience to that foundation. Hardware architecture and sizing are critical to the performance of SAP systems, and as such, SAP NetWeaver and Basis professionals have to work closely with their hardware expert counterparts to design and implement SAP systems. As part of this collaboration effort, valuable SAP experience can be gained and leveraged for a career in SAP.

In addition, if you have specific hardware experience with a certain vendor, you might want to consider talking to them about an in-house position. Cisco, HP, and IBM, for example, are SAP technology partners that can provide server, storage, and systems management platform experts specifically to their respective SAP customers. These companies are staffed by literally thousands of IT professionals worldwide, and the opportunities they provide make great stepping-stones for seasoned technology infrastructure experts.

---

[2] For example, one of the authors started his career as a plant engineer and later became the IT superintendent, and the other one started out programming in Basic and operating mainframe computers before becoming an SAP Basis consultant.

Platform Administrators

Hour 3, "SAP Technology Basics," discussed operating systems (OSs) and databases (DBs) and the platform combinations available for SAP. If you are already an administrator on one of these platforms, you might be able to leverage that experience as well. Microsoft Windows Server, UNIX, or Linux administrators and Microsoft SQL, IBM DB2, Oracle, and especially Sybase database administrators can have an advantage over the rest of the competition. If your company or another company runs SAP on the platform with which you are an expert, it might present just the right opportunity at the right time. If not, consider a position somewhere such as Microsoft or Amazon, for instance, where the company may be looking for individuals with existing skill-sets on their products to work on their own SAP (internal IT or consulting services) teams.

However, don't consider yourself a "senior" administrator simply because you've been running an SAP environment on AIX with Oracle for many years. A truly experienced senior platform administrator has a diverse set of experiences; such a person can log in and use different OSs and databases and has stayed current with new technologies as well.

In addition, network with your SAP NetWeaver peers whenever possible. Ask questions about how SAP runs on your OS or DB and what aspects affect performance. Find out why your company selected this specific platform to meet its business needs; computing platforms differ in terms of innovations, for example, that can minimize downtime, increase flexibility, and ultimately increase business agility. The information you uncover can provide priceless knowledge and can show interest on your part, which can be equally valuable if the right person is listening.

Developers and Programmers

As mentioned previously, SAP development and programming has gone from the more one-dimensional fourth-generation language called ABAP to a suite of options including object-oriented languages, Java, and web services. This shift to provide more web-based open access to SAP development could play right into your strengths, for instance, if you are an experienced HTML5 or .NET developer. As outlined in Hour 6, some IT scenarios call for the Java stack. Likewise, Microsoft and SAP continue to collaborate on tools such as the .NET connector for SAP, the .NET platform development kit (PDK) for SAP Enterprise Portal, and more. These changes present an assortment of opportunities for those willing to put in the time to adapt their programming knowledge to SAP.

Content management is also a popular topic in today's SAP environments. If you are a web developer, consider picking up SAP NetWeaver Portal and applying your web development and design expertise to the SAP world. SAP NetWeaver Portal integrates with existing company portal strategies and products such as Microsoft Office SharePoint Server (MOSS) and IBM WebSphere. Experience in one or more of these technologies can make you a valuable resource and put you in a position to broaden your skillset with SAP.

SAP HANA and Hadoop also present a host of development opportunities. These options bring the best of both the technical and functional worlds, as they are somewhat hybrids. SAP HANA and big data experts become the information management experts in a given enterprise. For this reason, technical experience in data mining, database administration, and so on and functional experience in specific business processes such as FI, HR, and MM are equally important. Therefore, try to get some experience in these areas and enhance your career in the process.

Working on the Intangibles

In Hour 22, we reviewed four broad areas benefitting both business and technology professionals. These are universal and should be reviewed by aspiring SAP technologists as well:

▶ The ability to network between teams and organizations

▶ The need for further education

▶ The need to present yourself professionally

▶ The need to conduct yourself responsibly and ethically

One final word is in order for the technology professional. Although it might seem a little cliché, there is a lot of truth to the statement a friend shared long ago: "There is no substitute for a little hustle." Often, the only distinction between those who achieve their goals and those who complain about how they cannot get out of their current situation is simply a lot of hard work. Many SAP professionals have done just that—*worked* their way into their positions. There is nothing in this hour that says you are guaranteed an SAP position if you follow these directions. However, there are some great tips and ideas to follow. And if you take advantage of what you have learned and work hard to connect to your prospective colleagues and peers, you will be well positioned to one day also work *your* way into an SAP technical career.

Summary

This hour covered many of the same themes outlined in the previous hour but from a technology perspective. Put what you've read here into practice and begin further developing the skills you have. Meanwhile, through an honest self-assessment, build new skills—technical, soft skills, and business skills alike—while you continue to pursue the avenues outlined this hour. Above all else, manage your own career. No one else has the same vested interest or as much to lose or gain.

Case Study: Hour 23

Consider this career development case study and the questions that follow. You can find answers to the questions related to this case study in Appendix A, "Case Study Answers."

Situation

With MNC's new SAP-on-Windows implementation scheduled to start in three months, you've heard about several new opportunities on the SAP technical team. You are ready for a change but unsure what to do first. Your manager seems uninterested in your ideas, much less your career, but you don't want to burn any bridges. You enjoy a broad and fantastically diverse background in infrastructure implementation, SQL Server administration, technical training, and a bit of project management. Answer the following questions as you consider your next move.

Questions

1. Reviewing your background again yields a thought about better managing your career. What's the rule you should follow?

2. Your experience could be useful to the new SAP project. How should you frame this experience?

3. If you eventually land a job in the SAP technical team as a generalist or jack-of-all-trades, how might you develop your career down the road?

4. A phone screen with the hiring manager revealed that the SAP technical team could use some testers after the system is physically implemented. What do technical testers do, and how do they do it?

5. During your interviews, a member of the SAP technical team asked what you thought about the SAP platform MNC had chosen. He alluded to the platform's innovative capabilities. How might you further this conversation?

Other Resources and Closing Thoughts

What You'll Learn in This Hour:

- ▶ Overview of professional resources
- ▶ Important user groups, journals, and more
- ▶ A review of online resources
- ▶ An introduction to select SAP career resources
- ▶ SAP-sponsored and other conferences and events

Because of its reach and popularity, the amount of available and often free resources for SAP isn't too surprising. What's really surprising is the breadth of these resources and the fact that they have only become available in the past five years. Today, you can find low-cost conferences and magazines, numerous books dedicated to SAP (many of which are provided online at little or no cost), and a great number of online materials. But if you just have a few questions and little to no money to spend, where should you go? To answer this question, we spend this final hour outlining SAP resources available to users, technologists, and other SAP business and IT professionals.

Professional Resources

Professional resources for SAP span the gamut from SAP's very own online resources to inexpensive books, magazine subscriptions, membership in professional user-based organizations, and more. Part of the reason for this diversity is SAP's size: Beyond its installed base and the hundreds of thousands of users who depend on SAP day in and day out, there's a supporting cast of another 100,000 or more consultants, contractors, developers, engineers, and other support personnel. Some of the most prominent and useful professional resources are described in the following sections.

SAP's Service and Support Resources

Before going elsewhere, turn to SAP's own online resources. From sites focused on serving the development and technical communities to those targeted at partners, SAP provides a wealth of readily accessible information. The following list is by no means exhaustive but should give you several excellent places to start:

▶ **SAP Ecosystem:** Accessed via www.sap.com/ecosystem, this site provides broad access to partner, thought leadership, and community sites, many of which do not require any special access or user IDs. The thought leadership site, for example, offers links to business innovation and trends, the Business Transformation Academy, Big Data, the Internet of Things, and various "expert" sites focused on mobile, the cloud, and more. The SAP ecosystem also enables connections with fellow academics via the SAP University Alliances Community and fellow colleagues via the ecosystem for SAP TechEd.

▶ **SAP Service Marketplace:** Accessed via service.sap.com, this is the primary portal into other SAP sites and resources. This portal is subdivided into Customer, Partner, and General Visitor sections, each of which provides links to relevant resources. For example, the General Visitor portal affords access to the SAP Community Network, SAP Help Portal, and SAP Education.

▶ **SAP Developer Network:** Accessed via www.sdn.sap.com, this site is a social network for SAP professionals. Use it to join and participate in numerous technical, business-oriented, and product-specific communities; access wikis and blogs; subscribe to newsletters; learn of upcoming events; and much more.

▶ **SAP Help Portal:** Accessed via help.sap.com, this site provides documentation and other library support materials spanning SAP Enterprise Resource Planning (ERP), SAP NetWeaver, SAP Business Suite, SAP R/3 and R/3 Enterprise, SAP for Industries, Composite Applications, SAP Solution Manager, and more.

▶ **SAP Partner Portal:** Accessed via partner.sap.com, this is an ideal site for partners interested in connecting with SAP's ecosystem, joining SAP's partner program, pursuing certifications, and obtaining access to partner-only SAP software and other materials.

▶ **SAP Support Portal:** Use this site, accessed via service.sap.com/support, for software downloads, license keys, and release and upgrade information. Also go to this site to use SAP's extensive knowledge base, referred to as SAP Notes.

If you are an SAP support professional, you might even consider setting the SAP Service Marketplace as your browser's home page. Keep in mind that you need an SAP Service Marketplace ID (sometimes still called an OSS ID) to access many of these sites.

SAP User Groups

In almost every facet of business, it is helpful to network with people who are using the same products and solutions you are using. SAP is no exception. The Americas' SAP Users' Group (ASUG) is an independent, not-for-profit organization composed of SAP customers and eligible third-party vendors, consulting houses, hardware vendors, and others. Visit ASUG's website at www.asug.com (see Figure 24.1). Although decidedly North American, the site offers a wonderful breadth of insight offered through its CIO council, events calendar, diverse community and special interest groups, industry-specific benchmarking capabilities, and best practices.

FIGURE 24.1
Look to ASUG for an independent view of SAP from a user's perspective.

ASUG's goals of educating members, facilitating networking among colleagues and SAP representatives, and influencing SAP's global product and service direction form the foundation of all that ASUG does. ASUG provides a forum for members to communicate mutual concerns to SAP, influence software development, exchange ideas and best practices, and establish future priorities.

The two types of ASUG membership are Installation Member and Associate Member. The former reflects membership at a corporate level for companies that have installed and run SAP. Fees range from $500 for SAP Business One customers up to $5,000 for large customers with more than $5 billion in revenue. This membership gives all employees of the company benefits from ASUG. Each company designates a "champion" (the single point of contact for the company), along with a primary contact, executive contact, and up to six secondary contacts.

Associate Members include licensed vendors (that is, entities that are licensed Logo, Platform, Alliance, or Implementation Partners) along with certified Complementary Software Program (CSP) participants. Noncertified partners such as small consulting firms can qualify for Associate Member privileges, too.

With ASUG membership comes access to the members-only site within the parent ASUG website. This provides access to a discussion forum, the Member Network, various ASUG-sponsored webcasts, and past presentations and other materials. ASUG members also enjoy discounted rates for attending the annual ASUG conference, access to local and regional chapter meetings, webinars, teleconferences, group meetings, symposiums, and more. Joining ASUG enables a member company to learn from the shared experiences of other users and to help forge solutions to common user challenges and influencing and shape SAP's product development over the next few years. With Installation Membership, the special opportunity to influence SAP SE makes for probably the most compelling reason to join the club. For more information about ASUG, email the group at memberservices@ASUG.com.

Beyond ASUG, there are numerous other SAP user organizations representing literally every region on the planet. The German-speaking DSAG (Deutschsprachige SAP-Anwendergruppe) is among the largest. The French-speaking user group (Utilisateurs SAP Francophones [USF]) and regional groups such as the African SAP User Group (AFSUG) and the Middle East and North African User Group (SUG-MENA) are popular as well.

Find the SAP user group representing your regional and language preferences at http://www.sap.com/communities/user-groups.html. Nearly all SAP user groups organize relatively inexpensive-to-attend annual conferences where you can get firsthand practical experience while networking with experienced experts.

Beyond the formal user groups around the world, many SAP departments of large companies in various cities organize an "SAP Stammtisch," where real-life experiences are shared. Finally, there are also periodicals independent from SAP, such as the German magazine *E3* (www.e-3.de), available online in English for iOS or Android.

SAP Professional Journal

A bimonthly publication, the *SAP Professional Journal* targets a wide cross-section of SAP professionals, from developers to systems administrators to infrastructure/Basis support personnel and more. But the journal also targets the business professionals who rely on SAP to keep their respective companies running. Within the pages of the *SAP Professional Journal*, you'll find technology tutorials, reviews of new products and options, coding and other technical tips, case studies, integration and systems management advice, migration and upgrade guidance, and a wealth of installation and support best practices. And these are not cursory articles or short abstracts; many are detailed articles that are immediately useful.

Perhaps even better than the printed journal is access to the online version. Take a look at www. sappro.com for a list of articles in the latest issue (plus abstracts). Even better, use this resource as a search engine to help find some of the best technical materials and SAP best practices available anywhere. With more than 8,000 pages of published articles and other documents, this investment will pay big dividends for the entire SAP support department.

SAPinsider

SAPinsider is published by the same organization that publishes the *SAP Professional Journal*: Wellesley Information Services (WIS). Its format is decidedly different, though, in that it's a quarterly publication, it's free to qualified subscribers (typically anyone supporting or using SAP), and it's sponsored directly by SAP SE. In fact, *SAPinsider* is a joint venture between WIS and SAP. To this last point, the editorial board of directors responsible for publishing valuable real-world *SAPinsider* content reflects a cross-section of some of SAP's most well-known executive and technical names. This helps ensure leading-edge insight. Important lessons learned are imparted every quarter, making *SAPinsider* an excellent addition to any SAP professional's reading.

In addition to providing solid technical advice, *SAPinsider* provides product walkthroughs and reviews, up-to-date news from SAP developers, and a number of useful regular columns—NetWeaver, Under Development, Recommended Reading (book reviews, slanted naturally toward SAP Press), and a New and Noteworthy section used by partners and SAP product organizations alike to share important findings. This variety of resources and information can help you stay well rounded and abreast of the most current developments in the SAP community. It's no wonder that more than 125,000 professionals who develop, implement, support, and use SAP applications depend on *SAPinsider*. For information, visit www.sapinsideronline.com.

InsiderPROFILES

The newest addition to the small circle of SAP-focused magazines on the market today is *InsiderPROFILES* (formerly *SAP NetWeaver*). Founded in 2005, its purpose is to share innovations and insights related to SAP NetWeaver, BusinessObjects, and SAP in general. This magazine does a good job aligning the business and IT sides of SAP. Managers will find the analysts' coverage, thoughts from industry experts, and real-world anecdotes and high-level case studies just what they need to build a business case for moving in a particular direction. Technologists and architects will find the best practices, detailed case studies, and independent insight proffered by SAP experts indispensable as well, enabling them to make better and bolder decisions while mitigating the risk of deploying products without the benefit of long histories (a nicer way of saying "less-mature products"). The magazine is free and delivered online. Go to insiderprofiles.wispubs. com/issue.aspx to learn more about why this might be the magazine you need.

Traditional and Online Books

Close to 1,000 books are available on the market today for SAP. Using online bookstores such as Barnes & Noble (www.bn.com) and Amazon.com, you can easily search for and uncover the latest SAP-related books. It's also worth your time to look at www.sap-press.com, which, unsurprisingly, offers a wealth of SAP books covering topics as diverse as SAP BusinessObjects, Solution Manager, Enterprise SOA, SAP Business One, performance optimization, ABAP and Java programming and performance tuning, SAP NetWeaver system administration, Workflow, SAP Customer Relationship Management (CRM) customization and development, SAP Business Warehouse (BW), security and authorization, SAP query reporting, and most every other product or capability related to SAP. Many other sites offer lists of popular books. These lists get stale quickly but can offer good insight into what's proven useful to other readers around the world.

Technical Newsletters

WIS Publications, the same entity that publishes the *SAP Professional Journal*, offers a number of well-received technical newsletters. Each newsletter is laser-focused on a particular topic, such as the following:

- ▶ *Financials Expert*: Geared toward finance and IT teams that use or support FI, CO, or SAP ERP Financials and covering quite a few reporting options, ranging from ERP and BW Reporting, to SEM, Financial Accounting, Profitability Analysis, G/L, Treasury, A/P, A/R, Controlling, and more. See www.ficoexpertonline.com for details.

- ▶ *BW Expert*: For those tasked with deploying, upgrading, optimizing, or supporting SAP's business intelligence solutions. For more information, check out www.bwexpertonline.com.

- ▶ *SCM Expert*: For SAP teams tasked with better understanding what it means to optimize an organization's supply chain. All the usual supply chain functions are covered, including procurement, warehousing, manufacturing schedules, sales, and distribution. But more than SAP Advanced Planner and Optimizer (APO) is targeted; *SCM Expert* targets core SAP ERP modules as well, including Sales and Distribution (SD), Production Planning (PP), Materials Management (MM), Quality Management (QM), and Project System (PS). Refer to www.scmexpertonline.com for details.

- ▶ *HR Expert*: For teams responsible for human capital management and more. From tutorials and case studies to real-world best practices and troubleshooting guidance, *HR Expert* provides the just-in-time advice an HR team needs to manage and optimize Employee Self-Service (ESS), Manager Self-Service (MSS), personnel administration, payroll, and more. See www.hrexpertonline.com for more information.

- ▶ *CRM Expert*: For teams responsible for unlocking critical CRM functionality, such as marketing, sales, service, and analytics, including CRM's new user interfaces, applications, and tools. Check out www.crmexpertonline.com.

Internet Resources

Many SAP Internet resources are available for you to communicate, learn, and share your own ideas and findings about your SAP system with SAP professionals, vendors, and the entire virtual user community. Always on and always available, the Internet is an ideal source for obtaining troubleshooting information in a pinch. It is a good idea to search the Internet every now and then for new SAP resources; an amazing wealth of new material is made available practically every day. The best of these resources and their content are covered next.

SAP ITtoolbox

One of the most popular and useful sites you can turn to is SAP ITtoolbox. It's been helping those of us in the SAP field for years and continually proves its worth. With more than 700 active discussion groups and a history of serving its community with facts and integrity, the ITtoolbox portal is a must-have subscription for nearly everyone. ITtoolbox takes care not to inundate you with weekly trash; instead, you choose, cafeteria-style, the topics that most interest you, and ITtoolbox works to provide you with updated topic-specific content as it becomes available. Interested in SAP careers, training, or certification? Want to review knowledge bases focused on SCM, ERP project management, or hardware platforms for SAP? SAP ITtoolbox has it all. Register at www.ITtoolbox.com.

SAP Fans

SAP Fans (www.sapfans.com) continues to be an excellent source of unbiased SAP information. (The site is not affiliated with SAP SE.) SAP Fans is designed as a forum to exchange ideas with other SAP customers working with SAP R/3, R/2, and other SAP systems. This website includes user-based, technical, and other discussion forums that provide you with opportunities to post questions, comments, and experiences about your SAP system and retrieve responses from other SAP professionals. These forums are grouped into a number of areas. Arguably the most useful is the Technical area. There's also a Non-Technical forum area, intended to host general discussions, share job postings and résumés, and focus on educational services, list training courses, and address certification questions. Finally, the Knowledge Corner, which is moderated in real time, lets you pose functional, technical, and ABAP-related questions. Using these discussion forums, you can easily post a question or problem that you are having with your SAP system. Other SAP Fans users will see your posting and (hopefully!) respond with possible solutions.

The network of contacts you gain as you discuss and share similar experiences can prove invaluable. As of this writing, SAP Fans boasts more than 108,000 registered users and nearly a million posts. And because it's an ideal source for SAP news, events, products, books, and employment opportunities, you should bookmark SAP Fans as one of your favorites. Yes, some of the material is outdated. But much of it is extremely current, making it one of the most useful (and very free!) resources available to aspiring and experienced SAP "fans" alike.

SAP FAQ

The SAP FAQ originated in 1994 as a web-based adjunct to the de.alt.sap-r3 Usenet discussion forum from Germany's University of Oldenburg, a pioneering SAP academic installation site. As a longstanding, not-for-profit, technology-specific resource, the SAP FAQ has earned and maintained a position of global credibility and respect. Its objective is to serve as a comprehensive point of information about SAP for those who work with SAP, companies that are implementing SAP, students, and those who are looking into SAP as a potential ERP solution or career option.

TechTarget and SearchSAP.com

What used to be termed the SAP FAQ's "by-subscription" discussion forum, ask-the-experts forum, and other similar resources are now accessed through TechTarget, the parent to SearchSAP.com. In fact, when you type www.sapfaq.com, you are rerouted to itknowledgeexchange.techtarget.com/itanswers, a wonderful portal into a wealth of materials, moderated discussions, salary surveys, events and conferences, great tips, useful newsletters, and much more. It's a great way to exchange ideas while staying on top of new trends and products. An awesome SAP product directory covers much more than the usual ERP, CRM, and supply chain topics. You can access hard-to-find information pertaining to disaster recovery and capacity planning, for example. You'll also find much to review if you're interested in trying to understand what kind of products are available in the hot areas of business process management (BPM) or reporting. From general, core FI and HR module-related discussions, to industry-specific dialogue, subscribers can select a customized combination of discussions that fit very specifically into their areas of interest and expertise. And given the no-cost approach to subscription, SearchSAP.com and TechTarget in general are no-brainers for SAP professionals on a budget. For more information or to subscribe, visit searchsap.techtarget.com.

SAP Conferences and Events

In addition to the ASUG conference and regular ASUG-sponsored events, a growing number of specialized SAP conferences are available to SAP professionals, users, and others. Some of these, such as SAP TechEd, are geared toward technologists and developers, whereas others, such as SAPPHIRE NOW, are geared toward executives and other decision makers. In addition, a wealth of product-specific conferences and events are hosted throughout the year by the same folks who publish the *SAP Professional Journal* and *SAPinsider* (WIS Publications, discussed earlier this hour).

Worried about the costs of attending a conference? Considering presenting a session or, better yet, co-presenting with a colleague or customer? Conference providers love bringing together practitioners and customers to share real-world experiences. Sharing your experiences and lessons learned is also a great way to contribute to the SAP community. The networking opportunities are fantastic, too, as is hearing from your peers on the latest and greatest on everything SAP.

In turn, nearly all the conference providers cover your airfare, hotel costs, and of course the conference fee for attending. They might even throw in a bit of a stipend for incidentals.

SAPPHIRE NOW

If you seek a high-level or executive-level perspective on SAP's current priorities and change-enabling initiatives, or if you're looking for an executive-level networking opportunity, consider attending the annual SAPPHIRE NOW conference. One is held every year in the United States, Europe, and other venues like Asia and India. Some technical sessions are offered, but SAPPHIRE NOW is better known for being a who's who of keynotes, customer case studies and success stories, and business-oriented presentation sessions. Go to www.sapphirenow.com for information regarding the most recent or upcoming SAPPHIRE NOW event.

SAP TechEd

There is no better way to get the inside SAP scoop on everything out there and everything coming around the corner than SAP TechEd. Because this event is not interested in hosting marketing sessions, you actually learn things that are immediately useful in your day-to-day life, whether optimizing your current system or planning for your next functional upgrade. SAP TechEd provides opportunities to easily, quickly, and cheaply take certification exams, which can save your travel and expense budget thousands because you can combine multiple training and certification trips into a single four- or five-day jaunt to great destinations such as Orlando, Las Vegas, Bangalore, Madrid, and Beijing. Bring your family along and start off your family vacation with SAP!

Managing Your SAP Projects

If you're on a team tasked with planning and deploying SAP, consider attending one of the proven SAP conferences out there: WIS's Managing Your SAP Projects. By offering real-world advice focused on resolving issues and duplicating successes, Managing Your SAP Projects gives you a chance to drill down into what makes or breaks a successful implementation or upgrade, walk through customer case studies, and hear about high-level strategies and leadership tactics used by SAP project leaders and their teams. Such practical guidance learned in the trenches is worth the nominal conference fee.

Because of the decidedly project management focus of this annual conference, certified Project Management Institute (PMI) Project Management Professionals will be glad to know that they can also earn professional development unit (PDU) credits by attending many of the more than 90 sessions, which is helpful in maintaining PMP certification. And because this is very much a vendor-neutral conference—SAP SE does not sponsor it, although many of the speakers hail from various SAP organizations—those interested in perhaps a less-biased view of SAP will find the sessions refreshingly straightforward.

Other WIS-Sponsored Seminars and Conferences

Wellesley Information Services offers a host of other content-specific and product-specific conference venues. In recent years, WIS has delivered more than 50 conferences and seminars in a variety of North American and European cities. Topics have ranged from SAP ERP for managers to technology-focused SCM, PLM, HR, BW, CRM, and IT. And the new SAP Solution Manager conference has received high marks from many SAP professionals. As with all of WIS's other conferences, the SAP-neutral stance makes this a great conference for absorbing great real-world information in just a few days. See www.wispubs.com/eventCalendar_SAP.cfm for a list of upcoming SAP-focused conferences near you.

Employment and Career Opportunities

One of the first things you will notice when you begin an SAP project is that you're suddenly in demand from others. Your email inbox and voicemail box will be bombarded with messages from recruiters offering to outdo your present salary, reduce your travel, increase your opportunities for advancement, and so on. Some of these are good deals, actually, but they can catch you off-guard. Therefore, you need to be prepared.

SAP knowledge is a hot commodity today; a wealth of positions are available, and the number of them is growing for people with the right skills. This includes functional as well as technical skills, development as well as configuration expertise. Possessing in-depth knowledge on how to configure and set up a module in SAP ERP is just as valuable as being able to write ABAP or Java code for SAP, or navigate an SAP system through a complex functional upgrade or OS/DB migration. And people with program management and project management skills gleaned through an SAP project are also in great demand. Unsurprisingly, a great number of websites are devoted to making their employment opportunities available to you. A sample of these websites is provided next.

Softwarejobs.com

www.softwarejobs.com is a great venue for posting and reviewing SAP employment opportunities. Its online career resources are free and useful, including consultation and résumé-writing help, links to free industry-related magazines and similar materials, access to career events and continuing education, and even access to a free personality test, a free career test, and a cadre of career-boosting and similarly inspired articles.

The site also offers free email, inexpensive background checks (to help the decision to hire you over 500 other candidates weigh in your favor), and a full-blown Resource Center portal site to provide access to all this and more. Finally, softwarejobs.com's Job Seeker Tools section makes it easy to build a portfolio, manage and post your résumé, conduct advanced job searches, and distribute your résumé through a number of venues.

ITtoolbox for Careers

As discussed previously, the ITtoolbox website provides outstanding career and job assistance. From the home page, you can launch the Career Center, which gives you rapid access to recently posted jobs, the capability to sign up for job alerts, the ability to introduce yourself to the IT industry's top recruiters, and access to the career-specific ITtoolbox knowledge bases.

Need to hire a couple of contractors for one of your own projects? ITtoolbox also features a section for employers. Use it to post a job opening and review the site's online Resume Database (access is fee-based; use your credit card), and you'll be knee-deep in thousands of résumés in no time. Be sure to bookmark this site as one of your favorites.

Up and Coming

As SAP opportunities continue to grow, a number of other sites have popped up, offering job databases worth checking out. A few popular sites are www.simplysap.com, www.justsapjobs.com, and www.sapcareers.com. In addition to these, it is wise to take a look at SAP job offerings on mainstream sites such as www.monster.com and www.careerbuilder.com and on IT job sites such as www.dice.com. These latter sites can be particularly helpful when looking for specific opportunities at firms in your region. With the wealth of jobs available, you are sure to find an opportunity worth pursuing.

Be sure to review Hour 22, "SAP Careers for the Business User," and Hour 23, "SAP Careers for the IT Professional," prior to pursuing or changing jobs in the world of SAP.

Summary

We've reached the end of the book and want to thank you for hanging in there. We trust that you've found this latest version of *SAMS Teach Yourself SAP in 24 Hours* a good use of your time. In this final hour, we looked at a number of SAP-related resources. Many of these are free, and all of them help you get the most out of your goal of becoming more familiar with SAP. Look to these resources every few months, if not more often; there's a wealth of knowledge captured in the Internet resources, for example, that benefit all of us from time to time.

Do you feel like you've matured from a SAPling to something a bit more experienced? We hope so. And we hope you have enjoyed our deeper focus on business users, new technical details, and new insight into how SAP has evolved over the past four years. On behalf of all of us, it's been our pleasure. Perhaps we'll get to work together soon. In the meantime, don't hesitate to contact us with your questions, experiences, and feedback.

Case Study: Hour 24

Consider this SAP resource-related case study and the questions that follow. You can find answers to the questions related to this case study in Appendix A, "Case Study Answers."

Situation

As the newest but one of the least-experienced SAP Financials developers at MNC, you have been tasked with quickly getting up to speed as the SAP project team prepares for a pending SAP ERP upgrade. Fortunately, your vast expertise in managing financial projects for several previous customers should come in handy. Not unexpectedly, you have also been told there's very little budget available for training.

Questions

1. With what group could you get involved to find out what other SAP customers are doing in the SAP Financials arena?

2. The big SAP Financials conference is coming up, and it's chock full of sessions you need exposure to. It looks like you can fit it into your schedule. With no budget for conference fees or airfare, how should you pursue attending?

3. How can you quickly find the top 100 books focused on SAP development?

4. How can you keep up-to-date with the latest SAP information available on the Internet?

5. What SAP conference might make the most sense for you to attend?

Case Study Answers

This appendix provides answers to the questions posed in each hour's case study. In some cases, note that other answers may also be correct.

Case Study: Hour 1 Answers

1. Although there are many smaller niche players in the business application market, three companies own the bulk of market share and mindshare in this space: SAP, Oracle, and Microsoft. Others, like Sage, Infor, Epicor, and NetSuite, could be interesting alternatives.

2. MNC needs to investigate SAP ERP first and foremost as it seeks to connect all its end users to a single financial system of record. At the same time, though, the company also needs to investigate SAP Customer Relationship Management (CRM) to address lost sales and other market opportunities. Finally, the board might be interested in investigating SAP NetWeaver Portal as perhaps a first step toward unifying how its end users "go to work," along with the SAP NetWeaver Process Integration (PI) product to integrate the company's diverse present-day solutions into a more cohesive solution.

3. SAP offers a mining industry solution and a milling solution, both of which should be of great interest to MNC. By implementing these industry solutions atop SAP ERP, MNC could immediately leverage mining-specific and milling-specific industry best practices.

4. With 100,000 employees, MNC faces several challenges. Questions related to the mix of front-end client devices need to be posed, along with details regarding network links between the 500 different sites and the site that would eventually be used to run SAP. Fortunately for MNC, the company's adoption of Microsoft Windows on its desktops and laptops will allow for several graphical user interfaces (including browsers).

5. The board needs to understand how SAP's client concept can enable business agility by providing different business units with their own legal entities or "clients" that can be customized for specific ways of doing business (in different countries or by line of business, for example).

6. Language and currency issues should be no problem for MNC, although the board needs to ensure that the organization's specific languages and dialects are supported by SAP.

Case Study: Hour 2 Answers

1. SAP is one of many different ERP solutions on the market today; it is premature to decide on SAP at this point, let alone specific SAP products and applications. Instead of focusing on vendors, solutions, or technologies, at this stage it's much more important to develop the business architecture and related business roadmap.

2. The business roadmap should connect business vision, strategy, and architecture to desired business functions and requirements (business blueprinting), which in turn become business processes or workstreams that ultimately are configured atop specific applications (SAP or otherwise).

3. MNC's lack of repeat customers speaks to a problem with the basic business tenet of how to increase revenue. Interestingly, the company might decide to fix this problem (a prudent move) or simply refocus its efforts on a new revenue opportunity (commodity goods direct sales).

4. The task force needs to look at MNC's situation from four perspectives: business, functional, technical, and project implementation.

5. The functional perspective addresses the "what" of a business solution. It answers the question "What will a particular business process do?"

6. The technical perspective addresses the "how" part of a business solution. It makes the business and functional perspectives possible through the deployment of specific applications and technologies.

Case Study: Hour 3 Answers

1. Doing nothing allows the combined company to pursue business as usual without risk of disruption; it's the least risky option.

2. Doing nothing is expensive in that many different server, operating system, and database products need to be managed and maintained. The SAP technology (Basis) teams will remain as disjointed as they were when they worked for two different companies. Little to no infrastructure standardization or consolidation is really possible, as well.

3. Consolidating servers, disk subsystem, network gear, and other assets into a common datacenter could help reduce the costs associated with managing and operating these infrastructure components, and it could allow MNC to retire one of its datacenters.

4. Standardizing computing platforms would decrease complexity, enable all systems to be managed by fewer people, and position MNC to eventually consolidate its like-for-like SAP instances.

5. Regardless of the number of instances associated with each SAP component, AMI currently supports three production systems.

6. HANA could prove useful in many ways. For example, HANA's compression technologies could help shrink AMI's huge databases, thus freeing up valuable disk space and enabling faster (and much smaller) database backups. HANA's in-memory performance will help the organization deliver faster analytics capabilities, too. Surely, the expense of HANA will raise additional budget concerns, however.

Case Study: Hour 4 Answers

1. In MNC's case, only SAP Enterprise Resource Management (ERP) and Supply Chain Management (SCM) seem to currently be in scope.

2. For the realization phase, the teams will probably be organized around functions and tasks. This might include teams focused on the business and teams focused on technology. For example, MNC might organize by Business and Configuration, Integration, Development, Test, Data, Security, and a host of various technical teams.

3. With regard to access strategies, explain the differences between the traditional SAPGUI fat client and web browser–based access. It's a good idea to avoid committing to one strategy or the other, however, because the blueprinting phase (where such matters are analyzed) has not yet been completed.

4. Tell the person that the SAP project lifecycle comprises seven steps or phases: project initiation, matching and prototyping, design and construction, system integration testing, business acceptance testing, cut-over preparation, and stabilization.

5. While the blueprinting phase definitely takes time and resources, the realization phase will consume much more time and much more budget.

6. The finance user's job will certainly be impacted by the SAP implementation. He will be trained in the new system, however, and will likely find the SAP ERP application a powerful and more capable replacement for his current system.

Case Study: Hour 5 Answers

1. SAP All-in-One is the best solution if the business processes are very complex and the system needs to support up to 2,500 users.

2. SAP Business One may be an ideal solution for a small company with straightforward business processes and a requirement for the system to be fully deployed in eight weeks or less.

3. SAP Business ByDesign is a good solution for companies that prefer to have their own employees customize the system's business functionality.

4. For subsidiaries of 2,500 or more employees, SAP's ERP application is probably most appropriate.

5. SAP Business ByDesign is a good fit for a company without an IT staff, as long you can accept the lack of features.

Case Study: Hour 6 Answers

1. Strategic benefits that MNC may realize by implementing new NetWeaver functionality include reduced total cost of ownership (TCO) and greater potential for innovation. The end users who need the Business Warehouse (BW) reports may then receive their reports via push technology (information broadcasting) instead of by logging on to the SAPGUI and manually searching for them. This reduces time spent on this task, and it allows the users to focus on other business challenges, which ultimately creates cost savings and a more efficient workforce for MNC. Alternatively, MNC might choose to invest in HANA to allow for instantaneous access to their reports.

2. Of the six SAP NetWeaver components areas or themes, the Composition and Business Process Management areas are most focused on solution development.

3. SAP provides several resources useful for planning and implementing information broadcasting on its SAP BW system. These include the SAP NetWeaver Master Guide as well as the installations guides for NetWeaver systems, standalone engines, and clients, which are broken out by OS and DB platform combinations. (Keep in mind that you must have a valid SAP Service Marketplace user ID to access these resources.)

4. SAP has changed its use of SAP BW and SAP BI several times over the past few years. They're generally interchangeable in much of SAP's documentation, with exceptions.

5. MNC could connect the chemical systems using the business-to-business chemical electronic data interchange (EDI) adapter. Alternatively, the legacy system might be supported by one of the application-specific adapters or technology standards, as well.

Case Study: Hour 7 Answers

1. SAP ERP Human Capital Management (HCM) includes a number of features. It is a compelling solution for many reasons, including its integration with SAP ERP Financials, Manufacturing, and other SAP solutions; its world-class talent management functionality; its ability to enable and empower global teams and ability to connect a firm's workforce to a single system of record and accountability; its built-in business intelligence capabilities;

its ability to be run as an outsourced business process, SAP's extensive SAP ERP Human Capital Management (HCM) partner network, the solution's open and extensible technology platform; and generally its reputation as a "safe choice" for HR organizations.

2. The components of plant maintenance include preventive maintenance, service management, maintenance order management, maintenance projects, equipment and technical objects, and plant maintenance information system.

3. SAP ERP Operations is an aging label for SAP's logistics offerings, composed of Procurement and Logistics Execution, Product Development and Manufacturing, and Sales and Service. Within these offerings are business processes related to purchasing, plant maintenance, sales and distribution, manufacturing, materials management, warehousing, engineering, and construction. The umbrella solution SAP Manufacturing comprises SAP ERP Operations.

4. SAP purposely engineers overlap between particular solutions and modules to enable companies to customize a business solution reflecting the specific business modules and processes necessary to meet their needs.

5. An important component of SAP ERP is the Analytics solution offering, which is a targeted solution consisting of financials, operations, and workforce analytics.

6. The SAP CRM features that help support new customers include marketing support, sales support, service support, web channel support, interaction center management support, partner channel management, business communications management, and real-time offer management.

7. No, SAP Manufacturing is composed of several components, all of which must be properly licensed.

8. SAP SRM's tight integration with PLM benefits SRM users by streamlining access to engineering documentation and other materials useful in optimizing product quality, manufacturing processes, and more; and providing visibility into ERP back-end data, such as materials management processes, financial documents, and bills of materials (BOMs).

9. The ERP component is the most mature, followed by SAP SCM.

10. The three general components of the supply chain include supply, manufacturing, and distribution.

Case Study: Hour 8 Answers

1. For the classic SAP solutions, you can choose between Infrastructure as a service (IaaS) and Platform as a Service (PaaS) offerings.

2. The responsibility of IaaS and PaaS providers reaches up to the virtual machine only. You are still responsible and have to install and maintain the operating system, the database, and the application code as in an on-premise installation. You also need to own the licenses for all these components and acquire the necessary maintenance contracts.

3. It has become a common best practice in the industry to combine on-premise installations for the productive mission-critical systems with development, sandbox, and training systems installed on the cloud.

4. In addition to SAP, which offers HEC, there are a wide variety of certified cloud providers offering HANA as part of their services (along with additional services beyond hosting HANA instances).

5. SuccessFactors focuses on cloud-based talent management, while paying people is still the domain of SAP HR.

6. Ariba provides a business network for purchases, while SAP SRM focuses on the demands of the company's buying department.

7. Fieldglass supports the management of contingent workers.

8. Concur helps its user avoid rekeying the same data multiple times by integrating travel booking with expense tracking. In addition, instead of collecting and mailing in paper receipts, travelers can take photos of train tickets or restaurant bills and submit them electronically.

9. hybris delivers a multi-channel retailing and catalog management solution that supports sales and marketing departments.

Case Study: Hour 9 Answers

1. The technical team needs the insight of MNC's power users in defining and reviewing how (and to what extent) SAP's applications may solve the company's business problems. Without the perspective of its power users, MNC risks "solving" the wrong problems—or worse, inventing new ones.

2. The prime integrator knows SAP and knows specific functional or business areas but is missing the firsthand knowledge held by MNC's power users. The power users working in the various accounting teams will serve as internal consultants to the prime integrator's consultants, coaching the implementation team in terms of how business is currently conducted and therefore how the work flows through the organization today.

3. With all the power users' knowledge of MNC's business processes and SAP's functional configuration, the biggest challenge faced by MNC after go-live might simply be retaining them.

4. The job of converting a firm's business requirements to functional specifications that may in turn be used to configure SAP appropriately is the responsibility of a special collection or matrix of people and teams—the functional business leaders, also called business process analysts, or "row" leaders.

Case Study: Hour 10 Answers

1. You will need the hostname or IP address, the system ID, and the system number.

2. Drill down into the SAP menu path until you reach sales order entry (select Logistics, Sales and Distribution, Sales, Order, Create).

3. SAP menus are good examples of the SAP tree structure.

4. No, the two-character language identifier is optional (unless you need to change to another language and that language has been pre-installed and configured in the SAP component).

5. Whereas SAP Fiori provides ubiquitous look and feel across mobile and traditional PC devices, SAP Screen Personas lets users and IT departments improve the usability and feel of the traditional SAPGUI. It's this create new-versus-modify existing UI perspective that marks the primary difference between SAP Fiori and SAP Screen Personas.

6. The SAPUI5 and its open-source equivalent OpenUI5 allow developers to create new SAP user interfaces that operate across mobile, tablet, and classic desktop environments.

Case Study: Hour 11 Answers

1. The four core business scenarios are SAP ERP Financials, SAP ERP Operations, SAP ERP Human Capital Management, and SAP ERP Corporate Services.

2. Materials management experience is directly applicable to the SAP ERP Operations scenario.

3. Real estate management experience is directly applicable to the SAP ERP Corporate Services scenario.

4. Your SAP MM purchasing experience means you're probably familiar with business transactions related to creating purchase orders (ME21N), creating purchase requisitions (ME51N), releasing PRs (ME54), listing PRs (ME5A), and automatically generating POs (ME59), among others.

5. SAP RE consists of many submodules ranging from those for real estate controlling, accounting, and contracting to rent adjustments, taxes, land use management, service charge management, and various sales-related processes. Discuss any of these to demonstrate your experience in SAP RE.

Case Study: Hour 12 Answers

1. An experienced CRM candidate should be able to talk about several of the following: sales, marketing, service, pricing, CRM analytics, Interaction Center (IC) system capabilities, or multi-channel capabilities.

2. A candidate who can talk intelligently about self-service procurement (classic shopping cart functionality), strategic sourcing, master data management (formerly catalog content management), spend analysis, or supplier evaluation is a prospective SAP SRM end user.

3. Candidates with knowledge of demand planning, production planning, transportation planning, and vehicle scheduling are probably good candidates for a supply chain management (SCM) end-user role.

4. A PLM end user with recipe management experience should be able to talk about creating, changing, and managing formulas, including substance types, management practices, roles, and parameters.

5. SAP PLM is tightly integrated with procurement management processes, material master data, engineering and document management functionality, safety and maintenance processes, and a host of various tools and other applications. Without this kind of broad experience, your PLM candidate is probably not a good fit in the short term.

Case Study: Hour 13 Answers

1. Three types of reporting users are lightweight executive or self-service users, BI users or decisions makers, and operational reporting users.

2. SAP offers several new and legacy visualization tools. While the SAP BO Xcelcius Enterprise tool is probably its most powerful visualization tool, the SAP BO Explorer, SAP BO Crystal Reports, SAP BO Web Intelligence, SAP Business Explorer, SAP Report Painter, and even the SAP QuickViewer afford a certain amount of visualization capabilities.

3. The SAP BO Web Intelligence tool provides business intelligence insight from existing reports, giving business intelligence users and decision makers a robust platform for business analysis and self-service BI mashups.

4. Several SAP reporting options are associated with SAP NetWeaver Business Warehouse, including SAP NetWeaver BW and BWA, SAP BW Powered by SAP HANA, and the SAP Business Explorer.

5. Most of SAP's legacy reporting options were built into the SAP ERP (previously SAP R/3) application.

Case Study: Hour 14 Answers

1. Replace the traditional FI/CO module in SAP ERP with SAP sFin.

2. Implement a centralized general ledger within an ERP on HANA system to collect all financial information from the source ERPs in real time.

3. Use the %pc command to easily download data directly into Word and Excel.

4. Select the appropriate customer addresses in SAP CRM and output the data into Word, using OLE connectivity.

5. Utilize SAP Interactive Forms by Adobe with one of the standard forms delivered by SAP.

6. The OpenText ECM Suite provides data and document archiving for SAP solutions.

Case Study: Hour 15 Answers

1. Given the timeframe, SAP's ASAP methodology and its accelerators are probably critical success factors. The Human Capital Management (HCM) module is quite mature, fortunately, with known risks, issues, and challenges. Perhaps ASAP's agile or iterative approach would prove useful in quickly delivering value throughout the year.

2. MNC's lack of SAP technical skills and leadership mandates that a senior enterprise architect familiar with MNC's industry and SAP HCM be contracted from SAP SE or from an experienced SAP systems integrator.

3. Given that MNC has a mature project management office (PMO), it should be assumed that the PMO is adept at creating project plans, contingency plans, communications plans, and escalation processes and is also well versed in managing quality and risk. Of course, without an available project manager to assist the program manager, an immense amount of tactical work will stack up quickly. A project manager with SAP experience needs to be made available or hired.

4. The VP of HR's past history with SAP is a major warning sign. Without the VP's buy-in, leadership, and activities aimed at promoting the new solution, the project will almost certainly fail. The VP of HR is probably the most important stakeholder, too, if not the project sponsor.

5. Considering the situation, you should tell the steering committee that the project is at high risk until the issues outlined here are addressed.

Case Study: Hour 16 Answers

1. MNC's current IT teams will need to be staffed and trained specifically for SAP. However, the datacenter team probably has the necessary knowledge to require only basic staff augmentation.

2. The SAP Basis team is responsible for planning, delivering, and maintaining the technical infrastructure necessary to run SAP.

3. Point the technical teams to SAP's Master Guides for detailed planning and preparation advice (see service.sap.com/instguides).

4. Though MNC's current use of a four-system landscape (development, test, pre-production staging, and production) is admirable, given the IT organization's technical gaps, the business's training gaps, and likely need for a business/functional sandbox as well as a DR solution, it will be necessary to deploy a broader system landscape.

5. Two additional DR solutions outside of basic tape backup/restore capabilities include using database log shipping and implementing a DR solution involving hardware-based storage replication technologies.

Case Study: Hour 17 Answers

1. The transaction code to launch the ABAP Development Workbench is SE80.

2. The name of the development environment for creating SAP Java applications is the SAP NetWeaver Developer Studio (NWDS).

3. The ABAP Development Workbench, Java NWDS, and the SAP Composition Environment represent the three primary toolsets used for SAP development.

4. The ASAP Implementation Roadmap for SAP NetWeaver Enterprise Portal is an example of a Run SAP roadmap.

5. The SAP Project Implementation Guide contains only the customizing steps necessary for the application components your company is implementing.

Case Study: Hour 18 Answers

1. Install SAP Solution Manager (after obtaining SolMan installation media and Installation Guides).

2. The first SAP landscape environment to be installed is typically a technical sandbox or "crash and burn" system.

3. SAP media is available at the SAP Software Download Center.

4. Yes, you can run a HANA PoC on Amazon using Amazon Web Services (AWS). Microsoft Azure has only limited HANA capability today, exposed in the SAP Cloud Appliance Library (with greater capabilities expected soon).

5. The HANA PoC needs to be finished within 90 days. After 90 days, the licenses will expire.

6. To immediately cut IT support costs related to changing and resetting passwords, MNC should consider implementing single sign-on (SSO).

Case Study: Hour 19 Answers

1. Generally speaking, a business's end users consume Software as a Service (SaaS), developers or programmers consume Platform as a Service (PaaS), and IT professionals consume Infrastructure as a Service (IaaS).

2. Less risky than the public cloud counterpart, hybrid cloud models represent the most reasonable and realistic first step into the cloud (although a good argument may also be made for pursuing a private cloud hosting model).

3. Many of SAP's new or acquired applications are delivered through SaaS.

4. Systems that might be good first movers into the cloud include CRM, end-user training systems, technical sandbox training systems, business demonstration and prototyping systems, any of the systems subject to seasonal spikes, the company's various test or quality assurance systems (and, to a lesser extent, the development systems), systems used to maintain data or storage backups, and perhaps MNC's disaster recovery systems.

5. While the ideas around deploying a homogenous SAP cloud might hold universal, Monsoon itself is for SAP's internal development and sales teams.

Case Study: Hour 20 Answers

1. Enable and activate the EEM_SLA dashboard to view End User Experience Service Level Reporting details.

2. Use CCMS transactions ST07, SM04, and AL08 to view end-user data such as the number of users logged into a particular functional area or on a particular application server, or users executing specific functional transactions.

3. SAP LVM lets you create new systems by dragging and dropping a newly described SAP system onto available hardware resources. It can also be used to deploy virtual machines and relocate SAP instances between physical and virtual machines.

4. Centrally monitor your entire SAP environment, including multiple SAP system land-scapes, by using SAP Solution Manager.

5. SAP Early Watch reports provide status on the health of a system, including platform and utilization figures that can be used to determine the actual resource consumption of the SAP solution. This information is important prior to go-live, upgrades, pending hardware refreshes, and so on.

Case Study: Hour 21 Answers

1. The idea of managing and minimizing risk, particularly the risk of downtime, is usually the most important matter surrounding a major change such as an upgrade.

2. No, this advertisement is not accurate. The ad should read, "Project Manager with SAP upgrade skills..." The fact that the SAP release is changing indicates this is a functional upgrade, whereas the term "migration" implies an operating system or database change.

3. MNC can later pursue an SAP OS/DB migration to move SAP to a platform that offers a lower total cost of ownership (TCO) or better opportunities to innovate. MNC might con-sider alternative hosting options as well.

4. Most changes to the computing platform are considered updates, changes to SAP function-ality are considered upgrades, and completely changing the OS or database release consti-tutes a migration.

5. While combined upgrade/migration projects are inherently riskier than performing these changes in stages (with a period in-between to allow the system to settle in), they're becoming easier to do and therefore more common. A combined upgrade/migration can also potentially minimize the overall business downtime required to perform these changes compared to doing them one at a time.

Case Study: Hour 22 Answers

1. To learn more about SAP's partners, review the partner search index at www.sap.com/ecosystem/customers/directories/SearchPartner.epx.

2. The banking industry is one of several industries specifically supported by SAP. With this knowledge, you can conduct your own research into the various business processes and functionality that will be required by MNC and therefore gain an advantage on several

fronts—developing your résumé, honing your experience, and ultimately interviewing for a position.

3. With a background in accounting and the ability to pick up technology quickly, you might be a fit for an SAP super user role at MNC's banking affiliate.

4. You might want to pursue Project Management Professional (PMP) certification from the Project Management Institute (PMI).

5. With success as a liaison between the business and IT, you likely have strong communication and networking skills in addition to solid business and technical skills, a combination that will certainly prove to be a valuable asset in your interview with MNC. Ensure that you highlight these sought-after qualities.

Case Study: Hour 23 Answers

1. The number-one rule is to manage your own career. Don't passively leave your career, your livelihood, in the hands of another—especially your manager.

2. With such a broad background in infrastructure, database administration, training, and project management, you can offer the project four very different yet very useful skills. Frame this as the project's opportunity to fill in its most critical or pressing gaps.

3. Your SAP jack-of-all-trades position could grow into a specialty focused on SAP Process Integration, SAP NetWeaver Portal, or a similar component.

4. Whether it is to test project-related enhancements to the system or quarterly patches and updates, SAP systems have to be tested to ensure changes are ready for production. This requires people who can create and exercise test scripts either manually or via automated testing tools.

5. The interviewer was likely interested in your thoughts regarding how computing platforms differ in terms of their ability to enable innovation. Further the conversation by discussing the platform's ability to minimize downtime, increase flexibility, and ultimately increase business agility. Take it even further by outlining cloud and other hosting options.

Case Study: Hour 24 Answers

1. It probably makes sense to join ASUG to find out what other SAP customers are doing in the SAP Financials arena.

2. If you had enough lead time, you could have worked with a colleague or customer to develop a session for the conference. With your background and expertise in managing financials projects and a compelling customer case study, your expertise would bode well

for being selected to co-present a session. In turn, the conference provider would cover your airfare, hotel, the conference fee, and perhaps other costs.

3. You can find the top 100 or so books covering SAP development topics by searching through Amazon, Barnes & Noble, or similar online sites. Sort by date to find current titles or by best-selling status to find titles that other people are actually buying. Some of the popular SAP sites offer their perspectives on useful titles, as well.

4. It is a good idea to use an Internet search engine, such as Bing, Google, or Yahoo!, to search for new SAP sites on a periodic basis to keep up-to-date with the latest SAP information available. Be sure to visit SAP's SDN and main web page frequently, as well.

5. As a financial analyst, you will want to attend the Financials Conference hosted by WIS. SAPPHIRE NOW could also be useful to learn about the latest SAP products in the financials area. On the other hand, if your goal is networking, ASUG is ideal for connecting with other financials experts face to face.

Index

O

Office

Access

importing SAP data into, 235-236

Report Wizard, 236-238

BusinessObjects Analysis for Office, 226

Excel, exporting SAP data from, 232

integration, 230

SharePoint, integration, 238-239

Word, creating SAP form letters, 233-235

OLAP systems, column orientation, 99-100

OLTP systems

Business Suite, 110

row orientation, 99-100

Onboarding module (Success Factors HCM suite), 137

on-premise model, cloud services, 132

on-premise SME solutions, 85

open source, Monsoon project, 336

OpenStack, Monsoon, 336-337

OpenText, SAP archiving, 239-240

OpenUI5, 177

operate (run) phase (ASAP), 251

operating systems

installation preparation, 312-313

landscapes, 42-45

migration, 363-365

Operational Management, Structural Graphics, 213

operational reporting users, reporting, 206

operations

administration and management, 285

staffing Basis team, 284-285

Operations (ERP), 73, 115, 184

Enterprise Asset Management module, 187-188

T-codes, 188

Materials Management (MM), T-codes, 189

Materials Management (MM) module, 188-189

Production Planning (PP) module, 186

submodules, 186

T-codes, 186

Quality Management (QM) module, 189-190

submodules, 190-191

T-codes, 191

Sales and Distribution (SD) module, 184

submodules, 184-185

T-codes, 185

Oracle, 7

organizational change management leads, 64

Organizational Management, 117

organizing projects by roles, 61-62

business, 62-63

functional, 62-63

general support, 63-64

leadership, 62

technical, 63-64

organizing projects by tasks, 59

access strategy, 61

blueprints and analysis, 60

communications, 59

configuration, 60

customizations, 60

cutover and go-live, 61

data, 61

defects, 60

post go-live, 61

pre-sales, 59

program management, 60

project management, 60

security, 61

technical team, 61

testing, 60

training, 61

orientation, row versus column, 99-100

OS-level profiles, 27-28

outbound delivery, changing, 158-159

Outlook, integration, 230

output lists, General Report Selection, 215

Overwrite mode, SAPGUI, 168

P

PA (Personal Administration) module, 116-117

PaaS (Platform as a Service), cloud services, 132, 329

pain points, identifying, 53

Partner Cloud (HANA), 105

Partner Portal, 400

Q

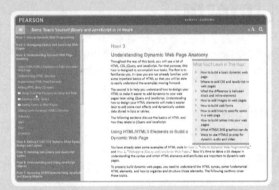

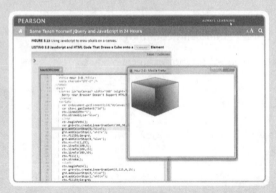
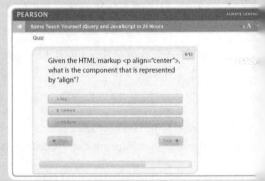